CISTERCIAN STUDIES SERIES: NUMBER TWO-HUNDRED ELEVEN

Thomas J. Bell

Peter Abelard after Marriage

CISTERCIAN STUDIES SERIES: NUMBER TWO-HUNDRED ELEVEN

Peter Abelard after Marriage

*The Spiritual Direction of Heloise
and Her Nuns Through Liturgical Song*

by

Thomas J. Bell

CISTERCIAN PUBLICATIONS
Kalamazoo, Michigan

Cistercian Publications
Editorial Offices
The Institute of Cistercian Studies
Western Michigan University
Kalamazoo, Michigan 49008-5415
cistpub@wmich.edu

*The work of Cistercian Publications is made possible in part by support from
Western Michigan University to The Institute of Cistercian Studies*

Library of Congress Cataloging-in-Publication Data

Bell, Thomas J.
    Peter Abelard after marriage : the spiritual direction of Heloise
and her nuns through liturgical song / by Thomas J. Bell.
        p. cm. — (Cistercian studies ; no. 207)
    Includes bibliographical references and index.
    ISBN 978-0-87907-311-4
    1. Héloïse, 1101–1164—Criticism and interpretation. 2. Abelard,
Peter, 1079–1142—Criticism and interpretation. 3. Church music—
France—500–1400. 4. Nuns as musicians—France. 5. Poetry,
Medieval—History and criticism. 6. Love songs—France—
History and criticism. I. Title. II. Series.

ML3027.2.B45 2007
782.32'35—dc22   2007013965

Printed in the United States of America

TABLE OF CONTENTS

PROLOGUE

THE COMBINED POWER of language and music forms the subject of this book, especially when the two are wielded by a master of rhetoric, poetry, and melody like the famous twelfth-century philosopher Peter Abelard (1079–1142). Scholars have long known of the liturgical sequences *Virgines castae* and *Epithalamica*, but only recently has it been argued by Chrysogonus Waddell that they are the work of Abelard. Richly layered and polysemous, like much of medieval art, these two sequences harmonize remarkably well in style and content with the large body of extant compositions that Abelard composed for his beloved Heloise (*c*. 1090–1164).

The two sequences, restored to their composer, offer us a new opportunity to explore the mature Abelard's exegetical skills, to witness his gifts as a liturgist, and to examine his role as spiritual adviser to Abbess Heloise. My work takes advantage of this opportunity by examining in detail the internal rhetoric of *Virgines castae* and *Epithalamica*. Abelard had a specific vision for how Heloise should understand her role as abbess of the Paraclete community, her relationship to Christ, and her feelings for Abelard himself. He displayed that vision to Heloise and her nuns through the rich tapestry of words and music that form his sequences. *Virgines castae* and *Epithalamica* speak directly to the life situation of the Paraclete abbess; their significance reaches all the way back to Abelard's earliest relations with Heloise. As with most students of the medieval period, my entrance into the world of Abelard and Heloise began with Abelard's 'Story of My Calamities', in which he tells how he seduced Heloise.

As he tells the story, the stage for Abelard and Heloise's life-long relationship was set by late 1113 or early 1114, when Abelard became master of the cathedral school of Notre-Dame. The most famous teacher, philosopher, and dialectician in all Paris, he had won distinction and droves of students. Invincible in rational argument, Abelard was, by his own account, also blessed with good looks. Perhaps as early as 1115 he set his sights on yet another challenge: seducing the most famous woman of his day, Heloise, who was known throughout France for a level of learning perhaps unsurpassed by any woman of her time.[1] Abelard was confident he could have his way with Heloise. Knowing her passion for classical letters, he seems to have asked himself, How could someone so in love with learning resist the advances of the most learned and handsome teacher in all of France?

Abelard did manage to win Heloise's heart, but, to his surprise, she also captured his. Like the legendary unicorn, Abelard

---

1. Heloise's age when she first met Abelard is uncertain. M. T. Clanchy, Abelard's most recent biographer, writes in *Abelard*, pp. 173–174 and 275): 'Abelard's description of Heloise as an "adolescent" does not mean she was a teenage bride, as her biographers have assumed. She may have been in her twenties . . . , or even close to thirty. He [Abelard] says that at the time they met, the fame of her learning "had made her most renowned in the whole kingdom" of France. Peter the Venerable confirms this: "I had not yet fully gone beyond the bounds of adolescence, nor had I yet passed into youthful years, when the fame of your name first reached me. I used to hear at that time of the woman who, although not yet disentangled from the bonds of the world, devoted the highest zeal to literary science." It can be inferred from this that Heloise was older than Peter: he was an "adolescent" reaching "youth" when she was a "woman". As he was born in 1092 or 1094, she had presumably been born around 1090 or earlier. She can hardly have been a teenager in 1117, as it would have taken her some time, years perhaps, to acquire (in the face of male prejudice) the scholarly renown which Abelard and Peter describe. As she was probably in her twenties, or even close to thirty, she may have been studying the ancient world intensively for the past ten or fifteen years. As Barbara Newman has argued, "Heloise came to Abelard with not only her mind but her imagination already well stocked"'. Clanchy 's quotation of Newman comes from her 'Authority, Authenticity and the Repression of Heloise', *Journal of Medieval and Renaissance Studies* 22 (1992) 121–158, quotation on 151. See also Mews, *Lost Love*, 32.

seemed indomitable to his enemies, but completely tame before Heloise. The two became entangled in an affair much more elaborate than the brief conquest he had originally schemed. Months passed, during which Abelard's love of philosophy waned and his concentration on students—with the exception of Heloise—wandered. Lost in the pleasures of love-making, he found inspiration only for writing songs in praise of Heloise. Soon Abelard's lyrics were on the lips of countless Parisian lovers, and news of the couple's affair was abroad. Ironically, Abelard became one of the most famous composers of love lyrics in Paris; at least one modern scholar has dubbed Abelard 'the first trouvère of France'.[2]

The exhilaration of these love lyrics soon turned to lamentation when the couple's intimacies were discovered by Heloise's uncle Fulbert. Notwithstanding the protestations of Heloise, Abelard sought to restore her and, even more, her uncle's lost honor by marrying the maiden—who now was with child. The marriage failed to quench Fulbert's thirst for revenge and he eventually retaliated by having Abelard castrated. The humiliated Abelard sought shelter in the monastic life (*c.* 1117). His public fame was reduced to infamy; he who had strutted around Paris like a peacock now hid his shame in a cloister. Heloise agreed to become a nun, and they both took religious vows.

Abelard was introduced to the monastic life at the monastery of Saint Denis, the most distinguished monastery in the Paris region. The monks of Saint Denis welcomed Abelard among their ranks until he applied his scholarly training to questioning the identity of their patron saint.[3] At this the monks were enraged;

2. Hans Spanke, 'St. Martial-Studien', *Zeitschrift für franzosischen Sprache und Literatur* 54 (1931) 282–422; 385–422; and 56 (1932) 450-478; reference, 410. A few reseachers have attributed individual songs to Abelard; see HP vol. 1, 17–18. Peter Dronke has attributed several poems to Abelard; see his *Medieval Latin and the Rise of European Love-Lyric* (Oxford: 1957), 2 vols., 1:313 ff. And 2:341ff. For every secular song attributed to him, however, there seem to be one or more scholars ready to gainsay the attribution.

3. Radice, p. 86.

Abelard was forced to flee, vowing to have no more contact with human society. In the territory of Troyes, five miles from Nogent-sur-Seine and fifty miles from the recently founded (1115) abbey of Clairvaux—hardly the wilderness that Abelard made it out to be—he established a little asylum for himself in 1122. But as always seemed to happen, eager students from across Europe soon found him. Eventually, they so overwhelmed his solitude that in late 1126 or early 1127 he sought escape, this time not as a hermit but as abbot of one of the holiest places in his homeland Brittany: the abbey of Saint Gildas-de Rhuys.[4]

In 1129, circumstances reunited Abelard and Heloise. Although Heloise was now an abbess, she had no cloister in which to house the nuns under her direction. As we shall see in more detail in Chapter One, Heloise and her nuns had lost possession of the abbey at Argenteuil when ecclesiastical authorities accused the nuns of some unspecified immorality. When Abbot Abelard learned of Heloise's homelessness, he reestablished contact with her and deeded his old asylum, the Paraclete Oratory, to the abbess and her nuns. In yet another ironic twist, Abelard found himself again inspired to write love songs for Heloise. However, these lyrics were no longer the poetry of youthful lovers; they were sacred songs, portraying the couple's descent into parallel lives of Christian humility and celebrating, at least from Abelard's perspective, an ecstasy higher than they had ever imagined in Paris: the transcendent love between Christ and virginal souls.

I had been a student of monasticism and liturgical music for some years when I first read and sang through Abelard's sequences and considered their vast and deep connections with his other writings for Heloise. I became captured as much by this Abelard *after marriage* as by the Abelard of scholarly fame. I began exploring how and why the topics of love, virginity, and marriage are so central to Abelard's sequences *Virgines castae* and *Epithalamica*. All three topics, I discovered, figure into the couple's early and late thought and action. No doubt Abelard dwelt on matters

---

4. Saint Gildas was the first historian of and apostle to post-roman Britain.

of romantic love in his secular songs. As we shall see, the language of love, virginity, and marriage fills many of the sacred songs and other works Abelard provided for, or exchanged with, Heloise. Yet I found that the place of song in the lives of Abelard and Heloise had never been seriously considered by scholars. That Abelard turned to song *both* in his early and his late relationship with Heloise seemed to me significant: Abelard found poetry and music a particularly appropriate medium through which to communicate his deepest thoughts and emotions to Heloise.

The rhetoric of his sequences and other Paraclete *liturgica* strongly suggest that the monk Abelard came to know the centrality of liturgical song in forming the christian virtues of willing obedience, well-ordered desire, deep remorse, and loving humility. Acquiring these virtues was a teleological process. Abelard came to realize that each liturgical act and song was to be performed in order to make the monk and nun approximate more and more the models and way of life embodied by Christ, his mother, apostles, martyrs, virgins, and the monk Abelard. Although Abelard's secular songs for Heloise have been lost,[5] the sacred songs he composed for her remain and, remarkably, invite us into the couple's world. Many years after the end of their affair and their entrance into the cloistered life, the two remained linked especially through the monastic disciplines of exhortation, exegesis, imitation, prayer, and song. Inspired by his love of Heloise, whom he now loved as his sister in Christ, the monk Abelard

5. Heloise writes at length of Abelard's love songs and their popularity in her 'first' letter to Abelard: 'You had besides, I admit, two special gifts whereby to win at once the heart of any woman—your gifts for composing verse and song, in which we know other philosophers have rarely been successful. This was for you no more than a diversion, a recreation from the labours of your philosophic work, but you left many love-songs and verses which won wide popularity for the charm of their words and tunes and kept your name continually on everyone's lips. The beauty of the airs ensured that even the unlettered did not forget you; more than anything this made women sigh for love of you. And as most of these songs told of our love, they soon made me widely known and roused the envy of many women against me'. English in Radice 115. The latin text is Muckle, 'Letters', 71–72.

sought through liturgical song to form Heloise and her Paraclete nuns in the proper moral dispositions and spiritual aptitudes that characterize the perfect bride Christ.

Many people have helped to make this book possible. I would like to thank William Flynn and Vernon Robbins, who offered encouragement and guidance in nurturing my original thoughts on Abelard into a sustained argument. Professor Robbins deserves special thanks for his patient reading and rereading of the many drafts of this work. Also, I cannot thank my friend Tim Long enough for reading drafts of this work as it went through many stages. Throughout this entire process he has offered me great encouragement and sound editorial advice. More than anyone, my wife Suzanne earns my highest praise and deepest thanks for applying her vast editorial and writing talent to many drafts of this project. Finally, I thank Rozanne Elder and her staff at Cistercian Publications for seeing this work through the publication process.

ABBREVIATIONS

AH
: *Analecta hymnica medii aevi.* G. M. Dreves and C. Blume, edd.. 55 volumes. Leipzig, 1886-1922.

ANF
: The Ante-Nicene Fathers, volume 5. Edinburgh, 1867; rpt. Grand Rapids: Eerdmans, 1981.

Astell, *Song*
: Ann W. Astell, *The Song of Songs in the Middle Ages.* Ithaca: Cornell University Press, 1990.

Asad, *Genealogies*
: Asad, Talad. *Genealogies of Religion: Discipline and Reasons of Power in Christianity and Islam.* Baltimore: The Johns Hopkins University Press, 1993.

Carruthers, *Memory*
: Carruthers, Mary. *The Book of Memory: A Study of Memory in Medieval Culture.* Cambridge Studies in Medieval Literature 10. Cambridge: Cambridge University Press, 1990.

CCCM
: E. M. Buytaert ed, *Petri Abaelardi Opera theologicae,* Corpus Christianorum Continuatio Mediaevalis, volumes 11 and 12. Turnhout: Brepols, 1969.

Clanchy, *Abelard*
: M. T. Clanchy, *Abelard: A Medieval Life.* Oxford: Blackwell, 1997.

CLS 3   *The Old French Paraclete Ordinary and the Paraclete Breviary I. Introduction and Commentary.* Cistercian Liturgical Series, 3. Trappist, Kentucky: Gethsemani Abbey–Kalamazoo: Cistercian Publications, 1985.

CLS 5   *Paraclete Breviary: IIIA Edition. Kalendar and Temporal Cycle.* Ed. Chrysogonus Waddell. Cistercian Liturgy Series 5. Trappist, Kentucky: Gethsemani Abbey-Kalamazoo: Cistercian Publications, 1985

CLS 6   *The Paraclete Breviary: IIIB Edition. The Sanctoral Cycle.* Ed. Chrysogonus Waddell. Cistercian Liturgy Series 6. Trappist, Kentucky: Gethesemani Abbey–Kalamazoo: Cistercian Publications, 1985.

CLS 7   *The Paraclete Breviary: IIIC Edition. Common of Saints, Varia, Indices.* Ed. Chrysogonus Waddell. Cistercian Liturgy Series 7. Trappist, Kentucky: Gethsemani Abbey–Kalamazoo: Cistercian Publications, 1985.

CLS 8   *Hymn Collections from the Paraclete I. Introduction and Commentary.* Cistercian Liturgical Series 8. Trappist, Kentucky: Gethsemani Abbey–Kalamazoo: Cistercian Publications, 1989.

CLS 9   Chrysogonus Waddell, *Hymn Collections from the Paraclete. Edition,* Cistercian Liturgy Series 9. Trappist, Kentucky: Gethsemani Abbey–Kalamazoo: Cistercian Publications, 1987.

CLS 20	Troyes, Bibliothèque Municipale MS 802, ff. 89r–90v, edited M. Chrysogonus Waddell, *The Paraclete Statutes. Institutiones nostrae* , Cistercian Liturgy Series 20. Trappist: Gethsemani Abbey, Kalamazoo: Cistercian Publications, 1987.
Copeland, *Rhetoric*	Copeland, Rita. *Rhetoric, Hermeneutics, and Translation in the Middle Ages: Academic Traditions and Vernacular Texts.* Cambridge Studies in Medieval Literature. Cambridge: Cambridge University Press, 1991.
CS	Cistercian Studies Series. Spencer– Kalamazoo, 1969– .
Diehl, *Lyric*	Diehl, Patrick S. *The Medieval European Religious Lyric: An Ars Poetica.* Berkeley: University of California Press, 1985.
Dronke, 'Virgines caste'	*'Virgines caste'. Lateinische Dichtungen des X. und XI. Jahrhunderts: Festgabe für Walther Bulst zum 80. Geburtstag, 93–117.* Heidelberg: Lambert Schneider, 1981; rpt Peter Dronke. *Latin and Vernacular Poets of the Middle Ages.* Chapter Six. Brookfield, Vermont: Gower Publishing Company, 1991. All references below are to the article as it appears in the German volume.
Flynn, 'Tropes'	Flynn, William T. 'Paris, Bibliothèque de l'Arsenal, MS 1169: The Hermeneutics of Eleventh-Century Burgundian Tropes, and Their Implications'. Ph.D. Dissertation, Duke University, 1992.
Freeland, *Hymns*	*The Hymns of Abelard in English Verse.* Translated and introduced by Sister Jane Patricia [Freeland]. New York: University Press of America, 1986.

Gilson, *Heloise*   Etienne Gilson, *Heloise and Abelard*. Ann
and Abelard   Arbor: University of Michigan Press,
                         1960, rpt 1968.
HP   *Peter Abelard's Hymnarius Paraclitensis*. 2
                         Volumes. Ed. Joseph Szövérffy. Wetteren,
                         Belgium: Cultura Press, 1975.
Mews, *Lost Love*   Constance J. Mews, *The Lost Love Letters
                         of Abelard and Heloise: Perceptions of Dia-
                         logue in Twelfth-Century France*. New
                         York: Plagrace, 2001.
Moncrieff, 'Nuns'   'Touching the Origin of Nuns' in C. K.
                         Scott Moncrieff, editor and translator, *The
                         Letters of Abelard and Heloise*. New York:
                         Knopf, 1942. Page 129–175.
Muckle,   'Abelard's Letter of Consolation to a
'Consolation'   'Friend'. Edited J. T. Muckle. *Mediæval
                         Studies* 12 (1950)163–213.
Muckle, 'Letters'   'The Personal Letters between Abelard
                         and Heloise: Introduction, Authenticity,
                         and Text'. Ed. J. T. Muckle. *Mediæval
                         Studies* 15 (1953) 47–94.
Muckle, 'Religious   'The Letters of Heloise on Religious Life
Life'   and Abelard's First Reply'. Ed. J. T.
                         Muckle. *Mediæval Studies* 17 (1955)
                         240–281.
McLaughlin, 'Rule'   'Abelard's Rule of Religious Women'. Ed.
                         T. P. McLaughlin. *Mediæval Studies* 18
                         (1956) 241–292.
NAH   Non-Abelardian Hymn
NPNF1   Library of Nicene and Post-Nicene Fa-
                         thers series 1. 14 volumes. Rpt Grand
                         Rapids: Eerdmans, 1983.
NPNF2   Library of Nicene and Post-Nicene Fa-
                         thers series 2. 14 volumes. Rpt Grand
                         Rapids: Eerdmans, 1983.

PL	*Patrologiae cursus completes*: Series Latina, ed. Jacques P. Migne, 222 volumes. Paris, 1844–1902.
Radice	Betty Radice, translator, *The Letters of Abelard and Heloise*. Harmondsworth-New York: Penguin Books, 1974.
SCh	Sources chrétiennes series. Paris-Lyons: Editions du Cerf.
Waddell, 'Chaste Virgins'	Chrysogonus Waddell. 'Abelard and the Chaste Virgins'. Unpublished Essay.
Waddell, *'Epithalamica'*	Chrysogonus Waddell. 'Epithalamica: An Easter Sequence by Peter Abelard'. *Musical Quarterly* 72 (1986) 239–271.

INTRODUCTION

THE WORLD HAS LONG KNOWN of Abelard the combative student, rakerous logician, seducer of fair Heloise, father out of wedlock, castrated husband, and philosopher-turned-monk. But Abelard after marriage remains a man largely undiscovered, except by a few specialists. Yet Abelard is as fascinating as a musical, poetic, and rhetorical genius as he is in any of his better known roles. In the pages that follow I will introduce the reader to Abelard the monk, abbot, and spiritual director of nuns. We shall enter the world of this monastic Abelard by following a path once well-worn by the founder of the Paraclete in the many written documents that he sent to Heloise and her nuns. At the center of these contributions stand the sequences *Virgines castae* and *Epithalamica*, two of many forms of liturgical song that Abelard created. As we shall see, by medieval standards Abelard was both a prolific and a gifted composer of liturgical poetry and melody.[1]

Scholars have long known of Abelard's six *planctus*—sacred songs of lament—composed for Heloise and her nuns.[2] In addition,

---

1. For an introduction to Abelard as a poet and musician, see Michel Huglo, 'Abélard, poète et musicien', *Cahiers de civilisation médiévale* 22 (1979) 349–361.

2. For more on Abelard's *planctus* see: W. Meyer and W. Brambach, edd. *Planctus virginum Israel super filiam Jephtae Galaditae* (Munich, 1885); W. Meyer, ed., *Planctus I, II, III, IV, V, VI* (Erlangen, 1890; reprint from *Romanische Forschungen* V, 2); Giuseppe Vecchi, ed. Pietro Abelardo, *I 'Planctus': Introduzione testo critico, trascrizioni musicali*, Testi e manuali no. 35 (Instituto di filologia romanza della Universitá di Roma; Modena, 1951); Wofram von den Steinen, 'Die Planctus

some one hundred thirty-three hymn texts written by Abelard for the Paraclete are extant.[3] Chrysogonus Waddell's recent studies of the surviving Paraclete Ordinary and Breviary have uncovered numerous antiphons, responsories, and collects that he contends were also written by Abelard.[4] Waddell has additionally discovered another *planctus*, *De profundis*, which he believes Abelard wrote, and, finally, uncovered the connections between Abelard and the sequences *Epithalamica* and *Virgines castae*.[5]

Medieval scholars of poetry, liturgy, and music generally agree on the differences among the various kinds of liturgical songs Abelard wrote for the Paraclete nuns. There are, however, similarities between the sequence, hymn, and *planctus* genres

Abelards-Jephthas Rochter', *Mittellateinisches Jahrbuch* 5 (1967) 122–144; A. Machabey, 'Les Planctus d'Abélard. Remargues sur le rythme musical du XIIe siècle,' *Romania* 82 (1961) 71–95; Lorenz Weinrich, '"Dolorum solatium" Text und Musik von Abelards Planctus', *Mittellateinisches Jahrbuch* 5 (1968) 59–78; Weinrich, 'Peter Abelard as Musician', *The Musical Quarterly* 55 (1969) 295–312, 464–486; Peter Dronke, *Poetic Individuality in the Middle Ages—New Departures in Poetry 1000–1150* (Oxford, 1970) 114–149; and Peter Dronke and Margaret Alexiou, 'The Lament of Jephtah's Daughter: Themes, Traditions, Originality', *Studi medievali* 3, ser. 12 (1971) 819–863.

3. Several editions of Abelard's hymns have appeared; the following are the three most important: 1) G. M. Dreves, *Petri Abaelardi Paeripatetici Palatini Hymnarius Paraclitensis sive hymnorum libelli tres ad fidem codicum Bruxellensis et Calmontani* (Paris, 1891). This edition was later reproduced (without commentary and annotations) in *Analecta hymnica*, vol. 48, 141–223. 2) Szövérffy, HP. 3) Chrysogonus Waddell, CL 9.

Details on the music of Abelard's hymns are in: Lorenz Weinrich, 'Peter Abelard as Musician', *The Musical Quarterly* 55 (1969) 295–312, 464–86; and Chrysogonus Waddell, CL 8.

4. On the many contributions Abelard made to the liturgical life of the Paraclete, see Chrysogonus Waddell, CL 3, 345 ff.; and Chrysogonus Waddell, 'Peter Abelard as Creator of Liturgical Texts', *Petrus Abelardus (1079–1142). Person, Werk und Wirkung*, Trierer theologische Studien, hrsg. von Rudolf Thomas (Trier: Paulinus-Verlag, 1980) 267–280.

5. *Virgines castae* is found in AH vol. 54, 133–135; and *Epithalamica* in AH vol. 8:45-47. Chrysogonus Waddell has made the case for attributing the two sequences to Abelard in several important studies; see especially his '*Epithalamica*' 239–271. His other important studies will be referred to below.

that make neat classification of them a less than tidy business. Indeed, as we shall soon see, the shades of likeness between these genres have figured in scholars' (mis)understanding of Abelard's musical contributions to the Paraclete nuns. Let us proceed by first presenting a standard description of the sequence as a genre. Then we shall consider Abelard's contributions to the Paraclete Abbey in light of the ambiguities surrounding the sequence, *planctus*, and hymn.

Scholars disagree over the earliest origins of the musical and poetic genre called the 'sequence'.[6] We do know that by the ninth century these long chants were sung in the Frankish kingdom after the Alleluia and its psalmodic verse at Mass on feast days, and before the reading of the Gospel. They were sometimes used elsewhere in the liturgy, especially as a substitute for the Vespers hymn. Typically the sequence took the form a, bb, cc, dd . . . x.

6. See the following standard discussions of the sequence: Hans Spanke, 'Aus der Vorgeschichte und Frühgeschichte der Sequenz', *Zeitschrift für französische Sprache und Literatur* 54 (1930) 282–317, 385–422; 56 (1931) 286–320; Hans Spanke, 'Sequenz und Lai', *Studi medievali* n.s. 11–12 (1938–1939) 12–68; Wolfram von den Steinen, *Notker der Dichter*, 2 vols. (Bern, 1948); Bruno Stäblein, 'Zur Frühgeschichte der Sequenz', *Archiv für Musikwissenschaft* 18 (1961) 1–33; Wolfram von den Steinen, 'Sequenz (Gesang)', in *Die Musik in Geschichte und Gegenwart: Allgemeine Enzyklopädue der Musik*, Friedrich Blume, ed., 17 vols. (Kassel, 1949–86), vol. 12: col. 522–554; Peter Dronke, 'The Beginnings of the Sequence', *Beiträge zur Geschichte der deutschen Sprache und Literatur* 87 (1965) 43–73; Richard L. Crocker, 'The Sequence', in *Gattungen der Musik in Einzeldarstellungen: Gedenkaschrift Leo Schrade*, vol. 1, edd. Wulf Arlt, Ernst Lichtenhahn, and Hans Oesch (Bern, 1973) 276–322; Richard L. Crocker, *The Early Medieval Sequence* (Berkeley: University of California, 1977); Stephen Ryle, 'The Sequence: Reflections on Literature and Liturgy', in *Papers of the Liverpool Latin Seminar 1976: Classical Latin Poetry/Medieval Latin Poetry/Greek Poetry*, ed. Francis Cairns (Liverpool, 1977) 171–182; Richard Crocker and Johan Caldwell, 'Sequence', in *New Grove Dictionary of Music and Musicians*, ed. Stanley Sadie (London, 1980), vol. 17:141–153; Richard L. Crocker and David Hiley, edd., *New Oxford History of Music*, vol. 2: *The Early Middle Ages to 1300* (2nd ed., Oxford: Oxford University Press, 1989) 256–264; Margot Fassler, *Gothic Song: Victorine Sequences and Augustinian Reform in Twelfth-Century Paris* (Cambridge: Cambridge University Press, 1993); and David Hiley, *Western Plainchant: a Handbook* (Oxford: Oxford University Press, 1995) 172–195.

The paired versicles were each sung to their own music. We shall more closely consider the history, function, and form of the sequence in Chapters Two through Four.

In these three chapters our analysis will show that Abelard's sequences have many of the characteristics of what is called an 'intermediate' sequence. Because sequences of this intermediate style are typically dated before 1100 AD, Abelard's sequences have a rather backward-looking character which places them in contrast to the sequence style of his twelfth-century Parisian contemporaries. Our analysis will further show that his sequences functioned in the Paraclete liturgy to 'sequence' the nuns' thoughts and lives from the Old Testament to the New Testament through the Church Fathers and into the world of the Paraclete. This movement suggests that the sequence's transitionary role in the medieval liturgy may in fact have been broader than is usually assumed. Finally, our rhetorical analysis of *Virgines castae* and *Epithalamica* will suggest that the rhetorical form of many sequences has its roots in the ancient techniques of composing discourse that go back to the thematic development of the *expolitio* and the elaboration of *chreiai*. These broad conclusions about the function and form of the medieval sequence genre will suggest themselves as we explore the central concern of this study: the meaning and significance of *Virgines castae* and *Epithalamica* in the lives of Abelard and Heloise.

Though Chrysogonus Waddell has only recently shown the remarkable connections between these two sequences and Abelard, we have long possessed evidence that Abelard wrote sequences for Heloise and her nuns. In the surviving cover letter that he attached to his *Sermonary*,[7] Abelard wrote:

7. Important studies of Abelard's sermons are: 1) Damien Van den Eynde, 'Le recueil des sermons de Pierre Abelard', *Antonianum* 37 (1962) 17–54, in which the author establishes the authenticity of all thirty-four sermons printed under Abelard's name in PL 178:379-610. 2) Chrysogonus Waddell, 'Peter Abelard as Creator of Liturgical Texts', *Studies in Medieval Cistercian History*, 2, ed. John R. Sommerfeldt, Cistercian Studies Series 24 (Kalamazoo: Cistercian Publications, 1976) 75–86. 3) Eileen F. Kearney, 'Master Peter Abelard, Expositor of Sacred

Having recently completed a certain little book of hymns
and sequences at your request, my venerated and beloved
sister in Christ, Heloise, I have also hastened to write some
sermons—a type of writing that is contrary to my usual
practice—for you and your spiritual daughters gathered at
our oratory.[8]

Understanding just what Abelard meant by *libello quodam
hymnorum vel sequentiarum* is not easy. Until Waddell's examination of *Virgines castae* and *Epithalamica*, no sequences arguably by
Abelard were known to exist. Many researchers simply assumed
that either Abelard's sequences had been forever lost or that the
sequences referred to in this prefatory letter were really his six
planctus.[9] Scholars have found this latter hypothesis appealing,
writes Waddell, 'because no sequences ascribable to Abelard were
known to exist, whereas six *planctus*, similar to sequences in some
respects, already had a secure place in the canon of Abelard's
compositions.'[10]

The supposition that the 'sequences' Abelard sent to Heloise
were really *planctus* points to certain ambiguities that exist between the *planctus* and sequence genres: Some *planctus* are written in typical sequence form and some sequences are written in
a form similar to that of the *planctus*. The typical sequence form
is a, bb, cc, dd . . . x; in other words, many sequences begin with
a single line of text with its own music (a) followed by a number
of double-line stanzas with parallel music (bb, cc, dd . . .) and

Scripture: An Analysis of Abelard's Approach to Biblical Exposition in Selected
Writings on Scripture', Ph.D. Diss., Marquette University, 1980, 244–247.

8. PL 178:379: *Libello quodam hymnorum vel sequentiarum a me nuper precibus tuis consummato, veneranda in christo et amanda soror Heloissa, nonnulla insuper opuscula sermonum, juxta petitionem tuam, tam tibi quam spiritalibus filiabus
tuis in oratorio nostro congregatis, scribere praeter consuetudinem nostram utcunque
maturavi.* My translation. All English translations in this study are mine except
where otherwise noted.

9. Waddell, 'Epithalamica', 241, n. 11. See also Peter Dronke, *Poetic Individuality in the Middle Ages*, 114–149.

10. 'Epithalamica', 241, n. 11.

conclude with a single line (x). Instead of the double stanzas so characteristic of the sequence, many *planctus* have triple and quadruple stanzas (with a single melody repeated to each line of a stanza). However, there are sequences—among them *Virgines castae* and *Epithalamica*—that have a mix of double, triple, and quadruple stanzas, like the typical *planctus*. Beyond similarity in form, there is some ambiguity about the performance of sequences and *planctus* in and outside the medieval liturgy. The sequence was performed usually at Mass and at times at Vespers. *Planctus* were songs of lamentation and existed largely outside the liturgy. There are, however, sequences that were performed outside the liturgy, and there are *planctus* that were sung in the liturgy, particularly at funeral Masses. These are the ambiguities that have led some scholars simply to assume that Abelard's sequences were in reality his surviving *planctus*. So if 'sequences' in Abelard's 'little book' are what we moderns tend to classify as *planctus*, Abelard wrote a little book of 'hymns' and *'planctus'* for the nuns at the Paraclete.

One could speculate that Abelard's *planctus* were a separate matter altogether and that he used the terms 'hymn' and 'sequence' interchangeably in the sermonary letter. This second theory points to another ambiguity, this time between the hymn and sequence genres. It is true that the *vel* in Abelard's letter can be translated 'or', and this could possibly mean that in Abelard's thinking hymns were sequences and vice versa.[11] Long before Abelard, Augustine of Hippo had defined 'hymn' as the praise of God with music.[12] Both the hymn and the sequence praise God in music; hence, sequences are hymns and hymns sequences.

11. A further argument for equating hymn and sequence is that sequences often were substituted for hymns, especially at Vespers on special feasts. Whatever Abelard meant by 'hymns' *vel* 'sequences', nothing in the Paraclete liturgical books suggests that the nuns substituted Abelard's sequences for hymns at Vespers or at any other time, or that Abelard intended them to do so, even on special occasions. Such a practice might, of course, have been so commonplace that neither Abelard nor the Paraclete scribe felt it necessary to mention it.

12. *Commentary on Psalm 148*.17; PL 37:1947; NPNF 1, vol. 8:677.

There are precedents for closely relating the hymn and the sequence. One of the finest creators of early sequence texts, Notker Balbulus, a ninth-century monk of Saint Gall, entitled his book of sequences a *Liber hymnorum*, a 'Book of Hymns'. Furthermore, by the mid-twelfth century, writes Patrick S. Diehl:

> many sequences . . . look exactly like hymns of the same period: a series of trimly rhymed trochaic stanzas of four, six, or eight lines of alternately eight and seven syllables that are all perfectly identical in form. Only the music (which is often borrowed) now identifies these texts as technically 'sequences,' since it retains the pair-wise progress of the sequence form (BB/CC/DD . . .).'[13]

Hildegard of Bingen, a contemporary of Abelard, wrote hymns that are virtually identical to her sequences.[14] In the absence of any Abelardian sequences, scholars have been left guessing just what might have distinguished a hymn from a sequence in Abelard's mind. The conclusion that he considered them essentially the same thing is not far-fetched.

With Waddell's attribution of *Virgines castae* and *Epithalamica*, we have reason to read Abelard's *hymnorum vel sequentiarum* as 'hymns or, more precisely, sequences'. If so, Abelard recognized, on the one hand, that sequences were sometimes in fact called hymns, and, on the other, that technically the two are not the same. His sequences were like hymns in that they praise God with music; but in form and function they were sequences. This theory would suggest that Abelard's little book of 'hymns' was actually a little book of sequences which he had written to facilitate the Paraclete nuns' praise of God with music.

---

13. Diehl, *Lyric*, 88, 89.

14. See Barbara Newman's discussion of Hildegard's sequences and hymns in *Saint Hildegard of Bingen: Symphonia, A Critical Edition of the* Symphonia armonie celestium revelationum *[Symphony of the Harmony of Celestial Revelations]* (Ithaca: Cornell University Press, 1988) 27–32.

We shall never know with certainty what the little songbook contained in its entirety. But this second theory makes the best sense of our evidence. It seems very unlikely that Abelard's little songbook included the complete collection of hymns he had provided for the nuns. For its time this collection was quite large, containing at least one hundred thirty-three hymns. We know that Abelard sent the hymn collection to Heloise in three install-ments: first, a group of twenty-nine hymns with a letter addressed to Heloise; then a group of forty-seven; and finally a group of fifty-seven hymns.[15] Unless he was being entirely facetious, Abe-lard could hardly describe this hymn collection, in whole or ac-cording to its individual parts, as 'little'.[16] It is my opinion that in his sermonary cover letter he was referring to a small group of sequences which he had recently sent to Heloise and which, in some general sense, he classified as hymns. If *Virgines castae* and *Epithalamica* were in fact written by Abelard, then it is prob-able that they were included in the *Libello . . . hymnorum vel se-quentiarum* he sent to Heloise.

These two sequences have been the subject of few scholarly studies. Peter Dronke has characterized *Virgines castae* as a 'tran-sitional' sequence. Scholars tend to differentiate a ninth-century sequence form, which they generally recognize as the beginning of the genre, from a final twelfth-century form, which they see as its culmination. Some sequences fall in the middle and are 'transitional' in nature. This classification basically means that, like other sequences between the ninth and twelfth centuries, *Virgines castae* has some features, such as unstressed rhyme, that make it like the ninth-century sequence, but four-line stanzas that make it like the twelfth-century sequence. Transitional se-quences were, Dronke adds, 'on the whole more likely to be datable before rather than after 1100'.[17] He did note one exception

15. See Mary M. McLaughlin, 'Peter Abelard and the Dignity of Women: Twelfth Century 'Feminism' in Theory and Practice', *Speculum* 42 (1967) 287–333, 292, n. 6.

16. On Abelard's light-heartedness see, M. T. Clanchy, *Abelard*, 131–134.

17. '*Virgines caste*', 97–98.

to this rule: Peter Abelard's *planctus*, written in the 1130s, 'are an unusual instance of a corpus of songs that are in sequence-form, or that take sequence-forms as a point of departure, and yet still show a studied avoidance of stressed rhyme.'[18] Dronke acknowledged that the pervasive unstressed rhyme of the sequence reminded him of Abelard's six *planctus*, and suggested that such rhyme may have been an 'archaizing technique' that Abelard had chosen as a way of setting his *planctus* apart from the Victorine repertoire—the classic 12th century form of the sequence genera. The structural and poetic similarities of *Virgines castae* and Abelard's *planctus* notwithstanding, Dronke stopped short of attributing the sequence to Abelard. His taxonomy of the sequence form led him to locate *Virgines castae* among the 'transitional' sequences which he dated before Abelard's time.

Chrysogonus Waddell's path to *Virgines castae* differed from Dronke's; he came to the sequence through the Paraclete liturgical books and by this approach perceived an even stronger connection to Abelard. In the Paraclete liturgical books he found references to several sequences which the editors of the *Analecta hymnica* had classified as anonymous. Among these were the sequences *Virgines castae* and *Epithalamica*, which he had found together in a late twelfth-century manuscript from Nevers. Upon cursory examination, he found the two chants to be Abelardian in style and content, and promised a monograph study of them.[19]

The present study helps confirm Waddell's argument that the two sequences were indeed written by Peter Abelard. By comparing these sequences to Abelard's extant sacred songs and music, I show that *Epithalamica* and *Virgines castae* possess oral-scribal, cultural, poetic, musical, rhetorical, historical, and social features that are characteristic of and in some cases unique to the work of Peter Abelard, especially to the sermons, hymns, and letters associated with Heloise. A range of conclusions based on close, systematic examination of the *internal rhetoric* of the two

18. '*Virgines caste*', 97.
19. Waddell, CL 3:347-350.

sequences. While not seeking to 'prove' that Abelard wrote these two songs, my study deepens and buttresses Waddell's hypothesis. I assume Abelard wrote them and then explore how and why the author wrote these exquisite works of poetry and melody.

Abelard's *liturgica*, the many texts with and without music he wrote for Heloise and her nuns, were not simply documents written down and safely stored away in the Paraclete library. His sequences and other *liturgica*, provided resources for the nuns' memory and sense of identity. Abelard sought to form the symbolic world of the Paraclete nuns by providing them with a *textus*, a word derived from the verb meaning 'to weave'. And, in Mary Carruthers' words, 'it is in the institutionalizing of a story through *memoria* that textualizing occurs.'[20] The Paraclete story as told by Abelard in *Virgines castae* and *Epithalamica* centers on the supreme virgin queen, her virginal intimates, and the heavenly bridegroom. Through this story Abelard sought to weave a particular 'community together by providing it with shared experience and a certain kind of language, the language of stories that can be experienced over and over again through time and as [liturgical] occasion suggests.'[21] The central claim of this study is that the language, imagery, and music of Abelard's sequences were designed to create and nurture a reality in which both the Paraclete nuns and Abelard and Heloise themselves could live and move and have their being.

Through the tropological and teleological formation of the liturgy, Heloise and her nuns would be habituated into heaven's mode of being. Their *habitus* as brides of Christ would be developed by repeatedly identifying with the queen's particular emotional responses (*pathos*) and by imitating her acts (*praxis*). Abelard sought to have his vision of the heavenly court so pressed into the being of the Paraclete nuns that they would be disposed to perceive, apprehend, experience, suffer, and rejoice just as passionately as the queen and her followers. The Divine Office

---

20. Carruthers, *Memory*, 12.
21. Carruthers, *Memory*, 12.

with its daily performance of liturgical song provided the indispensable means for the formation of the nun. Abelard's *liturgica* were, therefore, his way of textualizing, or weaving, together a particular institutional fabric at the Paraclete. In this tapestry the nuns could behold the mode of life into which they were ever journeying and the end to which they were destined.[22]

Interpreting *Virgines castae* and *Epithalamica* against the background of Abelard and Heloise's lifelong relationship, and a careful analysis of their intertexture (connections to phenomena outside the boundaries of their text) and rhetoric (internal discourse) shows that both sequences had deep persuasive significance in their original cultural environment. My exposition and analysis of the two sequences' various 'textures' or 'threads of discourse,' gives readers insight into how Abelard used his exegetical skills, poetic style, and rhetorical savvy in his spiritual direction of Heloise and her nuns.[23] Abelard directed his se-

---

22. I have gained great insight into the role of the liturgy in the monastic life from Asad, *Genealogies* 62-167. Alasdair MacIntyre's *After Virtue: A Study of Moral Theory* (Notre Dame: University of Notre Dame Press, 1981) also has been profoundly helpful in understanding the role of narrative in the virtue tradition and in the cultural world of communities like the Paraclete Abbey.

23. The metaphor of 'textures' I have drawn from Vernon Robbins, who argues that 'with socio-rhetorical criticism, the metaphor of texts as a thick tapestry replaces the traditional metaphor of texts as windows and mirrors. The idea has been that the interpreter who is truly interested in literature as literature treats all the characters, actions and episodes in a text as mirrors that reflect back and forth on one another. All of the reflections create the world 'inside the text'. Historians in contrast to literary interpreters, so the understanding goes, use the text as a window either to look briefly in at the text or to look out at the outside world, rather than as a set of mirrors, to find out what is inside the text. They look in or out of the windows of texts for the purpose of creating a story, namely a 'history', outside the texts.' *The Tapestry of Early Christian Discourse: Rhetoric, Society, and Ideology* (London: Routledge, 1996) 18–19. Socio-rhetorical interpreters like Robbins compare texts to tapestry, which when viewed from different angles reveals different configurations, patterns, and images. Robbins writes, 'when we explore a text from different angels, we see multiple textures of meanings, conviction, beliefs, values, emotions and actions. These textures within texts are a result of webs or networks of meaning and meaning effects

quences to the concrete life situation of the Paraclete nuns, especially Heloise, and used the affective force of the two songs' *literal*
imagery to move (*movere* or *saudere*) the nuns to love Christ, their
bridegroom. His strategy is fundamentally rhetorical, not dialectical; his primary goal for the nuns is application, not discovery,
of truth.[24]

Traditionally, rhetoric discovers truth by using training in
literacy to apply tradition to *praxis*. The rhetorician impersonates
or embodies the tradition he/she is teaching, and teaches his
students and audience to do likewise. This role-playing suggests
why narrative is so profoundly important to rhetoric. Truth is
found in re-living through imitation the truthful lives of those of
tradition. Dialectic, by contrast, sets itself over against tradition.
Its practitioners adopt a critical, not an imitative, attitude toward
tradition. As John D. Schaeffer writes, 'like Socrates, the dialectician impersonates one who does not know so that truth can be
discovered, whereas the rhetorician impersonates tradition so
that truth can be transmitted'.[25] Apparently Abelard was gifted
with the ability to assume the role of rhetorican as skillfully as
he could play dialectician. He applied his rhetorical skills for the
particular task of transmitting tradition and thereby shaping the

---

that humans create.' (*Tapestry*, 18) Robbins contends that the metaphor of tapestry, in contrast to the metaphors of windows and mirrors, avoids 'the problem
of separating the 'internal' mind of a text from the 'external' body of the world
in a manner that is not true either to the texts we read or to the lives we live. The
metaphor of windows and mirrors reflects a polarity between literature and history that is part of the dualism between mind and body in modern thought and
philosophy. This approach overlooks the nature of language as a social product,
possession and tool. Language is at all times interacting with myriads of networks of meanings and meaning effects in the world.' (*Tapestry*, 19.)

24. The similarity between my claim here and one of the main arguments
of Ann W. Astell in her splendid study *The Song of Songs in the Middle Ages*
(Ithaca: Cornell Univesity, 1990) is no accident. I shall show in this study that
Abelard's exegesis of the Song of Song fits exactly into Astell's study.

25. John D. Schaeffer, *Sensus Communis: Vico, Rhetoric, and The Limits of
Relativism* (Duke University Press, 1990) 115. I am indebted to Schaeffer's very
illuminating account of rhetoric and dialectic.

lives of the Paraclete nuns. This rhetorical process of transmission was very much about 'sequencing' present lives into the past and past lives into the present for the sake of moral formation. This concern with moral application indicates that *Virgines castae* and *Epithalamica* are characterized by a particular kind of rhetoric. Their overall rhetoric is not 'deliberative' or 'judicial'. On the one hand, Abelard does not focus on a specific action at the Paraclete that must cease or be taken in the immediate future; on the other, he does not seek to exonerate the nuns from some guilt nor does he pronounce judgment upon their behavior. Rather, the sequences' rhetoric is fundamentally 'epideictic'. Through them Abelard seeks to strengthen Heloise and her nuns' disposition toward their monastic way of life. In short, Abelard would have his vision of Christ's heavenly court and nuptial chamber so pressed into the being of the Paraclete nuns that each of them is predisposed to perceive, apprehend, experience, and enjoy life as do Queen Mary and her chaste virgins.

In studying the persuasive form, content, and goal of *Virgines castae* and *Epithalamica*, I have drawn heavily on the classical rhetorical tradition as mediated from antiquity through the Middle Ages, and in modern works by such figures as Chaïm Perelman and Vernon Robbins. The rhetorical tradition views historical sources, like the two sequences central to this study, fundamentally as perspectival discourses designed to persuade. They are instruments of persuasion. Through them Abelard seeks not merely to inform his Paraclete audience but also to persuade them fully to identify with the words within his sequences and the deeds they describe. The rhetorical tradition has developed a vast range of systematic strategies for probing the persuasive dimensions of oral and scribal discourse. It is fundamentally a hermeneutic that is not focused on universals but deals with particular speakers, in particular settings, addressing particular audiences, through particular modes of argumentation, with particular argumentative goals.[26] This is precisely the methodol-

26. See Chaim Perelman and L. Olbrechts-Tyteca, *The New Rhetoric: A Treatise on Argumentation* (Notre Dame: University of Notre Dame Press, 1969) 1–62;

ogy we need to enter into the symbolic world of the Paraclete and to appreciate Abelard's efforts to move Heloise and her nuns through song.

In addition to rhetorical criticism, sociological analysis has given me insight into the 'symbolic world' of the Paraclete and Abelard. Scholars in the social sciences, like Mary Douglas and Clifford Geertz, have used the concept of 'symbolic world' to refer to the world as it is known and experienced by a particular culture.[27] The term denotes the beliefs, practices, persons, rules, laws, objects, and myths, that define, legitimate, and give identity to a particular group of people—whether a community of nuns or an entire nation. Sociologists and anthropologists recognize that meaningful communication between human beings presupposes considerable sharing or overlapping of the symbolic worlds of speaker-author and audience. The persuasive communication Abelard sought to achieve through his sequences required that he and the Paraclete nuns shared the same symbolic world. His rhetorical goals required that he have the ability to play effectively upon the shared symbols which were most likely, in the nomenclature of the rhetorical tradition, 'to move' his Paraclete audience. In this the social science concept of symbolic world dovetails with the rhetorical tradition.

Through 'socio-rhetorical' analysis,[28] we hope to probe into the thickly textured world of the aged Abelard, the castrated, ascetic Abelard, the Abelard after marriage whom few people have closely studied. This Abelard is not the infamous dialectician or the bombastic Paris teacher; rather, it is Abelard the rheto-

---

David S. Cunningham, *Faithful Persuasion: In Aid of a Rhetoric of Christian Theology* (Notre Dame: University of Notre Dame Press, 1990) 28; and Carruthers, *Memory*, esp. 24–27.

27. Mary Douglas, *Natural Symbols: Explorations in Cosmology* (New York: Routledge, 1970); and Clifford Geertz, *The Interpretation of Cultures* (New York: Basic Books, 1973).

28. New Testament scholar Vernon K. Robbins first coined the term 'socio-rhetorical analysis' in his *Jesus the Teacher: A Socio-Rhetorical Interpretation of Mark* (Minneapolis: Fortress Press, 1984).

rician, father-founder, and spiritual director seeking to persuade Heloise and her virginal followers to enter fully into their role as Christ's brides.

Abelard's efforts at shaping the Paraclete nuns' identity were not limited to *Virgines castae* and *Epithalamica*. These two bridal songs stood at the center of a vast collection of hymns, sermons, prayers, and liturgical songs composed for Heloise and her nuns. What survives of it reveals a tightly crafted network of theological topics, images, and metaphors that Abelard wove together with the skill of a master weaver.

When we carefully piece together the fragments of this great Paraclete tapestry, we find as its central and most vivid images the bridal scenes of *Virgines castae* and *Epithalamica*.

Chapter One introduces the reader to the six primary sources that give us access to this great bridal gift that Abelard prepared for the Paraclete nuns:

1) the Paraclete Office book;
2) the Paraclete Ordinary;
3) the hymn collection that Abelard composed for the Paraclete;
4) Abelard's sermon collection written for the Paraclete;
5) the letters exchanged between Abelard and Heloise; and
6) the Nevers Prosary.

These sources enable us to piece together a large portion of the warp and weft that was once formed among Abelard's hymns, sermons, sequences, and other Paraclete *liturgica*. With this broad background sketched, we focus on the two sequences in Chapters Two through Four. In Chapters Five and Six we shall broaden our focus to consider how the rhetorical argument of the sequences is interwoven into Abelard's other Paraclete *liturgica*. As Chapters Two through Six unfold, the reader shall see that our analysis occurs on two levels, or, better stated, along two axes:

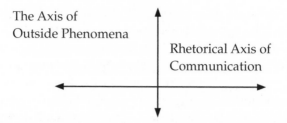

The Axis of
Outside Phenomena

Rhetorical Axis of
Communication

As the diagram suggests, our study proceeds linearly, on the one hand, closely examining the rhetorical discourse of *Virgines castae* and *Epithalamica*.[29] On the other hand, the study moves laterally, analyzing the dialogue that occurs between the sequences and a range of 'Abelardian phenomena' outside of the sequences— works Abelard contributed to the Paraclete liturgical life as well as the many sources, biblical, patristic, and medieval, that shaped Abelard's compositions.[30]

Vernon Robbins, in *The Tapestry of Early Christian Discourse: Rhetoric, Society, and Ideology*, calls this movement between the vertical and horizontal axes 'intertextual analysis.' It leads the interpreter to explore a range of phenomena outside of the text under investigation. The text and outside phenomena intersect on the 'oral-scribal' level where one discovers fragments of outside texts and oral traditions stitched into the text under investigation in the form of explicit quotations and allusions. Cultural, social, historical, and—in the case of *Virgines castae* and *Epithalamica*—poetic and musical phenomena are all woven together to create not only the tapestry of the individual sequences, but a larger tapestry formed by biblical, patristic, medieval, and Abelardian texts. This larger tapestry bears witness to the shared symbolic world of Abelard and the Paraclete nuns.

29. This diagram is adapted from Robbins, *Tapestry*, 31.

30. The range of dialogue between a given text and oral, scribal, cultural, social, poetic, musical, rhetorical, historical phenomena outside of it is infinite. I have concentrated my intertextual analysis on the field of biblical, patristic, and Paraclete sources that I think most reveal dialogue with Abelard's *Virgines castae* and *Epithalamica*.

Chapter Two explores the biblical and patristic intertexture of the two sequences at the oral-scribal level. This chapter is archaeological—a kind of excavation of Abelard's *memoria*. Here we unearth the sources out of which Abelard created *Virgines castae* and *Epithalamica*. While Abelard worked by gathering ('inventing') from his vast memory certain biblical and patristic building blocks, we get at this material only through the tedious effort of dismantling his artifice. Sometimes this intertextual analysis focuses on long passages; in other cases it centers on a single word found in a biblical or patristic source. Our goal is to discover the springs from which Abelard drew the *materia*, the subject matter, of the two sequences.

Chapter Two then considers *how* Abelard used his sources. We shall find that sometimes he quotes them word for word, other times he omits or adds words or phrases. We catch him rearranging his sources or restating them in his own words. The restraints of poetry and music by no means fully account for these variations. As we shall see, ancient and medieval speakers and writers were trained in how to shape and reshape their sources for rhetorical ends. Hence, Chapter Two not only identifies the sources Abelard used; it also shows that Abelard so consumed and assimilated the arguments and images of his sources that their meanings became expressions of his own thought. Having swallowed and digested his sources—to borrow an image from the Roman rhetor Quintilian[31]—Abelard skillfully redeployed them in a manner appropriate to his audience.

In Chapter Three, we examine Abelard's very careful *arrangement and elaboration* of his invented *materia*. This disposition is often systematic; Abelard moves his reader/singer step by step from one idea or scene to the next. Using insights from the *expolitio* and the epideictic elaboration of the ancient *chreia*—both exercises used well into the Middle Ages for training budding

---

31. Quintilian, *Institutio Oratoria*, X.1.16–19; trans. H. E. Butler, Loeb Classical Library 127 (Cambridge: Harvard University Press, 1966); Carruthers, *Memory*, 165–168.

young poets, preachers, and rhetors—we detail how Abelard develops the argumentative texture of his sequence.

Chapter Four shows that *Virgines castae* and *Epithalamica* possess poetic, musical, and rhetorical features that are particularly characteristic of Abelard's work. Here we rely in part on Chrysogonus Waddell's literary analysis of Abelard's hymns. We first present and illustrate many of the recurrent intertextual features and peculiarities of Abelard's hymns, and then subject the sequences to the same analysis and by this process draw results that correspond very closely to Waddell's. Chapter Four also gives careful attention to Abelard's musical setting of the two sequences. Here we build on the work of Ritva Jonnson, Leo Treitler, Calvin Bower, and William Flynn, who have produced important studies on the deep connections between text and music in medieval chant.[32] Their work also reveals how medieval musical training was grounded in the disciplines of grammar and rhetoric. We shall see that Abelard's sequences reflect the teaching of music theorists in his day: On the one hand, he had the ability to design melody that functioned primarily to articulate the syntactical structure of a text; and on the other, he could create a musical syntax that had its own independence from linguistic syntax.

In Chapter Five we probe directly into the connections between the *materia* of the sequences and Abelard's hymns, sermons, and letters to Heloise. Here we shall discover that Abelard drew on much the same source material in composing all of his many Paraclete contributions. We unearth in the sequences numerous turns of phrase, groups of words, and theological ideas that bear the fingerprint of Abelard and further confirm Waddell's argument for Abelardian authorship. As we discover how intertwined Abelard's Paraclete works are, moreover, we move ever deeper into the symbolic world that *Virgines castae* and *Epithalamica* very likely reinforced among Heloise and her nuns.

---

32. See Chapter Four, notes.

Chapter Six focuses directly on the place of *Virgines castae* and *Epithalamica* in the lives of Abelard and Heloise. Drawing on the 'personal' letters exchanged between Abelard and Heloise, we retell the story of their ill-fated love affair, short-lived marriage, and years in the monastic life.[33] Both she and Abelard knew that there was no merit in outward acts unmotivated by love of God. While considering Heloise's unhappy attitude toward her monastic life, her role as abbess of the Paraclete, and her continued obsession with Abelard, we see that the sequences were at least one way by which Abelard sought to convince Heloise, after their romantic relationship had ended, that she should love Christ above himself. He sought to move her heart to Christ as her bridegroom, though she confessed that she still considered Abelard her highest love. Externally she was a good abbess; yet both she and Abelard knew that there was no merit in outward acts unmotivated by love of God. Her intentions must match her deeds. The two sequences were a central means by which Abelard strove to create and nurture a symbolic world for Heloise that brought her affections in line with her life as abbess of the Paraclete.

33. I consider the letters authentic (and briefly state why in Chapter One), but do not reopen the debate over the genuineness of the correspondence.

1

THE PARACLETE
LITURGICAL TAPESTRY

Abelard was the greatest provider of devotional literature
for nuns in the twelfth century.

—*M. T. Clanchy*[1]

IN LATE 1129 Abelard made arrangements to hand over the
Paraclete Oratory, which he had founded some eight or nine
years earlier in the territory of Troyes, to Heloise and her
nuns.[2] Earlier that same year, on 14 April, the nuns had been
forcibly removed from their monastery at Argenteuil when
Adam Suger (1081–1151), the abbot from 1122–1151 of the royal
abbey of Saint Denis,[3] accused Heloise and her nuns of notorious

---

1. Clanchy, *Abelard*, 153.

2. Betty Radice writes: 'the Convent of Ste Marie of Argenteuil was founded as a monastery in the late seventh century by a nobleman Hermenricus and
his wife Numma, who presented it to the Abbey of St Denis. In the early ninth
century Charlemagne removed if from St Denis and made it independent, with
his daughter Theodrada as abbess. She intended it to revert to St Denis at her
death, but in the civil wars and the Norman invasions it was destroyed and
abandoned for about 150 years. At the end of the tenth century it was restored
by Queen Adelaide, wife of Hugh Capet, richly endowed and filled with nuns
of the order of St Benedict'; Radice 74–75, note 1.

3. The abbey of Saint Denis, the shrine of the martyr-apostle of France,
was the most sacred place in medieval France. Dead French kings were laid to
rest among the relics of Saint Denis and his holy companions, and the living—
kings, knights, peasants—made pilgrimages to the abbey in hopes of receiving

immorality and claimed that the monastic buildings and surrounding lands legally belonged to his monastery.[4] The lands of Argenteuil included a port on the Seine, without which Suger's plans for rebuilding the church of Saint-Denis would have been frustrated. Expelling the Argenteuil nuns on the grounds of moral impropriety—an act not unprecedented in Abelard and Heloise's day[5]—was easy enough in an age when male ecclesiastics generally viewed females as seductresses and an imminent danger to male purity.[6]

Argenteuil was a place of no little importance in Heloise's life. When she was a young girl, the nuns at Argenteuil had laid the foundation of Heloise's vast learning. Then, after their tragic marriage, Abelard had returned Heloise to Argenteuil and insisted that she take monastic vows. Eventually she became abbess. Under her tenure disaster struck when Abbot Suger dissolved the Argenteuil community and made little or no provi-

---

the saint's blessing. Control of the holy site made Suger very powerful; and as his building campaign progressed his power greatly increased. See Clanchy, *Abelard*, 234.

4. The charges Abbot Sugar brought against the nuns were endorsed by the papal legate Cardinal Matthew of Albano; by local leaders, including Geoffrey of Chartres, Ralph of Vermandois; and by King Louis VI and Queen Adelaide. Clanchy, *Abelard*, 249, writes: 'There is no way today of deciding the rights and wrongs of this [charge against the Paraclete nuns]. Suger was a very powerful man in France. But it may have been true that Heloise was unable to keep order at Argenteuil, just as Abelard could not control his monks at St Gildas. He [Abelard] makes no mention of the charge of immorality in his "history of calamities." His version is simply that "it happened that our abbot of St Denis some how or other acquired the convent of Argenteuil, as an ancient right pertaining to his monastery, and he violently expelled the nuns". Abelard's description of Suger as "our abbot" is significant, as it acknowledges the authority of St Denis over Abelard's oratory of the Paraclete, which is attested by its ancient connections with St Denis. Abelard's gift of his oratory to Heloise must have required "our abbot's" permission. This was a mutually beneficial arrangement, which made Suger look less violent and which gave Abelard a new role as a patron of nuns'. Mews, *Lost Love* 153–157, considers these charges against Heloise and her nuns as trumped up.

5. For details on the closing of other abbeys, see Mews, *Lost Love* 60–65.

6. See Christopher Brooke, *The Medieval Idea of Marriage* (Oxford: Clarendon Press, 1984) 69.

sion for its nuns. Abelard's *Historia calamitatum* relates that they suffered great hardship for several months after their displacement. Finally, late in the year 1129 Abelard learned of Heloise's calamities, and after ten years' separation from her, he came to the abbess and deeded the Paraclete to her.

Abelard probably never imagined that his remote Paraclete refuge would become the mother-house of other communities of nuns under Heloise's direction. Yet from the time of Abelard's death (21 April 1142) to the death of Heloise (probably 16 May 1164), the Abbey of the Paraclete founded no fewer than six communities following its observances.[7] The Paraclete and its daughter communities thrived for several generations after Heloise's death. Following the Protestant Reformation their numbers dwindled and the abbess, Jeanne Chabot, became a Huguenot. When she was finally ousted from her post in 1592, only three nuns remained to carry on the work that Abelard and Heloise had begun many years before.[8] Despite their small numbers, the community persisted until the late summer of 1795, when Madame Charlotte de Roucy, the last of the Paraclete abbesses, realized that the violently anti-monastic winds of the French Revolution were almost sure to strike the walls, indeed, the very foundations, of the Paraclete. She parceled out to select friends and retainers the most valuable books and manuscripts of the ill-fated community,[9] and the long history of the Abbey of the Paraclete ended.

---

7. In *Abelard*, 238, Clanchy writes, 'Within twenty-five years of its foundation, the Paraclete owned so much property that a map makes it look as if it had colonized the whole area around the Seine between Troyes and Provins'.

8. See Chrysogonus Waddell, 'Peter Abelard as Creator of Liturgical Texts,' in *Petrus Abaelardus (1079–1142). Person, Werk und Wirkung*, Hrsg. von Rudolf Thomas, Trierer theologische studien (Trier: Paulinus-Verlag, 1980), 267–286; see especially 284. Waddell cites in evidence *La regle de St-Benoist. Avec les Declarations et Constitutions sur icelle . . . Pour les Religeuses de Paraclit.* 1632.

9. Waddell, '*Epithalamica*' 239–271. For the details of the breakup of the Paraclete library, see C. J. Mews, 'La bibliothèque du Paraclet du XIIIe siècle à la Révolution', *Studia monastica*, 27 (1985) 31–60.

As is true of many past monastic communities, little remains today of what was once the Paraclete world. Its property has long been sold and its buildings and walls have crumbled into dust. Only a few of the abbey's books, with some of its liturgical texts and, even less, music, survive, bearing scant witness to the worship that once took place at the three altars of its cruciform oratory—the prototype of which Abelard himself had built of reeds and thatch in a lonely spot on the banks of the river Ardusson in Troyes.[10] The surviving Paraclete books suggest that the community's worship was formed by a unique combination of the cistercian liturgical office with hymns, sequences, *planctus*, prayers, sermons, and commentaries provided by Abelard.[11]

As in any monastery, the singing of Mass could easily require the officiating priest, his assistants, the choir, and the choir leader to draw on as many as eight interdependent books. It was common before and during Abelard and Heloise's day for a liturgical book to contain only those parts of the liturgy relevant to a single officiant in a service. Priests, monks, and nuns usually learned to sing their Mass parts from memory. The same was true of performing the daily hours of monastic prayer, the Offices. Special books preserved the Offices' texts and music, while the members of the worshipping community typically memorized their own part in the services. Mass and Office books were often very large; they served as a record of the web of prayers, scripture readings, songs, rites that constituted worship at a particular cathedral or monastery.[12]

Only two liturgical books survive from the Paraclete; fortunately, they allow us insight into the liturgical world of the Paraclete and, more importantly, they help us see how Abelard sought

10. For details on the Paraclete Oratory and cloister quadrangle, see Chrysogonus Waddell, CL 3:313-318.

11. Waddell, 'Peter Abelard as Creator of Liturgical Texts,' 270.

12. For a handy introduction to the principal forms, orders, and books of western liturgy, see John Harper, *The Forms and Orders of Western Liturgy from the Tenth to the Eighteenth Century: A Historical Introduction and Guide for Students and Musicians* (Oxford: Clarendon Press, 1991).

to shape that world by many of his own prayers, sermons, hymns, and sequences.[13] These books show us when, where, and how often *Virgines castae* and *Epithalamica* were prescribed for use at Mass; they also demonstrate that the themes of love, virginity, and marriage to Christ, so central to Abelard's sequences, permeated the nun's worship. The breadth and depth of Abelard's contributions surely justifies M. T. Clanchy's claim that 'Abelard was the greatest provider of devotional literature for nuns in the twelfth century.'[14]

This literary tapestry portrayed the symbolic world of Heloise and her nuns. Abelard the monk and abbot knew that daily performance of the liturgy, with its reading, singing, hearing, memorizing, and interpreting sacred texts—indeed, the entire *sequence* of monastic practices—constituted the material preconditions and material means for the formation of the Paraclete symbolic world. The rhetoric of *Virgines castae* and *Epithalamica* reflected the beliefs, practices, and persons that Abelard apparently thought best served to define, legitimate, form, and give identity to the Paraclete community. Careful analysis of the rhetoric of the two sequences suggests that Abelard sought to shape Heloise's character to eliminate any radical disjunction between her outer behavior and inner motives, and between her performance of monastic rituals and her personal sentiments.[15] Our first glimpse into this world of Abelard and Heloise after marriage will come through closer reflection on the surviving Paraclete Office Book and Ordinary.

13. A summary statement of the monastic observance at the Paraclete and its daughter-houses does survive. This little work, entitled *Institutiones nostrae*, guided the Paraclete nuns in applying the Rule of Saint Benedict to their lives. Chrysogonus Waddell has edited the manuscript, Troyes, Bibliothèque Municipale MS 802, ff. 89r–90v, as *The Paraclete Statutes. Institutiones nostrae* , CLS 20 (Trappist: Gethsemani Abbey,/Kalamazoo: Cistercian Publications, 1987).

14. *Abelard*, 153.

15. See Asad, *Genealogies* 63; Asad's treatment of the medieval liturgy and monastic moral formation has greatly helped me see what Abelard sought to do at the Paraclete.

THE SURVIVING PARACLETE OFFICE BOOK AND ORDINARY

The Paraclete Office book survives in a late-fifteenth-, early-six-teenth-century manuscript, Chaumont, Bibliothèque municipale, MS 31. This manuscript provides us with Paraclete texts *in extenso* for all the Day Hours of the Divine Office, as well as hymns, *capitula*, versicles, and collects for the Night Office, and contains:

1) the Paraclete's complete hymn repertory;
2) all the office collects and short readings recited by the hebdomadary, i.e., the weekly officiant at the Office;
3) the texts of all the chants—antiphons, responsories, and versicles—used throughout the Paraclete liturgical year; and
4) a complete calendar of feast days celebrating Christ's life and the lives of many saints.[16]

Among these various *liturgica* Chrysogonus Waddell has identified many contributions made by Abelard to the Paraclete. These contributions are profoundly interrelated, revealing that his Paraclete *liturgica* were, for the most part, all of one cloth. Given the Paraclete nuns' general faithfulness over the centuries to their traditional liturgical practices, this thirteenth-century manuscript probably gives us quite an accurate look at the liturgical life of Heloise and her twelfth-century nuns.

Alongside the Office book in importance is the abbey's *liber ordinarius*, or Ordinal, which survives in a late thirteenth-century manuscript—Paris, Bibliothèque nationale, MS français 14410.[17]

16. Chrysogonus Waddell has edited the entire manuscript in 3 volumes: CLS 5, CLS 6, and CLS 7.
17. Waddell has edited the entire manuscript in CL 4, and has provided notes and commentary on it in CL 3. Details on the history of the manuscript are also found in C. J. Mews, 'La bibliothèque du Paraclet du XIIIe siècle à la Révolution,' *Studia Monastica* 27 (1985) 31–60. The manuscript divides into three uneven sections: *Section I* (folios 5r–23r) contains a book of burials which indicates the obituaries and places where nuns and other persons connected with the abbey (Abelard included) are buried. *Section II* (folios 29r–116v) is essentially a *liber ordinarius*, a book of directions for the performance of the liturgy on particular days and feasts. References are made to readings in church, in refectory, and in

This work contains directions for how all the various texts and chants, once scattered throughout many different books, were to be coordinated and gives an outline of the Paraclete liturgy, including Mass, Office, readings in community, processions, and other occasional celebrations. Unlike the Chaumont manuscript, it contains no complete hymn texts, but it does frequently refer to particular hymns and sequences, giving their *incipits* and often noting the place(s) where they were to be sung. This provides some knowledge of hymn and sequence performance at the Paraclete in the late thirteenth century. Comparison with the Chaumont manuscript reveals that little changed in the abbey's liturgical life between the thirteenth and the fifteenth centuries.

Scattered throughout the Ordinal and Office book are many hymns, antiphons, responsories, and collects that we know were composed by Abelard for Heloise and her nuns. The hymnal— huge for its day with some one hundred thirty-three hymns—survives in part in two separate manuscripts: the Paraclete Office book referred to above; and a non-Paraclete source, Bruxelles, Bibliothèque royale, MS 10147-58. This third major source for our intertextual analysis consists of twelfth- and thirteenth-century *varia*, among which is found a collection of Abelard's hymns (ff. 81r–96v).[18] Here one finds ninety-six unnotated hymns (hymns

---

cloister before Compline; to the choice and arrangement of hymns for services; and to the processions and occasional celebrations connected to particular feast and fast days at the Paraclete. *Section III* (folios 117r–123v) is a directory for processions. It indicates only the incipits of the processional chants, which do not always agree with parallel references in the *Liber ordinarius*.

18. Hubert Silvestre has subjected this manuscript to detailed analysis in 'Le Ms Bruxellensis 10147-58 (S. XII-XIII) et son "Compendium artis picturae,"' *Bulletin de la Commission royale d'histoire* 119 (1954) 95–140; and in his critical review of Szövérffy's HP in 'A propos d'une édition récente de l'*Hymnarius Paraclitensis* d'Abélard,' *Scriptorium* 32 (1978) 91–100. For a list of modern editions of Abelard's hymns, see n. 6.

The contents of the divisions are as follows: *Libellus I:* Preface followed by Hymns 1–29: a complete cycle of Sunday and weekday hymns. *Libellus II:* Preface followed by Hymns 30–60: a cycle of hymns for the 'feasts of the Lord.' *Libellus III:* Preface followed by Hymns 61–105: a series of hymns for saints days. (This *libellus* is lacunose at the end; fortunately, the manuscript Chaumont 31 supplies most if not all of the missing material.)

without music). The collection is divided into three *libelli*, each of which is introduced by a Preface attributed to Abelard.

These three manuscripts bear witness to a vast network of *liturgica* that Abelard wove together for the Paraclete nuns. In this study we cannot draw on every thread of data, but will concentrate on one section of Abelard's great Paraclete tapestry: the image of Heloise and her bridal virgins with their bridegroom Christ.

ABELARD'S SERMONS FOR THE PARACLETE

Beyond these manuscript sources, Abelardian sermons and letters are central to the intertextual dimensions of this study. In addition to his hymns, Abelard sent a collection of his sermons for reading in refectory at community meals and before Compline at the end of the day. The frequent references to a book of *les sermons au mestre* (Sermons of the Master) in the Paraclete Ordinal, writes Chrysogonus Waddell, 'is proof that the sermons were still staple community fare in the later thirteenth century.'[19] The editors of *Patrologia Latina* attributed thirty-four extant sermons to Abelard and Damien Van den Eynde has convincingly demonstrated their authenticity.[20] His conclusion that these thirty-four sermons, with the possible exception of Sermon 24, formed the collection of sermons Abelard provided for the Paraclete, however, has proved to be less convincing.[21] Several sources attest to the existence of a collection of sermons for the Paraclete. The

19. 'Saint Bernard and the Cistercian Office at the Abbey of the Paraclete', in *The Chimaera of His Age: Studies on Bernard of Clairvaux*, edd. E. Rozanne Elder and John R. Sommerfeldt, Studies in Medieval Cistercian History 5 (Kalamazoo: Cistercian Publications, 1980) 76–109, here 105.

20. Damien Van den Eynde, 'Le recueil des Sermons de Pierre Abelard', *Antonianum* 37 (1962) 17–54.

21. See Chrysogonus Waddell, 'Peter Abelard as Creator of Liturgical Texts', *Petrus Abaelardus*, 75–86; and Eileen F. Kearney, 'Master Peter Abelard, Expositor of Sacred Scripture: An Analysis of Abelard's Approach to Biblical Exposition in Selected Writings on Scripture' (Ph.D. Dissertation, Marquette University, 1980) 244–247.

best-known of these is printed before Abelard's sermons in the *Patrologia Latina*: a dedicatory letter that Abelard apparently enclosed with the actual sermonary he sent to Heloise.[22]

> Having recently completed a certain little book of hymns and sequences at your request, my venerated and beloved sister in Christ, Heloise, I have also hastened to write some sermons—a type of writing that is contrary to my usual practice—for you and your spiritual daughters gathered at our oratory.[23]

Here he expressly refers to a sermon collection which he provided for the Paraclete upon Heloise's request.

Van den Eynde's conclusion that this letter was originally attached to the thirty-four sermons in *Patrologia Latina* is challenged by Waddell's analysis of the Paraclete Office book and Ordinal; he attributes only twenty of the PL sermons to Abelard's original book of sermons. The Paraclete Ordinary explicitly refers to eight of Abelard's extant sermons (1, 4, 7, and 18-22 in *Patrologia Latina*), all of which Waddell has identified in the book *Les sermons au mestre*.[24]

The twenty sermons Waddell associates with the Paraclete clearly address either nuns (Sermons 1, 13, 25-26, and 32) or an unspecified group (Sermons 2, 3, 9, 14-17, 23, and 34). Waddell contends that the sermons Abelard delivered to monks (Sermons 5, 6, 8, 10-12, 27, 28, 30, 33), or to monks and nuns (Sermons 29 and 31), did not form part of the original Paraclete sermonary, which, he argues, included all sermons preached explicitly to nuns, except Sermon 26—which the Ordinary suggests was in a volume separate from the original sermonary—and all sermons which do not specify a particular audience.

---

22. See my Introduction, above, page xxiii.

23. PL 178:379: *Libello quodam hymnorum vel sequentiarum a me nuper precibus tuis consummato, veneranda in christo et amanda soror Heloissa, nonnulla insuper opuscula sermonum, juxta petitionem tuam, tam tibi quam spiritalibus filiabus tuis in oratorio nostro congregatis, scribere praeter consuetudinem nostram utcunque maturavi.*

24. CL 3:385.

Waddell consequently proposes the following 'Table of Contents' for the collection of sermons Abelard sent to Heloise:[25]

Table I.1: *The Paraclete Collection of Sermons by Abelard*

PL #	Feast	Audience	Referred to in Paraclete Ordinary
1	Annunciation	Nuns	Yes
2	Christmas	Unstated	No
3	Circumcision	Unstated	No
4	Epiphany	Unstated	Yes
7	Palm Sunday	Unstated	Yes
9	Holy Week	Unstated	No
13	Easter Day	Nuns	No
14	Rogation Days	Unstated	No
15	Ascension	Unstated	No
16	Octave of Ascension	Unstated	No
17	Friday After Ascension	Unstated	No
18	Pentecost	Nuns	Yes
19	Pentecost Monday	Nuns	Yes
20	Pentecost Tuesday	Nuns	Yes
21	Pentecost Wednesday	Nuns	Yes
22	Pentecost Thursday	Nuns	Yes
23	St Peter	Unstated	No
25	St John the Evangelist	Nuns	No
32	St Stephen Protomartyr	Nuns	No
34	Holy Innocents	Unstated	No

25. CL 3:385-386.

In examining Abelard's Paraclete sermons, I have found that Sermons 1 (for the Annunciation) and 13 (for Easter) show profound interconnections with *Virgines castae* and *Epithalamica*, respectively. My analysis of the remaining Paraclete sermons also shows that Abelard used certain key topics to stitch together his hymns, sequences, and many of the sermons, and by them to keep these topics always before the Paraclete nuns.

ABELARD AND HELOISE'S LETTERS

A rich treasure of letters between Abelard and Heloise allows us to supplement the Office book, Ordinal and the sermons in analyzing the symbolic world of the Paraclete. Waddell has shown that, in addition to his sermons, hymns, and sequences, *le Mestre* provided the Paraclete nuns with numerous antiphons, responsories, and collects.[26] The letters reveal that many of Abelard's liturgical contributions were provided at Heloise's request and, moreover, provide some insight into the Father Founder's high aspirations and deep intentions for the Paraclete nuns. He clearly casts himself in the role of a Saint Jerome, with Heloise playing the part of the Virgin Mary and Mary Magdalene as well as Paula, Asella, and a host of other past female ascetics who guided other women in embracing Christ as their bridegroom.

Scholars have subjected Abelard's letters to much greater scrutiny than his sermons.[27] The authenticity of the correspondence has been doubted by many. With the publication of his *Héloïse et Abélard*[28] in 1938, Étienne Gilson seemed to have countered all the naysayers before him—at least he gave those who accepted the authenticity of the letters cause to continue believing. Then in 1972, John F. Benton jolted the abelardian scholarly world when he

26. 'Peter Abelard as Creator of Liturgical Texts', 277–279.

27. Critical editions of the correspondence are: Muckle, 'Consolation,' (Letter 1, the *Historia calamitatum*); Muckle, 'Letters,' (Letters 2–5); and Muckle, 'Religious Life,' (Letters 6 and 7). McLaughlin, 'Rule,' (Letter 8, Abelard's Rule for Religious Women).

28. *Héloïse et Abélard* (Paris, Librairie Philosophique J. Vrin, 1938); English translation, Gilson, *Heloise and Abelard*.

proposed that a third party had composed the correspondence.[29] Seven years later, in spite of his every effort to the contrary, Benton declared that new evidence had convinced him to abandon his earlier theory.[30] In its place, he proposed that the unity of literary style, the basic identity of characteristic terminology throughout the correspondence, the harmony of ideas and expressions with other works by Abelard—and the inability of himself and others to produce convincing cases of anachronisms or internal contradiction that could sustain his third-party hypothesis—all pointed to Abelard as the sole creator of the correspondence. Indeed, he conjectured that sometime after Abelard manufactured the letters, he attached the *Epistolae* and his *Historia calamitatum* to his Rule for the Paraclete nuns. Benton joined with Chrysogonus Waddell in arguing that Abelard combined the three 'to justify a Rule which departed from normal practices of Benedictine nuns and even from the *Institutiones* of the convent he had founded'.[31] The pendulum of scholarly opinion has now swung in the direction of accepting the correspondence in large part as genuine,[32] although the question has by no means been entirely settled.

Peter Dronke has shown deep stylistic links between Heloise's *Epistolae* and *Problemata*—the series of questions about scripture passages that Heloise addressed to Abelard and to which Abelard responded[33]—and a deliberate use of rhythmic cadences

29. John F. Benton, 'Fraud, Fiction and Borrowing in the Correspondence of Abelard and Heloise', in *Pierre Abélard—Pierre le Vénérable. Les courants philosophiques, littéraires et artistiques en occident au milieu du XIIe siècle. Abbaye de Cluny 2 au 9 juillet 1972* (Paris, 1975) 469–511.

30. John F. Benton, 'A Reconsideration of the Authenticity of the Correspondence of Abelard and Heloise', in *Petrus Abaelardus (1079–1142) Person, Werk und Wirkung*, ed. Rudolf Thomas (Trier: Paulinus-Verlag, 1980) 41–52.

31. Benton, 'Reconsideration', 49. Waddell has made much of the introductory role of the letters in his 'Peter Abelard's *Letter 10* and Cistercian Liturgical Reform', *Studies in Medieval Cistercian History, II*, ed. John R. Sommerfeldt, Cistercian Studies 13 (Kalamazoo: Cistercian Publications, 1976) 74–86; and CL 20:41-56.

32. Many scholars have participated in this long lived argument. Readers are referred to the vast bibliography contained in the works cited in the following notes.

33. *Problemata Heloissae*; PL 178:677-730.

which reveals a writing style unusual for the twelfth century. Dronke writes that Heloise 'has extended passages in which rhyme, assonance and parallelism have been sensitively interwoven, the cadences that depend on rhythm and those that depend on rhyme being artistically harmonized'.[34] Dronke shows that such stylistic features occur not only in Abelard's letters, but also in Heloise's letters to Abelard, in the epistle with which Heloise began the *Problemata*, and, even more prominently, in her letter to Peter the Venerable. Dronke would have us take seriously that the letters attributed to Heloise are indeed the work of Heloise.

Constant J. Mews' fascinating recent work *The Lost Love Letters of Heloise and Abelard*[35] has made an even more forceful claim for the authenticity of the letters. Mews argument for authenticity is linked to an anonymous collection of love letters written before their marriage. If truly authentic, this collection helps us better hear the voice of Heloise than we do in the traditional letters exchanged after their marriage. Concerning the authenticity of the two sets of letters, Mews declares: 'the doubts which have been raised about whether Heloise wrote the letters attributed to her, and about whether Abelard and Heloise could have written the love letters preserved at Clairvaux, reflect an unwillingness to accept that such a gifted and independently minded woman could have existed in twelfth-century France.'[36]

In sum, scholarship points in the direction of authenticity: Heloise wrote Abelard and Abelard wrote Heloise.[37] While

34. Dronke, 'Heloise's *Problemata* and *Letters*: Some Questions of Form and Content' in *Petrus Abaelardus (1079–1142): Person, Werk und Wirkung*, ed. Rudolf Thomas, Trierer Theologische Studien (Trier: Paulinus-Verlag, 1980) 53–73.

35. Mews, *Lost Love*.

36. Mews, *Lost Love* 170.

37. See D. E. Luscombe, 'The *Letters* of Heloise and Abelard since "Cluny 1972"', 19–39; P. Dronke, 'Heloise's *Problemata* and *Letters*', 53–73; Peter von Moos, 'Post festum', 75–100—all in *Petrus Abaelardus*. See also Peter Dronke, *Abelard and Heloise in Medieval Testimonies* (Cambridge: University of Glasgow Press, 1976); *idem*, 'Heloise,' in *Women Writers of the Middle Ages: A Critical Study of Texts from Perpetua (†203) to Marguerite Poret (†1310)* (Cambridge: Cambridge University Press, 1984) 107–143; Chrysogonus Waddell, CL 20:41–56; Barbara

conceding that one of the two, perhaps both, and maybe even a third party, may have 'tinkered' with the texts over the years before they appeared in thirteenth-century manuscripts, I agree with those scholars who accept the dossier, much as it stands, as a faithful transmission of the *epistolae* once exchanged between the Paraclete founder and its abbess. The letters figure in several profound ways in the bridal scene we are trying to recover. Most importantly, the letters and sequences fully harmonize in rhetorical intent: both genres contain rhetoric calculated to persuade Heloise to enter fully into her role as Christ's bride. As we process through this study, we shall see that this was no small matter to Abelard.

The Texts and Music of Abelard's Sequences

The music and full text of the two sequences *Virgines castae* and *Epithalamica* do not survive in any Paraclete liturgical book. The abbey's *Sequentiary*—its book of sequences—seems forever lost. Only the Paraclete Ordinary makes mention of the two sequences only by *incipit*. Fortunately, the two songs are found in a late-twelfth-century Nevers manuscript: Paris, Bibliothèque Nationale, MS nouv. acq. lat. 3126. Here one finds—on ff. 82v–91v—the oldest extant version of the texts and melodies of the two sequences.[38] The sequences appear in an appendix to the prosary. They seem never to have made their way into the Nevers liturgy; rather, hypothesizes Margot Fassler, they were among those sequences being considered, probably in the late twelfth

---

Newman, 'Authority, Authenticity, and The Repression of Heloise', *Journal of Medieval and Renaissance Studies* 22 (1992) 121–157; C. Stephen Jaegar, *The Envy of Angels: Cathedral Schools and Social Ideals in medieval Europe, 950–1200* (Philadelphia: University of Pennsylvania Press, 1994) 450, note 54; and Clanchy, *Abelard*, xi and 15–16.

38. Michel Huglo describes the manuscript and its contents in 'Un nouveau prosaire nivernais', *Ephemerides Liturgicae* 71 (1957) 3–30. Nevers is located on the river Loire in the geographical center of France, well south of the Paraclete, near the towns of Auxerre and Autun.

or thirteenth centuries, for addition to the local augustinian liturgy.[39] In the manuscript, *Virgines castae* appears first,[40] followed by two of Abelard's *planctus*: *De profundis ad te clamantium*, and *Dolorum Solatium*.[41] Then comes *Epithalamica*.[42] Chrysogonus Waddell speculates that these four pieces 'are grouped as they are because they are derived directly or indirectly from the same source, the Abbey of the Paraclete in Champagne, near Troyes'.[43] Unlike their situation in Nevers, at the Paraclete the sequences occupied a very important and prominent use, as we shall see.

There is as yet no critical edition of *Virgines castae* and *Epithalamica*.[44] Rather than attempt an analysis of the surviving manuscripts and printed versions of the two sequences here, I have transcribed and translated the latin text of each sequence as it exists in the late-twelfth century Nevers prosary. In my judgment, as in that of Chrysogonus Waddell[45], there is no reason to doubt that Heloise and her nuns sang the two sequences very much as they are notated in the Nevers prosary.

39. Margot Fassler, *The Gothic Song: Victorine Sequences and Augustinian Reform in Twelfth-Century Paris* (Cambridge: Cambridge University Press, 1993) 104.

40. *Virgines castae* on folio 84v.

41. *De profundis ad te clamantium*; on f. 87v, and *Dolorum solatium* on f. 88v. For discussion and a transcription of *Dolorum solatium*, see Lorenz Weinrich, 'Peter Abelard as Musician', *The Musical Quarterly* 55 (1969) 295–312, 464–86.

42. *Epithalamica*, f. 90r.

43. '*Epithalamica*', 242.

44. Chrysogonus Waddell has been collecting the various versions of *Virgines castae* and *Epithalamica* for many years. He has listed many of the variants of *Epithalamica* in his article '*Epithalamica*', 242–246. Variants of *Virgines castae* will appear in his promised work on the two sequences. I am grateful to him for having given me access to them through his unpublished essay on *Virgines castae*, 'Abelard and the Chaste Virgins'.

45. '*Epithalamica*', 246.

Virgines castae

1a. *Virgines castae*
   virginis summae
   decus praecinentes
1b. *Ceteras quoque*
   condignas laude
   post hanc venerantes

1a. Chaste virgins sing of
   the beauty of the supreme
   virgin
1b. and venerate after her
   the other worthy
   virgins by their praise

2a. *Psalmis et hymnis*
   canticis dignis
   sibi colloquentes
2b. *Solvant in istis*
   debitae laudis
   hostias sollemnes

2a. Speaking to one another in
   fitting Psalms and hymns
   and canticles
2b. Let them pay by these
   [songs] solemn sacrifices
   of due praise

3a. *Haec est adextris*
   assistens regis
   illa regina
3b. *Iuncta latere*
   sola cum rege
   praecedit ipsa
3c. *Aurata veste*
   varietate
   circiumamicta
3d. *Tamquam dominam*
   sequitur ipsam
   queque beata

3a. This one [the supreme virgin]
   is that queen serving at
   the right hand of the king
3b. United beside him
   she alone with the king
   proceeds
3c. In golden array
   clothed round about with
   variety
3d. Every blessed [virgin]
   follows her as
   her lady

4a. *Post eam adductae*
   virgines devotae
4b. *regi sunt oblatae*
   Christo consecratae
4c. *Tales erant Thecla*
   Agnes et Lucia
4d. *Agathes et multa*
   virginum caterva

4a. Led after her
   devoted virgins
4b. have been offered to the king
   [and] consecrated to Christ
4c. Such [virgins] were Thecla
   Agnes and Lucia
4d. Agathes and many
   a great throng of virgins

(Continued)

Virgines castae

5a. *Filiae Tyri*
    munera ferentes
	5a. The daughters of Tyre
	    bearing gifts

5b. *Et in his regis*
    vultum deprecantes
	5b. And entreating the favor of
	    the king by means of them

5c. *Hostias cunctis* *habent puriores*	[the gifts] 5c. Have offerings purer than

5d. *Corpore munde*
    Corde sanctiores
	all (other offerings)
	5d. (They are) clean in body
	    holier in heart

6a. *Holocaustum Domino*
    Offerent ex integro
	6a. As a burnt-offering
	    virgins offer to the Lord

6b. *virgines carne*
    integrae mente
	6b. the integrity of their flesh
	    and mind

6c. *immortalem sponsum*
    eligentes Christum
	6c. Choosing Christ as
	    their immortal bridegroom

7a. *O felices nuptiae*
    quibus nullae maculae
	7a. Oh happy nuptials where
	    there are no impurities

7b. *nulli dolores*
    partus sunt graves
	7b. No grievous pains of
	    childbirth,

7c. *nec pelex timenda*
    nec nutrix molesta
	7c. No rival mistress to be feared
	    no nurse who harasses

8a. *Lectulos harum*
    Christo vacantes
	8a. Their [virgins'] beds which
	    are left open for Christ

8b. *angeli vallant*
    custodientes
	8b. Guardian angels
	    protect

8c. *ne quis incestus*
    temeret illos
	8c. Lest any one impure
	    defile them

8d. *ensibus strictis*
    arcent immundos
	8d. They ward off the impure
	    with their drawn swords

9a. *Dormit in istis*
    Christus cum illis
	9a. In these (beds) Christ sleeps
	    with them (the virgins)

(Continued)

Virgines castae

9b. *felix hic somnus*
    requires dulcis
9c. *quo cum fovetur*
    virgo fidelis
9d. *inter amplexus*
    sponsi caelestis

9b. Happy the slumber [and]
    sweet the repose
9c. In which the faithful virgin
    is caressed
9d. In the embraces of the
    heavenly bridegroom.

10a. *Dextera sponsi*
    sponsa complexa
10b. *capiti laeva*
    dormit submissa
10c. *pervigil corde*
    corpore dormit
10d. *et sponsi grato*
    sinu quiescit

10a. The right hand of the bride-
    groom, clasps his bride
10b. His left hand
    cradles her head
10c. While wakeful in heart
    she sleeps in body
10d. and she quietly slumbers on
    the loving breast of her
    bridegroom

11a. *Approbans somnum*
    Sponsus beatam
11b. *inquietari*
    prohibet illam
11c. *ne suscitetis*
    inquit, dilectam
11d. *dum ipsa volet*
    ita quietam

11a. Favoring her sleep
    the Bridegroom
11b. Does not let her be
    disquieted
11c. he says: Do not awaken my
    beloved
11d. thus quiet as long as she
    wishes

12a. *Hic ecclesiastici*
    flos est ille germinis
12b. *tam rosis quam liliis*
    multiplex innumeris
12c. *quorum est fragrantiis*
    ager sponsi nobilis
12d. *naribus et oculis*
    aeque delectabilis

12a. Here the flower of the
    church is budding
12b. as many roses as lilies
    multiply beyond counting
12c. through their fragrance
    the bridegroom's field
12d. is equally delectable
    to scent and sight

(Continued)

Virgines castae

13a. *Ornatae tam byssina*
    quam veste purpurea
13b. *laeva tenent lilia*
    rosas habent dextera
13c. *et corona gemmea*
    redimitae capita
13d. *agni sine macula*
    percurrunt itinera

13a. Adorned in linen
    and in purple robes
13b. they hold lilies in their left
    hand, roses in their right
13c. and with their heads crowned
    as with a set of jewels
13d. they hasten along the paths
    of the Lamb without
    blemish

14a. *His quoque floribus*
    semper recentibus
14b. *sanctorum intexta*
    capitum sunt serta
14c. *His agnus pascitur*
    atque reficitur
14d. *hi flores electa*
    sunt illius esca

14a. Also from these flowers
    forever fresh
14b. the garlands on their holy
    heads are woven
14c. Among these the lamb
    pastures and is thereby
    refreshed
14d. these flowers are his food
    of choice

15a. *Hinc choro talium*
    vallatus agminum
15b. *hortorum amena*
    discurrit hac illac
15c. *Qui nunc comprehensus*
    ab his nunc elapsus
15d. *quasi quadam fuga*
    petulans exsultat

15a. Surrounded by this choir
    of such companies
15b. he races this way and
    that in the lovely gardens
15c. Now caught by them
    now slipping away
15d. he petulantly leaps about
    as if escaping

16a. *Crebros saltus*
    dat hic agnus
    inter illas discurrendo
16b. *Et cum ipsis*
    requiescit
    fervore meridiano

16a. This lamb leaps and bounds
    repeatedly prancing about
    among them
16b. And he rests among
    them [the virgins]
    in the noonday heat

(Continued)

Virgines castae

17a. *In earum pectore*	17a. In the middle of the day he
cubat in meridie	lies upon their breasts
17b. *Inter mammas virginum*	17b. He makes his sleeping place
Collocat cubiculum	among virgins' breasts
18a. *Virgo quippe*	18a. Since he himself
cum sit ipse	is a virgin, and was
Virgineque matre natus	born of a virgin mother
18b. *Virginales*	18b. He loves and longs
super omnes	for virginal embraces
amat et quaerit	above all others
recessus	
19a. *Somnus illi placidus*	19a. His sleep is serene when
in castis est sinibus	taken upon chaste laps
19b. *Ne qua forte macula*	19b. Lest otherwise perhaps a
sua foedet vellera	spot might soil his fleece
20a. *Hoc attende canticum*	20a. Attend to this song
devotarum virginum	of the illustrious college
insigne collegium	of devoted virgins
20b. *Quo nostra devotio*	20b. Whereby our devotion may
maiore se studio	with greater zeal adorn the
templum ornet Domine	temple of the Lord

Epithalamica

1a. *Epithalamica*
    dic Sponsa cantica
1b. *intus quae conspicis*
    dic foris gaudia
1c. *et nos laetificans*
    de Sponso nuntia
1d. *cuius te refovet*
    seper praesentia

2a. *Adulescentulae*
    vos chorum ducite
2b. *cum haec praecinerit*
    et vos succinite
2c. *Amici Sponsi vos*
    vocarunt nuptiae
2d. *et novae modulos*
    optamus Dominae

3a. *In montibus his ecce*
    saliens
3b. *ecce venit colles*
    transilens
3c. *per fenestras ad me*
    respiciens
3d. *per cancellos dicit*
    prospiciens

4a. *Amica surge propera*
4b. *columba nitens advola*

5a. *Horrens enim hiems iam*
    transiit
5b. *gravis imber recedens*
    abiit

1a. Sing, O bride,
    your bridal canticles
1b. Sing outwardly the joys
    you gaze upon within
1c. and gladdening us give
    tidings of the bridegroom
1d. whose presence renews
    you forever more

2a. O young maidens
    form your choir
2b. When she [the bride]
    begins singing, join in
2c. The bridegrooms's friends
    have
    called you to the nuptials
2d. let us welcome the songs
    sung by the lady

3a. Behold he comes leaping
    upon the mountains
3b. Behold he comes skipping
    over the hills
3c. Gazing upon me through the
    windows
3d. Peering through the lattices,
    he says

4a. Arise my friend make haste
4b. my beautiful dove fly to me

5a. For the bristly winter
    is now past
5b. the heavy rains have receded
    and gone

(Continued)

Epithalamica

5c. *ver amoenum terras aperuit*	5c. lovely springtime has opened earth
5d. *parent flores et turtur cecinit*	5d. flowers are appearing the turtle-dove has begun singing
6a. *Amica surge propera*	6a. Arise my friend make haste
6b. *columba nitens advola*	6b. my beautiful dove fly to me
7a. *Rex in accumbitum iam se contulerat*	7a. The king had already betaken himself to his chamber
7b. *et mea redolens nardus spiraverat*	7b. and my redolent ointment has breathed forth
7c. *in hortum veneram in quem descenderat*	7c. I had come into the garden into which he had descended—
7d. *at ille transiens iam declinaverat*	7d. but he passing through had already gone away
8a. *Per noctem igitur hunc quaerens exeo*	8a. And so by night I go forth from here seeking him
8b. *huc illuc anxia quaerendo cursito*	8b. anxious hither and thither I run in my seeking
8c. *occurrunt vigiles ardenti studio*	8c. the watchmen come upon me in my burning zeal
8d. *quos cum transierim Sponsum invenio*	8d. when I pass them I find my bridegroom
9a. *Iam video quod optaveram*	9a. Now I see what I had hoped for
9b. *iam tenco quod amaveram*	9b. now I clasp to what I had loved
9c. *iam redo quae sic fleveram*	9c. now I laugh at what I had so wept for
9d. *plus gaudeo quam dolueram*	9d. I rejoice more than ever I had grieved

(Continued)

Epithalamica

10a. *Risi mane flevi nocte*	10a. I laughed at morn I wept at night
10b. *mane risi nocte flevi*	10b. at morn I laughed at night I wept
11a. *Noctem insomnem dolor duxerat*	11a. Grief made the night sleepless
11b. *quem vehemetem amor fecerat*	11b. which my love made overpowering
11c. *dilatione votum creverat*	11c. desire intensified through delay
11d. *donec amantem aman vistat*	11d. until lover visited his beloved
12a. *Plausus die planctus nocte*	12a. Joy comes by day lamentations by night
12b. *die plausus nocte planctus*	12b. By day rejoicing by night lamentation
13a. *Eia nunc comites et Sion filiae*	13a. So come now companions and daughters of Zion
13b. *ad Sponsae contica psalmum adnectite*	13b. To the canticles of the bride add your psalm
13c. *quo moestis reddita Sponsi praesentia*	13c. wherein the presence of the Bridegroom restored to those in grief
13d. *convertit elegos nostros in cantica*	13d. turns our mournful elegies into canticles

THE SEQUENCES IN THEIR LITURGICAL CONTEXT

Now we are ready to discuss the overall liturgical context in which these two sequences were sung at the Paraclete. Table I.2 below (pp. 33–39) provides a tabulation of all the Abelardian *liturgica* associated with the feasts upon which the Paraclete nuns sung *Epithalamica* and *Virgines castae*. The right column combines Paraclete rubrics from both its Ordinary and Breviary. The left column gives the contents of Abelard's *Hymnarius Paraclitensis*, the collection of hymns he provided for Heloise and her nuns.

Comparison of the two columns reveals how important the Paraclete Ordinary and Office book are for our knowledge of Abelard the liturgist. Without them we would have no knowledge of the antiphons (ant.), responsories (resp.), and canticles Abelard wrote. We would not know that the sequences *Epithalamica* and *Virgines castae* were ever sung at the Paraclete. The Paraclete Ordinary and Breviary, combined with Abelard's hymnary, provide us, albeit in varying degrees of detail, with our closest estimate of Abelard's original liturgical intentions.

Of the ten feast days and hours of the Office outline below, Easter contains the greatest number of abelardian *liturgica*. For this greatest feast of the liturgical year Abelard provided hymns, responsories, antiphons, canticles, a sequence, and, almost certainly, his Easter Sermon 13. On Easter day and (in abridged form) on Easter Thursday and Saturday, moreover, the nuns of the Paraclete sang the sequence *Epithalamica*. Instead of leading her nuns in singing one of the sequences traditionally associated with Easter—*Victimae paschali laudes, Zima vetus,* or *Fulgens praeclara*[46]— Heloise substituted the relatively rare sequence *Epithalamica* as an expression of the nuns' joy over Christ's resurrection.

The popularity of *Virgines castae* among the nuns of the Paraclete is incontestable. Through Chrysogonus Waddell's study of the liturgical books of the Paraclete, we now know that *Virgines castae* was sung often at the abbey. It was prescribed for singing at six Masses: five for particular virgin saints and one for the feast of Saint Ursula and the Eleven-thousand Virgins. The six feast-days and their dates are:

---

46. Use of these three sequences in twelfth-century Easter liturgies was widespread; see Margot E. Fassler, *Gothic Song*, Appendix 5, 392.

Saint Lucy	13 December
Saint Agnes	21 January
Saint Agatha	5 February
Saint Margaret	20 July
Saint Faith	6 October
Saint Ursula and the 11,000 Virgins	21 October

Being sung at least six times yearly, *Virgines castae* was heard at Mass more than any other sequence in the Paraclete repertoire. The nuns sang most sequences no more than once a year.[47] Only one sequence, *Laetabundus*, approaches the use of *Virgines castae*, being sung five times yearly.[48]

The parallels between Abelard's *hymnarius* and the Paraclete liturgy notwithstanding, one wonders why all of Abelard's hymns were not used. Consider the Easter Vigil (Table I.2): Abelard prepared the hymns *Christiani, plaudite* for Vespers and *Da Mariae tympanum* for Vigils. But at the Paraclete a non-Abelardian hymn [NAH], *Hic est dies verus Dei*, was sung. *Christiani, plaudite* was therefore pushed to Vigils and the hymns that follow it to the Offices for Easter Day and Easter Week. We know from the Prefaces to each of the three *libelli* of Abelard's *Hymnarius* that he was very particular about which hymns were sung when. Yet the Paraclete nuns seem to have exercised considerable freedom in redistributing Abelard's hymns.

This redistribution of Abelard's hymns suggests that Heloise felt at liberty to pick, choose, and adapt hymns not only from those by the Paraclete Founder, but also from the primitive cistercian hymnal in use before Bernard's hymnal of 1147, and from gallican sources.[49] As best one can tell from the Paraclete Ordinary, Heloise followed traditions handed down from her prede-

47. Sequence singing at the Paraclete was limited to select feasts outside the penitential seasons of Septuagesima and Lent and to the octaves of a few of the principal feasts; see CL 3:349.

48. This sequence, Waddell writes, 'identified by only the first word shared in common with dozens of other sequence-incipits, is almost surely the famous *Laetabundus exultet fidelis chorus, alleluia . . .* '; CL 3:31.

49. See CL 3, especially 354–359.

cessors at Argenteuil and drew most of the Office hymns at the Paraclete from the primitive cistercian hymnary. The nuns' use of this early cistercian collection suggests that the thirteenth-century Paraclete Ordinary may well enshrine liturgical practices which extended as far back as Heloise's early abbacy. If the Ordinary does reflect practices from Heloise's lifetime, the nuns would have been singing cistercian hymns for a decade or more before Abelard sent his hymns to them.[50] Abandoning traditional chants for the new texts and music—even those composed by the Paraclete Founder—may have been more than a little difficult. Certainly, we should not underestimate Heloise's own vision for her nuns. Abelard provided the abbess and her nuns a great deal of liturgical material. But Heloise had a mind of her own and, what is more, so did her nuns. As Chrysogonus Waddell has rightly observed, 'we tend to reduce the Paraclete phenomenon to Peter Abelard—with Heloise, perhaps, playing an ancillary role, but with the community completely lost sight of.'[51] Heloise certainly must have had her own vision for the Paraclete nuns; our concern here, however, is primarily with Abelard's vision for the nuns.

50. CL 8, especially 83–114 and 140–144.
51. CL 20: 202.

Table I.2:
Easter and Virgins' Feasts at the Paraclete Abbey

EASTER VIGIL

Abelard's Hymnarius Paraclitensis	*Paraclete Ordinary and Breviary*
First Vespers:	First Vespers:
	Responsory.: *Respondens autem angelus*
	Versicle: *De torrente*
	Ant. to Magnificat: *Exierunt mulieras*
Hymn: *Christiani, plaudite*	Hymn: *Hic est dies verus Dei* NAH
Vigils:	Vigils:
Hymn: *Da Mariae tympanum*	Hymn: *Christiani, Plaudite*
	[Night reading: Gen 49:1]

EASTER DAY

Abelard's Hymnarius	*Paraclete Ordinary and Breviary*
Lauds:	Lauds:
	Canticle-formulary: *In lectulo meo per noctes* (Song of Songs: 3:1-5; 5:6b-8; 6:9-16)
Hymn: *Golias prostratus est*	Hymn: *Da marie tympanum*
	Mass:
	Sequence: *Epithalamica*
	[Sermon 13: Easter Sermon]
Second Vespers:	Second Vespers:
Hymn: *Veris grato tempore*	Hymn: *Golias prostaratus est*
	After dinner hymn: *Deus qui corpora creas et animas*

(Continued)

EASTER WEEK: FERIA 2-7

Abelard's Hymnarius	*Paraclete Ordinary and Breviary*
First Vespers:	First Vespers:
	Feria 6: Resp. *De resurrectione*
	tua
Hymn: *Christiani, plaudite*	Hymn: ?
Vigils:	Vigils:
Hymn: *Da Mariae tympanum*	Hymn: *Verio grato tempore*
Lauds:	Lauds:
Hymn: *Golias prostratus est*	Hymn: *Christinai, plaudite*
	Mass: Feria 5 & 7: last four
	strophes of *Epithalamica*
Second Vespers:	Second Vespers:
Hymn: *Veris grato tempore*	Hymn: *Christiani, plaudite*
	Weekday readings at Refactory:
	Song of Songs

EASTER OCTAVE

Abelard's Hymnarius	*Paraclete Ordinary and Breviary*
First Vespers:	First Vespers:
	Responsory: *Respondens autem*
	angelus
	Versicle: *De torrente*
	Ant. to Magnificat:
	Exieruntmulieras
Hymn: *Christiani, plaudite*	Hymn: *Christiani, plaudite*
Vigils:	Vigils:
Hymn: *Da Maria tympanum*	Hymn: *Da Maria tympanum*
Lauds:	Lauds:
Hymn: *Golias prostratus est*	Hymn: *Golias prostratus est*
Second Vespers:	Second Vespers:
Hymn: *Veris grato tempore*	Hymn: *Veris grato tempore*

SAINT LUCY (13 DECEMBER)

Abelard's Hymnarius	*Paraclete Ordinary and Breviary*
First Vespers:	First Vespers:
	Responsory: *Felix sterilis*
Hymn: *Sponsa Christi*	Hymn: *Sponsa Christi*
Vigils:	Vigils:
Hymn: *Cum in sanctis*	Hymn: NAH
Lauds:	Lauds:
Hymn: *Quantum sponso*	Hymn: NAH
	Mass:
	Sequence: *Virgines castae*
	[Sermon 1?]
Second Vespers	Second Vespers:
Hymn: *Ut aurora*	Hymn: *Ut aurora*

SAINT AGNES (21 JANUARY)

Abelard's Hymnarius	*Paraclete Ordinary and Breviary*
First Vespers:	First Vespers:
	Responsory: *Felix sterilis*
Hymn: *Sponsa Christi*	Hymn: NAH
Vigils:	Vigils:
Hymn: *Cum in sanctis*	Hymn: NAH
Lauds:	Lauds:
Hymn: *Quantum sponso*	Hymn: NAH
	Mass:
	Sequence: *Virgines castae*
	[Sermon 1?]
Second Vespers:	Second Vespers:
Hymn: *Ut aurora*	Hymn: *Ut aurora*

(Continued)

Saint Agatha (5 February)

Abelard's Hymnarius	*Paraclete Ordinary and Breviary*
First Vespers:	First Vespers:
	Responsory: *Felix sterilis*
Hymn: *Sponsa Christi*	Hymn: NAH
Vigils:	Vigils:
Hymn: *Cum in sanctis*	Hymn: NAH
Lauds:	Lauds:
Hymn: *Quantum sponso*	Hymn: NAH
	Mass: Sequence: *Virgines castae*
	[Sermon 1?]
Second Vespers:	Second Vespers:
Hymn: *Ut aurora*	Hymn: *Ut aurora*

Saint Margaret (20 July)

Abelard's Hymnarius	*Paraclete Ordinary and Breviary*
First Vespers:	First Vespers:
Hymn: *Sponsa Christi*	Responsory: *Felix sterilis*
	Hymn: *Sponsa Christi*
Vigils:	Vigils:
Hymn: *Cum in sanctis*	Hymn: NAH
Lauds:	Lauds:
Hymn: *Quantum sponso*	Hymn: NAH
	Mass: Sequence: *Virgines castae*
	[Sermon 1?]
Second Vespers:	Second Vespers:
Hymn: *Ut aurora*	Hymn: *Ut aurora*

Saint Faith (6 October)

Abelard's Hymnarius	*Paraclete Ordinary and Breviary*
First Vespers:	First Vespers:
	Responsory: *Felix sterilis*
Hymn: *Sponsa Christi*	Hymn: *Sponsa Christi*
Vigils:	Vigils:
Hymn: *Cum in sanctis*	Hymn: NAH
	[Night Office Reading: 1 Cor 7]
Lauds:	Lauds:
Hymn: *Quantum sponso*	Hymn: NAH
	Mass: Sequence: *Virgines castae*
	[Sermon 1?]
Second Vespers:	Second Vespers:
Hymn: *Ut aurora*	Hymn: *Ut aurora*
	Canticle: *In lectulo*

The 11,000 Virgins (21 October)

Abelard's Hymnarius	*Paraclete Ordinary and Breviary*
First Vespers:	First Vespers:
	Responsory: *Felix sterilis*
Hymn: *Sponsa Christi*	Hymn *Sponsa Christi*
Vigils:	Vigils:
Hymn: *Cum in sanctis*	Hymn: NAH
	[Night readings: I Cor. 7]
Lauds:	Lauds:
Hymn: *Quantum sponso*	Hymn: NAH
	Mass:
	Sequence: *Virgines castae*
	[Sermon 1?]
Second Vespers:	Second Vespers:
Hymn: *Ut aurora*	Hymn: *Vt aurora*
	Hymn: *Cum in sanctis*

Clearly it would be an error to equate the Paraclete hymn repertoire with Abelard's *Hymnarius Paraclitensis*. But that is an error made by moderns. The truth is, 'Abelard's contributions to the Paraclete liturgy were admitted selectively, and in no way replaced in any massive way a Paraclete liturgy that otherwise owed nothing to Abelard.'[52] The Paraclete nuns no doubt venerated their Father Founder, but they also continued liturgical practices familiar from many years of worship at Argenteuil. Any 'discrepancies' between Abelard's hymnal and Paraclete practices go back to the Paraclete nuns under the direction of Heloise. Apparently she chose, adapted, and rearranged Abelard's hymns as they fit within her community's preexisting liturgical tradition. As Mews writes, 'These liturgical manuscripts of the Paraclete may not affirm the voice of Heloise as an individual, but they give some clues to the liturgical direction that she chose for her community. She drew on the writings of both Abelard and the early Cistercians in order to implement her own vision of the religious life.'[53]

If we assume that the Paraclete liturgical books do indeed reflect the actual practices of Heloise and her nuns, then Abelard's hymns, sequences, and sermons featured prominently on many important Paraclete feasts. Their use at Easter and on the feasts of holy virgins became part of a tapestry of verbal, poetic, musical, narrative, rhetorical, cultural, theological, and ideological connections central to the Paraclete symbolic world. But even if Heloise and her nuns had never used a single hymn he offered them, the parallels between Abelard's hymns and the sequences *Virgines castae* and *Epithalamica* would remain. By bringing to light the web of connections among the Father Founder's *liturgica*, we would still gain insight into the world that Abelard intended to create, and sustain, at the Paraclete by his sequences. Our entrance into the symbols and textures of this cloistered world must therefore begin with the poetic and musical syntax of *Virgines castae* and *Epithalamica*.

52. Waddell, CL 8:94.
53. Mews, *Lost Love* 159.

2

THE WEAVER AND HIS MATERIAL

Ex hominis vicio ne culpes illius artem: est homo sepe malus qui bonus est opifex.

Do not fault a man's skills because of his failings: Many a bad man is a good artist.

—*Peter Abelard*[1]

IN COMPOSING *Virgines castae* and *Epithalamica*, Abelard drew on both oral and scribal sources. These sources were the fount from which he drew the images and language that he believed were essential to creating an appropriate symbolic world for the Paraclete nuns and for him and Heloise. Behind his sequences stand several biblical, patristic, and mythical sources that shaped Abelard's vision for the nuns. Into the two sequences are interwoven imagery and vocabulary from the Song of Songs and Psalm 44,[2] works by Jerome, Cyprian, and Ambrose, and the myth of the unicorn.

Nancy van Deusen has shown that medieval composers almost certainly modeled their sequences on the psalms, the cornerstone of learning among medieval monks and nuns. Both sequences and psalms 1) contain verses that vary in length from

1. Peter Abelard, *Carmen ad Astralabium: A Critical Edition*, ed. José M. A. Rubingh-Boscher (Groningen: J. M. A. Rubingh-Boscher, 1987) 113, lines 425–426. Epigraph quoted from C. Stephen Jaeger, *The Envy of Angels: Cathedral Schools and Social Ideals in Medieval Europe, 950–1200* (Philadelphia: University of Pennsylvania Press, 1994) 451, note 66.

2. Vulgate enumeration; Psalm 45 in the Hebrew enumeration.

pair to pair; 2) were written in long and short lengths; 3) center frequently on oral and instrumental praise; 4) make extensive use of allegorical language; and 5) bear witness to a range of emotive and affective states.[3] All these textual characteristics mark the sequence as a 'mixed' genre. Musically, the sequence—especially during its intermediate stage—was also 'mixed.' Many sequences are neither fully syllabic (set to a single tone) nor melismatic (set to two, three, or more tones). Historically, the genre also exhibited a mixture of texted and textless melody.[4] Modally, most sequences use both authentic and plagal forms of a mode.[5] Van Deusen argues that this mixed literary and musical style is by no means accidental; rather, it is characteristic of the liturgical function of the sequence.

The sequence genre gets its very name from its role within the liturgy. A 'transitional song, a copula between the Old and the New Testaments',[6] it appeared in the Mass between the Old Testament song; the Alleluia and its psalm verses; and the New Testament song, the chanted Gospel. Van Deusen writes: 'joined to the Alleluia, connected on the other hand to the Gospel, sequences included allusions to both and thereby provided a copulation between the two.'[7] Sequences had the particular function of making manifest the transition between the Old and New Testaments. The medieval church adorned its liturgy with sequences for the purpose of explicitly and systematically bringing into view the rich links between the Testaments. Hence, the genre's mixing on both the musical and literary levels gives it the unique function of performing the 'sequence' between the Psalm and the Gospel.

3. Nancy van Deusen, 'The Use and Significance of the Sequence', *Musica Disciplina* 40 (1986) 5–47; 8–9. She notes (page 8, note 13) that others have noticed analogies between the psalms and sequences, but no one else has explored this connection.

4. Van Deusen, 'Use and Significance', 20.

5. My thanks to William Flynn for reminding me of this modal mixture.

6. Van Deusen, 'Use and Significance', 24.

7. Van Deusen, 'Use and Significance', 22.

Through *Virgines castae* and *Epithalamica*, Abelard shows that the Old Testament Song of Songs and Psalm 44 speak eloquently of the love of Christ for his virginal brides. Yet the two sequences function not only as transitions from the Old to the New Testament, but also produce a sequence from the Old Testament to the Gospel message of Christ (New Testament), passing through the Church Fathers and arriving at the world of the Paraclete Abbey and its abbess, Heloise. As we analyze closely the intertexture of Abelard's two sequences, our study will suggest that, although van Deusen's hypothesis about the role of the sequence in medieval liturgy is essentially correct, scholars should consider whether the transitionary role of the sequence was in fact more broad. It may well be that the real force of a sequence's liturgical role rested in its power to move medieval women and men from the Old Testament to New Testament through the Church Fathers to the particular world in which the singer/auditor found her/his being.

INTERTEXTUAL ANALYSIS OF
VIRGINES CASTAE AND EPITHALAMICA

In creating *Virgines castae* and *Epithalamica*, Abelard juxtaposed a range of traditional images: the queen of heaven, Christ the bridegroom, and the lamb of God. These images stand beside one another like biblical scenes carved into a cathedral door or into the ivory covers of a liturgical book. Through a process of borrowing, reworking, and using traditional material in new ways, the artist Abelard reveals his talents in shaping a discourse appropriate to his audience. The rhetorical tradition refers to this conceptual process of 'discovery' as *inventio*. This process required the poet first to select the right sources for his composition from the vast stores of tradition; and then, from these selected sources to discover *materia*, proper subject matter, from which to develop his discourse.

　　We moderns err when we imagine a poet like Abelard beginning the process of composition with books and manuscripts piled high around him. *Inventio* began with the selecting and gathering of material long committed to the vast storehouse of memory. Like every medieval scholar, Abelard had been taught since his earliest days in school to impress the words, images, thoughts, and divisions of Scripture, the Fathers' writings, and other texts (sacred and pagan) into the wax of his memory. Long after he had studied with the master in Paris (*c.* 1133), Clanchy points out that Otto of Freising (*c.* 1110-1158) stood in awe of Abelard's memory.[8] Memory for ancient and medieval rhetoricians was a codex, a page or a wax tablet, upon which the past was inscribed. Memory, with its ability to store, sort, and retrieve, stood prior in importance to physical books, which were themselves memory cues and aids.[9]

Rhetoricians considered these sources to be 'external' means of persuasion, one of two categories of persuasion every author drew on. By Abelard's day a scriptural or nonscriptural source was considered 'external' in the sense that, as a means of persuasion it was 'not a creation of the mind of the speaker, though he has chosen and utilized it and may sometimes build a logical argument upon it.'[10] From his mental library the poet gathered and 'collated' 'external' sources out of which he built up a 'texture' of associations surrounding a common theme or set of themes.[11]

Inventio also included 'internal proof', the second category of persuasion, which was subdivided into *ethos*, *pathos*, and *logos*. These three dimensions of every speech inhere respectively in the speaker, the audience, and the discourse. As rhetorical scholar George Kennedy writes:

> Ethos means 'character' and may be defined as the credibility that the author or speaker is able to establish in his work. The audience is induced to trust what he says because they trust him, as a good man or an expert on the sub-

8. Clanchy, *Abelard*, 62.

9. See Carruthers, *Memory*, 16.

10. See George A. Kennedy, *New Testament Interpretation as Rhetorical Criticism* (Chapel Hill: University of North Carolina Press, 1984) 14.

11. Carruthers, *Memory*, 36.

ject . . . . Pathos inheres in the audience and may be defined as the emotional reactions the hearers undergo as the
orator 'plays upon their feelings. . . '. Logos refers to the
logical argument found within the discourse.[12]

Our focus here will be mainly upon Abelard's 'external' means
of persuasion. Yet, as we shall observe in Chapters Three and
Four, devices of style and figures of speech can and do awaken
audience interest and configure *materia* in new ways. *Ethos* is revealed to the audience by what the speaker says and how he says
it. *Pathos* is aroused in the audience by the emotional or affective
ideas and words used in the course of elaboration. *Logos*, the force
of the argument in its parts and as a whole, is manifest in the
persuasive order, art, and beauty of the rhetor's invented arguments. We will explore the 'internal proofs' in Chapter Four,
when we examine the rhetorical form of the two sequences.

An author may use his sources, external proofs, in a variety
of ways—quoting them word for word, omitting some of their
words, changing a few of their words, or restating them in his
own words. As one scholar, Rita Copeland, writes,

> To achieve difference with the given text is the test of the
> exegete's ingenuity, for his success depends on the skill with
> which he can suppress or conceal the very exegetical moves
> that govern his approach to the text. To amplify or abbrevi-
> ate the source, to avoid delaying where others delay, are the
> techniques that underscore the mastery of [medieval] exe-
> getical procedure by disguising that procedure as a form of
> invention.[13]

Classical and medieval teachers called this varied use of oral and
written sources *recitation*.[14] Yet in developing an argument, the

12. Kennedy, *New Testament Interpretation as Rhetorical Criticism*, 15.
13. Copeland, *Rhetoric*, 174.
14. Both Matthew of Vendome and Geoffrey of Vinsauf addressed the varied ways of handling invented sources; see Douglas Kelly, 'The Scope of the
Treatment of Composition in the Twelfth- and Thirteenth-Century Arts of Poetry,'
Speculum 41 (1966) 261–278.

medieval speaker or writer, often did not acknowledge his borrowings. According to the rhetorical tradition, when a rhetor presented wording without mentioning that the words were found elsewhere, he had not recited the source, but *recontextualized* it.[15] Like ancient and medieval painters, sculptors, and architects, rhetoricians began with traditional motifs, made them their own, and expressed through them a message appropriate to his audience. As Copeland observed,

> The text can be 'rewritten' as formally unified because its meaning or cause has been discovered. . . . But such exegesis does not discard the given text once its truths have been delivered up. Instead it invests the given text with a new tropological significance (as integument) and with a new structural rationale which makes the *modus agendi* the result of the exegete's own disclosive readings. (Copeland, *Rhetoric*, 78–81)

Psalm 44 and the Song of Songs provide the fundamental material out of which Abelard fashioned the two sequences. In Abelard's understanding, Psalm 44 and the Song of Songs are essentially of one cloth.

In elaborating the two biblical texts, Abelard draws heavily on works on virginity by Ambrose, Cyprian, and especially Jerome, and then enriches his sequence by drawing on the polysemous legend of the unicorn. Inventional analysis focuses on the material an author used as a resource to create the inner fabric of his or her discourse. Tracking every link—some of them only faint echoes—can be endless and eventually lead into the shadows of speculation. Not to identify the sources of *Virgines castae* and *Epithalamica*—both scriptural and nonscriptural literary sources as well as oral traditions—would be to ignore their very foundations. A range of juxtaposed and overlapping images combine to form these two sequences. This chapter will focus on the verbal images Abelard found and reconfigured in his own distinct manner.

15. Vernon Robbins, *The Tapestry of Early Christian Discourse: Rhetoric, Society, and Ideology* (London: Routledge, 1996) 102.

THE SONG OF SONGS: THE BRIDE AND BRIDEGROOM

Abelard's main source for both *Virgines castae* and *Epithalamica* is the Song of Songs, a collection of erotic love poetry[16] Modern scholars describe it as an anthology, dividing it into as many as thirty separate poems. The poems are lyric in so far as they express the feelings of a speaker to or about his or her beloved. There are monologues in which a male or female speaks; for example,[17]

dilectus meus mihi et ego	my beloved is mine and I am
illi qui pascitur inter lilia	his who pastures among the lilies
donec aspiret dies et	until the day breathes
inclinentur umbrae	and the shadows lean
revertere imilis esto	return my beloved, be
dilecte mi capreae aut	like the goat or a
hinulo cervorum	young herd of stags on the
super montes Bether	mountains of Bether.
(2:16-17)	

The lovers of the Song also enter into several dialogues.[18] In chapter one, we read:

ecce tu pulchra es amica mea	Behold you are fair my friend
ecce tu pulchra oculi tui	behold you are fair your eyes of
columbarum	doves
ecce tu pulcher es dilecte	behold you are fair
mi et decorus	my beloved and beautiful
lectulus noster floridus	our bed is flowery
tigna domorum nostrarum	the beams of our house are
cedrina	of cedar
laquearia nostra cypressina	our rafters are of cypress.
(1:14-16)	

16. See Marcia Falk, *Love Lyrics from the Bible: A Translation and Literary Study of the Song of Songs* (Sheffield, UK: Almond Press, 1982).

17. Other examples appear in Song 1:1; 1:19-21; 2:4-7; 2:14; 3:1-5; 4:1-7; 4:8; 4:9-11; 6:4-11; and 8:1-7. The Latin and English texts are from E. Ann Matter, *The Voice of My Beloved: The Song of Songs in Western Medieval Christianity* (University of Pennsylvania Press, 1990) xx and xxi. Her Latin is adapted from the critical Vulgate edition of R. Weber and her translation reflects medieval reading of the text.

18. Other love dialogues occur at 1:7-8; 2:1-3; 2:8-13; 4:12-5:1; and 8:13-14.

One of the unnamed lovers, usually the woman, addresses an audience outside the drama of the couple's love relations.[19] Several times an unnamed group offers its own commentary on love.[20] Occasionally, the female friend and lover of the poem(s) enters into a dialogue with a group about amatory matters.[21]

Several poems within the Song celebrate the beauty of the human body in a series of provocative metaphors. In Song 4:1-5 the poem's bridegroom describes his beloved from her eyes down to her breasts, elaborating on each of her members with an agricultural image. In 5:11-16 the bride extols the beauty of her beloved, from his head down, with various images:

dilectus meus candidus et	My beloved is white
rubicundus	and ruddy
electus ex milibus	chosen from thousands
caput eius aurm potimum	his head finest gold
comae cius sicut elatae	his hair exalted as
palmarum	the black palms of
nigrae quasi corvus	the raven
oculi eius sicut columbae	his eyes like doves on
super rivulos aquarum	streams of waters
quae lacte sunt lotae	which are washed with milk
et resident iuxta fluenta	and sit down beside the
plenissima	brimming streams
genae illius sicut areolae	his cheeks like gardens of spices
aromatum consitae a	planted by the
pigmentariis labia eius	perfumers his lips lilies
lilia distillantia murram	dripping finest myrrh
primam	
manus illius tornatiles	his hands crafted of
aureae plenae hyacinthis	gold full of hyacinths
venter eius eburneus	his belly ivory
distinctus sahhpyris	garnished with sapphires

19. Sg 1:5-6 and 8:11-12.
20. Sg 2:15; 3:6-11; 8:5a.
21. Sg 7:1-6 and 8:8-10.

crura illius columnae	his legs columns of marble
marmoreae	which are set upon golden
quae fundatae sunt super bases	bases his appearance
aureas species eius ut Libani	as Lebanon
electus ut cedri	chosen as the cedar
guttur eius suavissimum	his throat very soft
et totus desiderabilis	and all desirable
talis est dilectus meus	such is my beloved
et iste est amicus meus	and this is my friend,
filiae Hierusalem.	daughters of Jerusalem.

The mood of the Song is perhaps best captured by the female lover when she declares, in speaking to an audience of the 'daughters of Jerusalem': 'This is my beloved and this is my friend . . .' (5:16b).

At the core of *Virgines castae* and *Epithalamica* are Song of Songs 2:6-7 and 3:1-8, and central to the discourse of *Epithalamica* is Song 2:8-14. The poem opens at 2:1-7 on a note of irony: the female lover feigns modesty, declaring herself but one flower, one lover, among many women loved by her beloved. Her lover counters, insisting that she is unique—a lily among thorns, his darling among all maidens. The woman responds with similar praise, for he honors her with savory words and delicious fruits and wines. His words and deeds reveal the depth of his self-giving love to her. At verse 6 we find the young woman enfolded in the arms of her beloved, who charges the 'daughters of Jerusalem' not to disturb her rest:

ego flos campi	I am a flower of the field
et lilium convallium	and a lily of the valley
sicut lilium inter spinas	Like a lily among thorns so is
sic amica mea inter filias	my friend among daughters
sicut malum inter ligna	Like the apple tree among trees
silvarum	of the woods so is my

(Continued)

sic dilectus meus inter filios	beloved among sons
sub umbra illius quam	under the shadow of the one
desideraveram sedi	I had loved
et fructus eius dulcis	I sat and his fruit sweet to
gutturi meo	my throat
introduxit me in cellam	he brought me into the wine
vinariam	cellar
ordinavit in me	he has disposed charity in
caritatem	me
fulcite me floribus stipate	support me with flowers,
me malis	surround me with apples for
quia amore langueo	I languish with love
leva eius sub capite meo	his left arm under my head and
et dextera illius	his right arm will embrace
amplexabitur me	me
adiuro vos filiae	I adjure you, daughters of
Hierusalem	Jerusalem
per capreas cervosque	by the goats and the stags
camporum	of the field
ne suscitetis neque	neither arouse nor cause to
evigilare faciatis dilectam	awaken my beloved until she
quoadusque ipsa velit	wishes

Verses 8-17 of Chapter 2 form a unit that celebrates the feelings of love that come with spring. The gifts of spring rain abound: animals leap and frolic about, figs and vines emit their delectable odors, birds make new song, fresh flowers and new buds greet the day. Aroused by these sensual wonders the beloved makes haste over hill and dale to reach his dear lover. He bids her twice to come away with him. But as happens so often throughout the Song, he is vague and does not make known exactly where and when she can meet and depart with him. In her presence his attention drifts from their flight to the dulcet sound of her voice and the loveliness of her appearance. Finally, the woman presses her lover for a time when they can meet and depart. The unit closes with her proposal that the two rendezvous at night:

vox dilecti mei	the voice of my beloved
ecce iste venit saliens in montibus transiliens colles	behold, he comes leaping on the mountains springing across the hills
similis est dilectus meus capreae hinuloque cervorum	my beloved is like a goat and a young stag
en ipse stat post parietem nostrum	behold, he stands behind our wall
despiciens per fenestras prospiciens per cancellos	looking in through the windows watching through the lattices
et dilectus meus loquitur mihi	and my beloved speaks to me
surge propera amica mea formosa mea et veni	arise swiftly my friend my beautiful, and come for now
iam enim hiems transiit imber abiit et recessit	the winter has passed the rain has gone and departed
flores apparuerunt in terra tempus putationis advenit	flowers appear on the earth the time of pruning has come
vox turturis audita est in terra nostra	the voice of the turtle dove is heard in our land
ficus protulit grossos suos	the fig tree has put out its thick shoots
vineae florent dederunt odorem	the flowering vines have given off a smell
surge amica mea speciosa mea et veni	arise my friend my lovely one and come
columba mea inforaminibus petrae in caverna maceriae	my dove in the clefts of the rock in the hollow of the wall
ostende mihi faciem tuam sonet vox tua in auribus meis	Show me your face let your voice sound in my ears
vox enim tua dulcis et facies tua decora	for your voice is sweet and your face is beautiful.

Chapter 3 of the Song also provides important material for Abelard's discourse. In Song 3:1-5 the woman describes her desperate search for her beloved. Having run hither and thither about the sleeping city, she passes beyond the safety of the night watchmen and finally finds her beloved. The two return to the city and enter the house of the woman's mother. In verses 6-11 the woman, now unmistakably a bride, dreams about her approaching wedding day. She sees her bridegroom approaching her upon his bed or 'litter'; he is borne forward ceremonially by his servants, guarded by his warriors, and accompanied by a host of nobles. He is a Solomon, decked in attire befitting the greatest of kings. She sees herself brought before the king adorned in embroidered garments and gold ornaments. The daughters of Jerusalem come out to see her and behold her Solomon-like bridegroom:

In lectulo meo per noctes	On my bed through the nights
quaesivi quem diligit	I sought him whom my
anima mea	soul loves
quaesivi illum et non	I sought him and I did not
inveni	find
surgam et circuibo	I will arise and go around the
civitatem	city
per vicos et plateas	through the streets and the
	courtyards
quaeram quem diligit anima	I will seek him whom my soul
mea	loves
quaesivi illum et non	I sought him and I did not
inveni	find
invenerunt me vigiles qui	the watchmen found me who
custodiunt civitatem	guard the city
num quem dilexit anima mea	have you seen him whom my soul
vidistis	has loved?
paululum cum pertranissem	when I had hardly passed by
eos	them

inveni quem diligit anima mea	I found him whom my soul loves
tenui eum nec dimittam donec introducam illum in domum matris meae et in cubiculum genetricis meae	I held him nor will I let go until I lead him into the house of my mother and into the chamber of her who bore me
adiuro vos filiae Hierusalem per capreas cervosque camporum	I adjure you, daughters of Jerusalem by the goats and the stags of the field
ne suscitetis neque evigilare faciatis dilec tam donec ipsa velit	neither arouse nor cause to awaken the beloved until she wishes
quae est ista quae ascendit per desertum sicut virgula fumi ex aromatibus murrae et turis	who is this who comes up through the desert like a column of smoke from the spices of myrrh and frankincense
et universi pulveris pig- mentarii	and all the powders of the perfumer?
en lectulum Salomonis sexaginta fortes ambiunt ex fortissimis Israhel	behold, the bed of Solomon sixty strong men surround- ing it of the strongest of Israel
omnes tenentes gladios et ad bella doctissimi	all holding swords and most learned in warfare
uniuscuiusque ensis super femur suum	each one's sword on his thigh
propter timores nocturnos ferculum fecit sibi rex Salomon de lignis Libani	because of nocturnal fears King Solomon made a litter for himself from the wood of Lebanon
columnas eius fecit arenteas reclinatorium aureum ascensum purpureum media caritate constravit proper filias Heirusalem	its columns he made of silver the pillow of gold the ascent of purple the middle he has piled up with charity

(Continued)

egredimini et videte filiae Sion	for the daughters of Jerusalem go forth and see, daughters of Sion
regem Salomonem in diademate quo coronavit eum mater sua	King Solomon in the diadem with which his mother crowned him
in die disponsionis illius et in die laetitiae cordis eius	on the day of his betrothal and on the day of his heart's rejoicing.

Abelard stood in a very old and venerated tradition of interpreting the Song of Songs. Indeed, the Canticle was, writes Ann Matters, 'the most frequently interpreted book of medieval Christianity.'[22] Commentators from Origen to Aquinas flocked to its living waters.[23] Men and women, monastic and non-monastic, drank deeply from its flow, washed themselves in its purity, and meditated on its beauty. The Song's persuasive imagery notwithstanding, it posed two interrelated problems to medieval exegetes. First, it makes no mention of God and offers no explicit divine law, moral precepts, or sacred history. Second, it celebrates sensual pleasures and passionate sorrows of nameless lovers. Yet Abelard and every prior Christian commentator believed that God had spoken to the Church through the Song. The Song's sensual imagery and rhetorical immediacy, intensified through traditional interpretation, moved medieval men and women to love Christ, his Church, and his mother, the Virgin Mary, like no other biblical text. The intense love of the Song's bridegroom, the exegetes wrote, bore powerful witness to Christ's deep love of his bride, the Church and each individual soul. Equally, the persistent love of the Song's bride modeled the proper love the Church and every soul should have for Christ. The Canticle was in the Bible, the revelatory oration through which God, the grand

---

22. Matter, *The Voice of My Beloved*, 7.

23. For a collection of commentaries, see Denys Turner, *Eros and Allegory. Medieval Exegesis on the Song of Songs*, Cistercian Studies Series 156 (Kalamazoo: 1995).

rhetorician, speaks, teaching humans about their sinful condition and moving them to his ways. As Abelard observed, 'The intention of all divine Scripture is to teach and to move in the manner of a rhetorical speech.'[24] The Song's language, brimming with figures of speech and forms of argumentation, demanded interpretation and elaboration. The question was, How does one fully and properly understand God's message?

To medieval exegetes the deepest persuasive dimensions of Scripture resided in God's transference of language from its ordinary use to a use intended to convey christian content. The assumption that *veritas* (truth) is found hidden *sub umbra et figura* (under shadows and figures) stands at the core of medieval hermeneutics.[25] The rhetorical tradition provided exegetes with a range of interpretive tools that enabled them to dig into the fertile soils of Scripture, God's oration.[26] Eventually a four-fold method of treating the language of the Bible emerged in the West.[27] Medieval exegetes recognized in the language of Scripture at least four levels or modes of meaning. First is the 'literal mode' which clarifies the meaning of God's words and reads the divine text in order to understand its grammatical forms and its historical context. Second comes the 'allegorical mode' through which one elicits doctrine from the text that reveal relationships between the Old Testament narrative of Israel and the revelation of Christ in the New Testament. Third, the 'tropological mode' enables one to discern moral themes in the text and read it as a model for personal behavior; it turns the words of the text, like a mirror,

24. *Omnis Scriptura divina more orationis rhetoricae aut docere intendit aut movere;* in *Commentaria super S. Pauli Epistolam ad Romanos; PL* 178:783.

25. Matter, *The Voice of My Beloved,* 7.

26. Copeland, *Rhetoric,* especially Chapters 6 and 7.

27. On christian allegorical interpretation, see Henri de Lubac, *L'exégèse médiévale: Les quatre sens de l'écriture* (Paris: Aubier, 1959–61) 4 volumes. English translation by Mark Sebanc: *Medieval Exegesis,* volume 1: *The Four Senses of Scripture,* and *Medieval Exegesis;* Volume 2: *The Four Senses of Scripture* (Grand Rapids: Eerdmans, 1998 and 2000). See also Denys Turner, *Eros and Allegory* (above, note 23); and Andrew Louth, *Discerning the Mystery: An Essay on the Nature of Theology* (Oxford: Clarendon, 1983), especially 'Return to Allegory', 96–131.

upon a community's members.[28] Fourth, the 'analogical mode' gives insight into the *telos* of God's created order, the beatific vision, and the restoration of all things in Christ.

Patristic and medieval exegetes spent great energy probing the literal (or historical), allegorical, tropological, and anagogical levels of Song of Songs. Early commentators agreed that the Canticle is an *epithalamicum*, a wedding song, for a human king—most identified him as Solomon—and that it was probably composed for use at the wedding of an Israelite or Judean king to a foreign princess.[29] They were less interested, however, in the historical/literal level of the text than in its spiritual meanings. In their reading, the nuptial language of the Song pointed allegorically to the union between the divine Son and a human body in the Incarnation, and between the Son and his mystical body, the Church. This love language also spoke tropologically of the individual soul's contemplative *unitas* with Christ in the present, and anagogically anticipated the individual soul's and the universal Church's marriage with the heavenly bridegroom in the age to come.

While all christian commentators—from Origen in the third century, Gregory the Great, the Venerable Bede, and Alcuin in the early Middle Ages, to Hugh of Saint-Victor, Bernard of Clairvaux, Abelard, and a host of others in the twelfth—used each of the four modes to interpret the speech of God, they were all careful to shape their commentary to the understanding and needs of their contemporaries. Jean Leclercq has shown that social conditions in the monasteries of Abelard and Heloise's day predisposed twelfth-century exegetes to read and use the Song in ways quite different from those of their predecessors.[30] While benedictine monks typically replenished their ranks with children offered to and raised by them as oblates, the reformed Orders—the Cistercians, the Augustinians, the Premonstratensians,

28. Carruthers, *Memory*, 168.

29. Matter, *Voice of My Beloved*, 50–51, 70, and 107.

30. Jean Leclercq, *Monks and Love in Twelfth-Century France* (Oxford: Oxford University Press, 1979) 8–26. See also Astell, *Song*, 9.

and the Victorines, and, we may add, the Abbey of the Paraclete, recruited only adult members. Many were drawn from aristocratic circles, and more than a few had been married. Secular love songs had been upon the lips of many; some, like Abelard, had written love lyrics prior to entering monastic life. In expressing their devotion to God, such recruits created a body of monastic literature which focussed on love but was noticeably different from earlier writings on the Song.

By the third century, Origen, the first great christian exegete of the *Canticum*, had solved the problems of interpreting the Song of Songs by sharply distinguishing between the carnal literal level of the Song and the spiritual meaning hidden beneath the surface. The Song's hidden meaning comes to light when the exegete correctly identifies the principal actors veiled *behind* the *personae* of the Song's bridal drama. Origen identified the Song's bridegroom with Christ and its bride with both the Church and the individual soul. Every rational soul, *mens*, is to the body, what the *allegoria* is to the literal level of the Song. Just as the allegorical level of the Song is far superior to the literal, so the soul is far more important than the body. Hence, as Ann W. Astell writes,

> Origen's definition of the bridal soul led him to stress its higher, rational powers (*mens, spiritus, logos*) at the cost of supressing the body and its drives. Accordingly, his exegesis of the Song follows a two-part pattern—first, an examination of the literal meaning, followed by an exposition of its *allegoria* or spiritual sense. The procedure is dialectical, aimed at the discovery of truth, and characterized by unbroken ascent.[31]

Although Abelard and his contemporaries followed Origen in identifying the bridegroom with Christ and the bride of the Song with the Church and the soul, they did not identify the redeemed person with the *mens* alone. As we shall see, Abelard's sequences, like other bridal *liturgica* he composed for the Paraclete

31. Astell, *Song*, 7.

nuns, give 'prominence to the soul's lower, affective powers, which are intimately connected with the bodily senses and volition'.[32] Abelard held that the virginal soul experiences union with God not primarily as intellectual enlightenment, as did Origen, but as a living personal surrender of body and soul to Christ the bridegroom.

This is precisely the understanding of the soul and its redemption that Astell has found pervasive in twelfth-century interpretations of the *Canticum*. When twelfth-century commentators approach these two biblical bridal songs, whether they do so in sermons, devotional books, hymns or sequences,

> their exegesis moves beyond an exposition of hidden meaning (*allegoria*) to tropological exhortation—that is, they apply the interpreted text to the concrete life situation of their auditors and use the affective force of the Song's literal imagery to move them to virtuous action. In the process the allegory is reliteralized, joined again to the letter from which it was derived, and ascent turns into descent. The procedure as a whole is rhetorical, not dialectical; aimed at the application, not the discovery, of truth.[33]

Twelfth-century commentators like Bernard of Clairvaux and Hugh of Saint Victor—and Peter Abelard—envisioned a holistic redemption of body and soul.[34] Consequently, they did not seek to escape the carnal level of the Song or deny the affective powers of body and soul. Rather, they sought rhetorically to draw their auditors into the emotive language of the literal text—and to redirect their affections toward Christ in the manner of a bride to her bridegroom. For Abelard and his contemporaries, the tropological meaning of the Song—the dimension of the text that directly touches the ethical lives of its readers—best reveals divine eloquence. Through the ardent, personal surrender of the Song's bride, Christ seeks to teach, delight, and, above all, move every

32. Astell, 8.
33. Astell, 8.
34. Astell, 8.

soul to surrender to himself as to its bridegroom. The soul's learning to surrender was a teleological process.

Abelard, no less than Bernard of Clairvaux, realized 'that with adult recruitment the danger of sensual desire could not be dealt with directly by simple rejection: an authoritative redescription of pleasurable memory was necessary.'[35] Abelard's sequences stand at the center of his efforts to provide a vocabulary and vision by which the Paraclete nuns and especially Heloise could 'redescribe, and therefore in effect construct, their memories in relation to the demands of a new way of life.'[36] Abelard did not seek to manipulate the nuns' desires against their will and without their awareness; rather, he sought to create a *new* moral space in which their *old* desires and feeling were willingly surrendered to Christ as to their loving bridegroom. Like Bernard, Abelard courted the danger of the Song's erotic language so as to transform the nuns' memory of sexual love into love of God. As Talad Asad writes, the monastic life that

> aims to transform sensual desire (the desire of one human being for another) into the desire of God requires at the same time a change in the status of the monks [and nuns] as lovers. From being masters or equals of human lovers (male or female), they must now learn to become humble subjects of a heavenly lover. The transformation thus culminates in an unconditional subjection to the law [the monastic Rule], in desire becoming the will to obey God—the supreme Christian virtue.[37]

This surrender to God is precisely what Abelard portrays in stanzas 9-11 of *Virgines castae*. Stanza 9 marks the beginning of the central section of the sequence. Dronke has described this section as an '*epithalamium*', a 'bridal hymn'.[38]

35. Asad, *Genealogies*, 145.
36. Asad, *Genealogies*, 144.
37. Asad, *Genealogies*, 145.
38. '*Virgines caste*', 93. Ancient rhetoricians would have called this section a 'bedroom song' and identified the entire sequence as a 'wedding song'—a

In *Virgines castae* we find a virgin sharing her bed with Christ, who clasps her with his right hand and cradles her head with his left. The virgin's experience here is precisely that of the Song's bride. Consider the two texts in juxtaposition:

Song of Songs	*Virgines castae*
leva *eius sub* capite *meo*	Dextera *sponsi*
et dextera *illius*	*sponsa complexa*
amplexabitur me	capiti laeva
(2:6; 8:3)	*dormit submissa*
	*per*vigil corde
ego dormio et cor *meum*	*corpore* dormit
vigilat . . . (5:2)	*et sponsi grato*
	sinu quiescit
Adiuro vos filiae	*Approbans somnum*
Hierusalem	*Sponsus beatam*
per capreas cerboque	*inquietari*
camporum	*prohibet illam*
ne suscitetis *et*	ne suscitetis
evigilare faciatis	*inquit*, dilectam
dilectam *donec ipsa*	*dum ipsa volet*
velit (2:7; 8:3)	*ita quietam*

(Continued)

---

distinction that goes back at least to the third-century AD greek orator Menander Rhetor. In his treatise on epideictic speech—the discourse of praise and blame—Menander presents the *gamelios*—what the Latins would later call the *epithalamium*—as a form of epideictic speech. Along with the *epithalamium* there is a special, more narrowly focused, speech delivered at the nuptial room of the newlyweds. This speech he calls *kateunastikos*, or 'the bedroom speech'. See *Menander Rhetor*, ed. with trans. and commentary by D. A. Russell and N. G. Wilson (Oxford: Clarendon Press, 1981) 135–159. Notwithstanding Menander's terminology, I can find no evidence that Abelard and other medieval writers recognized a distinction between a 'wedding song' and a 'bedroom speech'.

His *left arm* under *my head* and *his right arm* will embrace me (2:6; 8:3)	The *right hand* of the bridegroom clasps his bride His *left hand* cradles her head
I *sleep and my soul keeps watch* (5:2)	While *wakeful in heart* she *sleeps* in body and she quietly slumbers on the loving breast of her bridegroom
I adjure you, daughters of Jerusalem by the goats and the stags of the field	Favoring her sleep the Bridgegroom Does not let her (the blessed one) be disquieted
neither arouse nor cause to *awaken my beloved* until she wishes (2:7; 8:3)	he says *Do not awaken my beloved* thus quiet as long as she wishes

Abelard is no slave to his source of inspiration. He 'recites' the Song text, but not word for word. It is enough for him to use key words that clearly link his work with the Song of Songs. Yet he changes words for poetic and rhetorical purposes. Abelard used the literal images of the Song to evoke, engage, and direct the feminine soul to set its affections upon Christ, the bridegroom. Abelard's Paraclete audience would have immediately recognized his language and imagery. In the symbolic world Abelard sought to create at the Paraclete Abbey, the voice of God spoke through the Song's bridegroom and the proper voice for Heloise and her nuns was found in the words and deeds of the Canticle's virginal bride.

Abelard introduces the bridal scene with another image from the Song which, once again resonates deeply with medieval culture, especially, the culture of husbands and wives. Before the virgin experiences the joys and intimacy of Christ's embrace, she finds herself in Christ's bed surrounded by guardian angels. The Song of Songs (3:7-8) inspires this scene in stanza 8.

Song of Songs 3:7-8	Virgines castae
en lectum *Salomonis*	Lectulos *harum christo*
sexaginta fortes	*vacantes*
ambiunt ex	*angeli vallant*
fortissimis Israhel omnes tenentes	*custodientes*
gladios	*ne quis incestus temeret*
et bella doctissimi uniuscuiusque	*illos*
ensis	*ensibus strictis arcent*
super femur suum	*immundos*
propter timores	
nocturnes	
Behold, *the bed* of	Their [virgins'] *beds*
Solomon	which are unoccupied
	for Christ
sixty strong men	Guardian angels protect
surrounding it of	
the strongest of	
Israel	
all holding swords and	Lest any one impure defile
most learned in	them
warfare	
each one's sword on his	They ward off the impure
thigh because of	with their drawn swords.
nocturnal fears	

The biblical passage tells us that three-score valiant men surround the bed of Solomon, each with a sword upon his thigh as protection against the fears of night; Abelard speaks of angels.

In the social world of Abelard and Heloise, gallant men guarding the family of a great lord was a social reality. Many monks had once belonged among the ranks of these men, some had even been lords. And many monastic women had known courtly life along with its courageous men and lordly patrons. Medieval nobles could see in Solomon's protection of his beloved the basis for the enclosed world of their 'courts.'[39] Abelard intends the scene, with its connections to the social world of Heloise and her nuns, to arouse them emotionally toward Christ. God— thought Abelard—wants the nuns to cast all of their cares upon their heavenly husband. As their patron and protector, Christ wants their full and complete devotion.

The angels who surround the bedded virgin brides of Christ are eternally on watch, warding off lascivious would-be lovers with drawn swords. Peter Dronke has proposed that the com- poser of the sequence, whom he stops short of identifying with Abelard, reads the Song's image of Solomon's bed guards through the lens of Saint Ambrose's *De virginibus* (1.51):

> And for you, holy virgins, there is a special guardianship, for you who with unspotted chastity keep the couch of the Lord holy. And no wonder if the angels fight for you who war with the mode of life of angels. Virginal chastity merits their guardianship whose life it attains to.[40]

Unlike *Virgines castae*, Ambrose does not speak specifically of angels fighting off human rivals to God's love; he does teach that virgins merit the special guardianship of the angels and that these heavenly guardians ward off anyone or anything that might bring harm to God's faithful virgins. As Ambrose says, 'they fight for us' and 'guard the fruit that is in us'.[41] The image of angelic knights with sword in hand had its parallel in the chivalrous protection earthly knights gave to their beloved ladies.[42] Abelard's

39. The word *court* comes from the Latin *curtis*, enclosure, specifically the enclosure that lords erected around their houses. See Georges Duby, ed., *A His- tory of Private Life 2: Revelations of the Medieval World* (Cambrige: Belknap Press of Harvard University Press, 1988) 12.

40. PL 16:202: *Vobis autem, virgines sanctae, speciale praesidium est, quae inem- erato pudore sacrum domini servatis cubile. Neque mirum si pro vobis angeli militant . . . .* Translation adapted from NPNFC 2, 10:371. See Dronke, 'Virgines caste', p. 103.

41. Quoted from NPNFC 2, vol. 1:371.

42. See Georges Duby, *The Chivalrous Society*, translated Cynthia Postan (Berkeley: University of California Press, 1980).

contemporaries sought to replicate the enclosed world of Christ's heavenly kingdom in their enclosed earthly courts.

The opening stanzas of *Epithalamica* seek to remind its reader-singers, with a few key biblical words, of its narrative sources as well as the appropriate socially determined response. Abelard 'invents' much of his sequence *Epithalamica* by drawing on the Canticle. In stanza 2 Abelard makes mention of the daughters of Jerusalem, the chorus of young women who appear frequently in the Song of Songs.[43] Yet, as Chrysogonus Waddell has observed, the sequence also alludes to Exodus 15:20-21; the daughters are not only the maidens of the Song, they are also the troupe of women who joined in the canticle of Miriam after the passage through the Red Sea:

> *Sumpsit ergo Maria prophetissa, soror Aaron, tympanum in manu sua; egressaeque sunt omnes mulieres past eam cum tympanis & choris, Quibus praecinebat, dicens: Cantemus Domino . . . .*[44]

With prophetic insight Miriam put into song the joy within her heart. Likewise, the bride is a seeress who sings outwardly of the connubial joys she has experienced within.

In stanzas 3-5, friends of the bridegroom appear, those who, like John the Baptist, summon all to the nuptials of bridegroom and bride (Jn 3:29). It is not surprising to find mention of these groomsmen; the great Song commentator Origen, known by every medieval commentator, had included among the participants in the sacred marriage, '. . . four groups: the two individuals, the bridegroom and the bride; two choirs answering each other—the bride singing with her maidens, and the bridegroom with his companions.[45] Here the bride and bridegroom each have

---

43. Sg 1:4, 2:7, 3:5, 5:8, 5:16, 8:4.

44. 'So Miriam the prophetess . . . took a timbrel in her hand; and all the women went forth after her with timbrels and with dances; and she began singing to them, saying: "Let us sing to the Lord. . . ."'

45. Translation by R. P. Lawson, *Origen. The Song of Songs. Commentary and Homilies,* Ancient Christian Writers (New York: Newman Press, 1957), 268. O. Rousseau analyzes this dramatic scenario in his edition, *Origene. Homélies sur le Cantique des Cantiques* (Paris, 1954) 39–44.

a chorus—the bride, a group of young maidens (*adulescentulae*), the groom, male companions (*sodales*).

These *dramatic personae* would have been familiar to most, if not all, of the Paraclete nuns, who surely had witnessed a wedding with its bride and bridegroom and their respective female and male attendants and family members. The scene to which the sequence alludes and which Origen evokes was ancient and solemn. Long before the couple were finally joined in matrimony, arrangements for their union had been afoot. For their joining was more than man and woman; it was the allying of one family with another for their mutual benefit and for the continuation of the family through offspring. Medieval women, like their ancient forbearers, bore the heavy responsibility of uniting two families—her father's and her husband's.

The marriage suggested by *Epithalamica* took place in stages. From her birth the bride's virginity had been guarded as a treasure by her father. At some point the bridegroom or his guardian had arranged his future union with her family. When old enough, the betrothed girl was blessed by a priest and she then publicly processed with her maiden attendants and family members to church. All gathered to witness the priest's public joining of the two before God and humanity, and the husband then took his bride into his household. The connubial scene of *Epithalamica* resonates with actual medieval social practice as well as images from the written texts that we have been exploring as the oral and scribal resources of Abelard's sequences.

The song of the bride in *Epithalamica* is an excellent example of 'recitation', i.e., 'the transmission of speech or narrative, from either oral or written tradition, in the exact words in which the person has received the speech or narrative or in different words'.[46] Words in roman type in stanzas 3-5 are taken from the Song of Songs 2:8-14.

---

46. Vernon K. Robbins, *Exploring the Texture of Texts: A Guide to Socio-Rhetorical Interpretation* (Valley Forge: Trinity International Press, 1996) 41.

Song of Songs	Epithalamica
Vox dilecti mei, ecce *iste* venit saliens in monti- bus transiliens colles (2:8)	In montibus *his* ecce saliens ecce venit, colles transiliens;
similis est dilectus meus capreae *himuloque cervorum* *en ipse stat post parietem nostrum* despiciens per fenestras pros- piciens per cancellos (2:9)	per fenestras *ad me* respiciens per cancellos *dicit,* prospiciens:
et dilectus meus loquitur mihi, surge propera amica *mea formonsa mea et veni* (2:10)	Amica, surge, propera! *columba nitens, advola!*
iam *enim* hiemps transiit imber abiit *et recessit* flores *apparuerunt in* terra *tempu* *putationis advenit vox* turturis *audita est in terra nostra* (2:11-12)	*Horrens* enim hiems iam transiit *gravis* imber recedens abiit; *ver amoenum* ter- ras *aperuit;* parent flores, *et* turtur *cecinit;*
ficus protulit grossos suos vineae *florent dedernt odorem* surge amica *mea speciosa mea et veni* columba *mea in foraminibus petrae in cav-* *erna maceriae* (2:13-14)	Amica, surge, propera columba *nitens, advola'*
The voice of my beloved *behold, he comes leaping* on the *mountains springing across the hills* (2:8)	*Behold he comes leaping* *upon the mountians* *Behold he comes skipping* *over the hills*

my beloved is like a goat and
    a young of stags
behold, he stands behind our wall
looking in through the
    windows watching through the
lattices (2:9)
	Gazing upon me *through the*
	    windows
	peering through the lattices
	        he says

Song of Songs	Epithalamica
and my beloved speaks to me *arise swiftly my friend my beautiful*, and come (2:10)	*Arise my friend make haste my beautiful* dove fly to me

for *now the winter has passed
    the rain has gone* and departed
	For the bristling *winter is
	    now past*
	the heavy *rains have* receded
	    and *gone*
	lovely springtime has
	    opened earth

flowers appear on
    the earth the time of
    pruning has come
	flowers are appearing the

the voice of the *turtle dove*
    is heard in our land
                (2:11, 12)
	turtle-dove has begun
	singing

the fig tree has put out its
    thick shoots
the flowering vines have
    given off a smell
arise, my friend, my *lovely* one,
    and come,
my dove in the clefts of the
    rock in the hollow of the wall
                (2:13, 14)
	Arise my friend make haste *my*
	    beautiful *dove* fly to me.

The Song here celebrates springtime love. Flora and fauna signal the beloved's coming to his bride: animals leap and frolic about, figs and vines emit their delectable odors, birds sing anew, fresh flowers and new buds greet the day. Upon his arrival, the bridegroom bids the bride twice to come away with him.

Abelard omits words from the biblical text. The abbreviation of both the narrative and 'the saying'—the spoken words of the bridegroom—creates a dramatic speech that features a short exhortation. The purest recitation of the biblical text occurs at the beginning of the bridegroom's song: one word of the biblical text is missing and the words are rearranged so as to create proper rhyme. The quoted words jog the singer's mind, cueing him or her to the biblical source of the bridegroom's song. As we shall see through analysis of rhetorical and cultural intertexture, the bridegroom is not imparting knowledge; he is presenting 'wisdom' that every soul should already know and to which every soul who hears his song should now respond.

The concluding lines of stanzas 3 and 4 clearly parallel the Song's refrain-like exhortation that the bride *surge et veni*, rise and come. Furthermore, Abelard's handling of the biblical text provides an example of omitting words to produce a remarkable rhetorical effect. The recitation adds two new words to Scripture and removes several words. In its abbreviated form the verse functions as a short, crisp, unmistakable exhortation in support of the bridegroom's argumentation. Abelard's unhesitating abbreviation and rearrangement of his sources for poetic impact are made for persuasive purposes: the sequence—as we shall see in our rhetorical analysis—is calculated to teach, delight, and above all, move the virginal auditor to follow in the steps of the virgin-bride.

In contrast to stanzas 3-5 of *Epithalamica*, which recite the text of the Song of Songs with only slight abbreviation and rewording, in stanzas 5 and 6 Abelard refashions the biblical text substantially into his own words. Words that occur in the Song of Songs are in roman type in the Latin . The italicized words differ from the biblical text. The sequence here is stitched together from phrases of the Song of Songs 1:11, 5:1a or c, 5:6a, and 3:1-4b:

Song of Songs	Epithalamica
dum esset rex in accubitu	Rex in accumbitum
suo nardus mea *dedit*	*iam se contulerat*
odorem suum (1:11)	*et* mea *redolens*
	nardus *spiraverat*
	in hortum veneram

(Continued)

pessulum ostii aperui delecto
meo at ille declinaverat
at*que* transierat
(5:6a)

in quem descenderat
at ille transiens
iam declinaverat

in lectulo meo per noctes
quaesivi *quem diligit anima*
mea
quaesivi *illum et non inveni*
surgam et circuibo civitatem
per vicos et plateas
quaeram *quem diligit anima*
mea
quaesivi *illum et non* inveni
invenerunt me vigiles *qui*
custodiunt civitatem.
num quem dilexit anima mea
vidistis
Paululum cum pertransissem eos
inveni quem diligit anima mea
(3:1-4b)

Per noctem *igitur hunc,*
quaerens *exeo*
huc, illuc, anxia
quaerendo *cursito*
occurrunt vigiles
ardenti studio

quos cum transierim
Sponsum invenio

while *the king* was *on his*
couch my nard gave out its
fragrance (1:11)

The King had already
betaken himself into his
chamber and *my* redolent
nard-oil has
breathed forth
I had come into the
garden into which
he had descended—
but *he passing through had*
already gone away

I opened the bolt of the door
to my love but *he had*
turned away and *gone over*
(5:6a)

On my bed *through the nights*
I sought him whom my soul loves
I sought him and I did
not find

And so *by night I* go
forth from here
seeking him

(Continued)

Song of Songs	*Epithalamica*
I will arise and go around the city	anxious hither and thither I run in my *seeking*
through the streets and the courtyards	
I will seek him whom my soul loves	
I sought and I did not *find* him	
The watchmen found me who guard the city	*The watchmen* come upon me in my burning zeal
have you seen him whom my soul has loved?	
when I had hardly *passed by* them I found him whom my soul loves	when *I pass* them I find my bridegroom

The bride's frantic search for the bridegroom sets the context for *Epithalamica*'s last stanzas. Abelard builds upon the link between the Song's affective language and similar language in biblical and patristic sources. The couplets of laughter/weeping and morning/evenings come respectively from Ecclesiastes 3:4, *Tempus flendi/tempus ridendi* (A time to weep/a time to laugh) and Psalm 29, *Ad vesperum demorabitur fletus, et ad matutinum laetitia* (In the evening weeping shall have place, and in the morning gladness).

Chrysogonus Waddell has observed that Abelard's development of these biblical phrases in stanzas 7-8 bear a remarkable likeness to Gregory the Great's *Homily* 25 on Mary at the tomb.[47] Abelard has drawn on many of the pope's ideas and used some of his vocabulary. Gregory wrote:

> *Qua in re pensandum est hujus mulieris* mentem quanta vis amoris accenderat, *quae a monumento Domini, etiam discipulis recedentibus, non recedebat. Exquirebat quem non invenerat,* flebat inquirendo, et amoris sui igne succensa, *ejus quem*

47. '*Epithalamica*', 262.

ablatum credidit ardebat desiderio . . . . *Sed Maria, cum* fleret, *inclinavit se, et prosperit in moumentum.* Certe jam monumentum vacuum viderat, jam sublatum Dominum nuntiaverat; quid est quod se iterum inclinat,* iterum videre desiderat. *Sed amanti semel aspexisse non sufficit, quia* vis amoris intentionem multiplicat inquisitionis. *Quaesivit ergo prius, et minime invenit; perseveravit ut quaereret, unde et contigit ut inveniret, actumque est* ut desideria dilata crescerent, *et cresentia caperent quod invenissent. Hinc est enim quod de eodem sponso Ecclesia in Canticia canticerum dicit: In lectulo meo per noctes quaesivi quem diligit anima mea; quaesivi illum, et non inveni. Surgam, et circuibo civitatem, per vicos et plateas quaerum quem diligit anima mea (Cant. 3:1). Quae defectum quoque inventionis ingeminat, dicens: Quaetivi illum, et non inveni (3:1). Sed quia diu inventio se non elongat, si inquisitio non desistat, adjungit: Invenerunt me vigiles qui custodiunt civitatem. Num quem diligit anima mea, vidistis? Paututum cum pertransissem eos, inveni quem diligit anima mea (3:4). Dilectum namque in lectulo quaerimus, quando in praesentis vitae aliquantula require Redemptoris nostri desiderio suspiramus. Per noctem quaerimus, quia etsi jam in ille mens vigilat, tame adhuc oculus caligat . . . .* Sancta enim desideria, *ut praedisimus,* dilatione crescunt. Si autem dilatione deficiunt, desideria non fuernt. *Hoc amore arsit, quisquis ad veritatem pertigere potuit . . . . Justum quippe est ut ex visione medici pertingat ad salutem, quae per aestum ejus desiderii vutnus amoris portat in pectore. Hinc rursus ait: Anima mae liquefacta est, ut dilectus locutus est (V.6). Mens namque hominis conditoris sui speciem non quaerentia male dura est, quia in semetipsa remanet frigida. At si* ardere jam ex desiderio coeperit ad sequendum quem diligit, *liquefacta per ignem amoris currit. Fit desiderio anxia . . . .*

We must consider in this woman's state of mind, that a great force of *love inflamed her.* When even the disciples departed from the sepulchre, she did not depart. She sought for him whom she had not found, *weeping* as she searched; *being inflamed with the fire of her love, she burned with desire for him who she believed had been taken away . . . .* But Mary [Magdalene], while she was weeping, stooped down and looked

into the sepulchre. It is true that she had already seen that
the sepulchre was empty, and had already reported that the
Lord had been taken away. Why did she stoop down again,
why did she again long to see? It is not enough for a lover
to have looked once, because the force of love intensifies
the effort of the search. She sought a first time and found
nothing; she persevered in seeking, and so it happened that
she found him. *It came about that her unfulfilled desires increased, and as they increased they took possession of what they
had found.* This is the reason the Church says of this person,
her own spouse, in the Song of Songs: 'Upon my bed during
the night I sought him whom my soul loves; I sought him
and did not find him. I will rise and go about the city,
through its squares and streets; I will seek him whom my
soul loves' (3:1-2). In her failure to find him she redoubled
her efforts saying, 'I sought him and did not find him' (3:2),
But since discovery is not long delayed if the search is not
abandoned, 'The watchmen who guard the city found me,
'Have you seen him whom my soul loved?' Scarcely had I
passed them by when I found him whom my soul loves'
(3:4) . . . . *Holy desires*, as I've told you before, *increase by
delay in their fulfillment;* if delay causes them to fail, they
were not desires. Anyone who has been able to reach out
for *the Truth has been on fire with this love* . . . . It is right that
the soul after bearing in its heart a wound of love brought
on by its *burning desire*, should reach out for healing at the
sight of the doctor. And so, again, it says: 'My soul melted
when he spoke' (5:6). The heart of a person who does not
seek the face of his creator is hardened by his ickedness,
because in itself it remains cold. But if it now begins to *burn
with the desire of following him whom it loves*, it runs since the
fire of love has melted it. Its desire makes it *anxious* . . . .[48]

In both *Epithalamica* and Gregory's sermon desire, burning love,
and anxiety flame up into a fierce emotional blaze. Both writers

48. Waddell, *'Epithalamica'*, 266. PL 76:1189B–1191A; translation adapted
from Dom David Hurst, *Gregory the Great. Forty Gospel Homilies* (Kalamazoo:
Cistercian Publications, 1990) 188–190. My emphases.

take up and amplify the theme of delay, found especially in Song, Chapter 3, with equal volume and intensity.

The alternation between desire and delay continues in *Epithalamica* in the next lines of stanza 7. The virginal bride's efforts to find her beloved fail at first; then she, like the bride of the Song, passes beyond the city watchmen, and beyond the gates finds her love (Song 3:1-4). In stanza 9 of *Epithalamica* appear two phrases, originally inspired by the Canticle, from the Office antiphons and responsories for the feast of Saint Agnes; Abelard recites them, changing a few words.[49]

Saint Agnes Office	Epithalamica
Ecce quod *concupivi*, iam video	iam video / quod *optaveram*
quod *speravi*, iam teneo	iam teneo / quod *amaveram*
Behold, *what* I yearned for, I *now see;*	*Now I see / wha*t I had hoped for
What I hoped for, I *now clasp.*	*Now I clasp / what* I had loved.

The verbs *optaveram . . . amaveram* differ from the *concupivi . . . speravi* of the antiphon for no other reason than the rhyme required for the sequence stanza.

This practice of forming phrases and lines by weaving bits and pieces of a source together (a skill called *collatio*) was common in both the ancient and medieval rhetorical tradition. The audience itself—assumed the rhetor—could easily supply the oral or written source that stood behind the new text. The ability to create such a mosaic implied that its author had extensive, detailed knowledge of the tradition stored in his memory and the skill to shape that tradition to meet his audience's expectations and to move its affections. A persuasive display of this vast knowledge brought the author much public honor and spoke eloquently of his noble *ethos*. Through their masterful songs, the

49. Hesbert, Corpus 3:189, note 2539.

bridegroom, the bride, the narrator, and ultimately the author of *Virgines castae* and *Epithalamica,* show that their person and words bear great authority, and are worthy of high respect and recognition.[50] Moreover, through their eloquence, God, the grand rhetorician, is honored, for ultimately it is God who speaks, through the author seeking to teach, delight, and move his people to deeper faithfulness.

PSALM 44: THE VIRGIN QUEEN

The Song of Songs is not the only biblical text that celebrates the love of unnamed lovers. Like the Canticle, Psalm 44 is essentially an *epithalamicum,* a wedding song, for a human king and queen bride. It was probably composed for use at the wedding of some Israelite or Judean king to a foreign princess.[51] Like the Song of Songs, the psalm makes no direct mention of God and on the surface reveals no divine commands, moral precepts, or sacred history.

Psalm 44 is essentially epideictic; that is, it is a song of praise. The unknown poet-singer begins by telling his reader that his task is to give a 'good word' about the bridal pair. He imitates the Canticle poet, but rather than create dialogical speech in which the bride and groom speak about each other, he speaks. He celebrates the physical beauty and moral virtues of the king and queen. For the royal bridegroom the psalmist declares:

50. The same aesthetic was true of Thomas Jefferson's drafting of *The Declaration of Independence.* 'By modern lights, Jefferson's use of texts by other authors (in writing the Declaration) might be considered to detract from his achievement. In the eighteenth century, however, educated people regarded with disdain the striving for novelty. Achievement lay instead in the creative adaptation of preexisting models to different circumstances, and the highest praise of all went to imitations whose excellence exceeded that of the examples that inspired them. Young men were taught to copy and often to memorize compelling passages from their readings for future use since you could never tell when, say, a citation from Cicero might come in handy'. Quoted from Pauline Maier, *American Scripture: Making the Declaration of Independence* (New York: Alfred A. Knopf, 1997) 104.

51. *The New Interpreter's Bible* (Nashville: Abingdon Press, 1996) 4:860–863.

Speciosus forma prae filiis hominum,	You are the most handsome of men;
diffusa est gratia in labiis tuis:	grace is poured upon your lips;
propterea benedixit te Deus	therefore God has blessed you
in aeternum	forever.
Accingere gladio tuo super femur	Gird your sword on your thigh,
tuum, potentissime.	O mighty one.

The poet then continues by praising the king's military might and admonishing him to use his power and majesty not for personal gain but to advance the good of his people. God has anointed the king to lead his people in fulfilling the divine will, and he must imitate God by loving righteousness and eschewing wickedness.

In verses 8 and 9 the poet describes the setting of the royal wedding. The elegant beauty of the king's palace forms the visual background for the celebration. The sounds of stringed instruments fill the air and make glad all who are present. Prestigious persons glide into place; the daughters of the king and numerous ladies of honor surround the queen bride, who stands at the king's right hand. With the queen now in view, the poet focuses on her new role and her noble dress (44:10-17). He admonishes her to embrace her new office and instructs her, describing the attitude she should assume in her new marital relationship: 'Forget your people and your father's house, writes the poet (v. 10), and to submit to her king. Her identity is now with her king; she must submit to him, which will only bring her recognition and honor (v. 12). Next the psalmist sings of the queen's beauty as she processes with a company of virgins in her train:

Et filiae Tyri in muneribus	The king shall greatly
vultum Tuum	desire your beauty,
deprecabuntur: omnes	for he is the Lord,
divites plebis. (v. 13)	your God.

(Continued)

Omnis gloria eius filiae	All the glory of her,
regis ab intus,	the daughter of the
in fimbriis aureis	king, is from within
circumamicata	with fringes of gold,
varietatibus.	she is robed in
	many colors.
Adducentur Regi virgines	Virgins are led in to the
post eam: proximae ejus	king after her.
afferentur tibi. (v. 14)	

With joy and gladness her companions escort her forward to be coupled with the king. Toward the end of the psalm, the lyricist returns to where he began, blessing the king and foreseeing many sons and much glory in his future.

Abelard constructed stanzas 3-5 of *Virgines castae* directly out of the material of Psalm 44. In stanzas 3 through 5 of the sequence Abelard depicts a cortège of virgins as it follows in the train of the supreme virgin. From the psalm he draws key words and phrases that any student of the Bible, certainly a monk or nun who sang through the psalms weekly, would recognize.

Psalm 44	Virgines castae
	(stanzas 3-5, 20)
Astitit regina a dextris	*Hec est* a dextris
Tuis in vestitue deaurato:	*assistens regis,*
circumdata varietate. (10)	*illa* regina
	Iuncto latere
audi filia, et vide,	*sola cum rege*
et inclina aurem tuam:	*precedit ipsa;*
et obliviscere populum tuum,	
et domum patris tui. (11)	
et concupiscet rex decorem	
Tuum:	
quoniam ipse est Dominus	
Deus tuus, et adorabunt	
eum. (12)	

(Continued)

Omnis gloria eius filiae
regis ab intus,
in fimbriis aureis
    circumamicata varietatibus.

Adducentur Regi virgines post
eam: *proximae ejus afferentur*
    tibi.   (14)

Et filiae Tyri *in* muneribus
vultum *Tuum* deprecabuntur:
    omnes divites plebis.   (13)

Afferentur in laetitia et
exsultatione: adducentur in
    templum *regis.*   (16)

Aurata veste,
varietate
circumamicta
Tamquam dominam
sequitur ipsam
queque beata.
Post eam adducte
virgines *devote*
regi *sunt oblate,*
christo consecrate.

Tales erant Thecla,
Agnes et Lucia,
Agathes et multa
virginum caterva.

Filiae Tyri munera *ferentes*
et in his regis vultum
deprecantes
Hostias cunctis habent
puriores,
corpore munde, corde
sanctiores.

Hoc attende canticum,
devotarum virginum
insigne collegium,
Quo nostra devotio
maiore se studio
templum *ornet Domine.*

Psalm 44	Virgines castae

The queen stands at *his right hand*
   in a vesture made from gold,
   clothed about
   with a variety of colors.
   (11)

This one [the supreme virgin]
is that *queen* serving *at the*
righthand of the king
United beside him she alone
with the king proceeds

Hear, O daughter, behold and
   incline your ear: Forget
   your people and the house
   of your father. (12)
The king shall greatly desire
   your beauty, for he is the
   Lord, your God. (13)

All the glory of her, the
   daughter of the king, is
   from within
   with fringes of
gold, *she is clothed round*
   about in a variety of
   colors.

In golden array *clothed round*
about with variety
Every blessed [virgin]
follows her as her lady.

Virgins are led in to the king
   after her. (14)

Led after her devoted virgins
have been offered to the king (and)
consecrated to Christ.
Such [virgins] were Thecla Agnes
and Lucia Agathes and many a
great throng of virgins.

And *the daughters of Tyre*
shall entreat him with
gifts. (12, 13)

The daughters of Tyre bearing *gifts*
And entreating the favor of the
king by means of them
Have offerings purer than all
[other offerings] [They are] clean
in body holier in heart

(Continued)

With joy and gladness they are led along: they enter into *the temple* of the king. (16)]

Attend to this song of the illustrious college of devoted virgins Whereby our devotion may with greater zeal adorn *the temple* of the Lord]

As Abelard uses imagery from Psalm 44, he is no slave to the biblical wording. In stanza 3 of *Virgines castae* he uses only two words of the parallel psalm verse, 44:10. By contrast, he interweaves many more words from Psalm 44:14 into stanza 4 of the sequence. Stanza 5 also draws heavily on the language of the psalm's thirteenth verse. Finally, stanza 20 concludes the sequence with a reference to the temple of the Lord, which resonates with the temple of the king lauded in Psalm 44:16. Abelard not only uses considerable discrimination in borrowing language from Psalm 44, he also feels free to rearrange the biblical text for his own purposes. In stanzas 4 and 5, Abelard moves texts around, presenting the psalmist's Daughters of Tyre (*filiae Tyri*: Ps 44:14) after describing the scene of virgins following the virginal queen (Ps 44:16).

Scenes of virgins following Mary, the Queen of Virgins, appear frequently in medieval literature.[52] This virginal band appears in many medieval lyrics such as the sequence *Exultent filiae Sion in Rege suo* reads:

Nunc inter virgines adducta
    post eam,
quae Mater est intacta,
virginum Virginis Mariae
digna est pedissequa . . . .[53]

Now amid virgins whom she leads after her is that Mother who is undefiled; the virgin is a worthy attendant to the Virgin Mary.

52. Adalbert de Vogüé has noted several such descriptions from the sixth century and provided references to many other later medieval depictions of Queen Mary and her virgins in 'Marie chez les vièrges du sixièmesiècle; Césaire d'Arles et Grégoire le Grand', *Benedictina* 33 (1986) 79–91.

53. I learned of the likeness between these two sequences from Waddell's 'Chaste Virgins' 27. See also Ulysse Chevalier, *Repertorium hymnologicum. Catalogue des chants, hymnes, latine depuis les origines jusqu'a nos jours, par la chanoine*

That Mary and her virginal attendants grace heaven's court was simply assumed by medieval people. Lords and ladies, kings and queens, all with their own attendants, sought to replicate the heavenly court on earth.

Abelard's *Virgines castae* and *Epithalamica* almost certainly reminded Heloise and her nuns who came from aristocratic circles of the earthly courts in which they had once lived. Every earthly procession, wedding ceremony, court, lady and her attendants, king and queen could be seen as symbolic of the heavenly realm. Every earthly marriage symbolized the most blessed of unions: the union of Christ and his Church as well as Christ and the individual soul.[54] Abelard rhetorically calculated his sequences to teach the Paraclete nuns what their bridal role was, to encourage them to delight in the honor of this role, and to move them to abandon all identification with their old lives and submit themselves completely to their heavenly bridegroom. Whereas many of the Paraclete nuns had once gracefully bestridden earthly courts, their abode was now among the honored court of heaven. Arousing the right emotions was key to successful persuasion. Through courtly imagery, Abelard sought to arouse the *pathos* of his audience; he wanted the nuns to understand the deep meaning of their lives in Christ. His 'internal' means of persuasion are intricately linked to the 'external' means uncovered by our analysis.

The addition of the phrase *iuncto latere* in stanza 3 of *Virgines castae* sets the sequence apart from both the psalm and the typical medieval description of the heavenly queen and her retinue of virgins. Here the queen is not alone in leading the chorus of virgins; the king and queen proceed side by side. In Psalm 44 the queen-bride is at her king's side only *before* the procession. In the wedding procession itself she and her virginal companions go forward to meet the king. Medieval texts influenced by Psalm 44

Ulysses Chevalier (Louvain and Brussels, 1892–1920) 6 vols., here vol. 1:345, note 5780; and vol. 5:144.

54. See Duby, *A History of Private Life*, 35–156.

typically have the bride and her virgins enter the heavenly temple in order to present themselves to Christ their King and Lord. Yet Abelard unquestionably reads Psalm 44 as placing Christ himself at the head of the processing virginal company and queen.

Is there a precedent for Abelard's description of Christ and his virgin queen? After an extensive inquiry into the question, Waddell has found very few descriptions of the heavenly procession that include Christ proceeding with a queen *at his side*.[55] Yet the source of *iuncto latere* seems to be Origen, who seems to have been the first commentator to use the phrase *iuncto latere*. In his first homily on the Song of Songs, he wrote,

> *Sponsa non post tergum sequitur, set iuncto ingreditur latere, apprehendit dexteram sponsi, et manus eius sponsi dextera continetur. . . .*
>
> The bride does not follow behind, she walks side by side with the bridegroom; she takes His right hand, and in His right hand her own hand is held.[56]

After Origen, however, the phrase was used infrequently until the twelfth century, when, as we shall see, it appears numerous times in the works of Peter Abelard.

NEW TESTAMENT TEXTS: THE LETTER TO THE EPHESIANS

Along with Old Testament sources, Abelard drew on several New Testament passages in 'inventing' his sequences. The first clear link occurs in *Virgines castae* stanza 2a, where the sequence, like Ephesians 5:19, exhorts its hearers to speak to one another in psalms and hymns and canticles.

---

55. 'Chaste Virgins', 27–30.

56. *Origène, Homélies sur le Cantique des Cantiques*, SCh 37 (Paris, 1954) 69. English translation R. P. Lawson, *Origen. The Song of Songs, Commentary and Homilies*, Ancient Christian Writers, 26 (New York: Newman Press, 1956) 274.

Ephesians 5:19	Virgines castae
Et nolite inebriari vino in quo est luxu-ria sed implemini Spiritu loquentes *vobismet ipsis* in psalmis et hymnis et canticis *spiritalibus cantantes et psallentes in cordibus*	Psalmis et hymnis, canticis *dignis* sibi *col*loquentes *Solvant in istis debitae laudis hostias sollemnes.*
Be not inebriated with wine, wherein is excess; but be filled with the Spirit, *speaking to one another in psalms and hymns and spiritual can-ticles,* singings and and making melody in your hearts	*Speaking to one another in fitting Psalms and hymns and canticles* Let them pay by these [songs] solemn sacrifices of due praise.

The exhortation in Ephesians to Spirit-filled singing figures into the broader moral admonition that forms the second half of the letter (chapters 4-6).[57] The letter's theological exposition (chapters 1-3) consists of a range of pauline topics that move Christians to speak to one another in psalms and hymns and canticles: humans are justified by God's free gift (grace) through faith (1:13; 2:5, 8-9), Christ made this gift available through his death on a cross (2:15-16), Christ's sacrificial death won redemption (1:7) for both Jews and Gentiles (1:12-13; 2:11-12; 3:6), Christ's death reconciled both Jews and Gentiles to God and each other, and these two 'races' or groups have now become one in Christ's body, the Church (2:14-16). If the Church is to bear witness in the world to God's reconciling power, it must manifest that unity in its life. Through his Holy Spirit, Christ makes possible a new form of humanity (2:15) and transforms the behavior of Jews and Gentiles alike.

Using baptismal imagery, the Letter to the Ephesians ad-monishes believers to 'take off' all their hostile attitudes and the

---

57. Abelard and medieval readers of the letter believed it to be the work of Saint Paul; many modern researchers insist that Ephesians was written pseud-onymously. See, for example, Luke Timothy Johnson's *The Writings of the New Testament: An Interpretation* (Philadelphia: Fortress Press, 1986) 367–380.

actions that formerly characterized them, when 'they were dark-
ened in their understanding, alienated from the life of God, because of their ignorance' (4:18). Abiding no longer in darkness,
they should adopt the pattern of 'lowliness, meekness, and pa-
tience' so characteristic of the life of Jesus (4:2-21). The letter
concludes with counsels on how to live carefully and wisely:

> Be careful then how you live, not as unwise people but as
> wise, making the most of the time, because the days are evil.
> So do not be foolish, but understand what the will of the
> Lord is. Do not get drunk with wine, for that is debauchery;
> but be filled with the Spirit, as you *sing psalms and hymns
> and spiritual songs among yourselves*, singing and making
> melody to the Lord in your hearts, giving thanks to God the
> Father at all times and for everything in the name of our
> Lord Jesus Christ. (5:15-20; my emphasis)

The letter goes on to say that this Spirit-filled life should
manifest itself in Christian marriages. Although wives are told
to submit to their husbands, Ephesians reserves its strongest
admonitions for husbands, who are to love their wives 'as Christ
loved the Church and gave himself up for her' (5:25). This self-
emptying love of Christ for the bride, the Church, is a 'profound
mystery'. As a husband and wife are made one flesh through
marriage, so Christ is one with the Church and in Christ both
Jews and Greeks are reconciled and made one. This union is the
fulfillment of God's plan 'to unite all things in him [Christ], things
in heaven and things in earth' (1:11).

On the surface this text seems to have little to do with the
virginal life; yet Ephesians uses several key words that may well
have linked the passage to virginity in the minds of Abelard as
well as the Paraclete nuns. The passage refers to two groups of
people: those who are 'wise' and 'unwise,' and those who are
'foolish' and not foolish. What paradigmatic group was known
for its wise and foolish members? The ten bridesmaids or virgins
in Matthew's gospel (25:1-13), five of whom were foolish and not
prepared for their bridegroom when he came, and five of whom
were wise and ready. This parable of Jesus resonates with the

argument in Ephesians. The wise virgin does not while her time away under the influence of wine, but is filled with the Spirit of Christ through the singing of psalms and hymns and canticles.

Beyond the possible link in Abelard's mind between the wise and foolish virgins and the exhortations in Ephesians, the letter draws an unmistakable parallel between Christ's marriage to the Church and human marriage. The Church—made up of Jews and Gentiles—is Christ's bride. Almost certainly Abelard presupposed the husband/wife and Christ/Church imagery of Ephesians. Abelard, however, recontextualizes the phrase. To be sure, Christians are speaking to one another in psalms, hymns, and canticles. But Abelard's attention is not upon the whole Church; it is upon that portion which is particularly qualified to be called the bride of Christ, the (wise) band of virgins, led by the supreme virgin, who have given themselves—as the sequence soon reveals—in body and mind to Christ and follow him wherever he goes.

PATRISTIC SOURCES AND THE SEQUENCES

Although Abelard drew heavily upon the Song of Songs and Psalm 44 in crafting his sequences, his understanding of these two biblical texts was greatly shaped by Jerome, Cyprian of Carthage, and Ambrose. These fathers of the Church wrote extensively on virginity and spiritual marriage to Christ and often drew on the Song and Psalm 44. These patristic texts contributed significantly to the content of the symbolic world that Abelard sought to cultivate among the Paraclete nuns.

The arguments against marriage in stanza 6 of *Virgines castae* evoke the world of Saint Jerome, and reflect the low view of marriage and high praise of virginity in his *Adversus Jovinianus*. In Rome sometime during the late 380s and early 390s, a monk named Jovinian began proclaiming that with the exaltation of virginity and asceticism, 'our religion has invented dogma against nature'.[58] Whatever merit Jovinian's arguments might have had,

58. *Adversus Jovinianus 1.41*; PL 23:211-338; quotation in column 211. English translation, Jerome, *Against Jovinian*, NPNFS 2, vol. 4, 346–416 at 379. Jovinian's

many Roman Christians, especially those of an ascetic disposition, could only see in them a threat to the much-honored virginal life. Leaders of the ascetic party reacted swiftly and decisively. Pammachius, a leading senator and member of one of the noblest and richest families of Rome, reported Jovinian to Pope Siricius (c. 334-399), who was himself a champion of celibacy. Pammachius also asked his childhood friend Jerome to respond to Jovinian's views.[59]

Jerome drew his mighty pen and set out to slay Jovinian. The result was his *Adversus Jovinianus*, in which he attempts to cut the heretiarch's position to pieces. Jerome's praise of virginity was coupled with a relentless attack on marriage. He had already made public his opinion that the good of marriage lies in the production of virgins.[60] He also had often recounted in letters and treatises the innumerable woes of marriage—screaming children, adulterous spouses, disobedient slave—all in an effort to persuade virgins from entering and widows from reentering the connubial state.[61] To a roman widow seeking spiritual guidance he suggested that remarriage is like a dog returning to his

---

teaching is known only through the works of his opponents, particularly Jerome and Augustine. Their anti-Jovinian works strongly suggest that his primary concern was not to challenge virginity or abstinence as legitimate christian practices, but to reject the view that asceticism was a truer form of christian life, a view which he believed led inevitably to Manicheanism. Only within the past decade or two have scholars begun to characterize Jovinian as a christian opponent of Manicheanism, rather than an anti-ascetic heretic. See Elizabeth A. Clark, 'Heresy, Asceticism, Adam, and Eve: Interpretations of Genesis 1–3 in the Later Latin Fathers', *Ascetic Piety and Women's Faith: Essays on Late Ancient Christianity* (New York and Toronto: Edwin Mellen Press, 1986) 353–85; and David G. Hunter, 'Resistance to the Virginal Ideal in Late-Fourth-Century Rome: The Case of Jovinian', *Theological Studies* 48 (1987) 45–64.

59. Pammachius, a scion of the ancient *gens Furia*, wielded considerable power in Rome at the time; see J. N. D. Kelly, *Jerome: His Life, Writings, and Controversies* (New York: Harper and Row, 1975) 19 and *passim*.

60. See Letter 22.20.

61. See Letters 22.2 and 22; 48.14 and 18; and 54.3-5; *Adversus Helvidium* 20; and *Adversus Jovinianus* 1.47.

vomit.[62] In *Adversus Jovinianus* he reckons the end of marriage 'death' and the end of virginity 'eternal life'.[63]

Jerome's *Adversus Jovinianus*, writes Christopher Brooke, 'became the basic medieval textbook for antifeminism'.[64] Particularly apt for satirizing marriage was Jerome's lengthy quotation of a lost book by the pagan philosopher Theophrastus. The essence of the philosopher's argument is that wives are a pest to philosophers, a view that Jerome reinforces with additional stories from pagan literature. Take Socrates: 'One day when he had withstood infinite abuse from [his wife] Xanthippe from an upper room, and she then drenched him with dirty water, all he did was to wipe his head and reply: "I knew that would happen, that a shower of rain would follow such a thunderstorm"'.[65]

Jerome's arguments appealed to both Abelard and Heloise, as we shall see again in the final chapter. As Christopher Brooke notes, 'When Abelard described in his *Historia Calamitatum* how he offered her marriage after he had made her pregnant, he gives a detailed account of her arguments against the fatal step, mostly based precisely on this passage in Jerome and quoting specifically the story about Socrates'.[66] Abelard made use of Jerome in de-

---

62. Letter 54.4.

63. *Adversus Jovinianus* 1.37, PL 23:211-82; NPNFS 2, vol. 6:374. Jerome's letters on virginity circulated widely in Rome, so Jovinian and his followers probably had knowledge of Jerome's asceticism and his teachings on the practice. If they did, they certainly deemed his slander of marriage a 'manichean' denial of the goodness of God's creation. *Adversus Jovinianus* 1.5 suggests that Jovinian had charged Jerome with Manicheanism. Pammachius apparently thought Jerome's views excessive, for he confiscated as many copies of the recently published *Adversus Jovinianus* as he could, fearing lest it circulate further. See Jerome, Letter 49.2.PL 22:512; NPNFS 2, vol. 6:79.

64. Christopher Brooke, *The Medieval Idea of Marriage* (Oxford: Clarendon Press, 1989) 62.See also Susan L. Smith, *The Power of Women: A Topos in Medieval Art and Literature* (Philadelphia: University of Pennsylvania Press, 1995), 27–29.

65. Jerome, *Adversus Jovinianum*, Bk. 1, 48; PL 23:278-279—quoted from Brooke, *The Medieval Idea*, 63. For more details on Jerome, see Kelly, *Jerome*, 91–103, 129–34, 273–282.

66. *The Medieval Idea*, 70–74.

scribing the woes of carnal marriage and weals of virginity in the sequence. Both teach that virgins are a *holocaustum* unto the Lord; in faith virgins offer their Lord a holy body and spirit. Consider the parallel between Jerome's depictions of virgins and Abelard's *Virgines castae* (stanza 6):

Adversus Jovinianus	*Virgines castae*
Grandis fidei est, grandisque virtutis, Dei templum esse purissimum, totum se holocaustum offerre Domino; *et justa eumdem Apostolum, esse sanctum et corpore et spiritu.*	Holocaustum Domino Offerent *ex integro virgines carne integrae mente immortalem sponsum eligentes Christum*
It is a mark of great faith and of great virtue, to be the pure temple of God, to *offer oneself to the Lord as a* whole *burnt-offering,* and, according to the same apostle, to be holy both in body and in spirit.	As a *burnt-offering* virgins *offer to the Lord* from their integrity the integrity of their flesh and mind choosing Christ as their immortal Spouse.

The theme of virgins offering their pure bodies and spirits to Christ is also present in *Virginitatis laus,* a letter believed in the medieval period to be by Jerome and used often by Abelard in his Paraclete *liturgica.*[67] Written in praise of virginity, *Virginitatis laus* begins with the claim that a special merit is attached to the recipients of virginal consecration. The letter writer develops his encomium with several topics found in both *Virgines castae* and

---

67. Though entered under Jerome's works as Ep 13 in PL 30:163-175, the work is no longer attributed to Jerome. Today scholars classify it as the work of the late fourth-century heretic Pelagius. For an english translation of *Viginitatis laus,* see B. R. Rees, *The Letters of Pelagius and His Followers* (Woodbridge: Boydell Press, 1991) 71–87. For details on Pelagius' life, see *idem, Pelagius: A Reluctant Heretic* (Woodbridge: Boydell Press, 1988). Both volumes provide extensive bibliography and analysis of Pelagius' life and works.

Epithalamica: virgins are described as the brides of Christ; their heavenly union is compared to earthly marriage; their path in life is the same as Christ's, the lamb, whom they follow wherever he goes; their lord was himself a virgin and the son of a virgin mother. The letter writer and Abelard are clear that of the holy and spotless flock of the Church, virgins are holier and purer offerings than all others made to God:

Viginitatis laus	*Virgines castae*

Nam cum universa turba creden-
tium paria dona gratia pererpiat, et
iisdem omnes sacramentorum bene-
dictionibus glorientur, istae aliquid
proprium prae caeteris habent, *cum*
de illo sancto et immaculato Eccle-
siae grege, quasi sanctories puriores *que* hostiae, *pro voluntatis*
suae meritis a sancto Spiritu eli-
guntar, et per summum sacerdotem
Dei offerunteur altario. Digna re-
vera Domino hostia *tam pretiosi*
animalis oblatio, et nullius magis,
quam suae imaginis, hostia
lacitura.

Filiae Tyri munera
ferentes

Et in his regis
vultum deprecantes

Hostias *cunctis*
habent puriores,

Corpore munde,
Corde sanctiores.

For while the whole multitude of believers receives similar gifts of grace and all rejoice in the same blessings of the sacraments, those to whom you (virgins) belong have something peculiar to themselves over and above what the rest possess: they (virgins) are chosen by the Holy Spirit out of the holy and spotless flock of the Church as *holier and purer offer-*

The daughters of Tyre, bearing gifts, and entreating the favor

(Continued)

Viginitatis laus	Virgines castae
ings on account of the merits given them for their choice of vocation and are presented at God's altar by his highest priest. The offerings of so precious a creature are truly worthy to be considered a sacrifice to the Lord, and there is none who will please him more than a victim in his own image	of the King by means of them [the gifts]*have offerings purer* than all: They are *cleaner* in body, holier in heart.

Both texts describe virgins as *hostiae*, victims sacrificed to the Lord. And, as Chrysogonus Waddell has rightly pointed out, the sequence's *cunctis* in combination with *puriores* parallels in meaning the letter's *prae caeteris*.[68] Both texts use the verb *habent* along with the comparatives *puriores* and *sanctories*.

THE WOES OF CARNAL MARRIAGE

Other works associated with Jerome also inspired *Virgines castae*'s stinging vituperations against carnal marriage. Abelard's deep knowledge of and identification with Jerome is further evident in stanza 7. By choosing Christ instead of worldly marriage, *virgines castae* have exchanged a host of worldly problems for heavenly nuptials. Stanza 7 lists a few of the commonplace woes of married life on earth: the pangs of childbirth, anguish over a husband's mistress, the annoyance of nurses. Jerome's Letter to Eustochium provides a common list:

> I write to you thus, Lady Eustochium (I am bound to call my Lord's bride 'Lady'), to show you by my opening words that my object is not to praise the virginity which you follow, and of which you have proved the value, or yet to recount the drawbacks of marriage, such as pregnancy, the crying

68. 'Chaste Virgins,' 30.

of infants, the torture caused by a rival, the cares of household
management, and all those fancied blessings which death
at last cuts short.[69]

Through a rhetorical sleight of hand (*paralipsis*), Jerome promises
not to enumerate the woes of marriage while he simultaneously
lists a string of marital woes. Later in the same letter, he speaks
(22.18) of the pangs of childbirth, pointing out that such pain
arises from sin—*in doloribus et anxietatibus paries, mulier*.[70] Though
'palpably traditional and familiar' these commonplaces, writes
Peter Dronke, 'can be found especially in the writings of Jerome'.[71]
In fleeing marriage, the virgin not only avoids pain, she forsakes
sin. In letter 54(.5) to the widow Furia, Jerome vividly describes
nurses and maids as venomous, self-seeking, and greedy—*cave
nutrices et gerulas et istius modi vinosa animalia*.[72] Chores, preg-
nancy, infants, nurses—all these and more would rob the virgin
of the time and quiet necessary for prayer and communion with
Christ.

Parallels between Jerome's letter to Eustochium and Abelard's
works for Heloise go beyond a shared antipathy for marriage and
its troubles. Jerome had used Psalm 44 in his advice to the virgin
Eustochium; surely Abelard knew and followed this usage in *Virgines castae*. Eustochium, like Heloise and her nuns, was to 'forget
her own people and her father's house' (Ps 44:15), which means,
wrote Jerome, 'it is not enough for you to go out from your own
land unless you forget your people and your father's house; unless
you scorn the flesh and cling to the bridegroom in a close embrace'.[73] Jerome closes his epistle with a cornucopia of topics we
find in both *Virgines castae* and *Epithalamica*:

69. Letter 22.2; PL 22:395; NPNFS 2, vol. 6:23.
70. PL 22:95 (alluding to Genesis 3:16).
71. 'Virgines caste,' in *Lateinische Dichtungen des X. und XI. Jahrhunderts: Festgabe für Walther Bulst zum 80. Geburtstag* (Heidelberg: Lambert Schneider, 1981)
93–117, quotation on 101; reprinted in *Latin and Vernacular Poets of the Middle
Ages* (Brookfield: Gower Publishing Company, 1991) Chapter 6.
72. PL 22:551.
73. 'Against Jovinian'; NPNFS 2, vol. 6:22.

Emerge, I pray you, for a while from your prison-house, and paint before your eyes the reward of your present toil, a reward which 'eye hath not seen, nor ear heard, neither hath it entered into the heart of man.' What will be the glory of that day when Mary, the mother of the Lord, shall come to meet you, accompanied by her virgin choirs! When, the Red Sea past and Pharaoh drowned with his host, Miriam, Aaron's sister, her timbrel in her hand, shall chant to the answering women: 'Sing ye unto the Lord, for he has triumphed gloriously; the horse and his rider has he thrown into the sea'. Then shall Thecla fly with you to embrace you. Then shall your Spouse himself come forward and say: 'Rise up, my love, my fair one, and come away, for lo! the winter is past, and the rain is over and gone.' Then shall the angels say with wonder: 'Who is she that looks forth as the morning, fair as the moon, clear as the sun?' 'The daughters shall see you and bless you; yea, the queens shall proclaim and the concubines shall praise you.' And, after these, yet another company of chaste women will meet you, Sarah will come with the wedded; Anna, the daughter of Phanue, with the widow. . . . Then shall the 'hundred and forty and four thousand' hold their harps before the throne and before the elders and shall sing the new song. And no man shall have power to learn that song save those for whom it is appointed. 'These are they who were not defiled with women; for they are virgins. These are they who follow the Lamb whithersoever he goes'. As often as this life's idle show tries to charm you; as often as you see in the world some vain pomp, transport yourself in mind to Paradise, essay to be now what you will be hereafter, and you will hear your Spouse say: 'Set me as a sunshade in thine heart and as a seal upon thine arm'. And then, strengthened in body as well as in mind, you, too, will cry aloud and say: 'Many waters cannot quench love, neither can the floods drown it'.[74]

74. PL 178:424, 425: *Egredere quaeso paulispet de carcere, et praesentis laboris ante oculos tues tibi pringe mercedem, quam nec oculus vidit, nec auris audivit, nec in cor hominis ascendit. Qualis erit illa dies, cum tibi maria Mater Domini choris occurret comitata Virgineis? cum post rubrum mare, submerso cum suo exercitu Pharaone,*

As in *Virgines castae*, this choir is included among those virgins 'who follow the lamb whithersoever he goes'. One day, when they are united with Christ the lamb, the virginal choir, which includes the virgin-martyr Thecla and a host of named and unnamed chaste women, along with Mary shall sing a new song. This lamb leads them into Paradise, where he is coupled with them—body and mind—as their spouse, their bridegroom.

The bridal imagery of Jerome's letter to Eustochium also figures in the Easter sequence *Epithalamica*. When Christ, the spouse, returns to receive his virginal martyrs he will declare to each: 'Rise up, my love, my fair one, and come away, for lo! the winter is past, the rain is over and gone'. In anticipation of the spouse's coming, virgins sing in one voice with Miriam, Aaron's sister, of his triumph over Pharaoh and all evil. By identifying Paradise as their true destiny, Eustochium and Heloise can 'essay to be now what they will be hereafter'—an utterance that is both tropological and teleological.[75]

---

tympanum tenes Maria soror Aaron in sua manu, praecinet responsuris: Cantemus Domino, gloriose enim honorificatus est: equum et ascensorem projecit in mare (Ex 15:1). *Tunc Thecla in tuos laeta volabit amplexus. Tunc et ipse sponsus occurret, et dicet: Surge, veni proxima mea, speciosa mea, columba mea, quia ecce hyems transivit, pluvia abiit sibi* (Cant 1:10, 11). *Tunc et Angeli mirabuntur, et dicent: Quae est ista prospiciens quasi diluculum, speciosa ut lana, electa ut sol* (Cant 6:9)? *Videbunt te filiae, et laudabunt reginae, et concubinae praedicabunt. Hinc et alius castitatis chorus occurret: Sara cum nuptis veniet: filia Phanuelis Anna cum viduis. . . . Tunc centum quadraginta quatuor millia in conspecia throni et seniorum tenebunt citharas, et centabunt Canticum novum. Et nemo poterit dicere Canticum illud, nisi numeras definitus. Hi sunt qui cum mulieribus se non coninquinavernit: virgines enim permanserunt. Hi sunt qui sequunter agnum quocumque vadit* (Rev 14:4). *Quotiescumque ve vana saeculi delectaverit ambitio: quoties in mundo aliquid videris gloriosum, ad paradisom mente transredere: esse incipe quod futura es, et andies a sponso tuo: Pone me sicut umbracalum in corde tuo: sicut siguaculum in brachio tuo* (Cant. 8:6), *et corpore pariter ac mente munita clambis, et dices: Aquae multae non potuerunt extinguere caritatem, et flumina non operient eam.* Translated adapted from NPNFC 2, vol. 6:41.

75. PL 178:42; NPNFS 2, vol. 6:41.

VIRGINITY AND THE FLOWERING OF THE CHURCH

In stanza 12 of Abelard's *Virgines castae* we discover words that Peter Dronke believes link the sequence to yet another work on virginity: the *De habitu virginum* by Cyprian of Carthage. Probably written shortly after Cyprian's consecration as bishop of Carthage in AD 249, the treatise centers on the virgin's *habitus*, a word that connotes for Cyprian (and the christian tradition) both an inner state of being as well as external clothing—as the monastic 'habit'. Cyprian's opening words suggest that virgins stand before the christian community as spiritual athletes who embody the christian virtues to a degree that inspires the awe of everyone. Cyprian writes:

> *Nunc nobis ad virgines sermo est; quarum quo sublimior gloria est, major et cura est.* Flos est ille ecclesiastici germinis, *decus atque ornametum gratiae spritalis, laeta indoles, laudis et honoris opus integrum atque incorruptum, Dei imago respondens ad sanctimoniam Domini, illustrior portio gregis Christi. Gaudet per illas atque in illis largiter floret Ecclesiae matris gloriosa faecunditas.* . . .
>
> My address is now to virgins, whose glory, as it is more eminent, excites the greater interest. *This is the flower of the ecclesiastical seed,* the grace and ornament of spritual endowment, a joyous disposition, the wholesome and uncorrupted work of praise and honour, God's image answering to the holiness of the Lord, the more illustrious portion of Christ's flock. The glorious fruitfulness of Mother Church rejoices by their means, and in them abundantly flourishes. . . .[76]

As Cyprian's address unfolds, he admonishes virgins to beware of the dangers that so easily beset those who dedicate themselves to this contest. The brides of Christ must dress plainly and avoid jewelry and cosmetics, all of which are the invention of the demons behind the pagan way of life. Virgins with wealth should support the poor. The virginal habit does not frequent boisterous wedding parties or go to promiscuous bath houses; Cyprian

76. PL 4:443 A; ANF 5:431; my emphasis.

exhorts them not to abandon the race they have begun but to have the habit of mind and heart that looks forward to the great reward that awaits them in the life to come.

Abelard agrees with Cyprian that virgins are the flowers grown from ecclesial seed and that much is at stake in faithfully embodying the virginal habit. Abelard binds his message in *Virgines castae* to Cyprian's treatise by reciting the bishop's memorable image of Christ's virgins: *Flos est ille ecclesiastici germinis.* Indeed, Abelard uses *ecclesiastici* in the same grammatical form as Cyprian, even though this violates strophe 12's rhyme-scheme, which should end in the same sound, *-is*, throughout:

Hic ecclesiastici	Here the flower of the
flos est ille germinis	Church is budding
tam rosis quam liliis	as many roses as lilies
multiplex innumeris	multiply beyond counting
quorum est fragrantiis	through their fragrance
ager sponsi nobilis	the bridegroom's field
naribus et oculis	is equally delectable
aeque delectabilis	to scent and sight.

Neither Dronke's nor Waddell's examination of the manuscript tradition shows that this 'error' of rhyme was 'corrected'.[77] By adhering to Cyprian's spelling, Abelard unequivocally links his sequence to Cyprian's text and very likely cued the Paraclete nuns' memory of the bishop's work at every singing of *Virgines castae*. Abelard avoided rhyme here for deliberate rhetorical reasons—as we shall see in the chapters to come. He inserts a little poetic road bump, so to speak, to mark an important transition in the song. The consummation of the bride and bridegroom's love is the flowering of the Church. Their spiritual marriage constitutes the great throng of the faithful who, as the sequence continues, follow the lamb wheresoever he goes.

---

77. Dronke, '*Virgines caste*', 96; Waddell, 'Chaste Virgins', 45.

THE LAMB PLAYS AMONG HIS VIRGINAL MARTYRS

With the appearance of the lamb in stanza 13, the scene shifts from the bridal chamber to virginal pastures, yet the imagery retains its sensual tone. A chorus of biblical and extra-biblical texts echo stanza 13. The lamb is the *agnus* of the Revelation 14:4. There the virgins are male; here female virgins follow the lamb wheresoever he goes. The lamb also is the *sponsus* of the Song of Songs; he leaps and prances, echoing Canticle 2:8, and following him, like the bride of the Song of Songs 1–2, are the virgins. Waddell has observed that these various biblical echoes are gathered up in the single source most likely behind the sequence passage: *Iesu corona virginum*, the much loved hymn for virgins, very likely by Saint Ambrose.[78] The following version of the hymn was sung at the Paraclete:

Ihesu, corona virginum,	Jesus, the virgins' crown,
quem mater illa concepit,	born of the mother who alone
que sola virgo parturit,	gave birth to a child and
hec vota clemens accipe.	yet remained a virgin,
	graciously
	receive these prayers.
Qui pas[s]cis inter lilia	You feed among the lilies,
septus choreis virg[i]num,	surrounded by choirs of virgins
sponsas decorans gloria,	—a bridegroom beautiful with
sponsisque reddens premia.	glory and divine rewards to his
	brides.
Quocunque pergis, virgines	Wherever you go virgins follow,
sequuntur atque laudibus	hastening after you with songs
post te canentes cursitant	of praise and making heaven
hymnosque dulces personant.	resound with melodious hymns.

(Continued)

78. A. S. Walpole, *Early Latin Hymns: With Introduction and Notes* (Hildesheim: Georg Olms Verlagsbuchhandlung, 1966) 112–114.

te deprecamur, largius	We implore you to give us this
nostris adauge sensibus	grace in our life of thoughts—
nescire prorsus omnia	not to have knowledge of anything
orruptionis vulnera.	that may wound or corrupt our
	virtue.[79]

In the hymn and *Virgines castae* the virgins are female and they
are *running* after the lamb wherever he leads: *Quocumque pergis,
virgines . . . post te canentes cursitant*. Stanzas 13 and 14 of the sequence reveal that the lilies and roses also wreathe the maidens'
heads—a ancient practice associated with marriage and perhaps
implicit in the bridal and flower imagery of Ambrose's hymn. At
stanza 14 we find the lamb feeding upon virginal flowers, as in
both the hymn (stanza two and in the Song of Songs 2:16, 6:2).
Stanza 15 of *virgina castae* begins *Hic choro talium vallatus agminum*,
and has essentially the same meaning as *septus choreis virginum*,
in the hymn's second stanza.

Elaborating on the identity of the virgins, Abelard says in
stanzas 13-14 that they are adorned with linen robes and purple
garments; they stand with lilies in their left hand, roses in their
right, and their hair braided with a twofold garland of lilies and
roses:

Ornatae tam byssina	Adorned in linen and
quam veste purpurea	purple robes
laeva tenent lilia	they hold lilies in their
rosas habent dextera	left hand, roses in their
	right
et corona gemmea	and, with their heads crowned
redimitae capita	as with a set of jewels
agni sine macula	they hasten along the paths
percurrunt itinera	of the Lamb without blemish

(Continued)

---

79. CLS 9:256; English by Joseph Connelly, *Hymns of the Roman Liturgy*
(Westminster: The Newman Press, 1957) 154–155.

His quoque floribus	Also from these flowers
semper recentibus	forever fresh
sanctorum intexta	the garlands on their holy
capitum sunt serta	heads are woven
His agnus pascitur	Among these the Lamb
atque reficitur	pastures and is thereby
	refreshed
hi flores electa	these flowers are his food
sunt illius esca	of choice.

Both the virgins' clothing and the flowers are standard medieval symbols drawn from the biblical tradition. Scripture pairs roses and lilies as well as linen robes and purple garments in Sirach 50:8 and Proverbs 31:22; lilies are often mentioned in the Song of Songs (2:1-2, 16; 4:5; 5:13; 6:1, 2; 7:2).

Drawing on the same biblical images, liturgical tradition has long associated roses and lilies with martyrdom and virginity. For example, the following responsory and verse from All Saints Day liturgy goes back centuries before Abelard:[80]

> R. *Beata vere Martyr Ecclesiae.* Quam victoriosorum gloriosus martyrum sanguis exornat, quam inviolata confessionis candida induit virginitas.*
> V. *floribus eius nec rosae nec lilia desunt.* Quam [etc.]*

As the versicle declares, 'neither roses nor lilies are missing from among her [the Church's] flowers', the blessed martyrs. These words link roses with the blood of martyrs and lilies with the brightness of virginity.

In creating *Virgines castae* and *Epithalamica*, Abelard has drawn to this point on a range of biblical and patristic texts. Often, however, a text recites, recontextualizes, and reconfigures whole stories, key ideas, central topics, and well-known motifs embedded in oral, as well as written, tradition. We shall now

---

80. Father Waddell uses this example in his 'Chaste Virgins,' x, note 87.

consider a few scribal and oral texts that Abelard wove into his scene of the lamb and his virginal florilegium.

THE UNICORN-LIKE LAMB IN VIRGINES CASTAE

With stanza 15 Abelard embarks on a literary development that neither Peter Dronke nor Chrysogonus Waddell has found in traditional literature on virginity. He describes a scene in which a lamb races among his virgin-martyrs, exhilarated and exultant at their failed attempts to catch him. He seems to take pleasure in their inability to apprehend and tame him.[81] If caught, he straightway wriggles away and continues with his merry play. Dronke writes, there is 'nothing quite comparable in earlier Christian tradition. Even hymns as prodigal in poetic inventiveness as those of Ephraim of Syria—cycles *De paradiso* and *De virginitate*, for example—appear to contain nothing of this kind'.[82] 'The Lamb may be, and is indeed, a Christ-symbol; but this is a remarkably pert, frisky lamb,' writes Waddell, 'one that leads the maidens on a merry chase.'[83]

Ovid's *Metamorphoses* (fairly often referred to by Abelard) relates a story parallel to the sequence.[84] In Book Seven of Ovid's masterpiece, we learn of the fateful encounter of the aged King Pelias and his daughters with Medea, a woman famous for magic. Driven by malice, she feigns friendship with Pelias' daughters and kills old Pelias. The daughters know that she has restored others to youth. Now she promises to do the same, through their assistance, for hoary-headed Pelias. To give the daughters greater confidence in her magic, Medea changes the oldest sheep in their flock into a little lamb. She cuts the elderly creature's throat and casts his carcass into a boiling pot. Immediately, Ovid writes,

---

81. Dronke discusses the 'sportiveness,' 'impulsiveness,' and 'wilful, wanton impudence' of the lamb's play in his *'Virgines caste'*, 102–112.
82. Dronke, *'Virgines caste,'* 103–104.
83. 'Abelard and the Chaste Virgins,' 46.
84. I am grateful to Father Waddell for pointing this out to me.

nec mora, balatum mirantibus exsilit agnus lascivitque fuga lac-
tantiaque ubera quaerit.

even while they were wondering at the sound, out jumped
a lamb and ran frisking away to find some udder to give
him milk.[85]

Granting a certain likeness in the friskiness of Ovid's lamb
and the pert lamb of the sequence, I do not believe that Ovid's
creature inspired Abelard. No twelfth-century man had to rely
on Ovid to learn of the spritely play typical of lambs at springtime. Abelard's frisky lamb may be unusual among medieval
Christ-lambs, but there is an unmistakable likeness between his
lamb and the mythological beast of long-told story: the unicorn.
Although the unicorn legend predates Christ, unicorn expert
Rüdiger Robert Beer writes that 'both the unicorn and the lamb
of God are symbols of the Savior, stemming from comparisons
made by early theologians . . . [and the unicorn's] similarity in
motif to the paschal lamb does admit christological interpretation'.[86] In his sermon on the conversion of Saint Paul, Abelard
shows his deep knowledge of these overlapping motifs and the
legends surrounding the unicorn. Drawing on Pope Gregory the
Great's commentary on the Book of Job, Abelard describes the
unicorn as altogether indomitable in its nature and yet easily
tamed by a virgin.[87]

Greek authors described the milky white unicorn as an ani-
mal so powerful and swift that no creature, human or beast, could
overtake it; yet the unicorn eagerly surrenders at the touch of a
virgin. Variants of the legend tell of the unicorn blissfully leaping

85. Latin and English translation found in Frank Justus Miller, *Ovid. Meta-*
morphoses, VII; Loeb Classical Library, 2 vols. (Cambridge: Harvard University
Press, 1916), 1:365.

86. Rüdiger Robert Beer, *Unicorn: Myth and Reality* (New York: Van Nostrand Reinhold Company, 1977) 41.

87. PL 178:529-532. In the sermon Abelard often refers to the unicorn as
a *rhinoceros*, for medieval people knew the rhinoceros only in the shape of the
unicorn, which bestiaries—popular handbooks on animals—described in great
detail.

into a virgin's lap, suckling at her breasts, and then following her to a kingly palace, where he is slain for his magical horn. After entering the symbolic world of early Christianity, the unicorn often 'stands right alongside the ecclesiastical symbolic beasts, namely the lion of Saint Mark, the bull of Saint Luke, the eagle of Saint John, and next to the dove and directly beside the lamb, the symbol of divine sacrifice'.[88]

Christian artists and scholars, in numerous medieval miniatures, tapestries, and bestiaries, identified the unicorn with Christ and the maiden with the Virgin Mary. One of the most widely used sources for allegorization of the unicorn myth was an early christian book on natural history, the *Physiologus*, or 'Natural Philosopher', a work that Abelard not only knew by memory but drew on in composing at least four of his hymns and to which he referred directly in his third Easter Hymn.[89] In the *Physiologus*, which Rüdiger Beer has claimed 'enjoyed a circulation second only to that of the Bible,'[90] the legend of the unicorn's capture by a beautiful virgin is interpreted both as a symbol

---

88. Beer, *Unicorn*, 43.

89. In stanza 4 of *Golias prostratus est* (hymn 60), Abelard writes:

Ut leonis catulus	As the lion's progeny,
Resurrexit Dominus	Risen is the Lord today,
Quem rugitus patris	Which the father hardily
Die tertia	Wakes at three days' end,
Suscitat vivificus	Following the victory
Teste physica	Nature's rites attend.

English translation by Freeland, *Hymns* 77. *Teste physica*, according to Szövérffy, is a direct allusion to the *Physiologus*. Abelard uses lion symbolism in hymns 53, 54, 55, and 56; he also referes to the legendary 'phoenix' in hymn 53; HP 2: 106–107. The authorship, date, and place of origin of the *Physiologus* is conjectural. The original seems to have been in Greek. It was translated into a range of Near Eastern languages, including Arabic, Coptic, and Armenian. Through Latin it eventually made its way into Italian, French, English, German, old Norse, Slavic, and Georgian. See Beer, *Unicorn*, 44–45. On the role of bestiaries in developing memory capacity in budding young students and monastic novitiates see Carruthers, *Memory* 126–127.

90. Beer, *Unicorn*, p. 44.

of chastity and as an allegory of the Christ's conception: as the unicorn surrendered his power to a waiting maiden, so Christ surrendered his divine nature and allowed himself to be captured in the womb of the Virgin Mary. Like the unicorn before a maiden, Christ stills his rage against human sin and honors the purity of Mary's chaste body by leaping into her lap, suckling at her breast, laying his head in her embrace, and falling asleep.

At times the Virgin and the unicorn are portrayed in an Eden-like, enclosed garden amid lilies and roses, symbolizing respectively the charity and purity of the courtly bride and the heavenly virgin. Contrary to the laws of nature, all the flowers depicted are in bloom at the same time. More often, the unicorn represents the passion of resurrection of Christ; once the unicorn takes his repose in the maiden's lap, he is surrounded by hunters and killed; he then rises from the dead. Hence, the unicorn could represent the all-conquering power of the Lord, while equally figuring meekness clad in the sinful garb of human flesh. Occasionally, the unicorn's maiden love is not Mary, but some other holy woman, especially those whose chastity is worthy of honor.[91]

Many artistic renderings of the unicorn legend have chivalric references, as the polysemous unicorn was also associated with courtly love. He was the symbol of monastic seclusion as well as knightly courage: a symbol of chastity and an embodiment of unrestrained licentiousness. The capture of the unicorn was symbolic, too, of a lover's passion for his lady. By contrast, the legend could represent the search and eventual capture of the beloved bridegroom by his adored lady, a topic that has more than a little semblance to the searching bride of the Song of Songs and *Epithalamica*.

The tale of the unicorn, in sum, consists of a vast interlocking network of symbols on which Abelard draws in his scene of the lamb and virgins in *Virgines castae*. The likeness between the unicorn legend and Abelard's lamb is simply remarkable. Surrounded, he races this way and that in lovely gardens of roses

---

91. Beer, *Unicorn*, 96–97.

and lilies. Like the hunted unicorn, Abelard's lamb is not caught; he leaps and bounds repeatedly, prancing about and escaping capture. Abelard's lamb is too powerful and swift to be subdued; yet he, like the unicorn, eagerly surrenders his fierceness to virgins.

In stanzas 16-19 of *Virgines castae* the scene shifts from playful leaping to gentle rest. Whereas the gentle bride reclined on the bridegroom's breast in stanza 10, the frisky lamb now makes the virgin's breast his resting place. Here Abelard unites the symbolism of the bride, the lamb, and the unicorn at rest, and then he inserts allusions to the Song of Songs into the sequence. On the one hand, Abelard's lamb is the Christ, born of the Virgin Mary's womb and nursed at her breasts. On the other, this lamb is the bridegroom, whom every virgin longs to hold and unite with in spiritual marriage. Careful as any miniaturist, Abelard places the entire scene against the background of redolent flowers. Roses and lilies abound, marking the marriage event and symbolizing the purity of the bride and groom.

Abelard is a weaver, carefully intertwining long and short, narrow and wide, small and large threads of color to form scenes of deep symbolic depth. He is, as it were, preparing a wedding tapestry for Heloise and her nuns. It is his gift for the brides of Christ, a gift, as we shall see, prompted by Heloise request. From biblical and non-biblical sources he has stitched their story. Its words, lines, stanzas, and sections all stress that God names himself a bridegroom because he desires Heloise and her nuns to respond to his call with 'the *affectus* of love' characteristic of a bride for her Bridegroom. In other words, God, the Rhetor of rhetors, appeals to Heloise in her whole being, her mind and her "lower body-linked powers"—that is, her *affectus*.[92]

Abelard joins other twelfth-century commentators on the Song of Songs as he presents the experience of love conveyed in

92. Astell, *Song* 6. See also Mews, *Lost Love*, 133–134, where he defines *affectus* as 'disposition or feeling' and discusses Saint Augustine's and Saint Bernard's use of the term to describe, respectively, 'interior disposition' or 'the interior state'.

his two sequences. What Ann W. Astell has written of early twelfth-century theologian Honorius of Autun's understanding of the biblical bride's song brilliantly captures Abelard's interpretation of the Song of Songs, Psalm 44, and the various patristic and medieval sources upon which he drew to create *Virgines castae* and *Epithalamica*. Abelard presents the biblical bridal experience to his Paraclete nuns by

> the typology of Bride-Bridegroom relationship, with its historical admission of new coupling, both in time and in the *anagogia* of eternity. The language of the Song itself, with its erotic images figuring forth the *amor Dei*, appeals directly to the human sense-nature in its sexual dimension. The reader's desire for ardent complementarity, with its ultimate trajectory toward metaphysical union with God, is immediately directed to the divine by the fusion of letter and gloss, text and interpretation, vehicle and tenor, in the reading [singing] process. The more contemplative that reading [singing] process, the more centered on the object of love, the more intoxicating and incantatory the words themselves become in their repetitive singularity of reference until the Song becomes, in rhetorical effect as well as in literary kind, a marriage song. Fusing together form and content, body and soul, letter and spirit, the *accessus* aim at unity the auditor of the Song with its divine *Auctor* in union of love—the 'causa finalis' of the whole work.[93]

These eloquent words apply well to the rhetorical intent of Abelard's sequences: Both are marriage songs designed in word, verse, and song to inspire Heloise and each of her nuns to unite their bridal selves with God. Within the Paraclete liturgy *Virgines castae* and *Epithalamica* function to 'sequence' the nuns and Heloise from the world of the Old Testament to the New Testament through the Church Fathers and the tale of the unicorn-like lamb into the world of the Paraclete. Abelard's sequences functioned in the Paraclete liturgy simultaneously to carry the nuns back

93. Astell, *Song*, 41.

into many biblical and non-biblical stories and to bring those same biblical and non-biblical stories into the nuns' present. Their anamnetic function parallels the overall role of medieval liturgy: The celebration of liturgy, especially the eucharist, was not simply about remembering something long over and done; rather, the repeated actions of the liturgy were the threshold over which the medieval church experienced the reality of all history summed up in Christ. Israel's story, the apostles' acts, the Fathers' teachings, the unicorn's life were all gathered up in the Son of God, the bridegroom, who was at the center of medieval worship.

3

SPINNING A BRIDAL TAPESTRY IN WORD AND SONG

Omnis Scriptura divina more orationis rhetoricae aut docere intendit aut movere.

The all divine Scripture is intended to teach and to move in the manner of a rhetorical speech.

—Peter Abelard[1]

T
HE DISCOURSE OF *VIRGINES castae* and *Epithalamica* is not deliberative; it is not designed to persuade the nuns to undertake or not engage in a future course of action. Nor is it judicial; their language is not calculated to convict the nuns of guilt or persuade them of their innocence. The speech of the sequences is best characterized as a rhetoric of praise. This epideictic language is tropological and teleological in nature; it is designed to configure, inculcate, nurture, and sustain a particular symbolic world through its *logos*, its pattern of argumentation.

Before looking at the sequence hymns as remarkable examples of *how* an individual medieval artist, working within the tradition would manipulate 'found' material, we shall pause to look briefly at ancient and medieval patterns of arrangement and composition and at epideictic rhetoric to explain why it was most fitting for cultivating the symbolic world of the Paraclete. Next we shall examine the *expolitio*, a particular form of epideictic

---

1. *Commentaria super S. Pauli Epistolam ad Romanos, Prologus,* PL 178:783–784.

discourse, to gain a deeper insight into the pattern of argumentation (*logos*) of *Virgines castae*; and then turn to another form of epideictic speech, *chreia,* elaboration, to probe the argumentative texture of *Epithalamica.*

ANCIENT AND MEDIEVAL PATTERNS OF ARGUMENTATION

The 'inventing' of material—analyzed in Chapter Two—was only the first step Abelard took in creating *Virgines castae* and *Epithalamica.* Next came *dispositio* ('arrangement') and then *elocutio* ('style'). The mature medieval poet made the first two steps in his mind; the last step, *elocutio,* might also be completely mental, but it often involved sketching out the poem on wax tablets to make stylistic polishing easier. Like an architect preparing to construct a great cathedral, the medieval poet considered carefully what he would put into his artifice before taking up parchment and *stylus,* a word that in the medieval period meant both pen and 'style'.[2] Once satisfactorily shaped and stylized, the composition, like an architectural sketch, was written out in full on a permanent surface like parchment.

After inventing his material, Abelard had to 'determine the rhetorically effective composition of the speech and mold its elements into a unified structure.'[3] He, like all great rhetors, gave heed to the *logos* of the speech which resides in storytelling—supporting assertions with reasons, clarifying assertions and reasons

---

2. Carruthers, *Memory,* 195.

3. On the shaping of speech in the Middle Ages, see Douglas Kelly, 'Theory of Composition in Medieval Narrative Poetry and Geoffrey of Vinsauf's *Poetria Nova*', *Mediæval Studies* 31 (1969) 117–148; Douglas Kelly, 'The Scope of the Treatment of Composition in the Twelfth- and Thirteenth-Century Arts of Poetry', *Speculum* 41 (1966) 261–278; Douglas Kelly, 'Rhetoric in French Literature: Topical Invention in Medieval French Literature', *Medieval Eloquence: Studies in the Theory and Practice of Medieval Rhetoric,* ed. J. J. Murphy (Berkeley: University of California Press, 1978) 231–251; Jane Baltzell, 'Rhetorical 'Amplification' and 'Abbreviation' and the Structure of Medieval Narrative', *Pacific Coast Philology* 2 (1967) 32–39; and Carruthers, *Memory,* 195.

with opposites and contraries, persuading through analogies, examples, citations of ancient testimony (usually written), and refuting possible counterarguments. Traditional grammatical and rhetorical education provided Abelard with skeletal outlines of judicial, deliberative, and epideictic speech; these outlines gave him the *topoi* ('topics') or commonplaces laid down according to a manner and method that everyone educated in rhetoric knew and expected in various forms of speech.[4] Yet every rhetor was also 'expected to hide the standard outline when crafting a speech, and to produce a composition that would appear to unfold naturally on a given occasion'.[5] The beauty and the seamlessness of the composition contributed to the rhetor's *ethos*, which helped render his audience open to persuasion In short, the rhetorical tradition made much of the importance of arrangement.

Yet much medieval poetry does not follow the patterns of arrangement so characteristic of classical rhetoric. In his very fine work *The Medieval European Religious Lyric*, Patrick Diehl describes medieval religious lyric as having a 'typically paratactic structure'.[6] It is stanzaic poetry whose strophes are nearly always 'autonomous units that occur without any clear logical or rhetorical order to specify their proper sequence. This paratactic relationship means that stanzas may be omitted, inserted, or rearranged without materially injuring the coherence and meaning of the text. . . .'[7] This explains in part, argues Diehl, why many scribes felt no compunction in omitting, adding, and rearranging the elements of many poems that survive in medieval manuscripts. To be sure, religious lyric had its unity, but to us moderns the unity is often said to lie in such repetitive (surface) structures as assonance, consonance, alliteration, and final or internal rhyme, not by the deeper step-by-step movement of argument

4. George A. Kennedy, *New Testament Interpretation as Rhetorical Criticism* (Chapel Hill: University of North Carolina Press, 1984) 23.

5. Burton L. Mack, *Rhetoric and the New Testament*, Guides to Biblical Scholarship series (Minneapolis: Fortress Press, 1990) 32.

6. Diehl, *Lyric*, 14.

7. Diehl, *Lyric*, 14.

from one stanza to the next. Yet such 'inorganically structured' lyric, explains Diehl, ultimately received unity from 'its cultural context and function.'[8] We shall explore further the significance of community for giving context and function to lyric when directly exploring *Virgines castae* and *Epithalamica* in their Paraclete symbolic world in Chapters Five and Six.

There are those medieval lyrics, fewer in number than the 'inorganically structured' poems described above, that Diehl recognizes as showing such an internal coherence that their argumentation can only be described as 'logical'. Linguistically, this coherence 'manifests itself in words that connect phrase to phrase, and sentence to sentence, in an active fashion, creating a forward, linear motion that counters the medieval tendency to simple juxtaposition of autonomous units, each looking upward to a controlling meaning somewhere above the level of the text.'[9] Such an 'organic structure' is, as Diehl has noted, characteristic of all Abelard's Paraclete poetry—hymns, *planctus*, and sequences.[10]

This organic structure reflected Abelard's own mode of reasoning about life at the Paraclete, and communicated to Heloise and her nuns his conviction that this same way of thinking should characterize their understanding and life at the Paraclete.

EPIDEICTIC SPEECH

Behind the organic structure Abelard gave *Virgines castae* and *Epithalamica* stand the traditional patterns of speech that constitute epideictic speech—as we have observed several times already. The discourse of the sequence is designed to strengthen its audience's adherence to a particular value and thereby induce it to carry out a general policy of action in the present.[11] Perelmann and Olbrechts-Tyteca have pressed the point that:

---

8. Diehl, *Lyric*, 15.
9. Diehl, *Lyric*, 122.
10. Diehl, *Lyric*, 122–123.
11. Kennedy, *New Testament Interpretation through Rhetorical Criticism*, 74.

. . . epidictic [*sic*] discourse sets out to increase the intensity of adherence to certain values, which might not be contested when considered on their own but may nevertheless not prevail against other values that may come into conflict with them. The speaker tries to establish a sense of communion [*sensus communis*] around particular values recognized by the audience and to this end he uses the whole range of means available to the rhetorician for the purposes of amplification and argument.[12]

Close reading of *Virgines castae* and *Epithalamica* suggests that Abelard did indeed seek through *Virgines castae* to persuade the Paraclete nuns to join the chaste virgins and the joyous bride and so to become imitators of those who are truly devout and participate in filling the temple of God with praise. Devotion, praise, song, love, and virginity are all practices central to the Paraclete symbolic world encoded into the two sequences.

Traditionally, epideictic speech is defined as the oratory of 'praise and blame'. It is used to address concerns of the present, rather than of the past. Epideictic rhetoric establishes the basis for honoring or memorializing a person by highlighting his or her exemplary deeds and many virtues. Hence epideictic speech tends to be broadly narrative in overall frame and topical in outline. As the noted scholar of classical rhetoric George A. Kennedy has written,

> In epideictic the body of the speech between proem [*exordium*] and epilogue [*conclusio*] is usually devoted to an orderly sequence of amplified topics dealing with the life of the person being celebrated or with the qualities of the concept under consideration, often adorned with vivid description (*ecphrasis*) [*narratio*] or with a comparison of the subject to something else (*synkrisis*).[13]

---

12. C. Perelmann and L. Olbrechts-Tyteca, *The New Rhetoric: A Treatise on Argumentation* (Notre Dame: University of Notre Dame Press, 1969) 51.

13. Kennedy, *New Testament Interpretation through Rhetorical Criticism*, 24.

The steps for constructing an effective epideictic speech were outlined, explained, and illustrated in the many *technai* and *progymnasmata* bequeathed by the Greeks to the Middle Ages. *Technai* were the rhetorical handbooks for students of advanced rhetoric, and the *progymnasmata* were handbooks written to introduce grammar students to rhetoric. Table III.1 (p. 103) gives the outline of epideictic discourse in four speech forms relevant to our analysis of *Virgines castae* and *Epithalamica*. The first outline comes from the *Rhetorica ad Herrenium*, a first-century BC rhetorical manual. The second outline is a composite sketch drawn from rhetorical manuals written between the first century BC and the second century AD. The third and fourth outlines come from Menander Rhetor's description of two specific forms of epideictic rhetoric: the wedding speech and the bedroom speech.

The *Rhetorica ad Herrenium*, a *technai* that Abelard and most-medieval academics assumed was by Cicero, refers to a sequencing process of elaborating epideictic speech called *expolitio*.[14] This is sometimes translated, as by Harry Caplan in his translation of the *Rhetorica ad Herrenium*, as 'refining'[15] but, it would not be off the mark to translate the term as 'sequencing'. Such a rendering would reflect its sequential elaboration of a theme. About *expolitio* the *Rhetorica ad Herennium* reads:

> Refining consists in dwelling on the same topic and yet seeming to say something ever new. It is accomplished in two ways: by merely repeating the same idea, or by descanting upon it. We shall not repeat the same thing precisely— for that, to be sure, would weary the hearer and not refine the idea—but with changes.[16]

14. See James J. Murphy, *Rhetoric in the Middle Ages: A History of Rhetorical Theory from St. Augustine to the Renaissance* (University of California Press, 1974).

15. *Rhetorica ad Herennium*, IV.xli.54, Trans. Loeb Library of Classical Literature (Cambridge: Harvard University Press, 1954) 365.

16. Quoted from *Rhetorica ad Herennium*, IV.xli.54: *Expolitio est cum in eodem loco manemus et aliud atque aliud dicere videmur. Ea dupliciter fit: si aut eandem plane dicemus rem, aut de eadem re. Eandem rem dicemus non eodem modo—nam id quidem*

Table III.1: *Epideictic Speech Forms*

Expolitio: The Sequencing of a Theme (*Rhetorica ad Herennium*—first century BC)	Standard Epideictic Speech (first century BC—2nd century AD *technai*)	The *Epithalamium* (Menander Rhetor—third–fourth centuries AD)	The Bedroom Speech (Menander Rhetor)
Res *Ratio*	*Exordium* *Narratio* *Partitio* (Theme or Proposition)	*Prooemium* Theme	*Prooemium* Theme
Pronuntio	*Confirmatio* (Confirmation or support of proposition)	*Encomia* on various topics: Marriage nuptial gods family the bride the groom flowers garlands bedchamber	*Encomia* on various topics with exhortation: Marriage nuptial gods family the bride the groom flowers garlands bedchamber
Contrario *Simile* *Exemplum*	Digressio (Digression or embellishment through: contrary, analogy, example)		
Conclusio	*Conclusio* (Conclusion or exhortation)	Conclusion	Concluding prayer

Rhetoricians by Cicero's time had noticed that a particular sequence of argumentation was most effective in epideictic speech, and they began to recommend it in the schools. Before then, roman rhetors had directed most of their attention to judicial and deliberative speeches. In fact, judicial speech dominated rhetorical education, and advice for deliberative speeches was based primarily on insights about the judicial speech.

When the *Rhetorica ad Herrenium* exhibits the sequencing of the 'refinement of a theme' in seven parts (IV.xliii.56-57), it presents an epideictic, rather than a judicial or deliberative, sequence. Here one learns that *expolitio*, 'descanting upon a theme', places great emphasis upon stating a theme (*res*) and providing it with a rationale (*ratio*). After this, instructs the writer, it is helpful to present a contrary that sharpens the theme by exploring the implications of something contrary or alternative to that theme. Then the refinement / sequencing process moves into argument from example and argument from analogy, both major means of adding new insight to the opening theme. At the end, it is wise to include a conclusion that contains within it an exhortation to act positively on the insights presented in the refinement.

Technai written after the *Rhetorica ad Herrenium* reveal that the form of epideictic speech was quickly standardized into six sections: (1) *exordium*, (2) *narratio*, (3) *partitio*, (4) *confirmatio*, (5) *digressio*, and (6) *conclusio*. In the *exordium* or introduction, the speaker established himself as qualified to address the praise or blame of a person or event. Rhetors knew that audiences that trust and respect a speaker are more likely to believe his speech. In the *narratio* the speaker presented the case in narrative form, describing the matter at hand as he saw it. He concluded his narration with a *partitio*, a thematic statement that he then went on to support through argumentation. The speaker crafted his argumentation so that it confirmed and embellished his theme. In conclusion the orator summed up his argument with exhortation.

---

obtundere auditorem est, non rem expolire—sed commutate. Trans. Loeb Library of Classical Literature (Cambridge: Harvard University Press, 1954) 365.

We know from the extant works of orators like Menander
Rhetor that the 'standard' outlines of epideictic speech were refined to meet specific occasions. By the late third and early fourth
centuries AD Menander offered his students details on constructing
standardized forms of epideictic speech for funerals, birthdays,
valedictions and greetings, weddings, and nuptial bedrooms.

Virgines castae and *Epithalamica* fit within the long history of
speech-making at weddings and over the nuptial bed. More narrowly focused than the *epithalamium*, the bedroom speech[17] was
designed for delivery at the nuptial chamber of the newlyweds.
The third and fourth columns of Table III.1 outline the epideictic
form of Menander's wedding and nuptial bed speeches. The *epithalamium* has four sections: (1) *prooemia*, (2) theme, (3) *encomia*
on various topics, and (4) conclusion. As in the latin *exordium* of
standard epideictic speech, the greek *prooemium* serves to present
the subject, invest it with grandeur, and explain the reason why
the speaker has come forward to discourse on the wedding occasion. The *prooemium* often includes narrative hymning of a
range of wedding topics, including bridal chambers, bride and
groom, family, and the god(s) of marriage. The theme, like the
latin *propositio* in standard epideictic speech, brings the narrative
discourse to a sharp focus. In the typical wedding song the theme
essentially makes the claim that marriage is a good thing. Next
the speaker supports his claim under a range of encomiastic topics, praising Nature's creation of marriage and the nuptial gods
and demigods. Tales of marriage's wonder are next celebrated
in narrative form. The speaker then dilates on the family and on
the goodness of the parents or guardians who have contracted
the marriage, before turning to laud the bridal pair. Finally, the
orator celebrates the beauty of the bridal chamber. With this last
topic the speech comes to its conclusion.

The bedroom speech that Menander describes has the same
four sections as the wedding speech but is intended to be much

17. *Menander Rhetor*, ed. with trans. and commentary by D. A. Russell and
N. G. Wilson (Oxford: Clarendon Press, 1981) 135–159.

shorter: (1) *prooemium*, (2) theme, (3) *encomia* on various topics, and (4) a concluding prayer. A brief *prooemium* opens the speech celebrating the purpose of the occasion and exhorts the bridegroom to fulfill his role as husband. This introductory material includes narrational discourse on marriage and closes with a theme in the form of an exhortation to the couple to consummate their union. In support of this exhortation the speaker celebrates the bride's beauty and virtue and the bridegroom's strength and prowess. This exhortation is also heightened by a reminder to the couple of how their long courtship has finally led to this moment of consummation. The bedchamber and the gods of marriage are celebrated for their contributions to the immanent sexual union. Finally, the goods of marriage are enumerated and the speech concludes with a prayer, asking the gods for a happy union and many children.

The *expolitio*, the standard form of epideictic speech, and the bridal forms of such discourse all form the background to the rhetorical tradition behind *Virgines castae* and *Epithalamica*. Yet the two sequences differ from each other in one important respect: *Virgines castae* has the characteristic shape associated with the ancient wedding speech; *Epithalamica*'s form, by contrast, is shaped less by ancient cultural practice and more by biblical discourse. Biblical passages—like Psalm 44 and the Song of Songs—were reshaped and embedded in the epideictic discourse of the ancient wedding speech. The Song of Songs gives the sequence its overall outline and narrative shape while epideictic forms of argumentation are embedded in the scriptural discourse. Hence, *Virgines castae* represents patterns of persuasion firmly embedded in the cultural world of greco-roman antiquity. *Epithalamica* represents patterns of persuasion embedded deeply in the cultural world of the biblical tradition.

THE ARGUMENTATIVE TEXTURE OF *VIRGINES CASTAE*

Table III.2 (p. 109) demonstrates that *Virgines castae* broadly follows the contours of ancient epideictic speech; the *exordium* and *rationale* set up the theme. Supporting argumentation follows, refining of the theme. We have argument from the contrary, examples, and analogy. Finally, as in the traditional epideictic speech, a conclusion restates the opening theme and closes the discourse with an exhortation.

Table III.2 also shows that the sequence's discourse is developed rhetorically around narrational exposition and argumentation. Careful reading through *Virgines castae* reveals that there are in the sequence four narrative parts, which I have labeled Narratives 1, 2, 3, and 4. The narrative texture 'sequences' through four events that stand over against and complement the song's argumentative texture. The opening statement, the *exordium*, is non-narrative. Narrative 1 describes events surrounding the queen and her virgins. A subsequent rationale speaks of previous events. Next comes argumentation from example and contrary, neither of which is narrative in function. Narrative 2 describes the nuptial bed of Christ and his virgin. The initial statement from the analogy is non-narrative. The argument by analogy soon shifts into two centers of narrative discourse: Narrative 3 focuses on the flowered virgins, and Narrative 4 describes the lamb's gamboling among and then resting with his virgins. The conclusion and its exhortation are non-narrative.

The rhetorical tradition considered narration the very fount of persuasiveness. Narration encompassed 'argumentation, realism in storytelling, plot, the negotiation of meaning, and the pursuance of common understanding'—notions that we moderns tend to separate.[18] Narration has come into English, and into Western culture generally, as a term divorced from argumentation. We moderns have been persuaded by our Enlightenment forebears to see narrative 'not as a mode of thinking but of not

---

18. John D. O'Banion, *Reorienting Rhetoric: The Dialectic of List and Story* (Pennsylvania State University Press, 1992) 61.

thinking, because narration lacks dichotomous abstractions that literates [like ourselves] take for granted as the mark of thought'.[19] If we are to begin to grasp the rhetorical force of *Virgines castae* and *Epithalamica*, we must suspend these Enlightenment prejudices as much as possible. Abelard's sequences stand in a tradition in which narration functioned as a form of thinking and arguing.[20]

With this overall view of the narrative and argumentative textures of *Virgines castae* in mind, let us examine the individual parts and topics of the sequence. Stanzas 1 and 2 constitute an introduction—called an *exordium* in the *Rhetorica ad Herrenium* and a *prooemium* by Menander—that is intended to arrest the singer's attention and make him or her receptive to the person and message of the speaker, who is Abelard. The *exordium* in epideictic speech typically presents, as a foundation upon which the speech will be built, several 'ideas or facts which will be constantly restated in different words, in different order, and in different form in what follows'.[21] The topics in the *exordium* of *Virgines castae* are: (a) virgins, (b) making music, (c) supreme virginity, (d) worshiping, and (e) offering. These topics combine to form the central theme of the sequences: virgins offer themselves in music. We soon learn that they offer themselves to Christ, their heavenly bridegroom.

The material of the *exordium* functions both as an introduction to the narrational exposition and its supporting argumentation. The highest form of virginity is represented by the Queen of virgins. Her *ethos* is truly wondrous and majestic. The narrator displays the queen's beauty through epideictic speech: she is worthy of praise because of her (1) proximity to the king, (2) royal garb, and (3) role as the lady of all virgins. The narrational exposi-

---

19. I have found no latin term for this; see O'Banion, *Reorienting Rhetoric*, 163; and Mark Johnson, *Moral Imagination: Implications of Cognitive Science for Ethics* (Chicago: University of Chicago Press, 1993).

20. See O'Banion, *Reorienting Rhetoric*, 183; and Alasdair MacIntyre, *After Virtue*, especially 206–225.

21. Kennedy, *New Testament Interpretation Through Rhetorical Criticism*, 79.

Table III.2: The Narrative and Argumentative Texture
of *Virgines castae*

Strophes	Narrational Exposition of Events	Epideictic Argumentation
1a		*Exordium*
1b		
2a		
2b		
3a	Narration 1:	*Narratio*
3b	The Queen and the Virgins	
3c		
3d		
4a		
4b		*Rationale*
4c		
4d		Examples
5a-d		
6a-c		
7a		
7b		
7c		Contrary
8a-d	Narrative 2:	
9a-d	The Nuptial Beds	
10a-d		
11a		
11b		Apostrophe:
11c		The Groom Speaks
11d		
12a		Analogy
12b		
12c		
12d		
13a-d		
14a	Narrative 3: The Flowered Virgins	
14b		
14c	Narrative 4: The Lamb	
14d		
15a-d		
16a-b		
17a-b		
18a		*Conclusio/Rationale*
18b		
19a		
19b		
20a		
20b		*Exhortatio*

tion is supported with a rationale that explains why the virgins are following after the supreme virgin: they have been offered to Christ. We can illustrate the rhetorical development of this material from *exordium*, narrative, to rationale as follows:

Topic: The Queen and the Virgins

    Introduction (*Exordium*: stanzas 1-2 *Virgines castae*)

virginis summae	Chaste virgins sing of
decus praecinentes	the beauty of the supreme
Ceteras quoque	virgin and venerate after her
condignas laude	the other worthy virgins
post hanc venerantes	by their praise
Psalmis et hymnis	Speaking to one another
canticis dignis	in fitting Psalms and hymns
sibi colloquentes	and canticles
Solvant in istis	Let them pay by these [songs]
debitae laudis	solemn sacrifices of
hostias sollemnes	due praise

Narrative 1: The Queen and the Virgins (stanza 3a-d)

    Praise of the Queen for her:

(1) proximity to King

Haec est adextris	This one [the supreme
assistens egis	virgin] is that Queen
illa regina	serving at the right
	hand of the King
Iuncta latere	United beside him
sola cum rege	she alone with
praecedit ipsa	the King proceeds

(2) royal clothes

Aurata veste	In golden array
varietate	clothed round about
circiumamicta	with variety

(Continued)

Narrative 1: The Queen and the Virgins (stanza 3a-d)
    Praise of the Queen for her:

(3) role as Lady of all virgins

Tamquam dominam	Every blessed
sequitur ipsam	[virgin] follows
queque beata.	[the supreme virgin] as her lady.

Rationale: Offered to the King (stanza 4a and b)

Post eam adductae	Led after her
virgines devotae	the devout virgins
regi sunt oblatae	have been offered to the king
Christo consecratae.	and consecrated to Christ.

Having sung the praises of the queen and explained the presence of the other virgins, Abelard gives examples of virgins who have followed the queen and offered their bodies and hearts to the king: Thecla, Agnes, Lucia, Agathes—all early christian virgin martyrs. Indeed, a throng of virgins too great to list by name was consecrated to Christ. Among this company one group is named: the daughters of Tyre. They offered the king gifts and won his favor. Christ is the king; the gifts were their pure bodies and holy hearts.

Examples typically were drawn from the arena of history. They show that specific saintly persons have actualized the general principle at issue. If the example is well-chosen, rhetoricians taught, the argument confirms the validity of the general rule by a specific and precedent case.[22] Like the examples favored by greco-roman orators, those used by Christians carried the evidentiary weight necessary to support the speaker's argument and the emotional resonances needed to win the audience to his position.

Abelard understood the psychological and philosophical power of examples as he began his *Historia calamitatum*, declaring in the opening lines: 'Examples often go further than words in

---

22. Mack & Robbins, *Patterns of Persuasion*, 60. See also Carruther's discussion of examples in *Memory*.

stirring or soothing human feelings (*affectus*)'.[23] Examples like Agnes and Thecla recalled the memorable deeds and words of celebrated individuals from the christian past. They represented the collective memory of the Church, handed down orally, taught in monasteries, cathedral schools, and churches, and preserved and disseminated in saints' lives.[24]

Abelard closes the argument from example with a statement that virgins do indeed present to the Lord the integrity of both their flesh and mind. In doing so, moreover, they make Christ their immortal bridegroom. Virgins accept the life of Christ's queen, the highest form of virginity, as a pattern for their own. Each soul chooses Christ as her own individual bridegroom.

Argument from Example: Scripture and Early Christianity
(stanza 4c, d, and 5)

Tales erant Thecla,	Such [virgins] were Thecla
Agnes et Lucia	Agnes and Lucia
Agathes et multa	Agathes and many
virginum caterva	a great throng of virgins
Filiae Tyri munera	The daughters of Tyre
ferentes	bearing gifts
Et in his regis	And entreating the favor of
vultum deprecantes	the King by means of them
	[the gifts]
Hostias cunctis	Have offerings purer than
habent puriores	all [other offerings]
Corpore munde,	[They are] clean in body
Corde sanctiores	holier in heart
Holocaustum Domino	As a burnt-offering
Offerent ex integro	virgins offer to the Lord
virgines carne	the integrity of their flesh
integrae mente	and mind
immortalem sponsum	choosing Christ as
eligentes Christum	their immortal bridegroom

23. Muckle, 'Consolation', 175. *Saepe humanos affectus aut provacant aut mitigant amplius exempla quam verba.*

24. Here I am indebted to Susan L. Smith, *The Power of Women: A Topos in Medieval Art and Literature* (Philadelphia: University of Pennsylvania Press, 1991) 6–7.

In stanzas 6 and 7, in Peter Dronke's words, 'the poetry moves into a rapturous, evocative style, laden with sensuous imagery'[25] as the relationship of the king and his virgin is developed through the topic of marriage. As we shall see in the following two chapters, Abelard's use of sensuous imagery plays an important role in achieving his rhetorical goal. In terms of rhetorical form, the sensual narrative of stanzas 4-7 forms a fitting introduction to the action of the new section. A contrary transitions into Narrative 2, which focuses on the nuptial beds.[26] In these beds virgins give their bodies, minds, and souls to Christ in complete devotion. Abelard then develops these topics in stanzas 8-11.

The spiritual marriage in which virgins join their holy flesh and minds to Christ, affirms *Virgines castae*, is the happiest of nuptials. The proof of this claim rests in a simple contrast between spiritual and carnal marriage. The latter is full of woes, a point Abelard drives home through the figure of speech called *anaphora*. He repeats the same word of negation in each clause of the strophe. Like a series of hammer blows the repetition of the negatives '*nullo*' and '*nec*' connect and reinforce successive thoughts. In happy, spiritual nuptials, by contrast, there is *no* impurity, *no* grievous pains of childbirth, *no* rival mistress to be feared, *no* nurse who harasses. This striking description of the commonplace 'woes' of carnal marriage is meant not only to inform but also to arouse the *pathos*, the emotions, of the singers.

The sequence then elaborates upon the good of marriage to Christ.[27] Stanza 8a seems at first glance to be a digression upon the angelic protection of the beds that Christ and his virgins occupy. But, in fact, it counters one of the strongest arguments in favor of carnal marriage made from antiquity through medieval times: every woman needs a protector—the traditional role of a

25. Dronke, *Latin and Vernacular Poets of the Middle Ages*, 101.

26. A topic central to both Menander's wedding and bedroom speeches; *Menander Rhetor*, 145, 147–149, and 157.

27. Dilation on the good of marriage was another topic central to Menander's wedding and bedroom speeches; *Menander Rhetor*, 137 and 157.

husband. But virgins need no mortal husband; they have Christ as their *sponsus* and to protect his *sponsae* he has placed his angels to watch over them.[28]

With the matter of marital protection settled, the sequence begins to amplify the happy nature of the spiritual marriage of the virgin and Christ's.[29] In what he suggests is an 'outrageous metaphor', Dronke describes the bedchamber as not 'the one divine thalamus, which the virgin enters when she becomes *sponsa*, but many beds, all awaiting the divine lover. . . . The connotations [are] of a divine potentate visiting the concubines in his harem.'[30]

The metaphor is striking; but as the nuptial scene unfolds in the ensuing stanzas the sequence's discourse seems designed to persuade virgins to put their affections on spiritual marriage, not carnal marriage. The many beds signify, not fleshly concubinage, but the many beds—like the many mansions—Christ has prepared for his followers. Each follower, indeed, each virgin, must experience nuptial union with Christ. That is why the highest form of virginity [i.e. Mary] leads virginal souls to Christ. Every soul must be wed to God if it is to participate in eternal life. Therefore, the image of the many beds seems designed to enkindle the love and longing of every virgin for Christ; it engages the human *affectus* on the sensual, literal level of the text and seeks to direct the soul's movement toward its heavenly bridegroom.

Virgines castae, therefore, tells the nuptial story, not of many virgin-concubines, but of every virgin in a single love-encounter. It describes the highest virgin's nuptials and every virgin's nuptials: Christ and his virgin-bride's bed is not characterized by fleshly relations; nor is the virgin's sound sleep the result of wearying carnal relations. Their embrace is heavenly; and her quiet

28. Menander also emphasized the importance of the topic of the bridegroom's strength and prowess in his bedroom speech; *Menander Rhetor*, 147.

29. Again, Menander included celebration of marriage as a fitting topic in the body of his wedding and bedroom speeches; *Menander Rhetor*, 141 and 157.

30. Dronke, *Latin and Vernacular Poets of the Middle Ages*, 101.

repose is due to spiritual lovemaking. The bridegroom watches his beloved as she sweetly sleeps and warns that no one is to awaken her. There is in spiritual marriage a silence that contrasts with the pains, grief, and distress of carnal marriage. This quiescence is so central to Abelard's argument that in lines 11b, 11c, and 11d he features the voice of the bridegroom himself, announcing with authority that his bride must be allowed to enjoy her quiet repose until she herself decides to awaken with joy. The bridegroom's voice heightens the drama and is calculated to stir feelings in the singer-auditor as no third-person narrative could do.

Statement of the contrary: Carnal vs. Spiritual Marriage
(stanza 7)

felices nuptiae	Oh happy nuptials
quibus nullae maculae	where there are no impurities
nulli dolores	No grievous pains of
partus sunt graves	childbirth [where there is]
nec pelex timenda	No rival mistress to be feared no
ec nutrix molesta	nurse who harasses

Narrative 2: The Nuptial Beds (stanzas 8-10)

(1) Angels, not mortal husbands, guard Christ's virgins

Lectulos harum	Their [virgins'] beds
Christo vacantes	[which are] unoccupied
angeli vallant	for Christ
custodientes	Guardian angels protect
ne quis incestus	Lest any one impure
temeret illos	defile them
ensibus strictis	They ward off the impure
arcent immundos	with their drawn swords

(Continued)

(2) Christ alone embraces and sleeps with his virgins

Dormit in istis	In these [beds]
Christus cum	Christ sleeps with
illis	them [the virgins]
felix hic somnus	Happy the slumber [and]
requires dulcis	sweet the repose
quo cum fovetur	In which the faithful
virgo fidelis	virgin is caressed
inter amplexus	In the embraces of the
sponsi caelestis	heavenly bridegroom.
Dextera sponsi	The right hand of the
sponsa complexa	bridegroom, clasps his
	bride
capiti laeva	His left hand cradles her
dormit submissa	head
pervigil corde	While wakeful in heart
corpore dormit	she sleeps in body
et sponsi grato	and she quietly slumbers
sinu quiescit	on the loving breast of
	her bridegroom
Approbans somnum	Favoring her sleep
Sponsus beatam	the Sponsus
inquietari	Does not let her be
prohibet illam	disquieted
ne suscitetis	he says Do not awaken my
inquit, dilectam	beloved
dum ipsa volet	thus quiet as long as she
ita quietam	wishes

This presentation shifts from argument from example—which led into the imagery of the nuptial beds—to argument from analogy, which leads into the image of Christ the lamb gamboling among meadow flowers until he finds midday rest on the breasts of the virgins.[31]

31. George A. Kennedy, *Classical Rhetoric and Its Christian and Secular Tradition from Ancient to Modern Times* (Chapel Hill: University of North Carolina Press, 1980) 94.

Virgines castae further amplifies the nature of the relationship between the virgins and Christ by the analogy of the flowering of the Church. In stanza 12a the emphatic demonstrative *hic* signals the importance of the argumentation that follows the attributed speech. The narrator is about to tell his audience something very remarkable about the quiescent bliss of spiritual nuptials: though no virgin is deflowered in the heavenly bridegroom's embrace, their relations lead to the flowering of the Church.

Argument from Analogy: The Flowering of the Church (stanza 12)

Hic ecclesiastici	[Here the flower of the
flos est ille germinis	Church is budding
tam rosis quam liliis	as many roses as lilies
multiplex innumeris	multiply beyond
quorum est	counting through their
fragrantiis	fragrance
ager sponsi nobilis	the bridegroom's field
naribus et oculis	is equally delectable
aeque delectabilis	to scent and sight]

Narrative 3: The Flowered Virgins (stanza 13, 14a and b)

Ornatae tam byssina	[Adorned in linen and
quam veste purpurea	purple robes they hold
laeva tenent lilia	lilies in their left hand
rosas habent dextera	roses in their right
et corona gemmea	and with their heads crowned
redimitae capita	as with a set of jewels
agni sine macula	they hasten along the
percurrunt itinera	paths of the lamb
	without blemish
His quoque floribus	Also from these flowers
semper recentibus	forever fresh the
sanctorum intexta	garlands on their holy
capitum sunt serta	heads are woven]

Between stanzas 12-13 the symbolic imagery of the company of virgins as the bridegroom's field, blooming with roses and lilies, yields to Narrative 3, a more realistic evocation of the maidens crowned with wreaths, holding in their hands bouquets of lilies and roses—well-known symbols of virginity and marriage.[32] The topic is still the virgin bride of Christ. The wreaths of stanzas 12b and 13a evoke classical marital rites, which included the crowning of the bride and groom, and function as a symbol of both virginity and marriage.[33] Stanzas 12-13 therefore function to develop further the main topic of the sequence: the relationship between Christ and his virginal bride. Among the virgins abides a lamb without blemish. Along his paths they hasten, following him whithersoever he goes.

The argument from analogy now turns from the fragrant and beautiful virgins of the bridegroom's field to the the lamb.

Narrative 4: The Lamb who Pastures among Virgins

(1) The Perky Lamb (stanzas 14c-d and 15)

His agnus pascitur	Among these the lamb
atque reficitur	pastures and is thereby
hi flores electa	refreshed these flowers
sunt illius esca	are his food of choice
Hinc choro talium	Surrounded about by
vallatus agminum	this choir of such companies he
hortorum amena	races this way and that in the
discurrit hac illac	lovely gardens

(Continued)

32. Menander had instructed his students that praise of the bride's garland of roses and adoration of the couple's nuptial room filled with flowers were very fitting topics for wedding and bedroom speeches; *Menander Rhetor*, 145 and 153.

33. Dyan Elliott, *Spiritual Marriage: Sexual Abstinence in Medieval Wedlock* (Princeton: Princeton University Press, 1993) 69.

Qui nunc	Now caught by them now
comprehensus	
ab his nunc elapsus	slipping away
quasi quadam fuga	he petulantly leaps
petulans exsultat	about as if escaping

(2) The lamb rests among virgins (stanzas 16 and 17)

Crebros saltus	This lamb leaps and bounds
dat hic agnus	repeatedly prancing about
inter illas	among them
discurrendo	
Et cum ipsis	And he rests among
requiescit	them [the virgins]
fervore meridiano	in the noonday heat
In earum pectore	In the middle of the
cubat in meridie	day he lies upon
	their breasts
Inter mammas	He makes his sleeping
virginum	place among virgins'
Collocat cubiculum	breasts

In an effort to appeal to the *pathos* of the nuns and draw them more deeply into the depths of the relationship between Christ and the virgins, Abelard resorts to a rather erotic image. Narrative 4 states that the lamb pastures among the virginal lilies and roses and is refreshed; they are his food of choice. As Dronke has noted, 'the erotic undertone may also be perceptible in the poet's choice of the expression *esca*, which can carry the suggestion both of food and of a sensual lure'.[34]

Rhetorically, the narrative of the lamb is developed around two centers of discourse, each corresponding to motifs central to the unicorn legend. In the first center, the unicorn-like lamb is too powerful to be caught. In the second, he willingly submits

34. Dronke, *Latin and Vernacular Poets of the Middle Ages*, 102.

to resting in the virgin's lap. As before, the preceding actions serve to introduce the points of action of this section.

Virgines castae closes with a rationale, a restatement of the sequence's overall argument, and an exhortation.

Conclusio (stanzas 18-20)

(1) *Rationale* (Stanza 18a)

Virgo quippe cum sit	Because he himself
ipse Virgineque matre	is a virgin and was
natus	born of a virgin mother

(2) Argument (stanzas 18b and 19)

Virginales super	He loves and longs
omnes amat et quaerit	for virginal embraces
recessus	above all others
Somnus illi placidus	His sleep is serene when
in castis est sinibus	taken upon chaste laps
Ne qua forte macula	Lest otherwise perhaps
sua foedet vellera	a spot might soil his fleece

(3) Exhortation (Stanza 20)

Hoc attende	Attend to this song
canticum	of the illustrious collegium
devotarum virginum	of devoted virgins
insigne collegium	Whereby our devotion may
Quo nostra devotio	with greater zeal adorn
maiore se studio	the temple of the Lord
templum ornet Domine	

The rationale recapitulates the reason for the entire sequence: Because the lamb Christ is a virgin and born of a virgin, he loves and longs to embrace virgins. Among them his sleep is serene and pure. From this reasoning an exhortation follows which recalls the opening song of the exordium and admonishes the singer to join her voice with heaven's virginal choir.

Having carefully gone through the rhetorical dimensions of *Virgines castae*, we can now display our results in outline form.

Table III.3 draws together the details of our analysis, showing both the sequence's narrative and argumentative texture. The left-hand column of the table labels the epideictic divisions of the sequence. Under each division the topics presented and developed are alphabetized. Finally, important rhetorical devices, such as example and apostrophe, are indicated with parentheses.

Table III.3: Argumentative Texture of *Virgines castae*

Rhetorical Analysis	Latin	English
Exordium: topics: (a) virgins (b) making music (c) highest virginity (d) worshiping	1a. *Virgines castae virginis summae decus praecinentes*	Chaste virgins sing of the beauty of the supreme virgin
	1b. *Ceteras quoque condignas laude post hanc venerantes*	and of the other virgins who worship after her
	2a. *Psalmis et hymnis canticis dignis sibi colloquentes*	Speaking to one another in fitting psalms and hymns and canticles
(e) offering	2b. *Solvant in istis debitae laudis hostias sollemnes*	Let them offer by these [songs] solemn sacrifices of due praise
Narration 1: The queen and the virgins (f) The queen; (g) The king	3a. *Haec est adextris assistens regis illa regina*	This one [the supreme virgin] is that queen serving at the right hand of the king
	3b. *Iuncta latere sola cum rege praecedit ipsa*	United beside him she alone with the king proceeds

Table III.3: Argumentative Texture of *Virgines castae*, cont.

Rhetorical Analysis	Latin	English
	3c. *Aurata veste varietate circiumamicta*	In golden array, clothed round about with variety
	3d. *Tamquam dominam sequitur ipsam queque beata*	Every blessed [virgin] follows her as her lady
Rationale: Offered to the king: Topics: (a) virgins; (c) Supreme virgin; (d) following; (e) offering; (f) queen; (g) king;	4a. *Post eam adductae virgines devotae* 4b. *regi sunt oblatae Christo consecratae*	Led after her devout virgins have been offered to the king [and] consecrated to Christ
Examples from Early Christianity	4c. *Tales erant Thecla Agnes et Lucia*	Such [virgins] were Thecla Agnes and Lucia
	4d. *Agathes et multa virginum caterva*	Agathes and many a great throng of virgins
expositio	5. *Filiae Tyri* *munera ferentes Et in his regis vultum deprecantes*	The daughters of Tyre bearing gifts and entreating the favor of the king

(Continued)

Table III.3: Argumentative Texture of *Virgines castae,* cont.

Rhetorical Analysis	Latin	English
	Hostias cunctis	by means of these [the gifts]
	habent puriores	have offerings purer than all [other offerings]
	Corpore munde	[They are] clean
	Corde sanctiores	in body and even holier in heart
	6. *Holocaustum Domino*	As a burnt-offering
	Offerent ex integro virgines carne integrae mente immortalem sponsum eligentes Christum	virgins offer to the Lord the integrity of their flesh and mind choosing Christ as their immortal spouse
Contrary: Carnal verses Spiritual marriage	7. *O felices nuptiae quibus nullae maculae nulli dolores partus sunt graves nec pelex timenda nec nutrix molesta*	Oh happy nuptials where there is no impurity no grievous pains of childbirth no rival mistress to be feared no nurse who harasses
Narrative 2: The nuptial beds Narrational exposition	8. *Lectulos harum Christo vacantes angeli vallant custodientes ne quis incestus temeret illos ensibus strictis arcent immundos*	These [virgins'] beds which are set apart for Christ guardian angels watch over Lest any one wicked defile them (the beds) they ward off the impure with drawn swords

(Continued)

Table III.3: Argumentative Texture of *Virgines castae*, cont.

Rhetorical Analysis	Latin	English
Narrative 2 cont. Narrational exposition	9. *Dormit in istis Christus cum illis felix hic somnus requires dulcis quo cum fovetur virgo fidelis inter amplexus sponsi caelestis*	In these (beds) Christ sleeps with them (the virgins) happy is the slumber sweet the repose in which the faithful virgin is caressed in the embraces of the heavenly bridegroom
	10. *Dextera sponsi sponsa complexa capiti laeva dormit submissa pervigil corde corpore dormit et sponsi grato sinu quiescit*	The right hand of the bridegroom clasps his bride His left hand cradles her head While wakeful in heart she sleeps in body and she quietly slumbers on the lov-ing breast of her bridegroom
(*apostrophe*: The groom speaks)	11. *Approbans somnum Sponsus beatam inquietari prohibet illam ne suscitetis inquit dilectam dum ipsa volet ita quietam*	Favoring her sleep the Sponsus Does not let her be disquieted he says Do not awaken my beloved thus quiet till she wishes

(Continued)

Table III.3: Argumentative Texture of *Virgines castae*, cont.

Rhetorical Analysis	Latin	English
Analogy: The Flowering of the Church Narrational exposition	12. *Hic ecclesiastici* *flos est ille germinis* *tam rosis quam liliis* *multiplex innumeris* *quorum est fragrantiis* *ager sponsi nobilis* *naribus et oculis* *aeque delectabilis*	Here the flowering of the Church is bud- ding as many roses as lilies multiply beyond counting through their fragrance the bridegroom's field is equally delectable to scent and sight
Narration 3: The flowered virgins	13. *Ornatae tam bys-* *sina quam veste pur-* *purea laeva tenent lilia* *rosas habent dextera*	Adorned in linen and purple robes they hold lilies in their left hand roses in their right
	et corona gemmea *redimitae capita* *agni sine macula* *percurrunt itinera*	and with their heads crowned as with a set of jewels they hasten along the paths of the lamb without blemish
	14. *His quoque floribus* *semper recentibus* *sanctorum intexta* *capitum sunt serta*	Also from these flowers forever fresh the garlands on their holy heads are woven

(Continued)

Table III.3: Argumentative Texture of *Virgines castae,* cont.

Rhetorical Analysis	Latin	English
Narration 4: The Lamb Narrative Embellish- ment of the analogy of the lovely gardens	*His agnus pascitur* *atque reficitur* *hi flores electa* *sunt illius esca*	This lamb pastures among them and is thereby refreshed these flowers are his food of choice
	15. *Hinc choro talium* *vallatus agminum* *hortorum amena* *discurrit hac illac* *Qui nunc* *comprehensus* *ab his nunc elapses* *quasi quadam fuga* *petulans exsultat*	Surrounded about by this choir of such companies he races this way and that in the lovely gardens Now he is caught by them now he slips away he heedlessly leaps about as if escaping
	16. *Crebros saltus* *dat hic agnus* *inter illas discurrendo* *Et cum ipsis* *requiescit* *fervore meridiano*	This lamb leaps and bounds repeatedly prancing about among them And he rests among them (the virgins) in the noonday heat
	17. *In earum pectore* *cubat in meridie* *Inter mammas* *virginum* *Collocat cubiculum*	In the middle of the day he lies upon their breasts He makes his sleeping place among virgins' breasts

(Continued)

Table III.3: Argumentative Texture of *Virgines castae*, cont.

Rhetorical Analysis	Latin	English
Conclusio (Begins with a rationale that moves into an exhortation)	18. *Virgo quippe cum sit ipse Virgineque matre natus Virginales super omnes amat et quaerit recessus*	Because he himself is a virgin and was born of a virgin mother He loves and longs for virginal embraces above all others
	19. *Somnus illi placidus in castis est sinibus Ne qua forte macula sua foedet vellera*	His sleep is serene when taken upon chaste laps Lest perhaps a spot should soil his fleece
	20. *Hoc attende canticum, devotarum virginum insigne collegium Quo nostra devotio maiore se studio templum ornet Domine*	Let us attend to this song of the illustrious collegium of devoted virgins Whereby our devotion may with greater zeal adorn the temple of God

The epideictic nature of *Virgines castae* suggests that Abelard appeals to themes, virtues, and practices that were already known and should be cherished by the Paraclete community. On the one hand, Christ cannot be mastered by human beings. On the other, he willingly takes his repose among virgins. Abelard wishes to intensify the community's commitment to virginity, purity, faith, and Christ by calling on the nuns to join in the bridal song of past and present followers of the lamb. Through the powers of *ethos, pathos,* and *logos,* Abelard's elaboration of the community's core practices and virtues perpetuates the Paraclete nuns' identity as Christ's bride.

EPIDEICTIC SPEECH AND CHREIA ELABORATION

We shall now observe Abelard doing much the same thing in the epideictic speech of his sequence *Epithalamica*. To do so, we turn from works like the *Rhetorica ad Herrenium* and the writings of rhetoricians like Menander Rhetor to surviving *progymnasmata*— the handbooks that contain the 'preliminary exercises' that ancient rhetoricians wrote for student use during the final stage of grammar school.[35] One of these classroom exercises was called the *chreia*, a term meaning 'useful'. Teachers of rhetoric employed it to indicate literary material useful in teaching rhetoric,[36] and to introduce the basic notions and skills necessary for composing epideictic speech; they considered it an essential tool for teaching students persuasive discourse and giving them guidance in proper conduct.[37] Because the *chreia* may be unfamiliar to modern readers, I have provided an outline of its nature. Knowledge of the *chreia* and its rhetorical elaboration will greatly add to our understanding of the epideictic discourse of *Epithalamica*.[38]

According to ancient teachers of rhetoric, a *chreia* was a concise statement and/or action aptly attributed to a definite person or something analogous to a person.[39] The following examples are of *chreiai* with a saying, with an action, and with both:

Sayings-*chreia*
> Antisthenes, on seeing an adulterer fleeing, said: 'You hapless fellow, how much danger you could have avoided for an obol'.

---

35. Mack & Robbins, *Patterns of Persuasion*, 13.

36. *Ibid.*, 45.

37. *Ibid.*, 16.

38. See Ronald F. Hock and Edward N. O'Neil, intro., trans., and edd., *The Chreia in Ancient Rhetoric. Volume I: The Progymnasmata, Texts and Translations 27, Graeco-Roman Religion Series 9* (Atlanta: Scholars Press, 1986). The broader educational context for the *chreia* is well described in Stanley F. Bonner, *Education in Ancient Rome* (Berkeley: University of California Press, 1977).

39. Hock and O'Neil, *The Chreia in Ancient Rhetoric*, 32.

Action-*chreia*

> In response to the one who said that there is no motion
> Diogenes got up and walked around.

Action- and sayings-*chreia* (mixed-*chreia*)

> Jesus, on entering the Temple, began to evict the sellers
> and said to them: 'It is written, "My house shall be a house
> of prayer, but you have made it a cave for brigands."'

Sayings-*chreiai* may contain sayings of general significance or short remarks understandable only in their context. They frequently indicate their occasion by means of a participial construction. Consider the participles 'seeing' and 'entering' in the examples above. Sayings-*chreiai* usually give the statement-response with a finite verb in a secondary tense, although the saying may occur either in direct or indirect discourse. Review the use of the past-tense verb 'said' above.

Action-*chreiai* steer the reader's thinking in a particular direction, inducing the reader to reflect on the meaning of an action performed by a noteworthy person. The participial and finite verb construction of the sayings-*chreia* are less typical in action-*chreiai*, but they do appear.

The mixed-*chreia* (action- and sayings-*chreia*), in its simplest as well as its most elaborate form, is a composition that stands between rhetorical and discursive speech, on the one hand, and, on the other, between rhetorical speech and narrative literature. Knowledge of the *progymnasmata*, with their graded curricula of lessons and exercises by which grammar students made the transition from literary studies to rhetoric, and their continued use in medieval education, provides a unique means for understanding the rhetorical effectiveness of *Virgines castae* and *Epithalamica*.[40]

40. The history of the *progymnasmata* is remarkably long. They began in the Hellenistic period and extended into the modern period. The most famous writers of *progymnasmata* were Theon of Alexandria (mid-first century AD), Hermogenes of Tarsus (mid-second century AD), and Aphthonius of Antioch (fourth century AD). Aphthonius' textbook eventually became the unrivaled standard among byzantine rhetoricians. It was not until the fourteenth or fifteenth century that Aphthonius's book made its way into the Latin West.

Throughout the medieval period only one *progymnasmata* was available for teaching students how to take a *chreia* and elaborate a speech upon it. Sometime in the sixth century the famous educator Priscian made a latin translation of a mid-second-century AD. *progymnasmata* by Hermogenes of Tarsus. Entitled *De praeexercitamentis*, this little translation has been for the most part overlooked by the scholarly world. Yet we know that lessons of the *praeexercitamina* formed typical classroom exercises in Abelard's time.[41] Indeed, Abelard's one-time student John of Salisbury (*c.* 1115–1180), in his *Metalogicon*, describes how Bernard of Chartres (d. *c.* 1130) used these ancient exercises in training his students in both declamation and composition. John's description is worthy of quoting at length, for it is an exceptional summary of the formal program of learning prose and poetic composition:

> Bernard of Chartres, the greatest fount of literary learning in Gaul in recent times, used to teach grammar in the following way. He would point out, in reading the authors, what was simple and according to rule. On the other hand, he would explain grammatical figures, rhetorical embellishment, and sophistical quibbling, as well as the relation of given passages to other studies. He would do so, however, without trying to teach everything at one time. On the contrary, he would dispense his instruction to his hearers gradually, in a manner commensurate with their powers of assimilation. . . . In view of the fact that exercise both strengthens and sharpens our mind, Bernard would bend every effort to bring his students to imitate what they were hearing. In some cases he would rely on exhortation, in others he would resort to punishments, such as flogging. Each student was daily required to recite part of what he had heard on the previous day. Some would recite more, others less. Each succeeding day thus became the disciple

41. See James J. Murphy, *Rhetoric in the Middle Ages: A History of Rhetorical Theory from St. Augustine to the Renaissance* (University of California Press, 1974) 131.

of its predecessor. The evening exercise, known as the 'declination,' was so replete with grammatical instruction that
if anyone were to take part in it for an entire year, provided
he were not a dullard, he would become thoroughly familiar
with the (correct) method of speaking and writing, and
would not be at a loss to comprehend expression in general
use. Since, however, it is not right to allow any school or
day to be without religion, subject matter was presented to
foster faith, to build up morals, and to inspire those present
at the quasicollation to perform good works. This evening
'declination,' or philosophical collation, closed with the
pious commendation of the souls of the departed to their
Redeemer, by the devout recitation of the Sixth Penitential
Psalm and the Lord's Prayer. He [Bernard] would also explain the poets and orators who were to serve as models for
the boys in their introductory exercises (*praeexercitamina*) in
imitating prose and poetry.[42]

42. English translation is from *The Metalogicon of John of Salisbury: A Twelfth-Century Defense of the Verbal and Logical Arts of the Trivium*, trans., intro., and notes Daniel D. McGarry (Westport: Greenwood Press, 1982), 67–69. Latin (PL 199:854) quoted from R. R. Bolgar, *The Classical Heritage and Its Beneficiaries* (Cambridge: Cambridge University Press, 1963) 417–418: *Sequebatur hunc morem Bernardus Carnotensis, exundantissimus modernins temporibus fons literarum in Gallia, et in auctorum lectione quid simplex esset, et ad imaginem regule positum ostendebat; figuras grammaticae, colores rhetoricos, cavillationes sophismatum, et qua parte sui propositate lectionis articulus respiciebat ad alias disciplinas, proponebat in medio; ita tamen ut non in singulis universa doceret, sed pro capacitate audientium dispensaret eis in tempore doctrinae mansuram. . . . Et quoniam memoria exercitio firmatur, ingeniumque acuitur ad imitandum ea quae audiebant, alios admonitionibus, alios flagellis et poenis urgebat. Cogebantur excoluere singuli die sequenti aliquid eorum que precedenti audierant; alii plus, alii minus; erat enim apud eos precedentis discipulus sequens dies. Vespertinum exercitium, quid declinatio dicebatur, tanta copiositate grammaticae refertum erat, ut si quis in eo per annum integrum versaretur, rationem loquendi et scribendi, si non esset behetior, haberet ad manum, et significationem sermonum, qui in communi usu versantur, ignorare non tem, ea proponebatur materia quae fidem adificaret et mores, et unde qui conuenerant, quasi collatione quadam, animarentur ad bonum. Novissimus autem huius declinationis, immo philosophice collationis, articulus pietatis vestigia preferebat; et animas defunctorum commendabat devota oblatione psalmi qui in poenitentialibus sextus est et in oratione Dominica Redemptori suo. Quibus autem indicebantur preexercitamina puerorum in prosis, aut poematibus imitandis poetas aut*

This intense educational program began with the rudiments of grammar, advanced to interpretation, and led to the *praeexercitamina*, the grammatical and rhetorical exercises of the ancient *progymnasmata*. Through the *praeexercitamina* Bernard's boys took their first steps into the world of rhetoric, the world of composition.

Like Hermogenes and Priscian, Bernard of Chartres used the *praeexercitamina* to show students how a brief *chreia* might be expanded by adding descriptive details of the circumstance, or explaining in detail who the characters were, or even expanding the dialogue into a little story with dramatic traits of its own.[43] Elaborated *chreiai* typically make their argument by evoking titles of honor, attributes of character, past events, emotions, and circumstantial actions in the narrative; they also feature exhortation, personal address, descriptive adjectives, and comparison. The elaborated *chreia* functioned much more like a complete epideictic speech, having an introduction, theme, argumentation, and conclusion.

When attributed speech and/or action and its rationale are present, the initial ingredients exist for an argument. For a complete rhetorical argument, however, an additional rhetorical figure or topic must be present. A complete argument, taught Hermogenes, Priscian, and (we can assume) Bernard, occurs by using a combination of one or more of the following:

—a contrary statement (which clarifies or restates the initial proposition, thesis, or statement of the case);

—an analogy (which introduces another sphere of human life or nature);

—an example (which introduces an authoritative person as a paradigm or model);

—a judgment (an authoritative saying or principle gleaned from written documents or a well-known saying);

---

oratores proponebat, et eorum iubebat vestigia imitari, ostendens iuncturas dictionum et elegantes sermonum clausulas.

43. Mack and Robbins, *Patterns of Persuasion*, 36.

—and a conclusion (which intensifies and focuses emotions and thoughts through summary, exhortation, and other techniques).

This teaching on the *chreia* emerged after several centuries of teaching students the 'sequencing' or 'refining' techniques of the *expolitio*. Hermogenes and rhetorical teachers applied this epideictic sequencing to the *chreia*, referring to the process as 'elaboration' rather than 'refining' or 'sequencing.' In this instance, a specific personage is introduced who then states the theme. *Chreiai* teachers taught that a theme attributed to a specific person becomes an authoritative pronouncement.[44]

The *chreia*, the authoritative pronouncement, is then elaborated upon in the same way as the theme of an epideictic speech is: rationale, contrary, example, analogy, perhaps citation of an ancient authority, and a concluding exhortation. These larger topics of argumentation work together on the macro level to form the overall dimensions of an epideictic speech. Table III.4 (p. 134) outlines the *chreia* elaboration form and places it in juxtaposition with the *expolitio* and standard form of the epideictic speech.

Understanding these basic facts about the *chreia* and its elaboration, and the epideictic theme and its refinement, we can now proceed to analyze the argumentative texture of *Epithalamica*. Like *Virgines castae*, the character and form of *Epithalamica* is unmistakably epideictic. Our analysis will identify the themes of Abelard's Easter sequence and show exactly how, in refining it, he follows the rules of *expolitio* and *chreia* elaboration. Further, we will see how carefully Abelard crafted his epideictic discourse so that he invites, if not outright lures, his Paraclete audience into conforming their lives to the mode of being to which he calls them.

---

44. Abelard's concerns, expressed in the Prefaces of his hymn collection, show that his thought followed something of the flow of the *chreia* teachers. They believed that a theme was given much more rhetorical force and authority if it was pronounced by a particular individual. Likewise, as we will see in Chapter Four, Abelard believed that a hymn—or any sacred song—was given authority when it was attributable to a particular person.

Table III.4: *Chreia* Elaboration

Standard Epideictic Speech	*Expolitio*: The Sequencing of a Theme	Hermogenes' *Chreia* Elaboration
1. *Exodium*		*Encomium*/Praise Paraphrase/*Chreia* Rationale
2. *Narratio*	*Res*	
3. *Partitio* (Theme or Proposition)	*Ratio*	
4. *Confirmatio* (Confirmation or support of proposition)	*Pronuntio*	
5. *Digressio* (Digression or embellishment through: contrary, analogy, example)	*Contrario* Simile *Exemplum*	Contrary Analogy Example
		Judgment
6. *Conclusio* (Conclusion or exhortation)	*Conclusio*	Exhortation

THE ARGUMENTATIVE TEXTURE OF *EPITHALAMICA*

Rhetorically, *Epithalamica* divides into three speeches, each with its own appeal to *logos*, *pathos*, and *ethos*. The first speech encompasses the entire sequence and is the argument of its narrator, which, we can assume, is the voice of Abelard. The second is the bride's song-speech: stanzas 3 through 11. The third speech is that of the bridegroom, which spans strophes 4 through 6 and is embedded in the opening of the bride's speech. In this last the sequence narrator employs the figure of *prosopopoeia*, the impersonation of a character. The dialogue between the bride and bridegroom is revealed in the following argumentative pattern:

Table III.5: The Narrational Texture of *Epithalamica*

Strophes

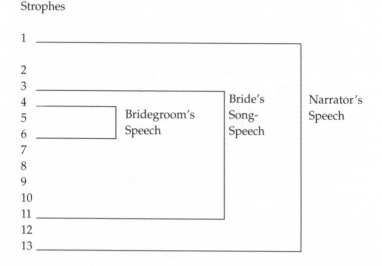

Table III.6 (pp. 139ff) shows the overall rhetorical outline of *Epithalamica*. *Epithalamica*, like *Virgines castae*, is epideictic in nature and its goal is therefore to strengthen adherence to a particular value and inspire the audience to carry out a policy of action.[45]

Moving from beginning to end, we can see how each of the three divisions of the sequence functions rhetorically. The *exordium* of the sequence consists of two exhortations: to the bride to share outwardly through song the inward joys she has with her bridegroom; to the bride's maiden-followers to form a choir and join in the nuptial song. The rationale for the bride's singing

45. Kennedy, *New Testament Interpretation through Rhetorical Criticism*, 74.

seems to be expressed in the words, 'his presence renews you forever more'. The rationale for the bridesmaids' song lies in the honor accorded them by the groomsmen.

THE BRIDE'S SONG

The bride begins her song with a description of the groom leaping and skipping as he comes to see her; it is a speech-derived from the Song of Songs. Direct quotation of the bride's song enlivens the narrative and imparts a sense of realism to her character. She describes his gazing upon her and includes words of her beloved bridegroom. Also drawn from the biblical Song, the discourse of the bridegroom in *Epithalamica* has the features of a sayings-*chreia*, a mini-speech complete with speaker, speech, and audience,[46] which often provide background by means of a participial construction, and then indicate action with a finite verb in a secondary tense, either in direct or indirect discourse.[47]

In *Epithalamica* we have not only the participial structure of the *chreia* (normal type), but the presence of four participial clauses!

In montibus his ecce saliens	Behold! He comes *leaping* upon the mountains
ecce venit, colles transilens	Behold! He comes *skipping* over the hills.
per fenestras ad me respiciens	*Gazing* upon me through the windows,
per cancellos dicit prospiciens	*Peering* through the lattices, he says:

The repetition of the participial structure enhances the description of the scene leading up to the bridegroom's speech—a narrative expansion called *amplificatio*—and, coupled with the repetition of a dramatic *ecce*, also builds great emotional anticipa-

---

46. Mack & Robbins, *Patterns of Persuasion*, 36.
47. Ibid., 46.

tion for direct speech by the bridegroom. Finally the bridegroom's words are preceded by the finite verb 'dicit,' a typical cue for the forthcoming sayings- or action-*chreia*.

The bridegroom's speech begins with a proposition (*propositio*): 'Arise, my Love, make haste! my beautiful dove, fly to me!' Immediately he provides a rationale for his proposal: 'For the bristling winter is now past' (stanzas 4 and 5). The bridegroom amplifies the rationale with a declaration that the heavy rains of winter have receded, springtime has opened the earth, flowers are appearing, and the turtledove has begun singing;[48] he specifies a natural process that emerges from analogical reasoning. The words that conclude the bridegroom's speech restate the *propositio*, forming an opening and closing (an *inclusio*) that reiterates the bridegroom's essential message and poetically gives his song a refrain form: 'Arise, my love, make haste my beautiful dove, fly to me'. The dramatic and impassioned refrain of the bridegroom raises the emotional tenor of the sequence to a new height and intensity.

The bridegroom's speech as a whole in *Epithalamica* is deliberative—a departure from Abelard's overall rhetorical strategy. The bridegroom, like the bridegroom in the Song of Songs, seeks to persuade the bride, his audience, to act immediately. The bridegroom in neither text seeks to intensify the bride's adherence to some values shared by the two, as is typical in epideictic discourse. Rather, in the spirit of deliberative speech, he calls her to hasten to him immediately. The question is whether he has persuaded her to 'hasten to him.' If so, she will 'fly to him.'

THE BRIDE'S SEARCH FOR HER BELOVED

The following four stanzas tell the bride's story. At stanza 7, the bride responds to the bridegroom's call, but finds upon her arrival in her beloved's garden that he has departed. This scene is

---

48. *Menander Rhetor*, 151–153, instructed his students to envoke the season as a fitting topic for the bedroom speech.

probably meant to create in the reader-singer a *pathos* of concern if not outright panic. 'Has he gone back on his word?' she might ask. The rhetoric of the sequence does not explore or seek to justify the ways of the bridegroom. All attention is focused on the response and emotional state of the bride.

Stanza 8, drawn from the Song of Songs, reveals her distress. Anxious, she goes forth by night, seeking her bridegroom throughout the city. She meets the watchmen, but they have no knowledge of the bridegroom. She presses on and finally finds him, apparently, somewhere on the outskirts of the city—socially a very dangerous place for a woman to be alone. The bride's grief is changed to joy.

At stanza 9 the bride pulls out the figurative 'stops' of her emotions. Through the clarion blast of *anaphora* she rejoices *iam . . . iam . . . iam* ('Now . . . now . . . now'). The bride describes a series of antithetical emotional states that have characterized her search. In stanzas 10 and 12 she tickles the listener's ear by the figure *commutatio*. In stanza 10, for example, she declares, *Risi mane, flevi nocte* ('I laughed at morn/I wept at night') and then repeats the same thought but reversing the words of each clause: *ane risi, nocte flevi* ('At morn I laughed/at night I wept'). This ornamentation provides aesthetic texture that is designed to lure the hearer / singer into the symbolic world of the song and to deepen the emotional appeal of the bride's song, thereby cultivating the *pathos* aimed to persuasion. Use of these rhetorical figures demonstrated the bride's, the narrator's, and, ultimately, Abelard's poetic skill and suggested a good *ethos* on the part of all three.

In the overall rhetoric of the sequence the bride's story serves as an *exemplum*. The term *exemplum*, as ancient and medieval rhetoricians used it, usually referred to a specific person—typically to historically well-known persons; but rhetoricians also made use of the general example 'whoever', 'anyone who', or 'the one who'.[49] *Exempla* show that a particular instance has actualized the general principle at issue. If the example is well

49. *Menander Rhetor*, 28.

chosen, the argument is confirmed in terms of a specific and precedent case.[50] Abelard's addressees likely saw in the bride of the biblical Song countless souls who, like her, have given themselves in spiritual marriage to the bridegroom, Christ.

The bridegroom has stated his *propositio* and its justification, and the bride has finally found her beloved. Now the narrator exhorts the daughters of Zion, with whom the Paraclete nuns would have identified, to add their psalm to the bride's and thereby experience the restoring power of the bridegroom's presence. The rationale for the exhortation rest upon the joy that day brings; the day is none other than Easter, the day of Christ's return to life and appearance before his disciples. Table III.6 gathers up all of the observations made above:

Table III.6: *Argumentative Texture in* Epithalamica

Rhetorical Analysis	Latin	English
Exordium:	1. *Epithalamica*	Sing O bride
FIRST EXHORTATION:	*dic Sponsa,*	Your bridal
Sing bride of what	*cantica intus*	canticle Sing out-
you see within	*quae conspicis*	wardly the joys you
Result (rationale?):	*dic foris gaudia*	gaze upon within
This song gladdens	*et nos laetificans*	and gladdening us
us	*de Sponso nuntia*	give tidings of
	cuius te refovet	the bridegroom
	semper praesentia	whose presence
		renews you for-
		ever more
SECOND	2. *Adulescentulae*	Young maidens form
EXHORTATION:	*vos chorum ducite*	your choir
Sing young maidens	*cum haec*	When she begins
with the bride	*praecinerit*	singing, join in
	et vos succinite	

(Continued)

50. *Menander Rhetor*, 60.

Table III.6: *Argumentative Texture in* Epithalamica, cont.

Rhetorical Analysis	Latin	English
Result (rationale?): This song gladdens us	*et nos laetificans de Sponso nuntia cuius te refovet semper praesentia*	and gladdening us give tidings of the bridegroom whose presence renews you for- ever more
SECOND EXHORTATION: Sing young maidens with the bride	2. *Adulescentulae vos chorum ducite cum haec praecinerit et vos succinite*	Young maidens form your choir When she begins singing, join in
Rationale: You have been invited to make her song yours.	*Amici Sponsi vos vocarunt nuptiae*	The bridegroom's friends have called you to the nuptials
Recapitulation of exhortation:	*et novae modulos optamus Dominae*	Let us welcome the songs sung the newly wed Lady
THE BRIDE'S SONG: *Chreia* Component: Setting *Amplificatio*: Description of Scene, Characters, Events	3. *In montibus his ecce saliens* *ecce venit colles transilens*	Behold he comes leaping upon the mountains Behold he comes skipping over the hills
Rhetorical Function: *Narratio*	*per fenestras ad me respiciens per cancellos dicit prospiciens*	Gazing upon me through the windows

(Continued)

Table III.6: *Argumentative Texture in* Epithalamica, cont.

Rhetorical Analysis	Latin	English
		looking through the lattices he says
CHREIA COMPONENT: bridegroom speaks Rhetorical Function: *propositio*	4. *Amica surge propera columba nitens advola*	Arise my friend make haste my beautiful dove fly to me
CHREIA COMPONENT: rationale Rhetorical Function: *Argumentatio* rationale/analogy (59)	5. *Horrens enim hiems iam transiit gravis imber recedens abiit*	For the bristling winter is now past the heavy rains have receded and gone
contrary/analogy	*ver amoenum terras aperuit parent flores et turtur cecinit*	lovely springtime has opened earth flowers are appearing the turtle-dove has begun singing
PROPOSITIO RESTATED:	6. *Amica surge propera columba nitens advola*	Arise my friend make haste my beautiful dove, fly to me
The Bride's Song:	7. *Rex in accumbitum iam se contulerat*	The king had already betaken himself into his chamber
	et mea redolens nardus spiraverat	and my redolent nard-oil has breathed forth

(Continued)

Table III.6: *Argumentative Texture in* Epithalamica, cont.

Rhetorical Analysis	Latin	English
	in hortum veneram in quem descend erat	I had come into the garden into which he had descended
	at ille transiens iam declinaverat	but he passing through had already gone away
EXAMPLE: The bride responds positively to the bridegroom's speech.	8. *Per noctem igitur hunc quaerens exeo huc illuc anxia quaerendo cur sito occurrunt vigiles ardenti studio*	And so by night I go forth from here seeking him anxious hither and thither I run in my seeking the watchmen come upon me in my burning zeal
	quos cum transierim Sponsum invenio	when I pass them I find my bridegroom
(*anaphora*)	9. *Iam video quod optaveram iam tenco quod amaveram iam redo quae sic fleveram plus gaudeo quam dolueram*	Now I see what I had hoped for now I clasp to what I had loved now I laugh at what I had so wept for I rejoice more than I had ever grieved
(*commutatio*)	10. *Risi mane flevi nocte mane risi nocte flevi*	I laughed at morn I wept at night At morn I laughed at night I wept

(Continued)

Table III.6: *Argumentative Texture in* Epithalamica, cont.

Rhetorical Analysis	Latin	English
	11. *Noctem insomnem dolor duxerat quem vehemetem amor fecerat*	Grief had caused insomnia a grief made my love over-powering desire
	dilatione votum creverat donec amantem aman vistat	intensified through delay until lover visited his beloved
Narrator's Conclusion Rationale	12. *Plausus die planctus nocte*	Joy comes by day lamentations by night
	die plausus nocte planctus	By day comes joy by night lamentation
EXHORTATION: Sing with the bride and her choir	13. *Eia nunc comites et Sion filiae*	So come now daughters of Zion!
	ad Sponsae contica psalmum adnectite	To the canticle of the bride, [and] add your psalm wherein
	quo moestis reddita Sponsi praesentia	the presence of the bridegroom restored
	convertit elegos nostros in cantica	to those in grief turns our mourn-ful elegies into canticles

Rhetorical analysis has enabled us to see the step-by-step movement of Abelard's sequences. The argumentative pattern of the *expolitio* and the *chreia* elaboration provided models for investigating the centers of narration and argument in *Virgines castae* and *Epithalamica*. We have seen that the steps for the elaboration of speech and action that had been passed down from the *Rhetorica ad Herrenium* to Hermogenes to medieval educators like Bernard of Chartres actually outlined the major moves in the construction of a complete epideictic argument. This link between rhetorical handbooks and school exercises calls scholars of medieval sacred lyric to consider more deeply the influence of grammatical and rhetorical training on the argumentative structure of medieval poetry.

This chapter has positioned the *expolitio* and the *chreia* elaboration pattern as a bridge between advanced rhetorical theory and the rhetoric of the liturgical sequence. Drawing on the *Rhetorica ad Herrenium*'s description of 'refining' and what Hermogenes' *Progymnasmata* says about the elaboration of *chreiai*, we have suggested that the Greco-Roman *expolitio* and *cheria* elaboration may indeed offer aid in compositional analysis of other medieval sequences, at least those of the logical type like Abelard's *Virgines castae*. Close rhetorical analysis of Abelard's hymns and *planctus* remains. The latter, being like the sequences in several ways, may well show a similar degree of careful rhetorical elaboration of narrative and argument as well as speech and action.

Also yet to be told is the story of epideictic speech, the *chreia*, and the *expolitio* in the Middle Ages. Exploring in depth these three patterns of speech in their medieval setting has been beyond the scope of this chapter—though one does suspect that the story is embedded in the larger story of the medieval french cathedral schools and the Paris University, places where Abelard spent much of his life being schooled and schooling others.

From our analysis of Abelard's *Virgines castae* and *Epithalamica*, we can draw the following general conclusions. The force of the two sequences' argument results from Abelard's conscious interweaving of a range of persuasive strategies analogous to those of the *expolitio*, the standard epideictic speech, and the elaborated *chreia*. The unity of epideictic compositional technique achieves a remarkable aesthetic effect which Abelard undoubtedly calculated to appeal to the nuns' sense of beauty and proportion. Further, Abelard develops the argument of each sequence through narrative and argumentative centers; as his discourse unfolds, he returns to his central proposition (theme) to take up some topic still in need of elaboration. Many of the topics central to *Virgines castae* and *Epithalamica* are precisely those topics Menander Rhetor had associated with the wedding and bedroom speeches.

As Abelard constructed his sequences, he united each division of his developing argument with the immediately preceding statement. Thus, each sequence carefully 'refines' its marital theme by 'sequencing' from one topic to the next.

Both sequences unfold like the petals of a rose until each flowers in full bloom. Abelard marks each level with elements of poetic, musical, and rhetorical style that are calculated to teach, delight, and move his audience. The epideictic nature of *Virgines castae* and *Epithalamica* suggests that the sequences contain traditions and display modes of being already understood and accepted by the Paraclete nuns. The epideictic rhetoric of Abelard's sequences calls them to enter into the world the sequences reveal. Abelard crafted his sequence to reach this tropological end.

We shall now see that along with masterful use of the figures *anaphora*, *apostrophe*, *prosopopoeia*, *commutatio*, and *antithesis*, Abelard's efforts at achieving this goal included a distinct poetic and musical style.

4

WEAVING POETRY AND SONG

Duo autem fateor tibi specialiter inerant quibus feminarum quarumlibet animos statim allicere poteras, dictandi videlicet et cantandi gratia quae ceteros minime philosophos assecutos esse novimus.

You had besides, I admit, two special gifts whereby to win at once the heart of any woman—your gifts for composing verse and song, in which we know other philosophers have rarely been successful.

—*Heloise*[1]

WHEREAS ARRANGEMENT orders the invented *materia* to render it harmonious, *elocutio* ('style') supplies poem or prose with appropriate words and figures of speech and thought. Elocution was often described as the becoming garment of speech. Style begins with harmonious disposition and clothes the poem with embellishment and ornamentation. Hence, elocution occupied in rhetorical theory the middle place between invention and disposition, on the one side, and memory and delivery, on the other.

This chapter explores how Abelard arranged his sequences and their elocution, and offers hypotheses on their delivery. Within the sequences's poetic and musical shape and characteristic organizing features—whether overall form or internal structure—we shall discover an abelardian style intimately familiar to Heloise and her Paraclete nuns because it pervades the hymns and *planctus* Abelard wrote for them.

1. Muckle, 'Letters', 71–72; Radice, 115.

Teachers of rhetoric, from Aristotle and Cicero to Perelman and Olbrechts-Tyteca, have recognized that an author's careful arrangement and elocution of a discourse have great force in shaping the symbolic world of the audience, and of evoking a well–ordered social world—a goal that Abelard considered central to his role as spiritual adviser to Heloise and her nuns. The well-developed and refined elocution of *Virgines castae* and *Epithalamica* likely evoked authority for their author and his message. Their polished delivery would have been aimed at arousing *pathos*, the positive response of the Paraclete nuns to the sequences' discourse. By their poetic and musical shape Abelard, following the canons of rhetorical tradition and the goals of Scripture itself, worked not only to stimulate the nuns' minds, but also to touch the emotive and sensual depths of the nuns.

This analysis will further confirm Chrysogonus Waddell's hypothesis that the poetic and musical style of Abelard's hymns and *planctus* perfectly parallels those of the sequences. Indeed, it will thrust us toward the conclusion that, if Abelard did not write the sequences, then some one put great effort into mastering the many details of both Abelard's poetic and musical style. Of course, such a copyist may have existed; history does include great forgers. However, I will follow William of Ockham's old rule of parsimony in theorizing: Don't multiply entities beyond necessity. So many dimensions of the sequences work together in abelardian fashion that the simplest hypothesis for explaining the amazing likeness between *Virgines castae* and *Epithalamica* and Abelard's hymns and *planctus* is that Abelard composed the sequences.

Before plunging into the details of our analysis, we need to place *Virgines castae* and *Epithalamica* in the broader history of liturgical genres and the sequence genre. With this background we will be able better to discern the distinctive formal and structural features of the two sequences, and so often associated with Abelard's hymns and *planctus*.

THE SEQUENCE AND LITURGICAL GENRES

For some time now medievalists and literary theorists have debated the status and meaning of the concept of 'genre'.[1] Here I am concerned with medieval 'liturgical genre' and by such a term refer to the prose and poetry 'that formed the spectrum of liturgical lyric that audiences clearly perceived as distinct in some important way or ways form other groups of poems'.[2] Table IV.1, adapted from William Flynn's study of the liturgical trope, shows the place of the sequence in the musical and textual forms of medieval liturgy at around the time of Abelard.

Table IV.1:
The Spectrum of Prose and Poetic Genres in Abelard's Day[3]

PROSE	POETRY
	Parallel stiches (Psalmody, Canticles)
Rhythmic cadences (Sermon, Oratory)	Rhythmic stiches & Prose stiches combined (Tropes)
Prose stiches (Most chant forms)	Parallel stiches with coordinated number & assonance (Early Sequence)
Prose or Narrative (Public Reading with coordinated /Cantillation)	Parallel stiches with number, rhyme, & often accent (Late Sequence)
Ordinary Speech (Conversation)	Stanzas with organization of number, rhyme, & accent (Hymn)

1. See Diehl, *Lyric*, 58.
2. *Ibid*.
3. Flynn, Tropes' 182.

Table IV.1 demonstrates that poetic syntax increases in prominence as one moves from the prose of ordinary conversational
speech to the highly—organized poetic syntax of the hymn genre.
The sequence genre is a sub-genre of liturgical poetry. Scholars
generally agree that as the medieval sequence developed it went
through three discernable stages, an early, middle, and late period. Though all sequences share certain characteristics, early,
middle, and late sequences do all have their own special
characteristics.

The origin of the sequence is hidden in the past, and scholars
have long debated the genre's origin.[4] Researchers do know that
by the ninth century these long Latin chants were sung at Mass
on feast days after the Alleluia and its psalmodic verse, and before the reading of the Gospel.[5] The creation of some four thousand five hundred sequences between the ninth and fourteenth
centuries is a sign of the enthusiasm which the medieval church,
particularly in its monastic centers, had for these songs. Because
sequences were composed and performed over an extended period, their poetic and musical style, not surprisingly, shows some
identifiable development over the centuries. Indeed, scholars
commonly speak of the early and late sequence. In this study, I
follow Peter Dronke by distinguishing between the 'early', 'transitional', and 'late' sequence.[6]

Whatever the provenance and date of the first sequence,
manuscript evidence reveals that sequences appeared in the
Carolingian liturgy as early as the ninth century. These 'early'

4. Richard L. Crocker, *The Early Sequence* (Berkeley and Los Angeles: University of California Press, 1977) 1–26, traces the origins of the sequence genre to
frankish monastic artists who consciously cultivated the sacred song; C. Hohler,
reviewing Crocker's *Early Sequence* in the *Journal of the Plainsong & Mediæval
Music Society* 2 (1979) 65–67, argues for an italian, not a frankish, origin for the
sequence. In his 'The Beginnings of the Sequence', *Beiträge zur Geschichte der
deutschen Sprache und Literatur* 87 (1965) 43–73, Peter Dronke argues that the
genre has its roots in both secular and sacred song; see esp. p. 69.

5. Sequences also appeared elsewhere in the liturgy, especially as a substitute for the Vespers hymn.

6. Dronke, *'Virgines caste'*, 97.

sequences typically were long chants in a prose style, which took the form a, bb, cc, dd, . . . ww, x. That is, they usually began and ended with a single line (a, x) between which were four or more double-line stanzas. Each couplet had its own distinct pattern of syllable accentuation. The single lines and couplets were usually set syllabically to their own melody; one note was given to each syllable of the text. The music mirrored the textual structure; there was a single melody at the beginning and the end, and a repeated melody for each of the double stanzas: a, bb, cc, dd, . . . ww, x. Most importantly, writes Patrick S. Diehl,

> The common denominator relating all of these ninth-century poetic structures is that they are a way of setting prose to music and that they are asymmetrical, to a greater or lesser degree. The first is simply an extension of the setting of Scripture to music, at least in Greek and Latin, where even the Psalter has been turned into prose. The second suggests a desire to replace the regularities of the Ambrosian hymn (or perhaps other sorts of strophic song, including the vernacular) with a structure closer to the structure of plainchant and art-prose (which was more 'classical' in fact than hymnody was) and royal acclamations. In itself, the contrast between conventional Latin poetic forms and the new song of the sequence must have been an important source of artistic effect.[7]

By the eleventh century, liturgical poets were slowly beginning to cultivate a new artistic effect in their sequences: rhymed, accentual latin poetry began to appear in sequence repertories. Many sequences from this time show an avoidance of stressed rhyme; i.e., their individual stanzas seldom have final accented syllables that rhyme. The eleventh century marked the advent of ever increasing rhyme, albeit 'half', and increased concern with accentuation in sequence composition. These changes tended to reshape both the texts and the melodies of the sequence genre. Still, the textual and musical symmetrical form (a, bb, cc,

7. Diehl, *Lyric* 83–84.

dd . . . ww, x) persisted. The couplets of most eleventh-century sequences also continued to reflect the general lack of uniformity in line-length characteristic of the early style. Scholars have characterized this 'mixed' style chant as the 'transitional' or 'intermediate' sequence.

A kind of geographical upheaval occurs in the world of the eleventh-century sequence that left no aspect of the genre untouched. By the twelfth century, the 'late' sequence had arisen, marked by regular, rhyming lines of accentual latin verse. The early prose sequence with its lines of varying length and structure was gone. Also gone were the single lines that had begun and ended past sequences. The new chant's syllable and accentual patterns were regularized and now conformed to a fairly small number of popular patterns (aabccb). Their meter was typically trochaic tetrameter (/./././.), with the third and sixth lines of individual strophes shortened by one syllable. The poetry of the late sequence was strophic. Hence, writes Diehl, 'many sequences . . . look[ed] exactly like hymns of the same period: a series of trimly rhymed trochaic stanzas of four, six, or eight lines of alternately eight and seven syllables that are all perfectly identical in form'.[8]

With this new regular syntax, a great fault line emerges between the text and music: in the twelfth-century sequence the music does not parallel the rhyme scheme aabccb. Yet sequence poets and composers tend to preserve the paired couplet structure characteristic of the early sequence by rhyming the ends of each half-stanza. Furthermore, they set the paired half-strophes to the same music, retaining in the music the pair-wise progress of the early sequence form (aa, bb, cc, dd, . . .). Notwithstanding the asymmetry between textual and musical rhyme, composers do manage to preserve something of the couplet structure of the pre-twelfth-century sequence.

Much scholarly energy has gone into studying the evolving poetry and musical form of the sequence genre, but only recently

8. *Ibid.*, 88–89.

has serious attention been given to the function of the sequence in the liturgy. As we saw in Chapter Two, Nancy van Deusen has argued that the sequence was a 'transitional song, a copula between the Old and the New Testaments'.[9] In the Mass the sequence occurs between the Old Testament song—Alleluia and its Psalm—and the New Testament song—the Gospel. Van Deusen writes, 'joined to the Alleluia, connected on the other hand to the Gospel, sequences included allusions to both and thereby provided a copulation between the two'.[10] Van Deusen is correct about the transitionary role of the sequence. In Chapter Two we saw that the transitionary function of Abelard's sequences goes beyond movement from the Old Testament to the New; his sequences produce a transition from the Old Testament to the Gospel (New Testament) by way of the Church Fathers to the world of the Paraclete nuns and Abbess Heloise.

As we consider how Abelard's known poetic and musical styles are reflected in *Virgines castae* and *Epithalamica*, we shall keep in mind the above sketch of the sequence genre's history and characteristics. As our analysis progresses over the next three chapters we will consider where the two sequences fit into and where they depart from the above sketch of the genre's history and function. We turn now to the poetic dimensions of the two sequences.

ABELARD'S SEQUENCES AS MEDIEVAL POETRY

Every medieval student began his study of poetic and musical forms and structures within his broader study of grammar. Abelard's early education very likely followed that of most medieval french students. All study began with grammar, which was divided into three stages.

---

9. 'The Use and Significance of the Sequence', *Musica Disciplina* 40 (1986) 5–47; quotation p. 24.

10. *Ibid.*, p. 22.

First, young students (starting at around the age of seven) were required to memorize vast passages of chanted Scripture for use in the liturgy. This also provided them with a working vocabulary of ecclesiastical Latin. Second, they studied the parts of speech and the rules of pronunciation and accent. This completed their elementary education, which equipped them to participate in the liturgy and to carry out the administrative tasks of the cathedral. Third, at some time between the ages of fourteen and eighteen, they studied advanced grammar, including the theory of ornamental language, which provided them with a foundation for studying the other liberal arts, and with a facility for understanding and appreciating more difficult and ambiguous language. The goal of this more advanced study was to gain a thorough knowledge of Scripture, which they acquired by directed reading of commentaries, starting with those of the book of Psalms. Finally, they could demonstrate their own mastery by adding to the scriptural glosses, by preaching, or by writing religious poetry.[11]

By the days of Abelard's youth, medieval grammar had become a subject of considerable complexity. Beyond the study of parts of speech and syntax, it included the analysis of such external features of poetic texts as rhyme, meter, diction, stanza structure, line length, and organizing schemes. It also included what today is typically called 'literature'. Students were taught to interpret existing literary works, especially the Scriptures. 'Ultimately', writes James Murphy, '[grammar] came to include a wide variety of linguistic subject matters, including not only syntax but metrics, rhythmics, modes of signification, and such 'rhetorical' matters as the arrangement of parts of discourse.'[12] Medieval grammar examined written and spoken discourse from its simplest components to its most complex structures. Such

11. Flynn, 'Tropes', 18–19.

12. James J. Murphy, *Rhetoric in the Middle Ages: A History of Rhetorical Theory from St. Augustine to the Renaissance* (Berkeley: University of California Press, 1974) 138. Murphy's work has been greatly advanced by two works: Copeland *Rhetoric*, see esp. 9–62; and Carruthers, *Memory*.

study was conducted for the final purpose of providing the student with the basic techniques necessary for understanding and commenting upon such non-scriptural texts as commentaries, hymns, and sequences, as well as Scripture.

Our concern here is mainly with the third stage of Abelard's grammatical training, the stage at which, as Flynn indicates, the student was plunged into the depths of 'ornamental language'. Analyzing the ornamental language of Scripture and using this language in prose and poetry required the student to gain a thorough knowledge of the 'poetic devices which were considered rhetorically effective and aesthetically pleasing'.[13] By the time Abelard entered this third stage of grammatical study, he was treading on the doorstep of rhetoric—the art of composing prose and poetry. At this stage grammar students were exposed to exercises in which they were required to craft short speech compositions, two of which were the *chreia* elaboration and the *expolitio*. Before composing these 'speeches', the student had first to demonstrate his ability to identify and create such poetic devices as 'schemes' and 'tropes'—all of which were components of extended discourse. Poetic form is rhetorically important because it helps to create an ordered world, to stimulate memory of the poetic discourse, and to provide aesthetic dimensions to speech that reach deep within the emotional and sensual being of an audience.

THE POETIC FORM OF *VIRGINES CASTAE* AND *EPITHALAMICA*

A cursory reading of *Virgines castae* and *Epithalamica* reveals that they share a characteristic use of half-rhyme (HR) and avoidance of regular accentuation except at caesuras and line endings. Abelard uses such schematic or figural repetition to ornament and give poetic form to the *materia* of his sequences. In Tables IV.2 and IV.3 below, I have analyzed the rhyme and accentuation of each sequence, designating lines with an interior caesura or minor articulation by a compound formula such as '6 + 6' to

13. Flynn, 'Tropes', 83.

Peter Abelard after Marriage

signify that the phrase consists of twelve syllables, with a caesura after the sixth syllable. The complexity of the stanzaic structure of both songs can be seen in the poet's variation of line lengths and his alternation between line-ending words with accent on either the antepenultimate or penultimate syllable, that is, on either the proparoxytone (ppo) or paroxytone (po). We shall refer to these two Tables repeatedly throughout this chapter. Our first concern is with the manifold use of half-rhyme (or monosyllabic rhyme) throughout the sequences. Then we shall consider their 'irregular' accentuation and complex strophic structure. Finally, the musical setting of the sequence texts will receive our full attention.

Table IV.2:
Poetic Features of *Virgines castae*

Text	Strophic Form	Incise Rhyme	Line Ending Rhyme	Last Word Accent
1a. *Virgines caste*		a (HR)		
virginis summe		a (HR)		
decus praecinentes	5+5+6	b (HR)	A (HR)	po
1b. *Ceteras quoque*		a (HR)		
condignas laude		a (HR)		
post hanc venerantes	5+5+6	b (HR)	A (HR)	po
2a. *Psalmis et hymnis*		a (HR)		
canticis dignis		a (HR)		
sibi colloquentes	5+5+6	b (HR)	A (HR)	po
2b. *Solvant in istis*		a (HR)		
debitae laudis		a (HR)		
hostias sollemnes	5+5+6	b (HR)	A (HR)	po
3a. *Haec est adextris*		a (HR)		
assistens regis		a (HR)		
illa regina	5+5+5	b (HR)	A (HR)	po

(Continued)

Table IV.2:
Poetic Features of *Virgines castae*, cont.

Text	Strophic Form	Incise Rhyme	Line Ending Rhyme	Last Word Accent
3b. *Iuncta latere*		c (HR)		
sola cum rege		c (HR)		
praecedit ipsa	5+5+5	b (HR)	A (HR)	po
3c. *Aurata veste*		c (HR)		
varietate		c (HR)		
circiumamicta	5+5+5	b (HR)	A (HR)	po
3d. *Tamquam*				
dominam		d (HR)		
sequitur ipsam		d (HR)		
queque beata	5+5+5	b (HR)	A (HR)	po
4a. *Post eam*				
adductae		a (HR)		
virgines devotae	6+6	a (HR)	A	po
4b. *regi sunt oblatae*		a (HR)		
Christo consecratae	6+6	a (HR)	A	po
4c. *Tales erant Thecla*		a (HR)		
Agnes et Lucia	6+6	a (HR)	B	po
4d. *Agathes et multa*		a (HR)		
virginum caterva	6+6	a (HR)	B	po
5a. *Filiae Tyri*		b (HR)	A	po
munera ferentes	5+6	c (HR)		
5b. *Et in his regis*		b (HR)	A	po
vultum deprecantes	5+6	c (HR)		
5c. *Hostias cunctis*		b (HR)	A	po
habent puriores	5+6	d (HR)		
5d. *Corpore munde*		b (HR)	A	po
Corde sanctiores	5+6	d (HR)		
6a. *Holocaustum*				
Domino	7+7	a (HR)		po
Offerent ex integro	7+7	a (HR)		po

(Continued)

Table IV.2:
Poetic Features of *Virgines castae*, cont.

Text	Strophic Form	Incise Rhyme	Line Ending Rhyme	Last Word Accent
6b. *virgines carne*	5+5	b (HR)		po
integrae mente	5+5	b (HR)		po
6c. *immortalem*				
sponsum	6+6	c (HR)		po
eligentes Christum	6+6	c (HR)		po
7a. *O felices nuptiae*	7+7	a (HR)		po
quibus nullae				
maculae	7+7	a (HR)		po
7b. *nulli dolores*	5+5	b (HR)		po
partus sunt graves	5+5	b (HR)		po
7c. *nec pelex timenda*	6+6	c (HR)		po
nec nutrix molesta	6+6	c (HR)		po
8a. *Lectulos harum*				
Christo vacantes	5+5		A (HR)	po
8b. *angeli vallant*				
custodientes	5+5		A (HR)	po
8c. *ne quis incestus*				
temeret illos	5+5		B (HR)	po
8d. *ensibus strictis*				
arcent immundos	5+5		B (HR)	po
9a. *Dormit in istis*				
Christus cum illis	5+5		A (HR)	po
9b. *felix hic somnus*				
requires dulcis	5+5		A (HR)	po
9c. *quo cum fovetur*				
virgo fidelis	5+5		A (HR)	po
9d. *inter amplexus*				
sponsi caelestis	5+5		A (HR)	po

(Continued)

Table IV.2:
Poetic Features of *Virgines castae*, cont.

Text	Strophic Form	Incise Rhyme	Line Ending Rhyme	Last Word Accent
10a. *Dextera sponsi* *sponsa complexa*	5+5		A (HR)	po
10b. *capiti laeva* *dormit submissa*	5+5		A (HR)	po
10c. *pervigil corde* *corpore dormit*	5+5		B (HR)	po
10d. *et sponsi grato* *sinu quiescit*	5+5		B (HR)	po
11a. *Approbans somnum* *Sponsus beatam*	5+5		A (HR)	po
11b. *inquietari* *prohibet illam*	5+5		A (HR)	po
11c. *ne suscitetis* *inquit, dilectam*	5+5		A (HR)	po
11d. *dum ipsa volet* *ita quietam*	5+5		A (HR)	po
12a. *Hic ecclesiastici* *flos est ille germinis*	7+7	b (HR)	A (HR)	ppo
12b. *tam rosis* *quam liliis* *multiplex* *innumeris*	7+7	b (HR)	A (HR)	ppo
12c. *quorum est* *fragrantiis* *ager sponsi nobilis*	7+7	b (HR) b (HR) b (HR)	A (HR)	ppo
12d. *naribus et oculis* *aeque delectabilis*	7+7	b (HR) b (HR)	A (HR)	ppo

(Continued)

Table IV.2:
Poetic Features of *Virgines castae*, cont.

Text	Strophic Form	Incise Rhyme	Line Ending Rhyme	Last Word Accent
13a. *Ornatae tam byssina*		a (HR)		
quam veste purpurea	7+7	a (HR)	A (HR)	po
13b. *laeva tenent lilia*		a (HR)		
rosas habent dextera	7+7	a (HR)	A (HR)	po
13c. *et corona gemmea*		a (HR)		
redimitae capita	7+7	a (HR)	A (HR)	ppo
13d. *agni sine macula*		a (HR)		
percurrunt itinera	7+7	a (HR)	A (HR)	ppo
14a. *His quoque floribus*		a (HR)		
semper recentibus	6+6	a (HR)	A (HR)	po
14b. *sanctorum intexta*		b (HR)		
capitum sunt serta	6+6	b (HR)	B (HR)	po
14c. *His agnus*				po
pascitur		c (HR)		
atque reficitur	6+6	c (HR)	C (HR)	
14d. *hi flores electa*		b (HR)		
sunt illius esca	6+6	b (HR)	B (HR)	po
15a. *Hinc choro talium*		a (HR)		
vallatus agminum	6+6	a (HR)	A (HR)	po
15b. *hortorum amena*		b (HR)		
discurrit hac illac	6+6		B (HR)	po
15c. *Qui nunc comprehensus*		c (HR)		
ab his, nunc elapsus	6+6	c (HR)	C (HR)	po

(Continued)

Table IV.2:
Poetic Features of *Virgines castae*, cont.

Text	Strophic Form	Incise Rhyme	Line Ending Rhyme	Last Word Accent
15d. *quasi quadam*				
fuga		b (HR)		
petulans exsultat	6+6	d (HR)	D (HR)	po
16a. *Crebros saltus*		a (HR)		
dat hic agnus		a (HR)		
inter illas				
discurrendo	4+4+8	b (HR)	A (HR)	po
16b. *Et cum ipsis*				
requiescit				
fervore meridiano	4+4+8	b (HR)	A (HR)	po
17a. *In earum pectore*		a (HR)		
cubat in meridie	7+7	a (HR)	A (HR)	po
17b. *Inter mammas*				
virginum		b (HR)		
Collocat cubiculum	7+7	b (HR)	B (HR)	po
18a. *Virgo quippe*		a (HR)		
cum sit ipse		a (HR)		
Virgineque matre				
natus	4+4+8	b (HR)	A (HR)	po
18b. *Virginales*		c (HR)		
super omnes		c (HR)		
amat et quaerit				
recessus	4+4+8	b (HR)	A (HR)	po
19a. *Somnus illi*				
placidus		a (HR)		
in castis est sinibus	7+7	a (HR)	A (HR)	po
19b. *Ne qua forte*				
macula		b (HR)		
sua foedet vellera	7+7	b (HR)	B (HR)	po

(Continued)

Table IV.2:
Poetic Features of *Virgines castae*, cont.

Text	Strophic Form	Incise Rhyme	Line Ending Rhyme	Last Word Accent
20a. *Hoc attende*				
canticum		a (HR)		
devotarum				
virginum		a (HR)		
insigne collegium	7+7+7	a (HR)	A	po
20b. *Quo nostra*				
devotio		b (HR)		
maiore se studio		b (HR)		
templum ornet				
Domino	7+7+7	b (HR)	B	po

Table IV.3:
The Poetic Structure of *Epithalamica*

Text	Strophic Form	Incise Rhyme	Line Ending Rhyme	Last Word Accent
1a. *Epithalamica*		a (HR)		
dic Sponsa cantica	6+6	a (HR)	A (HR)	ppo
1b. *intus quae conspicis*				
dic foris gaudia	6+6		A (HR)	ppo
1c. *et nos laetificans de Sponso nuntia*	6+6		A (HR)	ppo
1d. *cuius te refovet seper praesentia*	6+6		A (HR)	ppo
2a. *Adulescentulae vos chorum ducite*	6+6		A (HR)	ppo
2b. *cum haec praecinerit et vos succinite*	6+6		A (HR)	ppo
2c. *Amici Sponsi vos vocarunt nuptiae*	6+6	a (HR) b (HR)	B (HR)	ppo
2d. *et novae modulos optamus Dominae*	6+6	a (HR) b (HR)	B (HR)	ppo
3a. *In montibus his ecce saliens*	5+5		A (HR)	ppo
3b. *ecce venit colles transilens*	5+5		A (HR)	ppo
3c. *per fenestras ad me respiciens*	5+5		A (HR)	ppo
3d. *per cancellos dicit prospiciens*	5+5		A (HR)	ppo

(Continued)

Table IV.3:
The Poetic Structure of *Epithalamica*, cont.

Text	Strophic Form	Incise Rhyme	Line Ending Rhyme	Last Word Accent
4a. *Amica surge propera*	5+5		B (HR)	ppo
4b. *columba nitens advola*	5+5		B (HR)	ppo
5a. *Horrens enim hiems iam transiit*	5+5		A (HR)	ppo
5b. *gravis imber recedens abiit*	5+5		A (HR)	ppo
5c. *ver amoenum terras aperuit*	5+5		A (HR)	ppo
5d. *parent flores et turtur cecinit*	5+5		A (HR)	ppo
6a. *Amica surge propera*	5+5		B (HR)	ppo
6b. *columba nitens advola*	5+5		B (HR)	ppo
7a. *Rex in accumbitum iam se contulerat*	6+6		A	ppo
7b. *et mea redolens nardus spiraverat*	6+6		A	ppo
7c. *in hortum veneram in quem descenderat*	6+6		A	ppo
7d. *at ille transiens iam declinaverat*	6+6		A	ppo

(Continued)

Table IV.3:
The Poetic Structure of *Epithalamica*, cont.

Text	Strophic Form	Incise Rhyme	Line Ending Rhyme	Last Word Accent
8a. *Per noctem igitur hunc quaerens exeo*	6+6		A (HR)	ppo
8b. *huc illuc anxia quaerendo cursito*	6+6		A (HR)	ppo
8c. *occurrunt vigiles ardenti studio*	6+6		A (HR)	ppo
8d. *quos cum transierim Sponsum invenio*	6+6		A (HR)	ppo
9a. *Iam video quod optaveram*	4+5		A (HR)	ppo
9b. *iam tenco quod amaveram*	4+5		A (HR)	ppo
9c. *iam redo quae sic fleveram*	4+5		A (HR)	ppo
9d. *plus gaudeo quam dolueram*	4+5		A (HR)	ppo
10a. *Risi mane flevi nocte*	4+5	a (HR)	A (HR)	
10b. *mane risi nocte flevi*	4+5	b (HR)	B (HR)	
11a. *Noctem insomnem dolor duxerat*	5+5		A (HR)	ppo
11b. *quem vehemetem amor*	5+5		A (HR)	ppo
fecerat	5+5		A (HR)	ppo
11c. *dilatione votum creverat*	5+5		A (HR)	ppo

Table IV.3:
The Poetic Structure of *Epithalamic*, cont.

(Continued)

Text	Strophic Form	Incise Rhyme	Line Ending Rhyme	Last Word Accent
11d. *donec amantem aman*				
vistat	5+5		A (HR)	ppo
12a. *Plausus die planctus*				
nocte	5+5	a (HR)	A (HR)	
12b. *die plausus nocte*				
planctus	5+5	b (HR)	B (HR)	
13a. *Eia nunc comites*				
et Sion filiae	6+6		A (HR)	ppo
13b. *ad Sponsae contica*				
psalmum adnectite	6+6		A (HR)	ppo
13c. *quo moestis reddita*				
Sponsi praesentia	6+6		B (HR)	ppo
13d. *convertit elegos*				
nostros in cantica	6+6		B (HR)	pp

The columns marked 'Incise Rhyme' and 'Line Ending Rhyme' indicate the presence of half-rhyme. Let us examine more closely stanza twelve of *Virgines castae* (syllables in capital letters are accented) and its half-rhyme (HR):

Table IV.4:
Rhyme and Accentuation

Hic	ec-	CLE-	si-	AS-	ti-	ci	flos	est	IL-	le	GER-	mi-	nis,
tam	RO-	sis	quam	LI-	li-	is	MUL-	ti-	plex	in-	NU-	me-	ris,
QUO-	rum	est	fra-	GRAN-	ti-	is	A-	ger	SPON-	si	NO-	bi-	lis,
NA-	ri-	bus	et	O-	cu-	lis	E-	que	de-	lec-	TA-	bi-	lis.

As in lines one and two of this example, most stanzas of the two sequences are characterized by half-rhyme; only the final unaccented syllables of the four lines rhyme. The sequences have no stressed rhyme (disyllabic rhyme); i.e., their final accented syllables and following syllable(s) seldom rhyme. In the last two lines of stanza 12 (Table IV.4) the unstressed penultimate and final syllables rhyme; but again the accented syllable (capitalized) does not rhyme.

Half-rhymes

The use of half-rhyme except at caesuras (incises) and line endings and the occasional rhyming of the unstressed penultimate and final syllables was not characteristic of the sequences composed by Abelard's contemporaries such as Adam of Saint Victor.[14] Adam's sequences eventually set the standard for the genre and ushered in what scholars often portray as the golden age of the sequence. But the pervasive use of half-rhyme observed in *Virgines castae* and *Epithalamica* was a feature of the so-called 'intermediate' sequence, the type of sequence Peter Dronke considers more likely datable before 1100.

Yet Dronke himself has pointed out that Abelard's six *planctus*, composed in the 1130s, are the chief exception to the studied

14. Abelard was born in 1079; Adam of Saint Victor, whose date of birth is not known, flourished *c.* 1130. For details on Adam's life see Margot E. Fassler, 'Who Was Adam of St. Victor? The Evidence of the Sequence Manuscripts,' *Journal of the American Musicological Society* 37 (1984) 233–269.

use of stressed rhyme so characteristic of the late-sequence style that emanated from the victorine canons.[15] The twelfth-century Victorines, with their use of two-syllable and three-syllable accentual rhyme, were setting the pattern for the twelfth-century sequence. Abelard, by contrast, remained his own man. In his hands the *planctus*, typically a non-liturgical song of lamentation in sequence form, continues the style of the intermediate sequence. Dronke's observations regarding Abelard's avoidance of stressed rhyme in his *planctus* is no less true of his hymns.[16] Similarly, Diehl's study of medieval religious lyric shows that Abelard's hymns, when compared with twelfth-century hymns, are characterized by 'the old-fashioned austerity of monosyllabic rhyme'[17] Dronke has also ventured to speculate that Abelard might have wished to continue this old practice. He writes, 'Abelard may indeed have chosen this as an archaizing technique, one of his many ways of setting these compositions apart from the Parisian repertoire of the time'[18]

The reason Abelard used this 'archaizing technique' of half-rhyme may ultimately lie in his inveterate need to be master of his own school of thought and practice. Perhaps he inherited a love of battle and relish of praise from his knightly father; indisputably he had a passion for vanquishing his intellectual rivals. He tells us in his *Historia calamitatum* that he engaged more than one of his own teachers in public disputation, discrediting their teachings and dishonoring their reputation.[19] Perhaps, even after he had lost all in Paris and entered the monastic life, his ambitious nature would not allow him to follow the victorine sequence style. He had to place his own mark on the hymn, *planctus*, and, I would maintain, the sequence.

---

15. *'Virgines caste'*, 97–98.

16. Chrysogonus Waddell, CLS 8:42.

17. Diehl, *Lyric*, 94.

18. *'Virgines caste'*, 97.

19. *Historia Calamitatum*, Muckle, 'Consolation', 177–183; English in Radice, 58–65.

Abelard's three Prefaces to his *Hymnarius Paraclitensis* and his *Letter Ten* to Bernard of Clairvaux reveal that both he and Heloise were very knowledgeable about past and present musical and liturgical practices in the Church, and very keen on shaping their future use in the Church, especially at the Paraclete. In Preface One Abelard voices four complaints against current customs in hymn singing—problems that Heloise had pointed out to him in earlier correspondence:[20] too many hymns are anonymous and therefore without authority; authenticity requires that a hymn be traceable to an acknowledged authority. Similarly, the 'Gallican Psalter' so widely used among monastics and clerics had, in their opinion, no authority. No one knew who had translated it, yet the latin translation of the hebrew psalter by the authority of authorities, Saint Jerome, was readily at hand and should be used.[21] So some hymns and the Gallican Psalter had custom, but not authority, behind them; and by Abelard's and Heloise's reasoning, authority is always to be preferred to custom.[22]

The second argument in the preface rails against such well-known authorities as Hilary, Ambrose, and Prudentius who had left the Church poems that some people, in Abelard's opinion, have wrongly assumed were true hymns.[23] Following Augustine's definition of a 'hymn' as *laus Dei cum cantico* ('the praise of God with song'), Abelard (echoing Heloise) declares the work of these authorities unsingable; and if they are unsingable, they are not hymns. What makes them unsingable? They are full of elisions; by counting two syllables as one, many early christian poets preserved the metrical or rhythmical patterns of their poems. But by the twelfth century, the use of elision in venerable hymn texts seems to have been either misunderstood or little admired. '[M]onks *must* have understood the principles of elision well enough, schooled as many of them were in the dangerous

---

20. PL 178:1772; also in HP 2: 9. English in Freeland, *Hymns,* 31.

21. PL 178:1772; also in HP 2: 10. English in Freeland, *Hymns,* 31.

22. For a discussion of the material from Abelard's Prefaces from the perspective of Heloise, see Constant Mews, *Lost Love,* 160–161.

23. PL 178:1773; also in HP 2: 11. English in Freeland, *Hymns,* 32.

splendors of classical Latin poetry,' writes Waddell, 'but the evidence shows that they refused to chant a ten-syllable line as an eight-syllable line, even though the rhythmic pattern called for only eight syllables.'[24] Third, the *Hymnarius* complains that there simply are not enough authoritative hymns to meet the needs of the entire liturgical year. [25] Finally, too many of the authoritative hymns in use are sung at the wrong time; their texts clearly make them appropriate for day or night use, yet many monastic institutions are indifferent to their author's original intentions.[26] With his *Hymnarius Paraclitensis* Abelard intended to correct these problems, at least at the Paraclete.

Abelard's wide knowledge of the liturgical and musical practices is demonstrated again by exploring his *Letter Ten* to Bernard; here he shows himself fully informed about the early cistercian liturgy and alleges against Bernard's criticism of certain innovations at Heloise's Paraclete 'an elenchus of Cistercian liturgical novelties'.[27] Peter Dronke's suggestion that Abelard consciously cultivated a poetic style that set his hymns, *planctus*, and, I would add, sequences apart from the poetic style of such contemporaries as the Victorines has great merit. His sacred music (under the influence of Heloise) was pressed from a vineyard like no other in France; words and melody combined to create a savour and bouquet set apart as the recognizable harvest of Abelard's labors.

To sum up: *Virgines castae* and *Epithalamica* are permeated with the half-rhyme so characteristic of the intermediate sequence. A study of this half-rhyme in his *planctus* and hymns helps us place *Virgines castae* and *Epithalamica* in the abelardian

24. 'Saint Bernard of Clairvaux at the Abbey of the Paraclete', *The Chimaera of His Age: Studies on Bernard of Clairvaux*, CS 63 (Kalamazoo, 1980) 76–121; quotation on p. 103.

25. PL 178:1773; also in HP 2: 9–12. English in Freeland, *Hymns,* 33.

26. PL 178:1773; also in HP 2: 9–12. English in Freeland, *Hymns,* 33.

27. Waddell, 'Peter Abelard's *Letter 10* and Cistercian Liturgical Reform,' in *Studies in Medieval Cistercian History, II.*, ed. John R. Sommerfeldt, CS 24 (Kalamazoo, 1976) 75–86, quotation at 80.

milieu of the Paraclete. The two sequences abound in 'the old-fashioned austerity of monosyllabic rhyme' because Abelard composed them.[28]

ACCENTUATION

Rhyme is not all that links the sequences to Abelard's hymns and *planctus*. Table IV.4, above, also reflects Abelard's 'regular' use of 'irregular' accentuation. As Chrysogonus Waddell has observed: 'Abelard carefully safeguards the regularity of accentuation in the case of the line-endings, but in the preceding syllables lets the accents fall where they happen to fall.'[29]

The strophic pattern of stanza twelve (Table IV.4) consists of four fourteen-syllable lines, with a caesura after each seventh syllable and a proparoxytone (two unstressed syllables) at the end of each line. The accentuation of each line scans as follows:

Table IV.5: Abelardian Accentuation

```
. . / . / . .      . . / . / . .
. / . . / . .      / . . . / . .
/ . . . / . .      / . / . / . .
/ . . . / . .      / . . . / . .
```

Each stanza of *Virgines castae* shows this same deliberate effort to maintain regular rhythmic accents (/..) at each caesura and at the end of each line. The accentuation of each line of the sequence further reveals that Abelard was not concerned to make the accents preceding the caesura and the line endings regular. The steady alteration of accented (/) and unaccented (.) syllables is simply not characteristic of *Virgines castae* or *Epithalamica*.

The strophic structure of the two sequences also bears the mark of Abelard's preoccupation with varied strophic forms.

28. Diehl, *Lyric*, 95; he uses these words to describe the rhyme of Abelard's hymn collection.
29. CLS 8:32.

Tables IV.2 and IV.3 show the variety and the distribution of the sequence's meter. I have designated lines with an interior incise or caesura by a compound formula such as '6 + 6,' signifying that the phrase consists of twelve syllables, with a caesura after the sixth syllable.

The strophic demarcation of each section of *Virgines castae* is unusual among sequences, as the following examples demonstrate. Consider Table IV.2 (pp. 156ff), columns 2 through 4. The opening two strophes each consists of two sixteen-syllable lines and each sixteen-syllable line consists of three incises (5+5+6). Abelard has used an intricate rhyme-scheme to bind the four phrases together. The incises of each couplet rhyme, creating rhyme internal to each stanza. *Le Mestre* binds the two stanzas by rhyming the final syllable of each line. Only the final syllables of caesuras and lines rhyme. All of these figures give form and beauty to the sequences and most certainly were intended to appeal to and move the Paraclete nuns. Form and beauty seem to have been aimed at aesthetically reaching into depths of the nuns' feelings, sensations, and spirit, and thereby bringing not only their minds but also their bodies and souls into the world Abelard describes in the sequences.

Stanza three of *Virgines castae* shifts to four fifteen-syllable lines with three incises of five syllables each (5+5+5). The last syllables of each line rhyme (A-A-A-A), and, once again, Abelard binds each line internally with rhyming incises. As Table IV.2 shows, careful syllable enumeration and rhyme scheme continue throughout *Virgines castae*. One last example will demonstrate how Abelard's artful control and variation of rhyme helps keep the singer's attention. Stanzas nine through twelve share the same strophic form: a ten-syllable line with a caesura after the fifth syllable that is repeated in each line of the four stanzas. Abelard further weds the four stanzas by alternating between an AABB and an AAAA rhyme scheme. This time he makes no effort to rhyme the internal incises. The absence of this internal rhyme heightens the line-ending rhyme's role in unifying the four stanzas. Rhetorican David Cunningham's words nicely make my point: 'By getting the audience to appreciate the form in which a statement is cast, the speaker or writer will be better poised to interest the audience in identifying with the content of that statement.'[30]

The opening two strophes of the *Epithalamica* consist of four twelve-syllable lines in half rhyme (a-a-a-a) (see Table IV.3, pp. 163ff). Only the final syllables of the lines rhyme. The sequence shows none of the concern with internal rhyme between incises observed in *Virgines castae*. Stanzas three through six shift from two quatrains to two ten-syllable lines. Stanzas three and five have the rhyme a-a-a-a; stanzas four and six have the same eight-syllable rhyme, b-b. Stanzas seven and eight return to the twelve-syllable (6+6) lines of the first two strophes. The rhyme scheme of these quatrains is a-a-a-a. In stanza nine present-tense verbs mark the caesura in the nine-syllable (4+5) phrase, balancing the pluperfect verbs at the end. The result is rhyming at both caesura and at line end. Ten-syllable lines (5+5) of rhymed quatrain (a-a-a-a) constitute stanzas eleven and twelve. Stanza twelve forms a two-line refrain structured exactly like that of strophe ten, although with different words. Stanza thirteen is marked by the rhyme scheme a-a-b-b.

Chrysogonus Waddell has observed in the *Epithalamica* the same organizational technique we have already noticed in *Virgines castae*, and has shown that it is a characteristic feature of Abelard's sequence-like *planctus*.

> Each distinctive section has its own correspondingly distinctive strophic structure. Nothing like it is to be found so extensively and consistently in twelfth-century sequences of the more standard sort, where the strophic structure generally admits of relatively few variations. In the *planctus* as in the three sequences tentatively identified as Abelard's, the strophic forms vary considerably, corresponding to shifts in mood and the development of the text.[31]

30. David S. Cunningham, *Faithful Persuasion: In Aid of a Rhetoric of Christian Theology* (Notre Dame: University of Notre Dame Press, 1990) 46–47.
31. '*Epithalamica*', 259.

Abelard's concern with strophic forms is also apparent in his hymns. The strophic form of his individual hymns does not vary; the stanzas of a hymn by definition always have the same strophic form. What Abelard does is to give each group of hymns its own special strophic form. Consider, for example, the variety among the strophes of Abelard's hymns for Christmas, Epiphany, Easter, and Feasts of Virgins.

Christmas Cycle: Hymns 30-33

4 + 6   .   4 + 6   .   4 + 6   .   4 + 6

  a   a   b   b

Epiphany Cycle: Hymns 34-37

4 . 4 . 7 . 4 . 4 . 7

a   a   b   c   c   b

Easter Cycle: Hymns 42-45

7 . 7 . 7 . 6 . 7 . 6

a   b   a   c   a   c

Virgins Cycle: Hymns 92-95

4 + 7 . 4 + 7 . 4 + 7 . 4 + 7 . 4 + 5 . 4 + 5

  a   a   b   b   c   c

There is no repetition among Abelard's hymn cycles; each has its own strophic pattern.[32] 'No other body of medieval hymnody by a single author,' writes Chrysogonus Waddell,

> offers so rich a variety of strophic forms. Indeed, no other body of medieval hymnody contains more than a few instances of hymns whose strophic structures parallel any of those adopted by Abelard in this astonishing hymnic *tour de force*.'[33]

32. See CLS 8:24-27, for a complete listing of the strophic forms of each of Abelard's hymn cycles.
33. CLS 8:37.

Undoubtedly, strophic form distinguished Abelard's hymn cycles. The two sequences under investigation also show Abelard's sensitivity for strophic demarcation.

Our poetic analysis has shown that Abelard wraps the Paraclete world up in a poetic style that is distinct and unmistakable. He drew on a range of rhetorical devises in his effort to shape the nuns' symbolic world and to define Heloise's relationship to him. Yet his ability to nurture the Paraclete symbolic world was not limited to poetic style. In what follows, we shall consider how the music to which Abelard set the two sequences reinforces their form and articulates his vision for the nuns.

Musical Form, Structure, and Delivery

Abelard's masterful and distinctive handling of the poetic dimensions of *Virgines castae* and *Epithalamica* is equally present in the musical structure of each sequence. By medieval standards, Abelard was a very good composer of liturgical song. Although many of his sacred texts survive, only a few are extant with music. Scholars have long praised the musical setting he gave his hymn *O quanta qualia*. Equally laudable is the music for his *planctus Dolorum solatium*.[34] With *Virgines castae* and *Epithalamica* we have the opportunity further to appreciate his gifts as both poet and composer.

In fact, most medieval poets were composers and most composers were poets. Music and poetry went together like strings and a lyre; yet modern scholars have all too often underestimated their connection and equivalent importance. In recent years, however, Ritva Jonnson, Leo Treitler, Calvin Bower, and William Flynn have produced important studies that do indeed show deep connections between the text and the music of medieval liturgical

---

34. See Lorenz Weinrich, 'Peter Abaelard as Musician', *The Musical Quarterly* 55 (1969) 295–312 and 464–486. Beyond *Dolorum solatium* scholars have long known of five other *planctus* by Abelard. Unfortunately, these five *planctus* survive in staffless notation, so that the precise pitches of their melody cannot be determined.

chant.[35] Their insights provide a means of analyzing *Virgines castae* and *Epithalamica* that is grounded in the medieval disciplines of grammar and rhetoric. In the course of this chapter we shall see that, on the one hand, Abelard coordinated the musical syntax and textual syntax of his liturgical song so that the music articulated the syntactical structure of the text and thereby served effectively in proclaiming the meaning of the text; and, on the other, that he did not slavishly follow his sequences' linguistic syntax but created subtle associations between words and music, and gave both syntaxes a degree of independence. Through this independence, Abelard was able to create a musical syntax that encoded a particular reading of *Virgines castae* and *Epithalamica* that delivered the text both intelligibly and eloquently.

Like the rules that guided the sequences' poetry and music, so, too, there are boundaries that delineated Abelard's symbolic world. These rules are not intended to confine the nuns but to open to them a reality in which they can understand themselves. The sequences' poetic and musical syntax serve to characterize this world before the nuns; each syntax has its own manner of moving the nuns in their whole being. Sometimes the music and poetry work together, and other times each takes on its own mode of discourse. The interplay between words and music was central to medieval understandings of how to compose liturgical music.

Abelard's musical style shows his deep understanding of medieval music theory and composition. Music theorists from the ninth to the twelfth centuries had stressed the interconnection between text and music by their repeated recourse to the following *topos*: as individual letters are joined together to form syllables which in turn form words, and as words are linked together (by commas and colons) to form phrases and clauses which in turn

35. Ritva Jonnson and Leo Treitler, 'Medieval Music and Language: A Reconsideration of the Relationship', *Music and Language,* Studies in the History of Music, 1 (New York: Broude Brothers, 1983) 1–23; Calvin M. Bower, 'The Grammatical Model of Musical Understanding in the Middle Ages', *Hermeneutics and Medieval Culture,* ed. Patrick J. Gallacher and Helen Damico (Albany: State University of New York Press, 1989) 133–145; Flynn, 'Tropes', 76–185.

become complete sentences *(periodi),* so individual pitches *(voces)* are joined to form melodic gestures *(syllabae)* which in turn form subphrases (commas and colons), and these combine to make complete phrases *(distinctiones);* several such phrases join together to form a complete melody *(a periodus).*[36] Thus, musical *syllabae,* commas, colons, *distinctiones,* and *periodi* all play their proper role in articulating the musical syntax of a given mode.

As textual syntactic units are marked by punctuation, so, medieval theorists taught, musical syntax is marked by a mode's structural pitches. Theorists generally insisted that important structural points in the musical syntax should typically mark important structural points in the verbal syntax. Yet they also taught that a pause or cadence might mark significant musical gestures even where there was no such punctuation in the verbal syntax, and that punctuation in the verbal syntax might call for a pause to which the musical syntax might not correspond. Coordination of the syntaxes of music and words was the norm in liturgical chant, even though their independence was permitted in moderation.[37] Coordination seems to have been the norm in sequence composition, at least in the 'early' and 'intermediate' sequence. We have already observed many poetic features of *Virgines castae* and *Epithalamica* that place them in the 'intermediate' style; we shall now determine whether the music does much the same.

36. Bower, 'The Grammatical Model of Musical Understanding,' 136.

37. One might think this connection between text and music to be rather self-evident; indeed, Jonnson and Treitler write, 'everything we know of and about performed music in the early centuries of our recorded musical history centers on music sung with words—what was called *cantus'.* However, as they continue, fine music scholars like Howard Brown, Friedrich Blume, Ernest Sanders, and Richard Hoppins have written influential works claiming, in the words of Jonnson and Treitler, 'Medieval Music and Language', 1, that 'in the Middle Ages the relationship between music and language was at best minimal and that creating music which reflected its text was an achievement of the Renaissance'. This work includes (pp. 2–3) a list of works that have promoted the view that in medieval music words and melody coexisted but had little or no interaction.

Before plunging into the details of Abelard's two rather lengthy sequences, we shall consider how one medieval music theorist taught his students to analyze the relationship between music and verbal syntax. Known today only as John, this music theorist was a contemporary of Abelard. He provides a most coherent statement of the relationship between modal and verbal syntax:

> . . . just as in prose three kinds of *distinctiones* are recognized, which can also be called 'pauses'—namely, the colon, that is, 'member'; the comma or *incisio* and the period, *clausula* or *circuitus*—so also it is in chant. In prose, where one makes a pause in reading aloud, this is called a colon; when the sentence is divided by an appropriate punctuation mark, it is called a comma; when the sentence is brought to an end, it is a period. . . . Likewise, when a change makes a pause by dwelling on the fourth or fifth note above the final, there is a colon; when in mid-course it returns to the final, there is a comma; when it arrives at the final at the end, there is a period.[38]

John next proceeds to illustrate how musical syntax and verbal syntax are to be coordinated so that the melody properly cadences on notes that highlight the text's important divisions. Assuming that his reader has long had the text and music of his example memorized, John writes: 'So in the following antiphon: "Peter therefore" colon "was kept in prison" comma "but a prayer

---

38. *Sicut enim in prosa tres considerantur distinctines, quae in pausationes appellari possunt, scilicet collon id est membrum, comma, incisio, periodus clausura sive circuitus, ita et in cantu. In prosa quippe quando suspensive legitur, colon vocatur; quando per legitimum punctum sententia dividiture, comma, quando ad finem sententia deducitur, periodus est . . . Similiter cun cantus in quarta vel quinta a finali voce per suspensionem pausat, colon est; cum in medio ad finalem reducitur, comma est; cum in fine finalem pervenit periodus est.* Latin from Flynn, 'Tropes', 142, n. 17. English translation from Warren Babb, *Hucbald, Guido, and John on Music: Three Medieval Treatises* (New Haven: Yale University Press, 1978) 132–133.

was made" colon "for him without ceasing" comma "of the Church unto the Lord" period'.[39]

A modern reader—used to having the 'comma' mark a dependent clause and the 'colon' mark a independent phrase—may stumble at John's apparently odd reversal of the customary hierarchy of comma and colon. For the sake of clarity we shall use the modern hierarchy of colon and comma. Such liberty will not undermine John's point and it will allow us more easily to see the coordination among *syllabae*, commas, colons, *distinctiones*, and *periodi*. With the colon understood to mark an independent clause and the comma indicating a phrase, John's example now reads:

> So in the following antiphon, 'Peter therefore' comma 'was kept in prison' colon 'but a prayer was made' comma 'for him without ceasing' colon 'of the Church unto the Lord' period.

John is unequivocal in instructing that the structurally significant pitches of the mode should typically mark structurally important units of verbal syntax. His point is made clearer when both the text and music for his example are present. Although we do not have the exact variant of the antiphon *Petrus autem* that John had in mind, two closely related melodies (Example IV.6, a and b) survive that compare in many respects with John's example. These examples come from William Flynn's study of John's treatise.[40] Flynn also reverses John's use of colon and comma so as to preserve the ancient and modern hierarchy between the comma marking a clause and a colon marking a phrase.

---

39. Flynn, 'Tropes', 142. n.18; translation from Babb, *Hucbald, Guido, and John*, 132–133: *Petrus autem, colon; servabatur in carcere, comma; et oratio fiebat, colon; pro eo sine intermissione, comma; ab ecclesia ad Dominum, periodus.*

40. Flynn, 'Tropes', 143.

Peter Abelard after Marriage

Example IV.6: Antiphon

A. Pe - tus au - tem.
B. Pe - tus au - tem.

A. ser - va - ba - tur in car - ce - re:
B. ser - va - ba - tur in car - ce - re:

A. et o - ra - ti - o fi - e - bat,
B. o - ra - ti - o fi - e - bat,

A. si - ne in - ter - mis - si - o - ne:
B. pro e - o si - ne in - ter - mis - si - o - ne:

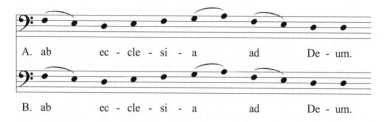

A. ab   ec - cle - si - a   ad   De - um.

B. ab   ec - cle - si - a   ad   De - um.

Like the version of the antiphon John had in mind, Flynn's examples are in the *protus* modality, the modern D mode. The structural tones of this mode are d, a, and f. D is the final; a, the fifth above or the fourth below the final; and f is the reciting tone, a third above the final. The fourth above the final, g, also has a kind of secondary structural importance in the authentic range of the *protus* modality. The c below the final is the flex of the mode and functions as a light cadential point. The following example (IV.7) gives the 'authentic' and 'plagal' forms of the D mode, the two forms of the *protus* modality, with their structural tones indicated. *Protus authenticus* starts with the final and extends to its upper *ambitus* or octave, while *protus plagis* starts a fourth below the final and extends to the fourth above the final. The tones and semitones that form the particular structure of the *protus* modality are the individual *voces* of the mode.

Example IV.7: The Protus Modality

protus authenticus   *protus plagis*

final   final

The structural tones of the D mode tend to encode songs in the *protus* modality with a particular musical syntax. Such musical marking cued the medieval singer as to which syntactic units were to stand alone and which were members of larger clauses.

In Flynn's two versions of *Petrus autem* (example IV.6), we can assume the same of John's variant: each musical setting of the antiphon has syntactic units (punctuated with **bold type** and labeled in the right-hand column) that can stand alone and units that cannot stand alone but are members of larger clauses. In these melodies, units that can stand alone cadence on the final, whereas those that cannot stand alone cadence on the fifth note above the final. Syntactic units that cannot stand alone in this antiphon could cadence on f, g, or c—all of which are structural tones that to varying degrees musically mark syntactic units in the *protus* mode. In lengthier chants, as we shall see in Abelard's sequences, the full range of cadential pitches is often used.[41]

Before we turn to *Virgines castae* and *Epithalamica*, we must consider one more dimension of medieval chant. As Calvin Bower has insisted, 'The full import of grammatical vocabulary in medieval theory is missed if it is viewed merely as a set of terms for analyzing a surface phrase structure independent of deeper, more basic musical meaning'.[42] Medieval theorists taught that the grammatical parts of text and music indicated which *voces* of a mode were to be lengthened so that they properly articulated syntactically significant points in the text and/or music. This theory of lengthening, called 'measured singing' *(numerose canere)*, prescribed that the last *vox* of (1) a syllable be slightly lengthened; (2) a *pars* (comma or colon) be lengthened more; (3) a distinction be even more extended; and (4) the period be held the longest. Further, some medieval theorists suggest that the lengthening of *syllabae, pars, distinctiones,* and *periodi* be proportional.[43] Thus, by recognizing a chant's mode, identifying its structurally significant pitches, and labeling the musical syntax with grammatical terms, one gets a clue as to its proper 'delivery' or performance.

41. John's theory of syntax does not work with every chant, but it is equally true that he does adumbrate a method of structuring melody that was the rule, not the exception, in singing and analyzing liturgical song in Abelard's day.
42. Bower, 'Grammatical Model of Musical Understanding', 138.
43. Bower, 'Grammatical Model of Musical Understanding', 140.

As we noted at the beginning of this chapter, delivery—or, as it was termed in Latin, *pronunciatio*—was the fifth and final part or species of rhetoric. Preparation for delivery occurred at the fourth part of rhetoric, appropriately called *memoria* ('memory'). No doubt, as the Paraclete nuns began to commit *Virgines castae* and *Epithalamica* to memory, the rhetorical development of their *materia*, the poetic ornamentation of their topics, the syntactical harmony between music and text, and the musical elaboration of structural pitches all combined to make the sequences easily memorable. An analysis of the textual syntax and musical syntax allows us to theorize as to how Abelard expected the nuns to sing the two songs.

In our analysis of the music of Abelard's sequences the following pattern will be used: First the text and music of the sequence will be presented with its grammatical units marked with bracketed capital letters, e.g. [A], and the musical punctuation indicated by bold type.[44] Detailed commentary will then follow. We will begin with *Virgines castae* and then move on to *Epithalamica*. Both sequences are in the *protus* modality; so we shall follow John's theory, identifying the structurally significant pitches of the sequences' melody and marking syllables with the letter s, subphrases (clauses) with a comma, *distinctiones* with a colon, and *periodi* with a period. Each period is indicated in the left-hand column as P 1, P 2, P 3, etc.

Careful analysis of the musical structure gives great insight into how the two sequences can be effectively delivered. By giving each cadential pitch its appropriate musical punctuation, the singer gains insight into how best to articulate the syntactical structure and meaning of the text. This articulation is effected by the singer giving each structural pitch its due proportional duration in respect to the period. Modern performers cannot know just what duration a period and its relative musical punctuation

---

44. Using William Flynn's suggestions, I have also indicated where the medieval hexachordal system would very likely have required the singer to flatten certain b's in the two sequences.

had in Abelard's day. No doubt, pitch length was fundamentally related to the singer's own culturally formed sense of how the text could be most clearly and persuasively delivered. By analyzing and performing melodies according to the principles set down by John, and other medieval theorists roughly contemporary with Abelard, one can perceive by both eye and ear the relationship between structural and nonstructural tones in a melody and determine the structural moments of melodies.[45]

45. Bower, 'The Grammatical Model of Musical Understanding', 143.

Virgines Castae

Virgines Castae

4a. Post e - am ad - duc - te: vir - gi - nes de - vo - te:

4b. re - gi sunt ob - la - te, chris - to con - se - cra - te.

4c. Tal - is e - rant Thec - la, Ag - nes et Luc - i - a:

4d. A - ga - thes ec mul - ta, vir - gi - num ca - ter - va.

5a. Fi - li - e ty - ri: mu - ne - ra fe - ren - tes.

5b. Et in his re - gis: vul - tum de - pre - can - tes.

5c. Hos - ti - as ba - bent: cunc - tis pu - ri - o - res.

5d. Cor - po - re mun - de: cor - do sanc - ti - o - res.

6a. ho - lo - caus - tum do - mi - no, of - fe - runt ex in - teg - ro,

Virgines Castae

6b. vir - gi - nes car - ne, in - teg - re men - te:

6c. im - mor - ta - lem spon-sum, e - li - gen - tes chris-tum.

7a. O fe - li - ces nup - ti - e, qui - bus nul - le ma - cu - le,

7b. nul - li do - lo - res, par - tus sunt gra - ves:

7c. nec pe - lex ti - men - da, nec nu - trix mo - les - ta.

8a. Lec - tu - los ha - rum, chris - to va - can - tes:

8b. an - ge - li val - lant, cus - to - di - en - tes:

8c. ne quis in - ces - tus, te - me - ret il - los,

8d. en - si - bus stric - tis, ar - cent im - mun-dos:

Virgines Castae

9a. Dor - mit in il - lis, Chris - tus cum ip - sis:

9b. fe - lix hic somp - nus, re - qui - es dul - cis:

9c. quo con - fo - ve - tur, vir - go fi - de - lis,

9d. in - ter am - plex - us: spon - si - ce - les - tis.

10a. Dex - te - ra spon - si, spon - sa com - plex - a:

10b. ca - pi - ti le - va, dor - mit sub - nix - sa:

10c. per - vi - gil cor - de, cor - po - re dor - mit,

10d. et spon - si gra - ta: si - nu qui - es - cit.

11a. Ap - pro - bans somp - num, Spon - sus bea - a - tum:

Virgines Castae

11b. in - qui - e - ta - ri,   pro - hi - bet   il - lum:

11c. ne   sus - ci - te - tis,   in - quid,   di - lec - tam,

11d. dum ip - sa   vo - let: i - ta   qui - e - tam.

12a. Hic ec - cle - si - as - ti - ci: flos est   il - le   ger - mi - nis:

12b. tam ro - sis quam li - li - is: mul - ti - plex   in - nu - me - ris:

12c. quo - rum est frag - ran - ti - is: a - ger spon - si   no - bi - lis:

12d. na - ri - bus   et   o - cu - lis,   e - que de - lec - ta - bi - lis:

13a. Or - na - te   tam bis - si - na: ves - te quam pur - pu - re - a:

13b. le - va   te - nent li - li - a: ro - sas ha - bent dex - te - ra:

Virgines Castae

13c. et co - ro - na ge - mi - nas: re - di - mi - tae ca - pi - ta:

13d. ag - ni si - ne ma - cu - la, per - cur - runt i - ti - ne - ra:

14a. His quo - que   flo - ri - bus: sem - per re - cen - ti - bus.

14b. sanc - to - rum   in - tex - ta: ca - pi - tum sunt ser - ta.

14c. His ag - nus pas - ci - tur, at - que re - fi - ci - tur.

14d. hi flo - res e - lec - ta, sun il - li - us es - ca.

15a. Hinc cho - ro ta - li - um, val - la - tus ag - mi - num.

15b. or - tho - rum a - me - na: dis - cur - rit hac il - lac.

15c. Qui nunc com - pre - hen - sus, ab his nunc   e - lap - sus.

Virgines Castae

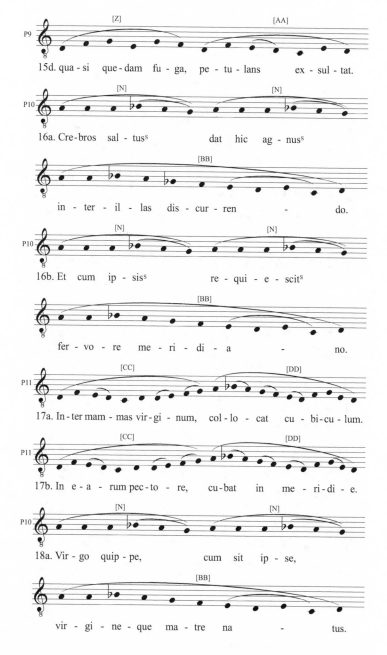

15d. qua - si que - dam fu - ga, pe - tu - lans ex - sul - tat.

16a. Cre - bros sal - tus[s] dat hic ag - nus[s]

in - ter - il - las dis - cur - ren - do.

16b. Et cum ip - sis[s] re - qui - e - scit[s]

fer - vo - re me - ri - di - a - no.

17a. In - ter mam - mas vir - gi - num, col - lo - cat cu - bi - cu - lum.

17b. In e - a - rum pec - to - re, cu - bat in me - ri - di - e.

18a. Vir - go quip - pe, cum sit ip - se,

vir - gi - ne - que ma - tre na - tus.

Virgines Castae

18b. Vir - gi - na - les,   su - per om - nes,

que - rit et a - mat re - ces - sus.

19a. Somp - nus il - li, pla - ci - dus in cas - tis est si - ni - bus.

19b. Ne qua for - te, ma - cu - la su - a fe - det vel-le - ra.

20a. Hoc at - ten - de can - ti - cum: de - vo - ta - rum

men - ti - um: in - sig - ne col - le - gi - um.

20b. Quo no - stra de - vo - ti - o: mai - o - re se

stu - di - o: tem-plum or - net do - mi - no.

Guided by the medieval principles of how music and text relate, we shall now examine each of the twelve musical periods of *Virgines castae* and their internal divisions. Period 1 begins with a clause [A] that starts and ends with a colon on d. A second clause [B] rises to a fourth above the final before again ending with a colon on d. A third clause [C] combines with the preceding two to form a period on d. The same musical period articulates the second line of stanza one. In this first period Abelard clearly establishes the *protus* modality through repetition of the final within and at the end of each clause. Moreover, clauses [A], [B], and [C] serve to articulate the rhyme and meaning of each clause of the text. Both music and text combine effectively to proclaim the opening two words and central topic of the sequence: *Virgines castae.*

In his musical setting of stanza 1, Abelard does not follow the early sequence tradition by beginning with a single line of text and music followed by double-line stanzas and music. By dropping the initial single line, he places his sequences well within the currents of change arising during the period of the 'intermediate' sequence and common in the time of the 'late' sequence. Abelard does, however, make each musical clause clearly articulate both modality and verbal syntax. Thus, the organic relationship between the text and music in stanza 1 may point back to the older style prose sequence in which music and text mirrored each other very closely. For the most part Abelard sets one note per syllable, a characteristic of the sequence genre throughout its development. Movement is by step with an occasional change of direction by leap of a third. We can already see that Dronke is right in saying the music of *Virgines castae* possesses the forward and backward-looking characteristics of the 'intermediate' sequence.

Period 2 (stanza 2) begins on A, a fourth below D, and thereby accentuates the plagal side of the D mode. Again, three short clauses combine to form a *periodus*. Here, however, the first clause [D] ends on c, the flex of the *protus* modality, which calls for a slight pause. Clauses two [B] and three [C] rhyme with the same clauses period 1. Like period 1, the three clauses combine to form a *periodus* on d. This period is repeated to line 2b. Again the music serves to articulate each clause of text and to emphasize the 5+5+6 strophic form with its internal and line-ending rhyme. Yet the music has its own role in guiding the delivery of the text. In clause [D] the cadence on c is but slight, resulting in an almost unbroken flow from clause [D] to [B] and a clear statement of the pauline phrase, *psalmis et hymnis canticus*. Through periods 1 and 2 Abelard has emphasized the structural moments of the text through the music and made clear the *ambitus* of the plagal form of the *protus* modality.

Period 3 (stanza 3) begins on d. Its first clause [E] rises to g before ending with a comma on f, the 'tenor' or reciting tone of the plagal D mode. The following clause [F] begins on f and rises to a, the highest *vox* sounded to this point in the sequence. A period, at [G], is formed as the music descends from a to d. This melody is repeated again with a noteworthy change in the cadential figure in [H].

In contrast to period 1, in which each clause cadences on d, period 3 sounds the final only at its beginning and end. By using other structural tones in the mode, Abelard keeps the music moving forward in search, so to speak, of its natural resting place, the final. The minor cadential articulations of clauses [E] and [F] continue to bring out the internal rhyme of its 5+5+5 strophic form, but they equally give the music its own independence that aids in a more flowing delivery of the text.

Another mark of the music's independence occurs with the cadential figure at [H]; Waddell contends that this figure is unique to Abelard's music.[46] *Le Mestre* created this four-note cadence around a two-note 'neume' which often occurs on a weak penultimate syllable of the final word.[47] He placed a single tone before and after the neume.

46. '*Epithalamica*', 257.

47. I have followed standard modern practice and translate all neumatic notation of the examples discussed throughout this chapter into modern notation.

Example IV.8: The Abelardian Cadence

3b.   . . . re - ge,   pre - ce   -   dit   ip   -   sa.

As the example shows, the initial tone moves up by step to the first tone of the two-note neume (at *ip-*). This second tone leaps down by a third, rather than taking the usual cadential movement by a step. This last note of the example (at *sa*) is approached downward by step. In *Virgines castae* this cadence is sung five times, in stanza 3b at [H], in stanza 17a and b at [HH], and in stanza 19a and b at [HH]. We encounter the cadence again in the first musical period of *Epithalamica*—where it is repeated four times.

According to Waddell, 'one looks in vain for a parallel [to this cadence] in the Victorine sequences or in those of other collections'.[48] The only other place one finds this cadential formula is in Abelard's *planctus Dolorum solatium*:

Example IV.9: *Dolorum solatium*, sect. 6

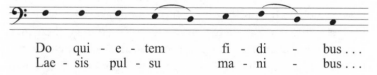

Do   qui - e - tem   fi - di   -   bus . . .
Lae - sis   pul - su   ma - ni   -   bus . . .

With this cadence, we may in fact have a musical figure that is unique to the musical style of Peter Abelard. This unusual cadence has its own charm that serves to ornament the musical syntax, much as figures of speech ornament rhetorical syntax.

Another significant abelardian feature of *Virgines castae* begins to occur in the third period and increases in frequency as the sequence progresses: Abelard does not predominantly set the syllables of words to simple neumes; rather he often gives neumes of two to four pitches to individual syllables. What is more, he very frequently places complex neumes—neumes of two or more

48. A point Father Waddell has made in correspondence.

tones—on unaccented syllables. Most twelfth-century sequence composers set one note per syllable, reserving the infrequent complex neume for stressed syllables. The famous twelfth-century sequence *Lauda crucis attollamus,* written by Abelard's contemporary Adam of Saint Victor, is the classic example of this practice:

Example IV.10: *Lauda crucis attollamus,* stanzas 1 and 2

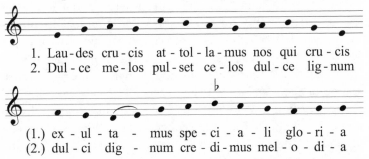

1. Lau - des cru - cis at - tol - la - mus nos qui cru - cis
2. Dul - ce me - los pul - set ce - los dul - ce lig - num

(1.) ex - ul - ta - mus spe - ci - a - li glo - ri - a
(2.) dul - ci dig - num cre - di - mus mel - o - di - a

Abelard, by contrast, not only makes frequent use of complex neumes, he also makes no effort to place these musical figures on accented syllables of text. Indeed, in terms of the ornamentation created by the presence of complex neumes, Abelard makes little effort to coordinate text and music. The two go their own way. Abelard seems to have been comfortable with melodic settings of words in which the single note assigned to the accented syllable is followed by a complex neume on the word ending, as at [E] in stanza 3; [D'] in 6c and 7c; [N] in stanza 8a and b, 9a and b, 10a and b; or [N] in stanzas 16a and b, and 18a and b. But he also is comfortable with neumed accents, as at [B'] in stanza 4a and b; [R] in 8d, 9d, 10d, and 11d; and [BB] in stanza 16a and b, and 18a and b.

After studying the musical style of Abelard's surviving hymn *O quanta qualia* and his six *planctus,* Lorenz Weinrich concluded that Abelard 'placed the neumatic formulas indiscriminately on accented and unaccented syllables alike'.[49] This hymn

49. 'Peter Abaelard as Musician—1', *The Musical Quarterly* 55 (1969) 303.

shows Abelard's penchant for placing complex neumes on any syllable—accented or unaccented (see Example IV.11). This style of hymn writing was characteristic of hymns composed before Abelard's time. Thus Weinrich's study shows that Abelard's hymns are 'old-fashioned' in style. The same can be said of his two sequences. Unlike the sequences written by Adam of Saint Victor and his followers, *Virgines castae* and *Epithalamica*, like many sequences written between the ninth and eleventh centuries, have many syllables—accented and unaccented—set to more than one note.

Example IV.11: O quanta qualia

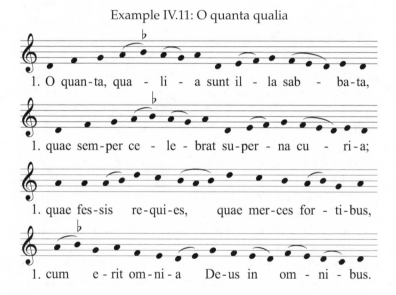

Abelard's 'old-fashioned' way of handling accented and unaccented syllables may help explain why his liturgical songs were not widely copied and sung throughout the late Middle Ages. An examination of the half-dozen or so melodic variants of the *Virgines castae* in manuscripts that date after the Nevers Prosary reveal that most of the variants indicate scribes attempting to 'update' the sequence by shifting Abelard's placement of neumes so that complex neumes accompany accented syllables and unaccented syllables receive simple neumes.[50] Two examples illustrate this point. A thirteenth-century Weingarten manuscript,[51] written with staffless neumes, substitutes single notes for complex neumes in all the above-mentioned instances except in [N] at stanza 8, and in [CC] at 17 and 19. Here the scribe was clearly seeking to 'correct' Abelard's style by simplifying his musical line. The person who transcribed a late-thirteenth-century noted gradual from Sankt Blasien[52] seems to have been less offended by Abelard's treatment of musical accent and verbal accent. Instead of replacing complex neumes with single neumes, as the Weingarten scribe, however, the Sankt Blasien scribe tended to replace single neumes on accented syllables with complex neumes, apparently in an effort to 'correct' the melodic imbalance cause by Abelard's style.

In *Virgines castae* in the Nevers Prosary, we next observe, period 3 is repeated two more times for lines 3c and d; the only exception is the abelardian final cadence at [H]. This fourfold repetition of period 3 departs from sequence tradition, and the unusual cadence at [H] tends to weaken the four-line verbal rhyme scheme of stanza 3 and to preserve something of the traditional sequence form of rhyming couplets at lines 3c and d.

---

50. Waddell, 'Chaste Virgins', 33. Waddell does not provide examples here, but describes the scribes' updating tendencies. He does give musical examples of the 'updating' efforts of several scribes who tinkered with Abelard's *planctus Dolorum solatium* in '*Epithalamica*', 257.

51. Stuttgart, Landesbibliothek, HB I Asc. 95

52. Karlsruhe, Badische Landesbibliothek, Blasien 102.

Period 4 (stanza 4) consists of four clauses, [A'], [B'], [D'], and [C]. In contrast to the undulating and leaping motion of period 3, period 4 moves in a graceful linear fashion that compares to periods 1 and 2. Clauses [A'] and [B'] are similar to clauses [A] and [B] in range and cadential pattern. They each end on d, calling for a colon; together the two clauses form a distinction. Furthermore, Abelard forms the last two clauses of period 4 from much of the musical material of clauses [D] and [C] in period 2. His restatement of [D]—labeled [D'] in period 4—is expanded by a single tone to accommodate a six, rather than a five, syllable phrase; [C] is repeated with no change.

The connections between period 4 and the melodic material of periods 1 and 2 are unmistakable. Indeed, with its six-syllable line-ending rhyme and reuse of melodic material from periods 1 and 2, period 4 serves to recapitulate the opening scene of the song. In stanzas 1 and 2 the singer tells of the supreme virgin and her virgin followers. Stanza 3 focuses on the beauty and honor of the supreme virgin, while stanza 4 shifts the singers' focus back to her chaste virginal cortège. The melody to which Abelard sets stanza 4 parallels the text's restatement of the opening topics of stanzas 1 and 2.

Rhetorical analysis in Chapter Three has shown that *Virgines castae* begins with an *exordium* that introduces the key topics of the sequence, and that at stanza 4 these topics are restated in a crisp *rationale*. Musical analysis now reveals that Abelard designed period 4 to reinforce the text's restatement of the sequence's opening topics. The use of earlier material in clauses [A'], [B'], [D'], and [C] links the named virgin-martyrs Thecla, Agnes, Lucy, and Agathes with the maidens of stanzas 1 and 2 who sing psalms and hymns and canticles to the supreme virgin. This link strengthens the argument from example of stanza 4, which provided specific examples of chaste virgins who have followed the queen and offered themselves completely to Christ the King.

Period 5 (stanza 5) begins on F. Its opening clause, [I], ends on d, forming a musical colon. A four-note descent from f to c ornaments the first syllable of text at [I] and may indicate a slight pause of a syllable at its lowest *vox*. Hereafter, this first clause continues with each syllable of text receiving a single pitch. A second clause, [C], a musical figure already observed as marking periods 1, 2, and 5, follows in similar fashion, also cadencing on the final. The two clauses combine to form period 5, which Abelard repeats for each of the four lines of stanza 5. Abelard repeats clause [C] throughout stanza 5, which, like stanza 4, is devoted to the elaboration of the deeds and the worth of the virgins who follow the supreme virgin. No doubt, clause [C] is one way that the music combines with the six syllable line-ending rhyme of stanzas 1-5 and helps to give structural integrity to the sequence. The musical rhyme Abelard created between his stanzas through the repetition of [C] also illustrates one way by which he has given his music its own independence and ornamentation.

Period 5, unlike period 3, does not have a cadence that musically breaks the four-line verbal rhyme. This deviation from the earlier sequence tradition is one of the features of *Virgines castae* that Peter Dronke has described as 'remarkable' in that such repetitiveness is characteristic of the *lai lyrique* of the twelfth and thirteenth centuries, but not of the early sequence.[53] What Dronke has described as lai-like in *Virgines castae* is the four-line strophic patterns so prevalent in Abelard's *planctus* and *Epithalamica*. The text of the vernacular *lai*, however, is typically not narrative in form, is often longer than the sequence, and is not strophic but composed of double, triple, or quadruple versicles which are often separated by the refrain-like repetition of textual and musical material used earlier in the song.[54]

Period 6 (stanzas 6 and 7) contrasts dramatically with period 5. Rather than setting each line of stanza 6 to the same melody, Abelard 'through composes' the melody so that each verbal unit has its own music. While period 5 is short, being formed of two

53. 'Virgines caste', 96–97.

54. On the *lai*, see John Stevens, *Words and Music in the Middle Ages: Song, Narrative, Dance, and Drama, 1050–1350* (Cambridge: Cambridge University Press, 1986) 140–155.

clauses, Abelard constructs period 6 from no fewer than six clauses, [J], [K], [L], [M], [D'], and [C]. He binds this long melody to earlier material by rounding it off with clauses [D'] and [C].

Period 6 begins on f, ascends to a before pausing on g to form a comma at [J]. Clause two, [K], climbs from A to c before descending by step back to f, thus marking a second musical comma. Clause [L] seems to call for a slight pause when its melody rises from g to a and then falls by step to c. The melody next leaps to f, where clause [M] eventually cadences on d to form a distinction. The melody continues with clause [D']. As in period 5, clause [C] functions to bring the melody to a close on d, marking a musical period. Abelard also sets stanza 7 to this same long musical period. On the one hand, he conforms to the traditional sequence couplet form by binding stanzas 6 and 7 together through strophic form and melody. On the other, he uses musical rhyme—through the repetition of clause [C]—to weave together the first seven stanzas and mark them off as a unit. This unit, as the earlier intertextual analysis has shown, centers on the heavenly scene of the supreme virgin with her king and virginal attendants portrayed in Psalm 44.

Period 7 (stanza 8) is formed from eight clauses. It begins on a, the fifth above the final; the a functions as a reciting tone in the first clause [N]. The end of clause [N] is marked by a three-*vox* neume that very likely indicates a musical syllable and the need for a slight pause at the end of the clause. Clause 2 [O] begins on a and cadences with a downward leap of a fifth from a to d to form a distinction. Abelard repeats this distinction twice, setting the first and second lines of stanza 8 to it. Stanza 8c and d are 'through-composed'; each has its own melody. Stanza 8c begins on a at clause [P] and ends on f, calling for a pause. The melody continues at [Q] with the a brief recitation of the text on g. The line cadences on f to form a musical comma. Stanza 8d begins on g. Here the music rises a 3rd to *b-flat* before descending by step to D, marking a colon at [R]. Finally the period is formed with a final clause, [S], that cadences on d. Abelard sets stanzas 9, 10, and 11 to the music of period 7. The repetition of the music combines with the subject matter of the text and the 5+5 strophic form to bind stanzas 8 to 11 into a unit. These four stanzas consist of material drawn primarily from the *Song of Songs*. Here poetic rhyme and musical repetition join to articulate the shape of Narration 2.

Abelard does not set stanzas 12 and 13 to a period. The melody to stanza 12 begins on the a above the final. Clause [T] cadences on a, and calls for a musical colon. At [U] a distinction is formed after the melody ascends by step to d', an octave above the final and then descends back to a. Stanza 12b begins on the c' above the final, the highest pitch to begin any clause in the entire sequence. The melody at [V] wanders downward, repeatedly sounding the fifth before finally pausing on a colon. Drawing again on earlier material, Abelard repeats clause [U] to form a second distinction. The melody for 12c consists of a restatement of [V] and a new musical clause at [W]. Once again Abelard seems preoccupied with the fifth. He does present the final at the opening of [X]. Twice the final is sounded before a leap to the fifth. The clause cadences on g, calling for a musical comma. Abelard concludes his setting of stanza 12 with a repetition of clause [V]. Abelard sets stanza 13 to the same melody as stanza 12, thus devoting two stanzas to the elaboration of the a above the final.

With the intonation of the text on a, the fifth above the final, in stanzas 12 and 13, Abelard seems interested less in shaping the text melodically and more in emphasizing the text by having it dramatically delivered through recitation on this 'dominant-like' structural pitch. Drawing on the Song of Songs in stanzas 8-11, Abelard relates the 'goods' of the virginal life, declaring that virgins rest in Christ's bed under the watchful care of guardian angels and that they sleep in the very embrace of Christ. In stanzas 12 and 13 he heightens the sexual intensity of the scene when, using Cyprian of Carthage's words, he declares that the consummation of this heavenly love is nothing short of the budding of the Church's flower. Abelard's musical interpretation of the nuptial intimacies of the virginal soul and her heavenly Bridegroom intensifies the climax of their love in at least three ways: in stanzas 12 and 13 Abelard (1) builds tension in the music by avoiding cadencing on the final, (2) heightens the intensity of the music by emphasizing the upper side of the D mode, and (3) constructs the melody like the rhetorical figure called climax.

Not once within clauses [T] through [X] does Abelard cadence on the final; all cadences are on the fifth above the final. In these stanzas Abelard is clearly determined to elaborate upon the fifth. His accentuation of this structural pitch of the D mode is something like a temporary modulation to the dominant in the major-minor tonality, a rhetorical device familiar to most modern listeners from the music of the eighteenth and nineteenth centuries.

Abelard further intensifies the song by moving to the upper range of the D mode. In the early periods of the sequence he emphasized the plagal side of the *protus* modality. Now he moves firmly into the authentic range, the upper side of the mode. Here his melody climbs to the extremes of the modes *ambitus* (range), several times reaching the d' an octave above the final.

Abelard heightens the climactic significance of stanzas 12 and 13 not only by dwelling on the fifth and the upper *ambitus* of the mode, but also by shaping the melody much like the rhetorical figure called *climax*. Through this figure a speaker's point is emphasized or clarified and given an emotional twist as if by climbing a ladder (the term means 'ladder' in Greek). As an example of this George A. Kennedy cites Romans 5:3-4: *We rejoice in our sufferings, knowing that suffering produces endurance, and endurance produces character, and character produces hope, and hope does not disappoint us.*[55]

In this passage the Apostle repeats the last word of each clause at the beginning of the next clause. This device has the structural effect of fixing the order of the clauses by concatenation. Abelard does much the same in the music of stanzas 12 and 13. Consider the following table of these two stanzas.

---

55. George A. Kennedy, *New Testament Interpretation through Rhetorical Criticism* (University of Chapel Hill, 1984) 28.

Table IV.12: Abelard's Musical *Climax*

Poetic Stanza	Musical Syntax	
12a	[T],5	[U]:5
12b	[V],5	[U]:5
12c	[V],5	[W]:5
12d	[X],4	[V]:5
13a	[T],5	[U]:5
13b	[V],5	[U]:5
13c	[V],5	[W]:5
13d	[X],4	[V]:5

In his concatendation of musical clauses Abelard creates a similar pattern: lines 12 a and b share [U], lines 12 b and c share [V]. and 12 c and d share [V]. He emphasizes this musical syntax by repeating it in stanza 13. Here both musical syntax and poetic texture support the argument from analogy and narrative that our rhetorical analysis of stanzas 12 and 13 revealed.

With stanza 14, Abelard's attention again returns to the final and its elaboration. Period 8 (stanza 14a) begins on the final, d, in [Y]. The melody rises to the a above the final and then closes with a leap of a sixth downward that eventually settles on the final, forming a colon. Much the same melody is repeated to form the period at [Y'] as the melody moves from d to a g and back to d. The melody is repeated to the words of stanza 14b.

Period 9 (stanza 14c) begins on the final and rises to mark a comma on f in [Z]. A period occurs in [AA] with a second musical figure that centers and cadences on d. This melody is repeated to the text of stanza 14d. Stanza 15a and b, and stanza 15c and d are essentially a repetition of the musical syntax of periods 8 and 9, respectively.

The melody in periods 8 and 9 is rather narrow in range and tends to abide around the final. Moreover, it is almost entirely syllabic. Abelard combines this musical texture with a 6+6 strophic form; the music and poetry work together in delivering his description of Christ's virginal martyrs with lilies and roses in their hands and wedding wreathes upon their heads. They follow Christ, the Lamb of God, wherever he goes, and the lamb feeds among and upon them as if they were a field most delectable.

As the Lamb begins racing among the virgins in stanzas 16 through 19, Abelard dramatically changes the character of the music. At that point (period 10, stanza 16) the Lamb ceases prancing and leaping about takes his rest in a virgin's lap. In contrast to the preceding two periods, periods 10 and 11 accentuate a, the fifth above the final, increase the range of the melody; and increase the use of two-note neumes. Through this elegant melismatic texture the entire drama of the Lamb among his virgins is effectively delivered.

Period 10 begins, at clause [N], with much the same melody which begins period 8. Here, however, Abelard repeats clause [N] twice, placing great emphasis on the text through repetition of the a above the final. As before, the three-note neume ending clause [N] calls for the slight pause of a syllable. The repetition of this 'old' material is balanced at [BB] by a melodic shape so far unheard in *Virgines castae*: the third clause begins on a, ascends one step, and then, after descending a sixth from b-flat to d, forms a period. As the descent is completed, Abelard introduces a four-note neume before the final that ornaments the (unaccented) penultimate syllable of the text. In good sequence style Abelard repeats period 10, setting stanza 16b to its melody.

Period 11 (stanza 17) begins on the final. In this period, formed from clauses [CC] and [DD], the musical syntax becomes much more florid with an increased presence of syllables set to two-note neumes. The melody rises up a third from the final before descending to the c below the final. From here to the end of the clause Abelard sets almost every syllable of text to two-note neumes. At [CC] the melody rises from c up a seventh to b-flat and then flows downward to the abelardian cadence we observed at period 3, clause [H]. Although a slight pause of a musical syllable on c might not have been out of place in articulating the text at the end of [CC], the music has in fact taken on considerable independence from the text here. The text speaks of the Lamb resting on the bosom of a maiden, while the music takes flight in a long ascending and descending line. The neumatic melody continues at [DD], flowing again to the abelardian cadence we observed in [H].

So Abelard alternates between periods 10 and 11 in stanzas 16-19. Period 10 supports stanzas 16 and 18, and period 11 supports stanzas 17 and 19. This pattern combines with the 4+4+8 strophic form of 16 and 18 and 7+7 strophic form of 17 and 19. Hence, music and poetry work together to emphasize the narrative development of the unicorn-like lamb among his virginal flowers.

Period 12 (stanza 20) returns to the three-clause periods we saw at the beginning of the sequence. The first clause, at [EE], begins on f above the final and forms a colon, ending on the final. In contrast to the previous two periods, the setting here is largely syllabic. But Abelard has not finished with musical ornamentation. The second clause [FF] begins with the first syllable of the text set to a five-note neume. The clause then continues syllabically, one *vox* per syllable. The last clause of the period, [GG], begins a step below the final, rises to g and ascends to the final through the ornamentation of a two- and four-note neume on the ante-penultimate and penultimate syllables of the text respectively. Once again, Abelard retains the couplet setting so characteristic of the sequence: he sets stanza 20b to period 12.

As in the first period, Abelard emphasizes the *protus* modality by his repetition of the final within and at the end of each clause of stanza 20. Like the clauses of period 1, clauses [EE], [FF], and [GG] articulate the tripart 7+7+7 strophic rhyme of the stanza. Both music and poetry unite effectively to recapitulate the sequence's overall argument and to exhort the Paraclete nuns to join other devout virgins who seek marriage with the heavenly Bridegroom.

Before drawing conclusions about Abelard's musical style and his setting of *Virgines castae*, we turn now to analyze the musical syntax of *Epithalamica*.

Epithalamica

1a. E - pi-tha - la - mi - ca, dic   Spon - sa,   can - ti - ca.

1b. in-tus quae con-spi - cis, dic   for - is   gau-di - a.

1c. et nos lae - ti - fi - cans, de   Spon - so   un - ti - a.

1d. cu -ius te   re - fo - vet, sem - per   prae - sen-ti - a.

2a. A - du - le   -   scen-tu - lae: vos cho -rum   du - ci - te.

2b. cum haec prae   -   ci - ne - rit: et vos suc   - ci - ni - te.

2c. A - mi - ci   Spon-si   vos: vo - ca-runt   nup - ti - ae.

2d. et no -vae   mo - du - los: op - ta-mus   Do - mi-nae.

Epithalamica

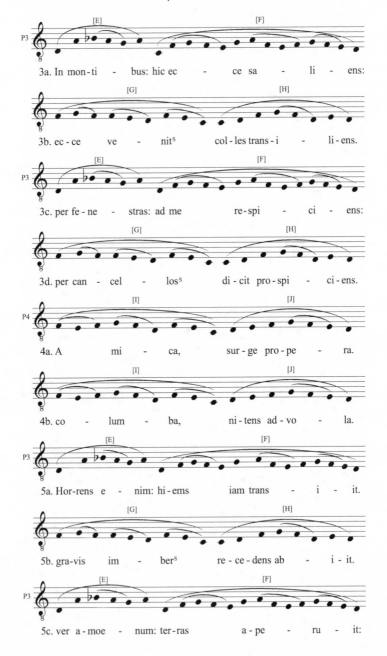

Epithalamica

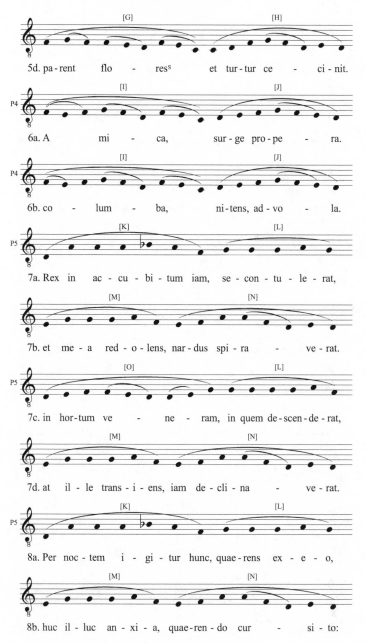

5d. pa - rent   flo - res[s]   et tur - tur ce - ci - nit.

6a. A   mi - ca,   sur - ge pro - pe - ra.

6b. co - lum - ba,   ni - tens, ad - vo - la.

7a. Rex in ac - cu - bi - tum iam, se - con - tu - le - rat,

7b. et me - a red - o - lens, nar - dus spi - ra - ve - rat.

7c. in hor - tum ve - ne - ram, in quem de - scen - de - rat,

7d. at il - le trans - i - ens, iam de - cli - na - ve - rat.

8a. Per noc - tem i - gi - tur hunc, quae - rens ex - e - o,

8b. huc il - luc an - xi - a, quae - ren - do cur - si - to:

Epithalamica

8c. oc - cur-runt vi - gi - les, ar - den - ti stu - di - o,

8d. quos cum trans - i e - rim, Spon-sum in - ve - ni - o.

9a. Iam vi - de - o, quod o - pta - ve - ram.

9b. iam te - ne - o, quod a - ma - re - ram.

9c. iam re - de - o, quae sic fle - ve - ram.

9d. plus gau - de - o, quam do - lu - e - ram.

10a. Ri - si ma - ne, fle - vi noc - te.

10b. ma - ne ri - si, noc - te fle - vi.

11a. Noc-tem in - som - nem, do - lor du - xe - rat.

Epithalamica

11b. quem ve - he - me - tem, a - mor fe - ce - rat.

11c. di - la - ti - o - ne, vo - tum cre - ve - rat.

11d. do - nec a - man - tem, a - man vi - si - tat.

12a. Plau - sus di - e, planc - tus noc - te.

12b. di - e plau - sus, noc - te planc - tus.

13a. E - ia nunc, co - mi - tes, et Si - on fi - li - ae.

13b. ad Spon - sae can - ti - ca, psal-mum ad - ne - cti-te.

13c. quo moe - stis red - di - to, Spon-si prae - sen - ti - a.

13d. con - ver - tit e - le - gos, no-stros in can - ti-ca.

We have already noted that *Epithalamica* is in the *protus* modality. Unlike *Virgines castae*, it begins and remains in the authentic range of the D mode, i.e., it abides mostly in the tones between the final and its higher octave. As before, we find *a* and *f* serving as major structural pitches along with d, the final.

Period 1 (stanza 1) begins on a, a fifth above d. Three clauses combine to form a period. The first clause, [A], ends on f, calling for a musical comma. Between the opening a and cadential *f*, the melody climbs to a c′ above the final. This c′ is the highest pitch in the entire song. The second clause ascends from *f* to a *b-flat* before making its way down by leap and step to end on the final. Abelard repeats this period in each of the four lines of stanza 1.

In its range, period 1 is dramatic, but several other features, Abelardian for certain, demand recognition. Indeed, one can say that period 1 offers a veritable cornucopia of Abelardian stylistic idiosyncrasies: (1) the syllables of text are set to a mixture of single-note neumes and two- and three-tone neumes, (2) accented and unaccented syllables are set indiscriminately to single tone and multitoned neuma, (3) each musical line ends with the abelardian cadence that we observed in *Virgines castae*, and (4) four lines of text are set to the same music. These features characterize almost every period of *Epithalamica*.

Period 2 (stanza 2) begins on the final and eventually cadences on the a above the final, marking a musical comma at [C]. A second clause follows; the two clauses combine to form a period at [D]. Abelard further joins the two clauses by beginning both with the same pitch, the final. This repetition achieves two important rhetorical goals: it makes for a proportioned delivery of the text of period 2, and it serves to narrow the wide-ranging melody of period 1. Although periods 1 and 2 differ, the two melodies work together to establish the mode and its range. Moreover, the cadential points of their melodies emphasize the strophic form that stanzas 1 and 2 share. By supporting this shared poetic form with music, Abelard indicates to this singer that these two stanzas work together. Indeed, we have seen in our rhetorical analysis that both stanzas serve as the sequence's exordium. Here two exhortations in the voice of the narrator initiate the connubial drama described in the remainder of the sequence.

Period 3 (stanza 3) begins and ends on the final, and is formed from four syntactic units: [E], [F], [G], [H]. From the opening d of clause [E], the melody leaps a fifth to a, which is then ornamented by a three-note neuma that leads to the pause of a comma on a. At clause [F] the melody once again begins on the final. Several three- and four-note neumes ornament the reciting tone f, bringing the melody eventually to form a distinction on d. Period 3 continues with figures that ornament f, and eventually rests on a period. The melody continues at [G] centering on the reciting tone f, which Abelard ornaments with several multi-toned neumes. The last of these musical gestures ends on c, calling for the slight pause of a syllable. At [H] the melody flows from the c below the final to d and upward as high as g, where it then turns downward and soon completes the period with a cadence on d. The melody of period 3 is now repeated for verses 3c and d. This repetition creates the couplet form we have observed in the traditional sequence.

Period 4 begins on f, which is ornamented thrice by three-note neumes at [I]. The last of these figures seems to call for the pause of a musical comma. This pause would assist in articulating the important first word of the bridegroom's speech, *amica*. Also, the clear articulation of phrase [I] would prepare for musical phrase [J], which begins on d and rises by step to g. From the g the melody descends on the unaccented penultimate syllable to the final. Here we have a period. The same musical line is repeated to stanza 6b, creating the characteristic musical couplet of the sequence.

Abelard sets stanza 5 to the musical period 3 and stanza 6 to period 4. This repetition of melody helps bind stanzas 3 through 6 together. Our rhetorical analysis has shown that this group of stanzas combines to form the bridegroom's speech-song. Poetry and music both undergird the rhetorical structure of stanzas 3-6. Once again, we see Abelard's artistry working on multiple levels. Here he binds the bridegroom's speech into a seamless unit through poetry, music, and rhetoric.

Stanza 7 returns full attention to the bride; and period 5 (stanza 7) marks this shift with a dramatic change in the musical style. In the preceding periods the music has largely been florid, with a concatenation of two- and three-note neumes ornamenting the key *voxes* of the *protus* modality. In period 5 Abelard begins setting one note per syllable of the bride's speech, with only the occasional ornamentation of a two- or three-note neume. This largely syllabic writing continues until the last period of *Epithalamica*, which takes on a style more like that of the opening period.

The syllabic setting beginning at period 5 signals that Abelard would have the bride's speech (stanzas 7 through 12) clearly articulated with little musical ornamentation. The first clause at [K] begins on d, leaps a fifth (just as does period 3), and eventually settles on f, calling for the pause of a musical comma. For the most part, clauses two [L] and three [M] parallel clause one [K] in musical shape and character; their cadences require at most a musical comma. A fourth clause [N] containing the only multi-tone neume in the melody, cadences on d, creating a period.

One expects Abelard to follow his custom and repeat the melody of period 5 for lines c and d of stanza 7. For the most part he does so; but in the first clause of the repetition of period 5, he introduces a change that makes the restatement less than exact. Here the melody, at [O], begins on d and rises by step to f, which is then ornamented by a three- and two-tone neume. Clause [O] cadences on g. From this point clauses [L], [M], and [N] follow as before to form a period. Almost certainly, Abelard introduced clause [O] because he did not wish to repeat the leap of a fifth that opens clause [K]. This leap is an important structural marker that he used to initiate the rhetorical section formed by stanzas 3-6 and the section formed by stanzas 7-8. Stanza 8 is also set to period 5.

In contrast to the preceding long distinction and period, Abelard next presents a short period of two clauses. Period 6 (stanza 9) begins on f and its first clause, [P], cadences on a two-tone neume, which may call for the pause of a comma on the *vox c*. Clause two [Q] begins on d and ends with a cadential formula reminiscent in terms of pitch to the abelardian cadence already discussed at length. Here the antepenultimate syllable receives a two-note neume rather than the penultimate, and is followed by a simple neume on the final two syllables of text. As before, the period is repeated three more times so that each of the four lines of stanza 9 are set to the same music. The repetition of [Q] and [P] through stanza 9 gives musical support to the anaphora identified here in the bride's speech. With the repeated declaration of *iam* (now!), [Q] gives musical support. Likewise, as *quod* or similar interrogatives follow in clause [P], the anaphora is amplified.

Period 7 (stanza 10) is created from four pitches. The first four syllables of stanza 10 are each set to a single pitch to form clause [R]. Abelard repeats the same four notes to the remaining four pitches of clause [R]. Hence, the musical syntax is ornamented by repetition. Abelard places this musical ornamentation in counterpoint to the textual figure *commutatio*, the repetition of clauses and words in a sentence in reversed arrangement, which we observed in Chapter Three.

Period 8 (stanza 11) consists of two clauses. Beginning on f, clause [S] is marked by a musical figure that descends from a to c. This figure calls for no more than the pause of a comma. The second clause [Q] is another example of Abelard creating rhyme between periods. Here clause [Q] of period 6 is again sounded to complete the period. Rather than a new period, one might consider [S] and [Q] as forming a variation on period 6. Thrice more the melody of the period formed by clauses [S] and [Q] is sounded.

At stanza 12, Abelard repeats period 7. And once again he sets the repetitive character of the music over against the repetitive figure *commutatio* in the text. Poetic analysis has shown that Abelard formed a textual unit in stanzas 9-12 by alternating between four- and two-line stanzas and through incise and line-ending rhyme. The music serves to bind the four stanzas in two important ways: (1) clause [Q] forms the second half of periods 6 and 8, and (2) stanzas 10 and 12 are both set to period 7. Hence, the music undergirds the strophic pattern and the poetic rhyme. Our rhetorical analysis has shown that stanzas 9-12 also form the climactic moment of the bride's song.

Period 9 (stanza 13) marks a change in musical character. Abelard brings *Epithalamica* to a close with a descending, neumatic melody that supports the sequence's opening 6+6 strophic form with a musical style much like that of period 1. Single and two-note neumes are combined to form a musical line that descends, via rising and falling by step, from f to d. Clause [T] begins and ends on f, calling for no more than the articulation of a musical comma. Clause [U] likewise begins on f but proceeds to cadence on d to complete the final period of the sequence. As periods 1 and 2 lend musical support to the exhortations that form stanzas 1 and 2, rhetorical analysis has shown that period 9 serves to articulate the final exhortation in stanza 13.

Having looked closely at the music of *Virgines castae* and *Epithalamica*, we can now make the following generalizations about the musical syntax of the two sequences.

1. d is clearly the most important pitch in their tonal hierarchy. It forms the end of more grammatical units than any other pitch, and is the final or modal center of each sequence. Pitches a third and fifth above *d*—namely, f and a—or the fourth below the final, form the next level in the tonal hierarchy of the pieces. These pitches end important structural units. The *g* a fourth above and the *c* a step below the final seem to occupy a secondary structural role in both sequences. Other pitches function to elaborate these structural tones.

2. The musical settings of the sequences do not fall well into the stylistic boundaries of the twelfth-century Victorine sequence. Syllables are not set predominantly to single notes; rather, neumes of two to four notes are given to individual syllables. Both sequences fit more into the style of the 'intermediate' sequence.

3. Beyond an 'archaic' use of multi-note neumes, the two sequences are also set apart from other twelfth-century sequences by their rather random 'mixing' of single and multi-note neumes. Abelard lets multi-note neumes and single-note neumes fall indiscriminately on accented and unaccented syllables, a practice not typical of twelfth-century sequence composers, who, when they used neumes of more than one note, ordinarily placed them on accented syllables.

4. This unusual practice carries an important abelardian fingerprint that supports Chrysogonus Waddell's argument that Abelard composed *Virgines castae* and *Epithalamica*. Not only did Abelard often place two- and three-note neumes on unaccented syllables within a word, he also was wont to place them on word endings. This is not to say that Abelard never makes an accented syllable coincide with two or more note neumes, but that Abelard's use of single-note and multi-note neumes was not governed by word accents.

5. With their series of three and four poetic lines set to the same musical phrase, *Virgines castae* and *Epithalamica* depart from sequence tradition. This extended repetition is atypical of sequences before the twelfth century, yet this practice of setting four lines to a single melody is a distinct feature of Abelard's musical style.

6. Abelard liked to bind musical periods together by the repetition and reuse of clauses and cadential figures. This practice gives the musical syntax its own rhetorical configuration. Structurally it helps divide the sequences into centers of musical development. Rhetorically the repetition helps guide the singer in delivering the clauses and periods as well as larger syntactical units of the text. Moreover, the charm of musical repetition, no less than strategic moments of textual repetition, help attract and hold the auditor's attention.

7. Abelard carefully coordinates the musical syntax so that it reflects the rhetorical structure of each sequence. Furthermore, the musical structure of each sequence is so shaped that it supports the strophic patterns that Abelard used to demarcate their internal poetic and rhetorical divisions.

In chapters Five and Six we shall explore how the sequences worked to create and nurture Abelard's vision for Heloise and her nuns. Chapter Five will show how the two sequences, combined with Abelard's other Paraclete *liturgica,* were designed to create a world characterized by certain key texts, principal teachings, dominant images, exemplary persons, and model deeds. All of these 'symbols' Abelard combined to form and support the symbolic world that he envisioned for the Paraclete nuns.

In the seventh and final chapter we shall see that both sequences fit squarely with Abelard's deepest concern for Abbess Heloise. I am of the opinion that Abelard rhetorically calculated *Virgines castae* and *Epithalamica*—like many of his hymns—to teach Heloise to desire to appropriate the experience of love conveyed in the sequences. The love language and the sensual images of the sequences—like the *Song of Songs* and *Psalm 44* that formed their scribal base—set forth the love between Christ and his bride. The sequence texts suggest that Abelard sought to direct Heloise's desire away from himself to the only true lover, Christ. The sequences would have served their purpose of *translatio*—conversion—into the abelardian symbolic world if indeed they did kindle Heloise's love and longing for God and move her soul's *affectus* toward Christ.

5

ABELARD'S PARACLETE BRIDAL
TAPESTRY

How great an interest the talent of your own wisdom pays
daily to the Lord in the many spiritual daughters you have
borne for him, while I remain totally barren and labour in
vain amongst the sons of perdition! What a hateful loss and
grievous misfortune if you had abandoned yourself to the
defilement of carnal pleasures only to bear in sufferings a
few children for the world, when now you are delivered in
exultation of numerous progeny for heaven!

—*Peter Abelard*[1]

WE HUMAN BEINGS are creatures who communicate
by means of language. We speak, sing, write, listen,
and read. Our communication is usually purposeful
and goal-oriented: we explain, demand, question, answer, praise,
blame, amuse, and plead. Often we speak in order to persuade
a listener to think or act in a particular way. The rhetorical tradition provides vast and varied insights into the intricacies of persuasive discourse. These insights were taught to ancient and

---

1. Abelard to Heloise, Letter 4: *Tuae vero prudentiae talentum quantas puo-
tidie Domino refert usuras, quae multas Domino iam spirituales filias peperisti, me
penitus sterili permanente, et in filiis perditionis inaniter laborante. O quam detestaile
damnum! Quam lamentabile incommodum, si carnalium voluptatum sordibus vacans
paucos cum dolore pareres mundo, quae nunc multiplicem prolem cum excultatione
parturis coelo!* Muckle, 'Letters', 90. Radice, 150.

medieval students under the five divisions of traditional rhetoric that have guided our analysis of Abelard's *Virgines castae* and *Epithalamica:*

> *inventio,* finding the available means of persuasion (Chapter Two);
> *dispositio,* arranging the discovered material in an effective order (Chapter Three);
> *elocutio,* choosing appropriate language (Chapters Five and Six);
> *memoria,* memorizing the speech (Chapters Five and Six);
> *pronunciatio,* delivering the speech (Chapter Four).

Skillful use of these five dimensions of classical rhetoric combined to achieve the goal of all oratory: so to marshal *res* and *verba*—thoughts and words, ideas and language—that one said what was most apt and congruent, fitting and proper, appropriate and decorous for teaching, moving, and delighting one's audience. The rhetorical tradition always emphasized that the activity of persuasion has three identifiable components: a speaker; an audience; and some form of communication.

Classical oratory insisted that truly efficacious communication between a speaker and his audience occurred only within a shared sense of community. Earlier we used the social-scientific term 'symbolic world' for this communal sense. Analysis of 'symbolic world' focuses upon the self-understanding of 'insiders', members of particular cultural group, and upon the symbols which bind them together. By reading a text on the cultural level, the social scientist gains insight both into an author's perception of the symbolic world of his insider audience, and into how the author seeks to influence that world through persuasive discourse. The researcher looks for symbols—persons, places, things, practices, beliefs, rules, myths, metaphors—central to the identity of the people who form a given culture.[2] The social scientists'

---

2. Vernon K. Robbins, *Exploring the Texture of Texts: A Guide to Socio-Rhetorical Interpretation* (Valley Forge: Trinity International Press, 1996) 74.

idea of symbolic world overlaps in many ways with the rhetoricians' concept of *sensus communis*.

Teachers of rhetoric spoke of *sensus communis* when referring to the speaker and audience's common sense of propriety, their shared but often unstated mores and manners. The *sensus communis* roots the individual in the past and present of the community through *narratio*, a commonly held story of identity. The story constitutes '[a] living tradition', writes Alasdair MacIntyre, 'an historically extended, socially embodied argument, and an argument precisely in part about the goods which constitute that tradition'.[3]

In this chapter we explore how the two sequences are part of an historically extended and socially embodied argument over the identity of Heloise and her nuns. Abelard wove his argument into an intricately related tapestry of texts by which he set out to form, in Brian Stock's words, a 'textual community'.[4] Abelard meticulously brought threads of language, image, metaphor, theology, and prescribed practice and examples together into a whole. Through the tightly stitched argument of his sequences and other Paraclete *liturgica*, he labored to cultivate a particular *sensus communis* and symbolic world—a particular self-understanding and mode of being—at the Paraclete.

Virgines castae and *Epithalamica* with their topics of the supreme virgin, heavenly virgins, and marriage to Christ, are part of a great network of abelardian *liturgica* designed to train Heloise and her nuns to see and to conduct themselves as Christ's brides. As Mary Carruthers' work helps us see, Abelard's sequences provided a temporal and spatial meeting ground, a 'common place', between a vast storehouse of culturally shared exemplary

3. Alasdair MacIntyre, *After Virtue: A Study in Moral Theory* (Notre Dame University Press, 1981) 207.

4. Brian Stock, *The Implications of Literacy: Written Language and Models of Interpretation in the Eleventh and Twelfth Centuries* (Princeton: Princeton University Press, 1983) especially 88–240. On the textualization of culture, see also Vernon K. Robbins, *The Tapestry of Early Christian Discourse: Rhetoric, Society, and Ideology* (New York: Routledge, 1996).

stories and the Paraclete nuns' particular situation; this meeting ground offered the nuns a way of understanding themselves.[5] Carruthers' 'common place', the social sciences' 'symbolic world', and the rhetorical tradition's *sensus communis* are overlapping concepts that will lead us deep within the social and cultural world of the Abelard and the Paraclete nuns.

THE CULTURAL TEXTURE OF VIRGINES CASTAE

Virgines castae was sung at least six times a year at the Paraclete; it was an integral part of the year-round worship of the Paraclete nuns. A comparison of the sequence with the numerous other contributions Abelard supplied for the celebrations at which *Virgines castae* was sung makes clear the common threads (topics) between them. By painstakingly reconnecting these threads we can restore the warp and weft of Abelard's tapestry well enough to discern the symbols that he considered central to Heloise's and her nuns' identity.

Our intertextual, rhetorical, poetic, and musical analyses have shown that Abelard shaped *Virgines castae* in way that put four figures and their stories before the Paraclete nuns: 1) the supreme virgin and her virginal court; 2) heaven's nuptial bed; 3) the virginal flowers of the Church; and 4) the unicorn-like Lamb. By an analysis of key words and phrases we shall see how Abelard enriched these figures with the color and depth of the life he expected of the Paraclete nuns.

The Supreme Virgin and Her Virginal Court

In the exordium of *Virgines castae*, stanzas 1-2, we encounter the words *virginis summae*; this exalted title, 'the supreme virgin' most certainly refers to the Virgin Mary, and was calculated to arrest the Paraclete nuns' attention. As Chrysogonus Waddell has observed,[6] medieval liturgical texts made little use of this

---

5. Carruthers, *Memory*, 181.
6. 'Chaste Virgins', 22–23.

expression. The expression shows up once in a prayer by Maurilius of Rouen in the eleventh century,[7] and again in a single fifteenth-century text.[8] Yet the phrase turns up several times in Abelard's works, always related in a very particular way to Heloise and the Paraclete nuns.

In Letter Four of the couple's extant correspondence, while Abelard seeks to convince Heloise that God justly punished them for their sin, he speaks of the 'supreme virgin':

> After our marriage, when you were living in the cloister with the nuns at Argenteuil and I came one day to visit you privately, you know what my uncontrollable desire did with you there, actually in a corner of the refectory, since we had nowhere else to go. I repeat, you know how shamelessly we behaved on that occasion in so hallowed a place, dedicated to *the supreme Virgin*. Even if our other shameful behaviour was ended, this alone would deserve far heavier punishment.[9]

Sex in the refectory dedicated by the Argenteuil nuns to the supreme virgin was shameful, even for a married couple, and worthy of God's heavy judgment.

When Abelard refers to the *virginis summae*, he almost always describes a context very much like that of the sequence *Virgines castae*:

7. G. G. Meerseman, '*Der Hymnos Akathistos im Abendland* (Freiburg, Switzerland: Universitätsverlag, 1960, 2 vols.) 2:166, apparatus line 8.

8. H. Barré, *Prières anciennes de l'Occident à la Mère du Sauveur* (Paris: P. Letheilleux, 1963) 184, line 61.

9. Muckle, 88: *Nosti post nostri foederationem coniugii, cum Argenteoli cum sanctimonialibus in claustro conversareris, me die quadam privatim ad te visitandam venisse, et quid ibi tecum meae libidinis egerit intemerantia in quadam etam parte ipsius refectorii, cum quo alias videlicet diverteremus, non haberemus. Nost, inquam, id impudentissime tunc actum esse in tam reverendo loco et* summae virgini *consecrato. Quod, et si alia cessent flagitia, multo graviore dignum sit ultione.* Translation Radice, 146.

Virgines castae	Chaste virgins
virginis summae	sing of the beauty
decus praecinentes	of the supreme virgin
Ceteras quoque	and venerate after her
condignas laude	the other worthy virgins
post hanc venerantes	by their praise
Psalmis et hymnis	Speaking to one another in
canticis dignis	fitting psalms and hymns
sibi colloquentes	and canticles
Solvant in istis	Let them pay thereby
debitae laudis	solemn sacrifices
hostias sollemnes	of due praise.

The supreme virgin, in all of her regal beauty and sinless nobility, is surrounded by a choir of virgins. The articulation of these topics—virgins, making music, supreme virginity, and worship—resonates with the same topics in Abelard's other Paraclete *liturgica*.

Compare, for example, the sequence with Abelard's sermon for the feast of the assumption. In the sermon the supreme virgin is accompanied by virgins who follow her as their model for the virginal life:

> And so you virgins, and every female devoted to Christ, are the disciples of this *supreme virgin*, from whom you have received an example from her manner of life, and through following her vow of continence have been prepared for the temple of the Lord, as it is written: 'Virgins of the king are led after her; they are brought near to him by her [the supreme virgin]. They are brought forth in joy and exultation and led into the temple of the king'. (Ps 44:15)[10]

---

10. PL 178:544 A: *Et vos ergo, virgines, vel quaeeunque feminae Christo devotae, hujus* summae Virginis *discipulae, a qua sancti propositi documentum suscepistis, et per continentiae votum eam secutae, templum Dominicum estis factae, sicut scriptum est: Adducentur Regi virgines past eam, proximae ejus afferentur tibi. Afferentur in laetitia et exsultatione, adducentur in templum Regis'* (Ps 44:15). . . . See also PL 178:542A.

As in *Virgines castae* so here, too, Abelard identifies the *summae virginis* with the queen-bride of Psalm 44. These and similar texts suggests that he—and probably Heloise and her nuns—considered this psalm a core source for visualizing the heavenly world of the supreme virgin; and the supreme virgin's world is filled with song.

Virgines castae's exordium begins with a choir of virgins singing of the supreme virgin and her virginal retinue. The term *praecinentes* (singing) in stanza 1 occurs again in Abelard's Easter sermon and in the sequence *Epithalamica*. In Abelard's writings the verb *praecinere* has a very particular connection to female monastics: it figures deeply in his efforts to encourage Heloise to set her affections on Christ as her bridegroom and to live out her role as leader of the Paraclete community. Abelard would have Heloise model herself after the supreme virgin and the Paraclete nuns identify with heaven's virginal choir, enraptured in bridal song. This imitation is deeply related to the Paraclete nuns' daily practice of singing the liturgy.

In Chapter Two we noted that the pauline phrase *loquentes vobismetipsis in psalmis, et hymnis, et canticis spiritualibus* (Eph 5:19) underlies stanza two of *Virgines castae*. This phrase is also used by Abelard in his preface to the second part of his hymn collection,[11] and is again echoed in three of Abelard's hymns: *Christiani plaudite*,[12] an Easter hymn; *Ecce domus Domini*,[13] a dedication hymn; and *Iustorum memoriam*,[14] a hymn for feasts of confessors. While the appearance of this pauline phrase in the preface to a collection of hymns, or in a hymn is certainly not unusual, yet in the context of the Paraclete, it becomes one more way in which Abelard exhorts the nuns to identify themselves with the sequence's bride and to find their deepest identity in singing their bridegroom's praises. If, as we suggested in that earlier chapter, Abelard's sequence does indeed link the pauline distinction

11. Waddell, CLS 4:7.
12. CLS 9:63.
13. CLS 9:84.
14. CLS 9:121.

between persons 'wise' and 'foolish' (Eph 5:15) with the gospel parable of the wise and foolish virgins (Mt 25:1-13), then the phrase 'singing psalms and hymns and spiritual songs among yourselves' must have taken on a special significance in the Paraclete world, for by *Virgines castae* and *Epithalamica* Abelard is exhorting Heloise and her nuns to be numbered among the wise virgins. Moreover, the pauline description of Christ's self-giving love for his bride the Church (Eph 5:23), which appears after the exhortation to sing psalms, hymns, and canticles, suggests the spiritual marriage so central to Abelard's bridal song.

In his hymn *Iustorum memoriam* Abelard preceded the phrase from Eph 5:19 with the words *dignam laudibus*. Then, within a few lines, he followed the pauline phrase with the terms *sollemnes hostiae*, which he linked with the verb *exsolvuntur*. This chain of words forms a noteworthy parallel between the hymn and the sequence:

Iustorum memoriam	*Virgines castae*
Iustorum memoriam,	Psalmis *et* hymnis
dignam laudibus,	canticis dignis
Psalmis, hymnis, canticis	*sibi colloquentes*
spiritalibus	
Mater ovans	
celebrat ecclesis,	
Quorum fidens	
postulat suffragis.	
Summe pater,	
Tibi grates	
Et sollemnes hostiae	Solvant *in istis*
De collatis	*debitae laudis*
Tuae donis	hostias sollemnes
Exsolvuntur *gratiae*	

(Continued)

Iustorum memoriam	*Virgines castae*
Worthy praise of godly men *offered heartily,* *Psalms and hymns and canticles* with sincerity, Now the Church awards her sons forever sure, Trusting them in turn for prayer intense and pure. Highest Father, to you we give thanks.	Speaking to one another in fitting *psalms* *and hymns and canticles,* *Let them pay* by these (songs) *solemn sacrifices* of due praise.

If we put like terms in juxtaposition, a fundamental verbal link becomes visible between the hymn and *Virgines castae.*[15]

Seq.	*condignas laude . . . Psalmis et hymnis, canticis . . .*
Hymn	*dignam laudibus . . . psalmis, hymnis, canticis . . .*

Seq.	*Solvant . . . hostias sollemnes*
Hymn	*sollemnes hostiae . . . exsolvuntur*

Both songs begin with an introductory invitation to praise God. The *exordium* of the sequence exhorts the nuns to sing with the verb *solvant;* the hymn does the same but with the verb *exsolvuntur.*[16] Both verbs have the same meaning.

So great is the web of connection between Abelard's hymns and his other works that abundant quotation, parallelism, reference, allusion, and echo between Abelard's works and the sequences is precisely what one expects from him. That we should find Abelard quoting himself is only routine, contends hymnologist Joseph Szövérffy:

> In the Sunday and weekday hymns, we find numerous passages taken from Abelard's own writings, in the first place from his *Expositio in Hexaemeron* (PL 178. 731-784); Abelard's

15. Szövérffy, HP 1:118.
16. In the Waddell edition, the text is reading of Chaumont 31 is preferred to that of Brussels 10147–10158 followed by Dreves and Szövérffy.

use of Orosius and Macrobius in both his Sermons as well
as in his hymns was already indicated. In hymn #35, we
find a series of wordings, ideas, etc, which all come from
his *Sermo* IV (PL 178.409-417) word for word ('verus sol,'
'ortus,' 'occasus,' Herod and the *magi* etc.) For hymn #37,
we find parallels in his Commentary on Paul's letter to the
Romans and in his *Sermo* III (PL 178:398ff.) etc. The hymns
for Candlemas (#38-41) are linked up again with *Sermo* V
(PL 178.417 ff.) but some passages are found in *Sermo* II (PL
178.395), etc.) and in *Ep.* VII (ibid. 237); the same applies to
Hymn #39 (cp. PL 178.419). For hymn #40, we find material
from the *Theol. Christ.* (CC 12.173, 12.292, etc.) and from
Sermo XI (PL 178.461). The Passion hymns can be derived
from his *Sermo* XI, Commentary on Paul's letter to the Romans, his *'Ethica'*, etc., also from Sermons XXX, XXXII, the
Expositio symboli quod dicitur Apostolorum (PL 178.617-630).
Practically all the sermons could be quoted as sources for
the interpretations of the hymns.[17]

By repeating images and phrases Abelard wove a verbal tapestry
by which he sought to inculcate the virtuous christian bridal-self
at the Paraclete.The rhetoric of *Virgines castae* and *Epithalamica*
suggests that this virtuous self would take shape at the Paraclete
as the nuns individually and communally developed the ability
to live in accordance the saintly example of Psalm 44's supreme
virgin and her virginal followers.

We have already observed[18] that Psalm 44 is the source for
stanzas 3-5 of *Virgines castae;* and that Abelard tells the story of the
queen and her virgins through the argumentative force of narration, rationale, examples, and contrary.[19] Medieval people commonly identified the queen and the daughters of Tyre 'by *figura*
with Mary and the early Christian virgin martyrs'.[20] We can be
certain that Heloise and her nuns connected Psalm 44 with Queen

17. Szövérffy, HP 1:118.
18. See Chapter 2, pp. 38, 66ff.
19. See chapter 3, pp. 110ff.
20. Dronke, '*Virgines caste*', 99.

Mary with her virginal retinue. Indeed, by its placement at Mass *Virgines castae* made manifest the links between the Old Testament queen and her virginal followers and the New Testament virgin Mary and hers—which included the Paraclete nuns.

Abelard's use of Psalm 44 suggests that he considered it central to the Paraclete nuns' understanding of their vocation and their *sensus communis*. In his sermon for the Annunciation, he teaches that the Old Testament queen alluded to in Psalm 44 is the shadow of the New Testament Virgin-Mother Mary.[21]

> So Mary is called blessed among women more than among men, because the grace of her virginal manner of life has multiplied through imitation mostly among females; just as the psalmist before proclaimed, saying: 'The queen assists at his right hand,' etc. and again: 'The virgins of the king are led after her; they are led into the temple of the king'. After her, he says, they are led into the temple of the king because through imitation of this supreme queen, innumerable virgins have been consecrated in the true temple of God.[22]

In his Letter Six to Heloise on the origin of nuns, Abelard refers to Psalm 44:16, 17 when explaining why, unless there is imminent peril of death, the consecration of virgins may not be celebrated at any other season other than during Epiphany, Easter week, and on the feast days of the Apostles.[23] Because virgins are precious

---

21. See Eileen Kearney, 'Master Peter Abelard, Expositor of Sacred Scripture: An Analysis of Abelard's Approach to Biblical Exposition in Selected Writings on Scripture' (Ph.D. diss. Marquette University, 1980) 275.

22. PL 178:383-384: *Benedicta igitur Maria in mulieribus potius quam in viris dicitur, quia haec ejus gratia virginalis propositi in feminis maxime per ejus imitationem mulitplicanda fuerat, sicut et Psalmista antea praedixerat, dicens: Astitit regina a dextris tuis, etc. (Psal. XLIV, 10). Et rursum: Adducentur regi virgines post eam, adducentur in templum regis (Ibid. 15). Post eam, inquit, adducentur in templum regis, quia per imitationem hujus summae reginae, virgines innumerae in verum Dei templum sunt consecrandae.*

23. PL 178:242: *Virginum quippe consecrationem nisi periculo mortis urgente celebrari alio tempore non licet quam in Epiphania et Albis paschalibus, et in apos-*

and rare[24] the Church consecrates them only on chief festivals devoted to Christ. Because they are his virgin brides, special recognition of their purity is only fitting. Again, he turns to Psalm 44 to
confirm the recognition accorded the virgin brides of Christ:

> Over the marvelous virtue of [virgins] the whole church
> greatly rejoices, just as the psalmist has proclaimed in these
> words: 'The virgins of the Queen are led after her;' and
> again, 'With joy and exultation shall they be brought: they
> shall enter into the king's temple'.[25]

Stanza 3 of *Virgines castae* possesses another unmistakable
verbal connection with Abelard's use of Psalm 44. In it Heloise
and her nuns surely would have heard the echoes of Abelard's
hymn *Quantum sponso,*[26] Sermon One[27], and Letter Five[28]:

Virgines castae (stanza 3)

Hec est adextris	This one is assisting at the
assistens regis,	right hand of the king
illa regina	that queen

---

tolorum natalitiis. Translation in Montcrieff, 'Nuns', 154; this letter, summarized,
appears as Letter Six in Radice, 180–182.

24. On the significance of virginity in the early church, see Peter Brown,
The Body and Society: Men, Women and Sexual Renunciation in Early Christianity,
Lectures on the History of Religion, vol. 13 (New York: Columbia University
Press, 1988). Virginity in medieval Christianity is treated by John Bugge, *'Virginitas:' An Essay in the History of a Medieval Ideal.* Archives internationales d'histoire
des idées, series minor, 17. (The Hague: Martinus Nijhoff, 1975).

25. Muckle, 'Religious Life', 267–268: *De quarum scilicet virtute mirabili universa amplius congaudet ecclesis, sicut et psalmista praedixerat his verbis: Adducentur
regi virgines post eam et rursum: Afferentur in laetitia et exsultatione, adducentur in
templum regis.* Translation, Moncrieff, 'Nuns', 155.

26. Hymn 94, stanzas 2 and 3, in CLS 9:132; PL 178:1815; AH 48:216; HP
2:249.

27. PL 178:387.

28. PL 178:200A.

Virgines castae (stanza 3) Cont'd

Iuncto latere	*united beside*
sola cum rege;	alone with the king
precedit ipsa	she processes
Aurata veste,	clothed round about in
varietate	golden variety
circumamicta;	
Tamquam dominam	every blessed virgin follows
sequiter ipsam	after her [the queen] as her
queque beata.	lady.

Sermon I

Magnum est, est filia, incomparabile bonum te coelestis regis sponsam . . . ; ut quasi regina coelorum et iuncto latere *assistas, et cum eo, ceteros omnes praecedas in vestitu deaureato . . . .*

She [Mary] is great; she is the daughter, the incomparably good bridegroom of the king of heaven . . . ; so that as the queen of heaven, she stands *united beside* him [the king], and together with him, she goes ahead in front of all others in golden vestments . . . .

Quantum sponso

Subsequuntur sponsum	Others follow after the
ceterae,	bridegroom
Haec incedit iuncto latere.	she processes *united beside* [him]
Et regina sponsi tenens dexteram,	and the queen holds the right
Subsequentem turbam habet	hand of the bridegroom
ceteram,	with the remaining throng
	following

(Continued)

Letter V

Astitit Regina a dextris tuis. . . . Ac si aperte dicatur, ista iuncto latere *sponso familiarissime adhaeret, et pariter incedit, caeteris omnibus quasi a longe assistentibus vel subsequentibus.*	On your right stands the queen. . . As if it were openly stated [in Psalm 44], she is *united beside* the bridegroom, clinging to him most intimately, and walking in procession with him, while all the others stand at a distance or follow behind.

Anunciation Sermon

quasi regina caelorum ei iuncto latere *assistas, et cum eo, caeteros omnes praecedas . . . .*[29]	You [Mary], as queen of heaven, stand close, *united beside him,* and, with him, go ahead in front of all others . . .

All four works speak of the queen being *iuncto latere*—a turn of phrase that goes back at least to Origen.[30] 'United beside' the king, she leads the procession of virgins. Linking these works by such a simple, yet very unusual utterance is completely in keeping with Abelard's style. As Szövéffy has observed, Abelard often employs only a word, an expression, or an image that indicates his source—whether from his own works or from the Church Fathers.[31] *Iuncto latere* is but one of many phrases Abelard repeats to knit his Paraclete *liturgica* into one seamless cloth.

As we saw in our oral-scribal analysis in Chapter Two, Abelard rarely confined himself to servile reproduction of his sources. As Szövéffy writes, 'He nearly always interprets, expands, or symbolically exploits the biblical [and nonbiblical] passages used as a starting point'.[32] *Virgines castae* teems with material traceable to Abelard's favorite passages from the Bible and the Fathers.[33]

---

29. PL 178:387 D.
30. See Chapter 2, p. 73.
31. HP 1:89.
32. HP 1:88.
33. See HP 1:91 and 109.

Abelard draws on his much-loved Psalm 44 and follows Origen in adding to its narrative the words *iuncto latera*. The brief phrase was likely enough to remind the Paraclete nuns of Origen's text and to allow Abelard to claim that the Virgin Queen processes at the side of her King while dedicated virgins follow close behind them. In the following stanzas of *Virgines castae* he then shifts his focus from the king and queen to the queen's virginal cortège.

Stanza 4 refers to personages well known to medieval Christians.[34] Our rhetorical analysis identified this material as argumentation via example. By the early Middle Ages the virgin-saints Agnes, Thecla, Lucy, and Agatha were social rather than simply textual figures.[35] That is, people throughout medieval society could speak of them without reference to any particular text. Many clerics and lay persons, for example, would have known of little Agnes's dramatic martyrdom. Ardently courted by the son of a prestigious Roman, she refused his advances, declaring that she was already espoused to her heavenly bridegroom. When the young man fell sick with love, his father summoned Agnes and, upon learning of her christian faith, demanded that she make formal sacrifice to the roman gods or be thrown into a brothel. Again Agnes refused. She was then led naked through the streets of Rome to a brothel, where her suitor's attempt at ravishing her was met by instant death. Her enemies sought next to burn her; when they failed, one managed to behead her.[36]

Virgin martyrs like Agnes had a particular significance in certain cultural contexts, especially among female ascetics, among them Heloise and her nuns at the Paraclete. The combination of

34. Our rhetorical analysis identified this material as argumentation via example.

35. On the distinction between 'cultural' and 'textual' features, see Robbins, *Tapestry of Early Christian Discourse*, 110 and 117.

36. The stories of Agnes, Lucy, and Agatha are told in the classic thirteenth-century collection of saints' lives, Jacobus de Voragine's *The Golden Legend: Readings on the Saints*, translated by William Granger Ryan, 2 vols. (Princeton: Princeton University Press, 1993).

Thecla with Agnes, Lucy and Agatha, which we noted above,[37] led Peter Dronke to propose a possible north italian provenance for *Virgines castae*.[38] Thecla's cultus was minimal in medieval France during Abelard and Heloise's day, yet she was one of the virgin-saints added to the early Paraclete calendar (under the date 23 September).[39] Agatha, Agnes, and Lucy were three of four virgin martyrs on whose feasts twelve lessons were read at Vigils. Cecilia is the fourth, but in *Virgines castae*, Cecilia is missing from the traditional quartet of principal virgin martyrs. At the Paraclete, Thecla—while not accorded the maximum twelve lessons—was considered important enough for her *Life* to be read aloud to the community before Compline.[40]

What might have led the Paraclete nuns to replace Cecilia with Thecla? If we imaginatively enter the cultural context of Abelard and Heloise, a possible explanation appears. In the letters exchanged between the couple, we discover that several texts by Jerome loom large in their correspondence. Perhaps the most important of these is the famous letter (22) he wrote to the virgin Eustochium, a veritable spiritual directory for consecrated virgins.[41] Near its conclusion, Jerome describes a procession headed by Mary, Mother of the Lord, who has in her train choirs of virgins:

> What will that day be like when Mary, Mother of the Lord, comes forth to meet you, accompanied by her choirs of virgins? . . . Then Thecla will fly joyfully into your embrace.[42]

Perhaps Abelard singled Thecla out as one of the queen's attendants because the great Jerome had included her in his own nar-

37. See Chapter Two, p. 84.

38. Dronke, '*Virgines caste*', 96.

39. On the Paraclete liturgical calendar and Thecla's place in it, see CLS 3:269.

40. CL 3:269.

41. See our scribal analysis above, Chapter Two.

42. PL 22:422: *Qualis erit illa dies, cum tibi maria Mater Domini choris occurret comitata Virgineis? . . . Tunc Thecla in tuos laeta volabit amplexus.*

ration of the supreme virgin's world. Or perhaps he did so because he knew that Heloise and her nuns already honored the virgin on their calendar and respected Jerome's authority.

We know from Abelard's letters to Heloise that he identified closely with Jerome. Describing Jerome as 'the greatest doctor of the Church and glory of the monastic profession',[43] Abelard declared himself the saint's heir 'as regards slanders and false accusations'.[44] Unquestionably, Abelard drank deeply from the works of Jerome; one might call Jerome his mentor in the ascetic life. In Abelard's symbolic world Jerome's story and writings loomed large; his Paraclete writings suggest that Abelard determined that the same should be true of the nuns' world.

The echoes between *Virgines castae* and Jerome's writings would not have been lost on Heloise. Her summary of Jerome's arguments against marriage in his *Adversus Jovinianum* make it clear she equally knew and admired Jerome's work.[45] In the final chapter we shall look more closely at Heloise's own argument against marriage and her contention that Abelard's marrying her would fundamentally undermine his self-understanding and public recognition as a philosopher and cleric. For now we are concerned with Abelard's efforts to shape the cultural identity, the *sensus communis*, of the Paraclete nuns as a choir of virgins following their abbess, the embodiment in their community of heaven's highest virgin.

It was through Jerome's letter to Eustochium that Abelard justified his addressing Heloise as one of heaven's bridal ladies. In one of his letters Abelard greeted Abbess Heloise as 'my lady', adding, 'you were previously the wife of a poor mortal and now

43. McLaughlin, 'Rule', 289; Radice, 264.

44. Muckle, 'Consolation', 211; Radice, 105.

45. Abelard reports Heloise's 'argument in his *Historia calamitatium*; see Muckle, 'Consolation' 186–189; Radice, 70–75. On Abelard's knowledge of Jerome's *Adversus Jovinianum*, see P. Delhaye, 'Le dossier anti-matrimonial de l'*Adversus Jovinianum* et son influence sur quelques écrits latins du XIIe siècle,' *Mediaeval Studies* 13 (1951) 70–75.

are raised to the bed of the King of Kings'.[46] Certainly Abelard and Heloise were more than casual readers of Jerome. Abelard not only saw his own personal trials in the light of Jerome's calamities, he also turned to Jerome, the experienced counselor of women ascetics, as a guide in directing the Paraclete nuns. Abelard was keen to convince Heloise to play the same role among her nuns as Jerome's beloved Paula had with the women and girls under her care. This role—as our analysis of *Virgines castae* and *Epithalamica* increasingly suggests—was nothing short of being a Queen Mary, a Miriam, a Mary Magdalene, and leading her virginal followers in seeking after marriage to Christ. Abelard did not see Heloise as these Marys in the sense of role-acting; rather, the Marys' experience, articulated by Scripture and Abelard, should so stamp Heloise's character that she may find her identity by following in the footsteps of these saints.[47]

The 'self' that Abelard expected Heloise and her nuns to find in and through his texts was not the autonomous, individual self of modern western culture. In Mary Carruthers' words, 'Self-expression is a meaningless term in medieval context'.[48] The medieval 'self' was not defined over and against society; society constituted and completed the person. Medieval personality was 'dyadic', group-oriented. For medieval people, the most elementary unit of social reality was not the individual person but the 'dyad', the person in relation with and connected to some group, whether family or community. As Scripture scholar Jerome Neyrey has stated,

> A dyadic personality is one that needs another person constantly to know who he or she is. Such a person perceives himself as always interrelated to other persons, while occupying a distinct social position both horizontally (with others sharing the same status, ranging from center to pe-

46. Letter IV; Muckle, 'Letters', 83; Radice, 137.
47. On the importance of character as a mark stamped on a person much as a character is impressed on a coin or seal, see Carruthers, *Memory*, 179–182.
48. Carruthers, *Memory*, 182.

riphery) and vertically (with others above and below in social rank). Group oriented persons internalize and make their own what others say, do, and think about them because they believe it is necessary, if they are to be human beings, to live out the expectations of others.[49]

The society in which the individual nun lived included not only her sisters but every deceased saint and sinner whose presence and past experience was mediated to her through oral tradition, sacred texts, and liturgical song. Reciting and singing texts constituted a highly active communal dialogue between her mind and the voices called forth by memorized or written texts. The dialogue occurred most profoundly on the stage of the monastic liturgy and was central to the teleological process of morally transforming the individual nun and her community into perfect brides of Christ. The stage upon which this dialogue occurred was the Paraclete *sensus communis*. Past and present persons engaged in a historically extended, socially embodied exchange that was fundamentally ethical or tropological. The dialogue occurred most profoundly through the readings and songs of the monastic life and was central to the teleological process of morally transforming Heloise and her community into perfect brides of Christ.

Gregory the Great nicely summed up the moral goal of *lectio*—reading—and liturgical song, when he declared, 'We ought to transform what we read [and sing] into our very selves, so that when our mind is stirred by what it hears our life may concur by practicing what has been heard'.[50] The point of reading and memorizing Scripture, hymns, sequences, and commentaries was to identify so deeply with Jesus' and the saints' mode of being

---

49. Jerome H. Neyry, ed., *The Social World of Luke-Acts: Models For Interpretation* (Peabody: Hendrickson, 1991) 73. See also Bruce J. Malina and Jerome H. Neyrey, *Portraits of Paul: An Archaeology of Ancient Personality* (Louisville: Westminster John Knox Press, 1996).

50. Gregory, *Moralia in Job*, 1.33 (PL 75:542C), quoted from Carruthers, *Memory*, 164.

that one's character was marked by their image and likeness. This lifelong process began in obedience, by conforming outwardly to right living. As we shall see in Chapter Six, Heloise knew that external conformity did not transform one's character. Virtue must abide deep within; goodness must become habitual, a state of being in which the ways of God and his saints abide in the fabric of one's soul.

In his Annunciation sermon,[51] just a few lines before the *iuncto latere* passage quoted above, Abelard styled Agatha the Virgin Mary's *imitatrix*. Abelard's *liturgica* were calculated to move Heloise, like Agatha *imitatrix*, to identify with the experience of the highest virginal bride who presents her virgina followers, the nuns under her charge to Christ the King. Understanding the tropological significance of *Virgines castae*, which is closely related to this sermon, helps us better understand van Deusen's earlier point that medieval sequences served to make manifest the transition from the Old Testament to the New Testament.[52]

This movement from Old Testament to New Testament, from exemplary story to exemplary story, was fundamentally ethical. The chorus of voices that filled medieval Christendom's memory was formed not only habits of thought, but also habits of character. As Mary Carruthers states, 'Character indeed results from one's experience, but that includes the experiences of others, often epitomized in ethical commonplaces, and made one's own by constant recollection'.[53] In fact, medieval culture lived less by ethical rules than by ethical memories.[54] 'One sometimes gets the impression', Mary Carruthers writes:

> that a medieval person . . . could do nothing (especially in duress) without rehearsing a whole series of exemplary stories, the material of their experience built up board by

51. PL 178:387C.
52. Above Chapter Three.
53. *Memory*, 179.
54. *Memory*, 182.

board in memory, and, as Gregory [the Great] says, transformed into their very selves, so that even in moments of stress the counsel of experience will constrain a turbulent and willful mind'.[55]

The ethical content of Abelard's sequences arose out of the topics of love, virginity, marriage, faith, and Christ the Lamb as they were recollected and embodied in the characters of the sequences and thereby lodged as an experienced event in the memories of the Paraclete nuns. The tropological exhortation of Abelard's sequences suggests that he expected the nuns to work long and hard to internalize and impress into their memories the exemplary deeds and words of others, and so to make them their own.

Not that this 'sequencing' between the Testaments was *only* tropological. Both *Virgines castae* and *Epithalamica* foreground their tropological emphasis against the background of the literal and allegorical levels of the Old and New Testament texts they evoke. Moreover, their tropological emphasis contains within it a deep sense of the anagogical significance of the biblical text. The moral life urged in the sequences (and the biblical texts between which they mediated) is an anticipation of the life to come. The sequences functioned to transition the Paraclete nuns not only between the Testaments, but also between this life and the age of the resurrection.

The nuns could hardly have missed the range of saintly deeds and words that echoed between *Virgines castae* and the works Abelard wrote at Heloise's request. For example, Agatha and Agnes are paired in Abelard's Letter Six (On the Origin of Nuns) in a passage thematically and verbally related to *Virgines castae*.[56] In celebrating the great zeal women have for chastity, Abelard marshals the example of these two virgins. The passage begins with a host of ideas spun together in *Virgines castae*.

55. *Memory* 180.
56. PL 178:250A-C.

> Who, lastly, does not know that women embraced the ex-
> hortation of Christ and the counsel of the Apostles with so
> great zeal of chastity that, to preserve the integrity of flesh
> and mind alike they offered themselves as a holocaust to
> God in martyrdom, and triumphant in the twofold crown,
> sought to follow the Lamb, the Bridegroom of Virgins,
> whithersoever he should go? . . . Who also has shown the
> devotion of holy virgins to be so pleasing to Himself that a
> multitude of Gentile people hastening to seek the protection
> of Saint Agatha, spreading out her veil against the terrible
> fire of boiling Etna, He saved from the loss both of body
> and of soul. . . . This also not a little commends the dignity
> of holy women, that they consecrated themselves by their
> own words, saying: 'With His Ring He hath espoused me:
> I am Betrothed to Him'. For these are the words of Saint
> Agnes, whereby the virgins who make her profession are
> betrothed to Christ.[57]

Many christian women have preserved the *integrity* of *flesh* and
mind, offering themselves as a *holocaust* to God in martyrdom and
following the lamb, the bridegroom of virgins, whithersoever he goes.
Abelard develops each of these topics in the stanzas following
the appearance of Thecla, Agnes, Agatha, and Lucy. In Abelard's
Letter Six, he tells of Agatha giving witness to Christ before Gentiles, and being protected from the torment of boiling Etna. Her
story gives proof of God's profound love of virgins, reasoned

57. Muckle, 'Religious life', 275: *Quis denique ignoret feminas exhortationem
Christi et consilium apostoli tanto castimoniae zelo esse complexas ut pro conservanda
carnis pariter ac mentis integritate Deo se per martyrium offerrent holocaustum, et
gemina triumphantes corona agnum sponsum virginum quocumque ierit sequi studerent? . . . Qui etiam sanctarum devotionem virginum in tantum sibi gratam esse
monstravit ut gentilis populi multitudinem ad beatae Agathae suffragium concurren-
tem velo eius contra aestuantis Aethnae terribilem ignem opposito tam a corporis quam
animae liberaret incendio. . . . Illud quoque non modicum sanctarum dignitatem com-
mendat feminarum, quod in suis ipsae verbis consecrantur, dicentes: anul suo subar-
ravit me etc; ipsi sum desponsata, etc. Haec quippe verba sunt beatae Agnetis in quibus
virgines suam professionem facientes Christo desponsantur.* Translation Moncrieff,
'Nuns', 166–167.

Abelard, and also reveals the depths of divine love. Indeed, Agnes's faithful words of betrothal had become for Abelard the precise words of every virgin who makes her profession to Christ.

Abelard further explains the special grace of virginity in stanza 5 of *Virgines castae*, where the words *puriores . . . sanctiores* have a remarkable parallel to a pseudo-Jerome letter, *Virginum Laus*.[58] Abelard and Heloise, and very likely the Paraclete nuns, knew this text and accepted it as one of Jerome's letters. Abelard quotes it extensively in his praise of virgins in Letter Seven (Abelard's Rule for the Paraclete Nuns).[59] Having quoted Jerome's praise of virginity from his Letter 22 to Eustochium, Abelard continues lauding the virginal state by quoting *Virginum Laus*.

> [Jerome] also writing to a virgin dedicated to God of the virgins consecrated to God, what blessedness in heaven and what dignity they enjoy on earth, thus beginning says: 'How great blessedness holy virginity shall enjoy in heavenly things, apart from the testimony of Holy Scripture, we are taught also by the custom of the Church, wherefrom we learn that a special merit subsists in those who are spiritually consecrated. For whereas each and all of the multitude of the faithful receive equal gifts of grace, and all alike glory in the same sacramental blessings, these have something special beyond the rest, when out of that holy and spotless flock of the Church, as *holier and purer* victims of the merits of their intention, they are both chosen by the Holy Spirit and are offered by the High Priest on the Altar of God'.[60]

58. PL 30:168.

59. PL 178:242B.

60. Muckle, 'Religious life' 275: *Qui etiam ad virginem Deo dicatam scribens de consecratis Deo virginibus, quantam in coelo beatitudinem, et in terra possideant dignitatem, ita exorsus, ait: 'Quantam in coelestibus beatitudinem virginitas sancta possideat, praeter Scripturarum testimonia, Ecclesiae etam consuetudine edocemur qua addiscimus peculiare illis subsistere meritum quarum spiritalis est consecratio. Nam cum unaquaeque turba credentium paria gratiae dona percipiant, et hisdem omnes sacramentorum benedictionibus glorentur, istae proprium aliquid prae eteris habent, dum de illo sancto et immaculato Ecclesiae grege quasi* sanctores puriores *que hostiae pro*

Embedded in *Virgines castae* are language and symbols that echo Jerome, Abelard's most highly regarded authority on the consecration of virgins. Once again Abelard, the master rhetorician, connects his hymns with each other and with biblical and patristic sources by a single key word.

That the Paraclete nuns could not have heard connections between Abelard's hymns and stanza 6 of *Virgines castae* is unlikely; the chaste virgins are described as a *holocaustum*, a 'burnt offering' to the Lord. Abelard uses the word *holocaustum* in at least five of his hymns.[61] *Da Mariae tympanum* (stanza 1), celebrating Christ's resurrection, directs Jacob (Israel) to join Miriam in offering God a *holocaust* of song. *Pugnant mundi principes* (stanza 2) applies the term to Christ's martyrs. Abelard describes virgin-martyrs as holocausts in *Sponsa christi* (stanza 3) and *Quantum sponso* (stanza 1)—two of his four hymns for virgins. *Peccatricis beate sollemnitas* (stanza 2) declares that no *holocaust* can relieve the guilt of sin like heartfelt repentance.

Virgines castae and *Epithalamica* were designed to remind Heloise and her sisters that at profession they—like Thecla, Agnes, Lucy, and Agatha and all the martyrs—had given themselves as a burnt offering to Christ in the integrity of both body (*carne*) and mind (*mente*). We have already seen the parallels between the virginal holocaust of Jerome's comments in his *Adversus Jovinianum* and Abelard's *Virgines castae*.

---

voluntatis suae meritis a Spiritu Sancto eliguntur, et per summum sacerdotem Dei offerunter altario. Item: Possidet ergo virginitas . . . et quod alii non habent, dum . . . et peculiarem obtinet gratiam et proprio, ut ita dixerim, consecrationis privilegio gaudet'. Translation adapted from Moncrieff, 166–167.

61. Hymn 29, *Da marie tympanum* (stanza 1), directs Jacob (Israel) to join Miriam in offering God a holocaust, a sacrifice of song (CLS 9:43; PL 178:1786; AH 48,:163; HP 2:76). Hymn 82, *Pugnant mundi principes* (stanza 2), applies the term to martyrs (CLS 9:117; PL 178:1809; AH 48:202; HP 2:206). Virgin martyrs are so designed in Hymn 92, *Sponsa christi* (stanza 3) (CLS 9:130; PL 178:1814; AH 48:215; HP 2:244) and Hymn 94, *Quantum sponso* (stanza 1) (CLS 9:132; PL 178:1815; AH 48:216; HP 2:249). Hymn 96, *Peccatricis beate sollemnitas* (stanza 2), declares that no holocaust can relieve the guilt of sin like heartfelt repentance (CLS 9:134; PL 178:1816; AH 48:220; HP 2:264.).

Adversus Jovinianum	*Virgines castae*
Grandis fidei est, grandisque virtu-	Holocaustum *Domino*
tis, Dei templum esse purissimum,	*Offerent ex integro*
totum se holocaustum *offerre*	*virgines carne*
Domino; et justa eumdem Apos-	*integrae mente*
tolum, esse sanctum et corpore et	*immortalem sponsum*
spiritu.	*eligentes Christum*
It is a mark of great faith and of	As a burnt-offering
great virtue, to be the pure	virgins offer to the Lord
temple of God, to offer oneself a	the integrity of their
whole burnt-offering, and, ac-	flesh and mind
cording to the same apostle, to be	choosing Christ as
holy both in body and in spirit.	their immortal Spouse.

In the marvelous way Abelard had of quoting his sources—whether the source is himself or others—he could transform the relatively mediocre wording of prose texts into superb poetry by changing a single word or phrase.

Both Jerome's *Adversus Jovinianum* and Abelard's *Virgines castae* agree that it is not enough for the virgin to give her flesh; the true virginal soul gives all she is to God. It is in describing this 'all' that the two texts show a subtle but important difference. Jerome makes the traditional distinction between *caro* and *spiritus*. *Virgines castae*, by contrast, makes the less typical distinction between *caro* and *mens*.[62] Waddell has recognized Abelard's tendency to prefer the pair *corpus-mens* or *caro-mens* to the more common *caro-spiritus*.[63] For example, in his Annunciation sermon, where he is discussing the *desponsata* of Mary to Joseph, Abelard asks,

> *Sed quae, quaeso, est dignitas, esse virginem in* carne, *si jam per consensum corrupta fuerat* mente?

> But where, I ask, is the dignity of being a virgin in the *flesh* if the *mind* through consent [to marriage] has been corrupted?[64]

62. Waddell, in 'Chaste Virgins' 30–31, notes that most other medieval writers made a distinction between *caro*, the 'flesh', and *spiritus*, the 'spirit'.
63. Waddell, in 'Chaste Virgins', 31–32.
64. PL 178:381C. My translation.

He uses the couplet again in his sermon for the Circumcision of the Lord. Discussing circumcision in the Old and New Testaments, he makes his point by contrasting the exterior circumcision of the *carnis* with the interior circumcision of *mentis*.

> *Pro signo autem justitiae jam habitae circumcisionem suscepit, ut videlicet interiorem* mentis *vitiis circumcisionem, hoc est justitiam fidei, exterior circumcisio* carnis *ostenderet potius quam faceret.*

> Now the sign that one has received a just and habitual circumcision is most clearly in the interior life of one's *mind*, that is, through the righteousness of faith, more than through the exterior circumcision of the *flesh*.[65]

Often, as Waddell has noted, Abelard links some form of the word *integritas* to his *caro-mens* pairs,[66] as he does in his Annunciation sermon:

> *Unde nequaquam de hac promissione dubia, de modo requirebat quo esset complenda, utrum scilicet per admissionem viri sine dilectione peccati, sicut in paradiso fieret si homo non peccasset, an* integritate corporis *partier et* mentis *conservata, sicut in ejus proposito fuerat.*

> About this promise there should be no doubt; it must be fulfilled, whether, to be sure, it is through the work of a man without the love of sin, just as it would have been done in paradise if man had not sinned, or through one who preserved the *integrity of her body and mind*, just as it is stated in his [the angel's] announcement [to the Virgin Mary].[67]

This grouping also appears with *holocaustum*, in Abelard's Letter Six: *pro conservanda* carnis *partier ac* mentis integritate . . . offerent holocaustum.[68] Although Abelard most frequently joins the *caro-*

---

65. PL 178:398D. My translation.
66. 'Abelard and the Chaste Virgins', 30–31.
67. PL 178:385 B.
68. Above, note 53.

mens pair with *integritas* and *holocaustum*, in his hymn *Sponsa christi*, Abelard also used the more traditional pairing, *caro* and *spiritus*,[69] and joins with it *integritas* and *holocaustum*.[70]

Integratam spiritu quam corpore	With integrity of spirit and body,
holocaustum verum fit	she offers a true offering
ex virgine	from her virginity.

We can now see that verse 6 of *Virgines castae* not only uses words found in Abelard's sermons and hymns, it uses these words in the same combination. In the pages to come, we shall see similar word groupings shared by the sequence and Abelard's works for the Paraclete.

Let us turn now, however, from the axis of intertexture to the axis of rhetoric. We need to go beyond the identification of common words and phrases to the rhetorical goals of all of this language. Rhetorical analysis will help us see the significance of Abelard's *caro-mens* pairing within his broader argument before the Paraclete nuns.

Nothing in Abelard's use of the *caro-mens* suggests that he followed Origen, who identified 'the redeemed person with the *mens* alone, and who predicate[d] a flight from the body and its affects as a necessary precondition for holiness'.[71] Origen considered the literal meaning of the Song of Songs so erotically intoxicating as to endanger readers; hence, he insisted that 'the literal carnality of the Song veils a spiritual meaning (*allegoria*), even as the human body houses a [rational] soul'.[72] By overcoming fleshly desires, the rational soul (*psyche* or *anima*) takes flight to its original state and becomes once more a *mens*. Abelard, by contrast, did not teach the Paraclete nuns that the perfected soul (*anima*

---

69. Hymn 92; CLS 9:130; PL 178:1814; AH 48:215; HP 2:244.

70. Hymn 90, a hymn for virgins; CLS 9:130; PL 178:1814; AH 48:215; HP 2:245.

71. Astell, *Song,* 6.

72. Astell, *Song,* 2.

perfecta) was a *mens* free from the body and its lower, body-linked sensitivity or *affectus*.[73]

The Paraclete spiritual director must be included in that wide circle of twelfth-century commentators on the Song of Songs—Anselm of Laon, Bernard of Clairvaux, Rupert of Deutz, William of Saint Thierry, Gilbert of Hoyland, John of Ford, Alan of Lille, and Isaac of Stella—who envisioned 'a holistic redemption of body and soul made possible through a firm identification with, and engagement of, the lower, body-linked powers—that is, the affects'.[74] Bernard of Clairvaux, for example, taught that the soul's union with God is experienced not primarily as intellectual enlightenment, but as a deeply loving, personal surrender to God.[75] Richard Weingart and Paul L. Williams have shown that Abelard, no less than Bernard, placed love of God at the center of Christian faith.[76] He never ceased to marvel at Christ's great love for humanity, or to exhort his readers to yield their whole being—mind, *affectus*, and body—to God's love in Christ. One interpreter of the atonement has written of Abelard, 'Paradoxically enough, this man, whose life was broken because of the tragic consequences of his love of Heloise and whose theological career was lived out in the midst of a storm of controversy,

---

73. On Abelard's theology, see Richard E. Weingart, *The Logic of Divine Love: A Critical Analysis of the Soteriology of Abailard* (Oxford: Clarendon Press, 1970); and Paul L. Williams, *The Moral Philosophy of Peter Abelard* (Lanham: University Press of America, 1980).

74. Astell, *The Song of Songs*, 6. See also, Denys Turner, *Eros & Allegory: Medieval Exegesis of the Song of Songs* (Kalamazoo, Mich.: Cistercian Publications, 1995) especially 38–43.

75. See, for example, Bernard, Sermo 7:2.2, in *Sermons super Cantica Canticorum*, in *Sancti Bernardi Opera*, 1, edd. J. Leclercq, C. H. Talbot, H. M. Rochais (Rome: Editiones Cistercienses; , 1958) 31-32; translated Kilian Walsh and Irene Edmonds in *Bernard of Clarvaux: On the Song of Songs*, 1, Cistercian Fathers Series, 4 (Spencer, Massachusetts-Kalamazoo, Michigan: Cistercian Publications, 1971) 38–39.

76. Weingart, *The Logic*; and Williams, *The Moral Philosophy* (above, note 73), especially 80–84; 151–172.

became the greatest advocate of that interpretation of the work of Christ which sees in it supremely love enkindling love'.[77]

In *Virgines castae* and the Paraclete works linked to it, Abelard seeks to draw his audience into the divine embrace by identifying each nun with bride in the Song of Songs and with the emotive directives of the Song's literal meaning. While Abelard allegorized the Song of Songs' lushly erotic celebration of two unnamed lovers' passionate joys and sorrows, he *'reliteralized* the spiritual meaning of the Canticle by clothing it in poetry and prose replete with the moving *sensual* power of the original text'.[78] Whereas Origen had used allegory to escape the Song's embarrassing and potentially dangerous literal meaning, Abelard, like his contemporaries, valued the Canticle 'for the affects it awakens, the example it sets, the images it provides for the communication of personal and communal experience'.[79] *Virgines castae* suggests that Abelard, no less than Bernard in his sermons on the Song, seized upon the emotive force of the Song's *literal* meaning—the union of woman and man—to arouse *pathos* in his audience and to move them to identify with the bride of heaven. Once again we see that the discourse of *Virgines castae* was designed to 'sequence' the Paraclete nuns from the literal level of the Old Testament song to its Gospel significance—union with God in Christ.

Abelard uses language and symbols throughout his Paraclete works that stresses affection, sweetness, desire, heat, emotion, and passion. *Virgines castae* and its companion Paraclete *liturgica* articulate Abelard's teaching 'that the proper human response to the divine call issued through the inspired text is that of the *Sponsa'*.[80] He assumes and expects the Paraclete nuns to agree that the sexual union of earthly marriage bears some metaphoric

---

77. Robert H. Culpepper, *Interpreting the Atonement* (Grand Rapids, Michigan: William B. Eerdmans Publishing Company, 1966) 88.

78. Astell, *Song,* 18—my emphasis.

79. Astell, *Song,* 28.

80. Astell, *Song,* 10.

likeness to union with God through spiritual marriage.[81] Hence, Abelard's sequences are fundamentally tropological readings of the Song of Songs, designed to inspire his audience to appropriate the experience of love and to awaken longings in *caro* and *mens* for the embrace of Christ. Through the sequence he seeks to make manifest the Gospel message adumbrated in the Old Testament Song and have it embodied in the Paraclete world.

Let us return to *Virgines castae* and see further how the liturgical song worked to 'sequence' the Paraclete nuns into heaven's mode of being.

Having chosen Christ as their bridegroom (*sponsum eligentes Christum*), true virgins like the Paraclete nuns are wedded, according to stanza 6 of *Virgines castae*, to their immortal bridegroom (*Immortalem sponsum*). At least two of Abelard's sermons echo this same idea: Sermon 30 declares that virgins join themselves to the immortal bridegroom (*sponso immortali se copulant*)[82]; Sermon 1, Abelard's Annunciation sermon, proclaims: 'you [Paraclete virgins] have chosen not a man, but God as your bridegroom' (*non virum sed Deum elegistis sponsum*).[83]

By choosing Christ instead of worldly marriage, the Paraclete nuns exchanged a host of problems for heavenly nuptials.[84] Stanza 7 of *Virgines castae* marshals a few of the commonplace woes of married life that Saint Jerome often held before the ascetic women under his tutelage: the pangs of childbirth, the torments caused by a husband's mistress, the annoyance of nurses.[85] In

81. Metaphoric language here is used not simply in the sense of poetic imagination and rhetorical flourish; metaphors can and do create reality. See George Lakoff and Mark Johnson's *Metaphors We Live By* (Chicago: The University of Chicago Press, 1980) especially 139–146.

82. PL 178:569C.

83. PL 178:383A.

84. Theologia Christiana, II; PL 178:1198D-1200C; CCCM, 171. In *Abelard*, 195, Clanchy notes that Abelard 'wrote in *Theologia Christiana*, "how great are the obstacles, the burdens, and the dangers in which marriage abounds".

85. Jerome, *epp* 22, 18, 54; and *Adversus Helvidium*, 20. See Dronke, '*Virgines caste*,' 101.

our rhetorical analysis we observed that these woes serve as argument from the contrary. Anaphora and contrary argumentation contrast the weal of heavenly marriage with worldly union. The virgins in the train of the supreme Virgin offer themselves in spiritual marriage to Christ, the heavenly bridegroom. Anaphora and contrary argumentation contrast the weal of heavenly marriage with worldly union.

Stanza 7's pessimistic description of some of the woes suffered by wives takes us once again to Abelard's references in both sermons and letters to Jerome's Letter 22 to the virgin Eustochium. Both Abelard and Heloise knew and used it—she to persuade Abelard to be her Jerome and write her a word of consolation, he to persuade Heloise that she was Christ's bride and that Christ was her only consolation.

HEAVEN'S NUPTIAL BED

Stanzas 8-11 sought to lead the Paraclete nuns into the virgin's sweet heavenly nuptial chambers and to focus their attention upon the beloved's bed. In them *Virgines castae* narrates the story of every virgin's spiritual marriage. This nuptial story reaches its climactic moment when the bridegroom himself breaks the narrative flow with his own words of love and authority.

In stanza 8, we find the word *vacari*, a frequently used word in the medieval vocabulary.[86] Abelard, Heloise, and the Paraclete nuns all knew the word and its contemplative meaning well. In Letter 5 Abelard uses the term in the contemplative way when he exhorts Heloise (and her nuns) with these words:

---

86. *Vacantes* ought to be in the same case as *harum*, but *Lectulos harum Christo vacantium* would violate both rhyme and meter. It is for reasons of grammar, I assume, that Dronke, *'Virgines caste'* 100, translates: 'These maiden's beds, awaiting Christ . . .'.) For more on the significance of *vacari* in monastic teaching, see J. Leclercq, *'Lectulus.* Variazioni sul un tema biblico nella tradizione monastica,' in *Bibbia e Spiritualita* (Rome, 1967), 417–436; or in *Otia monastica. Etudes sur le vocabulaire de la contemplation au Moyen Age,* Studia Anselmiana, 51 (1963) 134.

*Vos autem, quae in cubiculum caelestis regis ab ipso introductae
atque in eius amplexibus quiescentes . . . ei toto vacatis.*

But you, you who have been led by the king of heaven
himself into his bedchamber, and who, resting in his embrace . . . , *give yourselves* wholly to him.[87]

In *Virgines castae, vacare* is used in combination with the term
lectulos ('narrow bed'). With the joining of these two words, one
truly enters the cultural world of the Paraclete. The Paraclete
nuns would have been very familiar with the symbol of the 'narrow bed'; it was a major theme in many of Abelard's liturgical
contributions to the abbey. He began his night office canticles
and the canticles assigned to Easter, and the feasts of Mary Magdalene and of Virgins with the Song of Songs text, *In lectulo meo
per noctes quaesivi quem diligit anima mea . . . .* (3:1-5).[88]

In stanzas 9-11 we are told that the soul who gives herself
to Christ enjoys the connubial bed of her immortal bridegroom.
In his Letter Four to Heloise Abelard writes:

[*Sponsa*] *introductam se dicit in cubiculum regis, it est in secretum vel* quietem contemplationis, *et lectulum illum de quo
eadem alibi dicit:* In lectulo meo *per noctes quaesivi quem diligit
anima me*a . . . .

She, the bride, has been led into the king's bedchamber, that
is, to that secret, quiet place of contemplation, and into the
narrow bed of which she elsewhere says: '*On my narrow bed*,
night after night, I sought my true heart's love . . . .'[89]

Contemplatio, meditatio and *ruminatio* are terms that referred to
the process of memory-training, storage, and retrieval by which
monks and nuns internalized Scripture, liturgical texts, and commentary on such texts. *Meditatio* was the discipline of committing
the substance of a text to memory, re-presenting it in order to
make it one's own.[90] *Ruminatio*, writes Mary Carruthers, evoked

87. PL 178:203A.
88. CLS 3:360 and 386.
89. PL 178:201D.
90. Carruthers, *Memory*, 222.

'an image of regurgitation, quite literally intended; the memory is a stomach, the stored texts are the sweet-smelling cud originally drawn from the meadows of books (or lecture) [and liturgy], they are chewed in the palate.'[91] Abelard wanted Heloise and her nuns so to masticate and digest his sequences and other liturgical contributions that they become lodged in their collective and individual memory, thereby becoming part of their very being and experience.

In a lengthy section toward the beginning of his Rule for Women Religious (Letter Eight), Abelard writes approvingly of the virgin who refuses to rise from her bed of contemplation for any earthly man, no matter how wealthy, powerful, or honorable.[92] Women saints have excelled at withdrawal from the world, contends Abelard and draws on his most trusted authority, Jerome, in telling the story of a virgin who graciously begged Saint Martin's indulgence in not visiting her, for, she declared, 'I have never been visited by a man'.[93] Of this virgin, Abelard writes approvingly, *Haec revera de contemplationis suae* lectulo *surgere dedignata vel verita.* ('This woman in fact disdained or feared to rise *from the bed* of her contemplation'.[94]) In Abelard's Paraclete *liturgica* the bed of the virgin is a narrow bed of *contemplatio*; disturbing it is to be avoided.

Abelard returns to the same topic toward the end of the Rule, where his treatment of separation from the world is largely a commentary on the symbol of the *lectulus*:

> Whoever therefore wishes to learn the secret of monastic quiet must be glad to have a *narrow bed* and not a wide one. From the wider bed, as the Truth says, 'one will be taken, and the other left'. But we read that the *narrow bed* belongs to the bride, that is, to the contemplative soul which is more

91. *Ibid.*, 165.

92. PL 178:265A.

93. McLaughlin, 'Rule' 249: *Ibi, pater, ora quia numquam sum a viro visitata.* McLaughlin notes (n. 69, p. 249) that she was unable to locate the passage in Jerome's works.

94. *Ibid.*

closely joined to Christ, and clings to him with the strongest
desire. None, we read, have been left who lay on this, and
the bride herself says of it: 'By night on my *narrow bed* I
sought him whom my soul loves'. She also refuses or fears
to rise from this *bed*, but answers, as we said above, to the
knocking beloved. For she believes that the dirt she fears
will soil her feet is only outside it.[95]

As Chrysogonus Waddell has noted,[96] phrases such as *lectulum nostrae quietis* abound in Abelard's sermons and letters. In
one of his sermons for the feast of Saint Stephen, Abelard takes
as his text precisely a verse from the Song of Songs (3:7): *En* lectulum *Salomonis sexiaginta fortes ambiunt* ['Around *the narrow bed* of
Solomon there are sixty mighty men']. The bed is not the Church
as a whole, but 'the narrow bed' big enough only for the relatively
few who choose, like the Paraclete nuns, the 'quiet of holy continence'.[97] The Paraclete nuns are 'brides' because their life is
wholly given over to God, *vita Deo penitus vacans.*[98] *Lectulus, quies,
contemplatio,* and *vacare* are all terms that Abelard places at the
heart of Paraclete identity. These metaphors are more than flights
of poetic imagination and rhetorical flourish, they help create
and preserve the cultural and spiritual reality of the Paraclete
world.[99]

This characteristic language was not entirely gender-specific:
In his sermon for the Dedication of a Church—a sermon not

95. PL 178:305A: *Quisquis itaque quietis monasticae secretum desiderat,* lectulum *magis quam lectum se habere gaudeat. De* lecto *quippe, ut Veritas ait, unus assu-
metur et alter relinquetur.* Lectulum *vero sponsae esse legimus, id est animae contem-
plativae Christo arctius copulatae et summo ei desidero adhaerentis. Quen quicumque
intraverit neminem esse relictum legimus. De quo et ipsamet loquitur: In* lectulo *meo
pernoctans quaesivi quem diligit anima mea. A quo etiam* lectulo *ipsa surgere dedig-
nans vel formidans pulsanti dilecto quod supra meminimus respondet. Non enim sordes
nisi extra* lectum *suum esse credit quibus inquinari pedes metuit.* English adapted
from Radice, 255–256.

96. 'Chaste Virgins,' 37.

97. PL 178:570A: . . . *sanctae continentiae quietem.* . . .

98. PL 178:570A.

99. See Lakoff and Johnson, *Metaphors We Live By*, 143–146.

written for the Paraclete but for a male monastic community—he writes:

> To Christ the *faithful soul* unites herself, as though *bride,* and dedicates herself, and sleeps, as it were, in his *embraces* in the *narrow bed of contemplation—sleeps in body,* but *keeps watch in mind,* in keeping with the *bride*'s words: '*I sleep, but my heart keeps watch'.*[100]

Abelard recognized that in relation to God every human soul is feminine. A few paragraphs earlier, Abelard had spoken of the betrothal of the faithful soul (*fidelis anima*) to which Christ unites himself as his bride (s*e . . . quasi propriam sponsam Christo se copulat*), so that henceforth she (*anima*) may totally give herself to him (*ut ei deinceps tota vacet*).[101] Christ embraces every responsive soul in the narrow bed of contemplation.

Fidelis is another term in stanza 9 calculated to shape the Paraclete nuns' understanding of themselves and their symbolic world. *Fidelis* is not found in the Song of Songs, yet in numerous instances Abelard linked the term with the virginal bride. In his hymn for feasts of virgins he writes: *Quantum Sponso* fidelis *haec (sponsa) fuerit* [102] ('How faithful is this bride to her bridegroom') and *hic in* fide *facta foedera* ('Here in faith she has been united').[103]

In several of these non-Paraclete works Abelard uses *lectulus, vacare, sponsa, amplexus, contemplatio, dormire, cor, corpus, vigilare,* and *fidelis* in a short span of text and in the same theological context as he does in stanza 9 of *Virgines castae.* This complex of interrelationships of language and topic points to Abelard's particular vision for Heloise and her community. Through his hymns,

---

100. Sermon 28, *In dedicatione Ecclesiae;* PL 178:551-552D . . . . *cui* (i.e., Christo) *se* fidelis anima *quasi* Sponsam copulat, *et dedicat, et velut in* amplexibus *eius* lectulo contemplationis dormit corpore, *sed* vigilate mente, *iuxta illud* Sponsae: Ego dormio et cor meum vigilat. . . . My translation.

101. PL 178:551D.

102. Hymn 94; CLS 9:132; PL 178:1815; AH 48:216; HP 2:252.

103. Hymn 95;CLS 9:133; PL 178:1816; AH 48:217; HP 2:252.

sermons, and sequences he is seeking to shape the symbolic world of Christ's faithful and vigilant virginal brides who are being called to his narrow bed where in his embrace they may contemplate his great love for them (stanzas 10-11).

Returning to stanza 8, we find that angels—rather than the soldiers of Solomon—are standing guard (*custodientes*) about the Paraclete virgin's nuptial bed, reserving it alone for Christ and his bride.

We know that Abelard insisted on safeguarding the chastity of the Paraclete nuns—perhaps remembering all too well his seduction of the maiden Heloise. In his Rule, he requires the male *praepositus* (prior) promise before community and bishop that he will scrupulously protect the nuns against 'carnal contagion'.[104] Even the lesser clerics must swear in their profession-formula to safeguard the bodily purity of the nuns as best they can.[105] Comparison between the Rule and *Virgines castae* suggests that, in Abelard's mind, the *praepositus* was the Paraclete nuns' angelic custodian.

As in *Virgines castae*, so in Abelard's Saint Stephen's Day sermon and his hymn for the feasts of virgins, guardians protect the narrow bed lest it be violated by the adultery of diabolical temptation, defiled by the contagion of fleshly pleasures, or disturbed by the tumults of worldly concern.[106] Every October 21, on the feast of the 11,000 Virgins, the Paraclete resounded with the singing of *Virgines castae* at Mass and Abelard's hymn *Ut aurora* at Vespers. Both pieces are bridal songs, *epithalamica*. Both also tell of angels who guard Christ's virgins, as we read in stanza 2 of the hymn:[107]

104. McLaughlin, 'Rule' 260: *carnali contagio*. . . ; PL 178:277A; Radice 213.

105. McLaughlin, 'Rule', 260; PL 178:277A.

106. *The Saint Stephen's Day Sermon; PL* 178:570C. Hymn 95; CLS 9:133; PL 178:1816; AH 48:217; HP 2:252.

107. Hymn 95; CLS 9:133; PL 178:1816; AH 48:217; HP 2:252. The feast for the 11,000 virgins commemorated the death of the 11,000 virgins who met their death with Saint Ursula. The earliest accounts of Ursula's story go back to the eighth century. The number of the virgins who perish varies from five to eight and eleven, but by the early twelfth century their number had soared to a veritable army 11,000 strong.

Paranimphos illic habet angelos	Here there are Paranymphic angels,
quos custodes habuit hic proprios	who are watching over this property.
ad superna thalamorum gaudia	These angels in procession lead
illam pompa deducit angelica	her above to the joys of the bridal
hinc obuiam uirgo uirgines	bed.
illinc martir habet martires	Here the Virgin meets the virgins,
	there the Martyr holds the martyrs.

Christ and his betrothed Paraclete virgin are being joined in wedlock before heaven's hosts. Angels, *paranimphos*, both sing of their nuptials and guard the couple's marriage bed.

Virgines castae goes further than *Ut aurora*, adding that guardian angels ward off lascivious individuals with drawn swords. Dronke has linked the stanza to Saint Ambrose's *De virginibus*.[108] Yet Ambrose does not speak specifically of angels fighting off rival human lovers; he simply taught that virgins merit the special guardianship of the angels.

Stanza 8 has one other word that calls for commentary: *Incestus*, meaning generally 'impure' and more narrowly 'incestuous', appears quite frequently in Abelard's sermons and letters. It shows up in cognate form in a text by Gregory the Great[109] on which Abelard drew in his Saint Stephen sermon. There Abelard, following Gregory, claims that an angel extinguished the fleshly lusts that seriously defiled (*incestabatur*) a certain Abbot Equitius. A few lines later Abelard speaks of an *incestuosam vitam*, an incestuous life.[110] Against this impure life driven by libido angels guard Christ's virgins.

THE VIRGINAL FLOWERING OF THE CHURCH

Virgines castae (stanza 12) and Cyprian agree that virgins are the flowering of the Church. Abelard used this metaphor to describe the Paraclete virgins in his very fine hymn *Quantum sponso*. As in *Virgines castae*, Abelard there describes the virgins who follow

108. 'Virgines caste,' 101.
109. PL 77:165.
110. PL 178:571C.

the heavenly queen of Psalm 44. She is, according to the hymn's verse 2, *iuncto latere* with the heavenly bridegroom. Having guarded the integrity of her body (*corpus integrum*, stanza 1), she offers herself whole to her bridegroom. A garland of lilies and roses is woven into the virgin-bride's hair. She wears purple and white linens, symbolizing royalty and purity, and, as in the sequences, she also carries lilies and roses. A reference to Revelation 14:4 occurs in stanza 2, together with a further reference to the cortège of virgins who follow the virgin bride. In stanza 4 we see a further parallel between the sequence and the hymn in a combination of the words *sertum* and *intextum*, a reference to the fragrance Christ finds so sweet and to the garlands and bouquets the virgins bear.

Quantum sponso (vv. 1-4)[111]

Quantum sponso fidelis haec fuerit,	How the bride is constant in her faith to Christ
Tam ipsius vita quam mors docuit,	All her life has witnesses, though her death sufficed
Illa corpus integrum custodiens,	Guarding well her body whole and undefiled,
Haec ipsius holocaustum offerens;	this she offered freely, fully reconciled.
Virgo sponsa, *Virgo sponsus est,* *Sponsa martyr,* *sponsus martyr est.*	Virgin bride and virgin bridegroom both, Martyrs with their first espousals' oath.
Talem sponsum talis sponsa decuit,	Such a bridegroom rightly merits such a bride.
Quae secuta sit, quocunque ierit,	She will follow in the way— wheresoever his footsteps guide.

(Continued)

111. Hymn 94; CLS 9:132; PL 178:1815; AH 48:216; HP 2:251. Translation Freeland, *Hymns,* 129–130 (hymn 122).

Quos nec sacrae carnis decor dividat,

Like in beauty of their consecrated flesh,

Nec in morte dispar amor pateat;

so in death this love unites the
two afresh.

Sub sequuntur sponsum ceterae,

Other maidens walk behind the
spouse,

Haec incedit iuncto latere.

but for her more favor he allows.

Et regina sponsi tenens dexteram,
Subsequentem turbam habet ceteram
In vestitu deaurato renitet
Et coronas supradictas possidet;
Certe aurum hor est optimum,
Incorruptum est et rutilum.

Heaven's queen is held upon the
bridegroom's right; Others follow in a throng in virgin white.
She, resplendent in her robe of
cloth of gold, Leads on those
whose crown it is her right to
hold. Surely this is gold of quality, Uncorrupted, shining
splendidly.

Sertum rosis intextum et liliis
Sunt insigne martiris et virginis,
In odorem christo suauissimum
martir rosam, uirgo profert lilium
indumenta dant insignia,
candens bissus, rubra purpura.

Garlands woven with the lily
and the rose Mark the virtue
that the virgin martyr shows.
Odors brought to Christ are
sweetly redolent; Martyrs bring
the rose, and virgins lily's cent.
Even clothes denote their holy
place; Royal scarlet, whiteness of
their grace.

Pulchri gressus Eius sunt in calceis,
Quos et sponsus collaudat in canticis,
Quis sit eius ornatus, praedictum est,
Quo sit eius progressus, dicendum
est.
Ipsi decus, ipsi gloria,
Qui tot fecit mirabilia.

Beautiful processions, sandals
on their feet, Hear the bridegroom's praise in songs their
hearts repeat. What their course
and order is has been designed;
Where their movement carries
them must be defined.
His the beauty, his the majesty
Who created so amazingly.

Once again we find another abelardian hymn intertwined with *Virgines castae*. Written for the third nocturn of the Feast of All Saints, *Communis celebritas* (stanzas 4 and 5) reads:[112]

His chorus adiungitur Virginum	Here the virgins' chorus stands,
Et rosis intexitur Lilium,	Here among the roses and lilies
Flos insignit corceus Medium.	Purple flowers mark the land.
Trina florum talium Specie	Three ways are the flowers bred:
Sertum odoriferum, Domine,	You, O Lord, sweet odor spread
In te nitet omnium Capite.	Flourishing as flowers' head.

Chorus virginum, rosis intexitur lilium, sertum, odoriferum—terms characteristic of *Virgines castae* appear in Abelard's hymns *Quantum sponso* and *Communis celebritas*.

The language of *Virgines castae* in stanzas 12-19 finds parallel in several of Abelard's prose works linked to Heloise and the Paraclete. In his sermon for Saint John the Evangelist (Sermon 25), for instance, Abelard combines Revelation 14:4 with the roses and lilies metaphor.[113] More striking is Abelard's Sermon 32 for Saint Stephen's Day, where *le Mestre* encourages Christians—male and female—to imitate the first martyr:

> who is the example of those who following the lamb wheresoever he goes are clothed in linen and purple together with a diadem of freshly harvested, interwoven roses and lilies.[114]

Revelation 14:4, linen and purple, roses and lilies, roses and lilies linked with the term *intextum*: this combination offers a significant parallel to the sequence, and once again reveals the rich intertexture of Abelard's Paraclete *liturgica*.

---

112. Hymn 105; CLS 9:140; AH 48:222; HP 2:271; Freeland, *Hymns,* 137 (hymn 132).

113. PL 178:537B.

114. PL 178:576D: . . . *qui exemplo eius Agnum sequens quocumque ierit, et bysso pariter indutus et purpura, rosis simul et liliis intextum percipiet diadem.*

Beyond Abelard's sermons, the same preponderance of terms appears in his Letter VII, on the origin of nuns, in a text on chastity:

> Having conserved equally the integrity of their flesh and mind, they [virgins] offer themselves to God as a holocaust through martyrdom, and win a double crown. Having given their solemn promise to God, the virgins strive to follow the lamb wheresoever he goes.[115]

Abelard would have the Paraclete symbolic world characterized by the same persons and actions.

The Unicorn-like Lamb

As we observed in our scribal analysis of *Virgines castae*, Abelard embarks in stanzas 14-18 on a literary development of the lamb topic that seems on the surface to be quite his own. The number of 'beast motifs' in Abelard's hymns is limited. One he does use is Christ as the 'Lamb of God',[116] yet no lamb like that of *Virgines castae* is apparent in his hymns or letters. In his Sermon 24, on the conversion of Saint Paul, Abelard reveals a deep knowledge of the unicorn legend, and applies the motifs of the legend to the life of Paul. Drawing on this myth, one that Heloise and her nuns, like almost anyone else in twelfth-century Europe, would have known, Abelard in *Virgines castae* describes a lamb who, on the one hand, cannot be stopped by humans and, on the other, takes his rest among virginal breasts. As our oral-scribal analysis in Chapter Two suggested, Abelard's development of the unicorn-like lamb metaphor is unprecedented, making it a uniquely abelardian contribution to the symbolic world of the Paraclete nuns.

---

115. PL 17:250A: . . . *ut pro conservanda carnis pariter ac mentis integritate, Deo se per martyrium offerent holocaustum, et gemina triumphantes corona, Agnum sponsum virginum quocumque ierit sequi studerent.* My translation.

116. HP 1:107.

The unicorn-like lamb evokes a vast range of ideas central to Abelard's message. The lamb has the strength and power to escape any human efforts to control him; nevertheless, he so loves virgins that he willingly lies in their laps The unicorn's association with both chastity and courtly love deepens the lamb's connection with the bridal and the sensual topics already voiced in the sequence. Finally, one cannot help but conclude that, in writing for Heloise, Abelard sought to contrast himself with Christ. His own story paralleled the tragic death of the mythical unicorn: once under the spell of his maiden (Heloise), the unicorn (Abelard) was surrounded by his enemies (Fulbert's henchmen) and dehorned (castrated). By contrast, Christ the unicorn is ultimately victorious. He gives his life for his beloved maiden and rises again to return to her lap. We shall see in Chapter Six that *Virgines castae* and *Epithalamica* offer an insight into Abelard's efforts at convincing Heloise that Christ is a bridegroom whose love is true and unfailing; she should seek after marriage with him.

The edges of the great cultural fabric that Abelard wove together and in which he sought to enfold the Paraclete are now coming into view. Abelard is engaged in a great project that has at its center the formation of a particular Paraclete symbolic world. At the center of Abelard's tapestry stands the king of heaven with his noble queen with her virginal attendants. Analysis of his sequences suggests that Abelard recognized the power of language, image, metaphor, and music to nurture a Paraclete common ground and *sensus communis*. His language of virginity and spiritual marriage are means of making and maintaining the conceptual system and kinds of liturgical and devotional activities of monastic Christianity.

We have seen Abelard intricately weave *Virgines castae* into the tapestry of Paraclete culture through word, phrase, metaphor, allegory, theology, and music. We now turn to Abelard's *Epithalamica* to seek further evidence of Abelard's efforts to form the identity of Heloise and her nuns.

THE CULTURAL TEXTURE OF EPITHALAMICA

On Easter day and, in abridged form, on Easter Thursday and Saturday, the nuns of the Paraclete sang *Epithalamica*. On this most sacred Sunday of the liturgical year, the Paraclete Ordinary suggests that Heloise did not lead her nuns in singing the sequences traditionally associated with Easter—*Victimae paschali laudes, Zima vetus, Fulgens praeclara*. This departure from long tradition is remarkable in light of the widely held assumption among modern liturgiologists that days of greatest solemnity are most resistant to change.[117] In place of traditional sequences the Paraclete nuns expressed their joy in Christ's resurrection through Abelard's sequence *Epithalamica*.[118] This choice showed their identity as disciples of Abelard.

For Abelard the *Song of Songs* was above all a paschal canticle. It is one of the major sources for his Easter and Ascension hymns.[119] *Le Mestre* also drew all three of the canticles he provided for the Paraclete Easter Sunday Office from the great scriptural canticle.[120] In addition, during Easter Week Heloise and her nuns seem to have read from the Old Testament's great drama of love in refectory.[121]

Epithalamica is an Easter play in miniature, as Chrysogonus Waddell has observed, and a condensed version of the Song of

117. E.g. Anton Baumstark, *Comparative Liturgiology* (London: A. R. Mowbray, 1958) 27.

118. Fassler, *Gothic Song*, Appendix 5, lists and discusses the Easter sequences sung at other monasteries.

119. The Easter hymns are 58–61, in CLS 9:65; PL 178:1795; AH 48:180; HP 2:131-132. The Ascension hymns are 62–65; CLS 9:71; PL 178:1797; AH 48:184; HP 2:133-141.

120. CLS 7:386-387. On the uniqueness of the Paraclete canticle repertory, see Waddell's commentary in CLS 3:359-361; or Waddell, 'Peter Abelard as Creator of Liturgical Texts,' in *Petrus Abaelardus (1079–1142). Person, Werk und Wirkung*, Hrsg. von Rudolf Thomas, Trierer theologische Studien (Trier: Paulinus-Verlag, 1980) 270–272.

121. CLS 7:140-141, with reference to a marginal addition to the Paraclete Ordinary, f. 59v.

Songs.[122] The four persons and groups identified long ago by Origen are present: the bride; her maidens; the bridegroom; and his companions. There is also a narrator who addresses the bride and then the first collective *persona*, her maiden companions, the daughters of Zion. The second collective person comprises the groomsmen, who bid the maidens welcome to the nuptial feast.

The two principal characters are the bride and the bridegroom. Only the bride actually appears on stage. It is she who makes the bridegroom present by narrating his speech to her audience. Her song tells of his hasty visit and pressing demand that she slip away with him; his sudden disappearance; her wild search for him by night; and their ecstatic reunion. Finally, the narrator returns to the stage, exhorting the daughters of Zion to make the bride's nuptial song their own.

THE NARRATOR'S EXHORTATION TO NUPTIAL SONG

The backdrop for the actors is set by the position and novelty of the sequence's very first word: *Epithalamica*. Abelard seems to have been among the first, if not the first, to use this adjective derived from *epithalamium*, 'bridal hymn'.[123] *Epithalamica cantica* would immediately remind the Paraclete nuns that patristic tradition had long described the Song of Songs as the 'bridal song' *par excellence*, the bridal song that celebrates the love of God for his people, of Christ for his Church, of the Word for the loving soul.

The sequence would also direct the thoughts of Heloise and her sisters to Abelard's contributions to the Paraclete Easter liturgy. Every nun would have chanted at Lauds, just a few hours before Easter Mass, Abelard's paschal hymn *Da Mariae tympanum*;[124] and heard a public (and perhaps private) reading of Abelard's Easter sermon.[125]

---

122. Waddell, 'Epithalamica', 239–71; see especially 247.

123. Waddell, 'Epithalamica', 254.

124. Hymn 43; CLS 9:64; PL 178:1794; AH 48:179; HP 2:129; in Freeland, *Hymns*, 75–76 (Hymn 59).

125. Sermon 13; PL 178:484B–489A.

Hymn	Sermon	Epithalamica
Da Mariae tympanum,	*Quod quidem femina-*	*dic Sponsa cantica,*
Resurrexit Dominus	*rum canticum quanto*	*intus quae conspicis*
Hebraeas ad canticum	*mysterio plenum de-*	*dic foris gaudia*
Cantans provocet,	*scribatur, diligenter at-*	*et nos laetificans*
Holocausta carminum	*tendite. Hic quippe*	*de Sponso nuntia*
Iacob immolet.	*Maria, quae choro illi*	*cuius te refovet*
Subvertens Aegyptios	*feminarum praecine-*	*seper praesentia*
Resurrexit Dominus,	*bat, quae cum virum*	
Rubri maris alveos	*habuisse non legatur,*	
Replens hostibus,	*virgo intellegi-*	
Quos involvit obrutos,	*tur . . . non solum*	
Undis pelagus.	*cantasse memoratur,*	
Dicat tympanistria,	*sicut Moyses vel popu-*	
Resurrexit Dominus,	*lus, sed etiam proph-*	*Adulescentulae*
Illa quidem altera	*etes esse describitur, et*	*vos chorum ducite*
Re non nomine,	*tympanum in manu*	*cum haec praeci-nerit et*
Resurgentem meritia	*tenuisse. Quid enim*	*vos succinite*
Prima cernere.	*prophetes, nisi videns*	*Amici Sponsi vos*
	interpretatur? Cum vi-	*vocarunt nuptiae*
	sionem autem. . . can-	*et novae modulos*
	tat, cui verborum	*optamus Dominae*
	quoque mysteria domi-	
	nus revelat; cum in illa	
	videlicet populi libera-	
	tione, et hostium sub-	
	mersione non tam	
	corporum salutem at-	
	tenderet, quam ani-	
	marum figurari	
	propspiceret . . . .[126]	

(Continued)

---

126. PL 178:484.

Hymn	Sermon	*Epithalamica*
Give to Miriam the drum. Risen is the Lord today. With her singing let her come to the Hebrews' throng. Let not Jacob render dumb Sacrifice with song. Binding Egypt mightily risen is the Lord today. God has made his people free But in flooded graves Overcomes the enemy In the Red Sea's waves.	O how much does the exultation of the solemn Passover belong to the devotion and honor of women, as the pages of the Old and New Testaments bear witness. Indeed, according to the Old, with the completion of the first Pascha celebrated in Egypt by the people of God on the night that they were liberated through the affliction of the sons of Egypt, as the book of Exodus narrates, not only the men, but also the women rendered a song of joy to the Lord. As the same Scripture says, 'Now Moses and the sons of Israel sang this song to the Lord, and they said: "Let's sing to the Lord . . ."' Thereupon the same text directs the reader to the song sung alone by the	Sing O bride Your bridal canticles Sing outwardly the joys you gaze upon within and gladdening us give tidings of the bridegroom whose presence renews you forever more O Young maidens, form your choir When she [the bride] begins singing join in The bridegroom's friends have called you to the nuptials Let us welcome the songs sung by the lady

(Continued)

Hymn	Sermon	*Epithalamica*
Let melodists resound.	women: 'So Mary the prophetess, sister of Aaron, took a timbrel in her hand; and all the women went forth after her with timbrels and with dances; and she began the song to them singing, "Let us sing to the Lord . . .'" (Ex 15:20-21). Listen closely to how this mystery was fully and sonorously told of in the song of these women. This Miriam began to sing her song to this choir of women	
Risen is the Lord today.		
She, the other Mary, found		
Truth, not only name;		
Risen body, clothes unwound;		
Hers the first acclaim.		

Abelard's hymn, sermon, and sequence call for singing unto the Lord much as Exodus 15:20-21: *So Miriam the prophetess . . . took a timbrel in her hand; and all the women went forth after her with timbrels and with dances; and she began the song to them, exhorting: 'Let us sing to the Lord . . .'* .

The principal person in the sequence is the bride; she is at one and the same time Miriam of the Exodus, Mary Magdalene of the Gospels, the beloved of the Song of Songs, and, almost certainly, Heloise. By connecting the Paschal Vigil baptism with Miriam's canticle celebrating the Hebrews' miraculous passage through the Red Sea Abelard has followed tradition. Miriam, the *Maria* of the Old Testament, is both virgin (Scripture mentions no husband) and prophetess (one who speaks on behalf of God). Abelard undoubtedly understood *quibus praecinebat* ('she began the song to them'—Ex 14:21) to mean that Miriam served as song leader for the women who joined her in singing of God's victory over the Egyptians. As she sings her canticle, leading her women companions in song and dance, she tells of her inward vision, a revelation not only of passage through the death-dealing waters of the Red Sea, but also of the liberation of God's People through the sacrament of baptism. Hence, Abelard's rhetorical question: 'How can she be a prophetess, unless seeing she can also interpret? Now, in her visions, the Lord reveals to her every mystery in words, that is, she sings of her revelation'.[127] Abelard's explanation of Miriam's song provides the context for the narrator's exhortations to bridal song in the exordium of the *Epithalamica*. The narrator enjoins the bride-prophetess to describe in song the joys that she gazes upon within her heart. For the bride is, like Mary-Miriam, a prophetess.

Miriam's vision of baptismal waters at the Red Sea anticipates New Testament baptism. Hence Abelard's sermon moves to yet another Mary and her group of female companions: Mary Magdalene and the holy women who were the first to see the risen Lord and to proclaim his resurrection to the apostles. Abelard declares Mary Magdalene *apostolorum apostola* (apostle to the apostles), whom God sent to proclaim the joy (*gaudium*) of the resurrection to the first apostles.[128] Here phrase after phrase of the sermon parallels the topics and images of the first stanza of the sequence.

> Now if we also read over the series of events in the New Testament, we shall understand that Mary and the other women with her correspond with Miriam and her devout female companions, and that they were the first to exhibit joy over the Lord's resurrection, for we find that they alone gathered at his tomb. Therefore, Mary is remembered as a prophetess, that is, she is called the apostle to the apostles. She took in hand a corporal timbrel, that is, she had a spiritual timbrel. Because she loved the living Lord more than

127. PL 178:484D: *Quid enim prophetes, nisi videns interpretatur? Cum visionem autem, id est revelationem cantat, cui verborum quoque mysteria Dominus revelat.*
128. PL 178:485B.

others, she was more afflicted, shakened, and mortified by his death. For this reason she was the first to merit consolation from his resurrection, for she was the most anxious about and distressed by his death. Now she is called the apostle to the apostles; she is the legate to the legates. The Lord directed her to the apostles that she might announce the joy of the resurrection to them. That same Mary first proclaimed it to the others in song, and she, before the other women, attained the joy of the resurrection and she first proclaimed it by declaring what she had first seen to the apostles and the other men present gathered with them.[129]

Like her Old Testament namesake, Mary Magdalene leads a troupe of women in song. At their Lord's death the whole company of his followers had been distraught, but Mary and her sisters by their faith merited the honor of proclaiming the joyous news of Christ's resurrection. Abelard is explicit that Mary Magdalene, like Miriam of old, was the first to sing of what she had been the first to see: *et haec ante alias, gaudio resurrectionis primo est potita, et haec prima nuntiando praecinit quod prima viderat.* Then, like Miriam, Mary Magdalene leads her troupe in singing. Abelard makes the same point about the women 'meriting' the honor of being the first apostles in his Letter VII, on the origin of nuns.[130]

---

129. PL 178:485B: *Quod si Novi quoque Testamenti revolvamus seriem, et in hac Maria et ceteris cum ea feminis alteram Mariam, et cum ipsa devotas feminas, quibus primum Dominus suae resurrectionis gaudium exhibuit, competenter intelligamus, reperimus singula his convenienter aptari. Illa quippe prophetes memoratur, haec apostolorum apostola dicitur. Illa corporale tympanum sumpsit, haec spiritale habuit. Quo enim hae viventem Dominum amplius dilexerat, super ejus morte amplius afflicta, et quati mortificata fuerat. Unde et prima de resurrectione consoltionem meruit, quae de ejus morte amplius anxia et moesta fuit. Apostolorum autem apostola dicta est, hoc est legatorum legata: quod eam dominus ad apostolos primum direxerit, ut eis resurrectionis gaudium nuntiaret. Maria illa caeteris in cantico praecinebat, et haec ante alias, gaudio resurrectionis primo est potita; et haec prima nuntiando praecinit quod prima viderat. Post ipsam vero, ad caeteras geminas hos gaudium resurrectionis priusquam ad apostolos vel quolibet viros perventi.*

130. Muckle, 'Religious life,' 258; Moncrieff, 'Letters', 139.

The bride of the sequence exhorts her maiden followers to do likewise, and Heloise should do the same with her Paraclete nuns. In yet another way, we see *Epithalamica* serving in the Mass to 'sequence,' to make manifest the transition, between the Old and New Testaments, the passage from an old into a new life.

Each of these great women song leaders—Miriam, Magdalene, and the bride—functions as an *exemplum*. Their stories merge into one through a kind of rhetorical superimposition which invites their continuance by the Paraclete choir. In the sequence, the historicized allegory of the women's stories serves as a bridge, setting the songs of Miriam/Mary in direct contact with the bride's song. Abelard likens the bride's midnight search for her beloved to Miriam's emotional horror at the impassable Red Sea and the people's joyous escape through its parted waters, as well as to Mary Magdalene's sorrowful vigil at the tomb and her joyous realization of Christ's resurrection.

Stanzas 3-6 of *Epiphalamica* lack a distinctively abelardian content or expression; they are simply paraphrases of lines in *chreia*-like form of the Song of Songs. Yet in the context of Abelard's Easter hymns and sermon, the stanzas point to a particular rhetorical goal: to convince the Paraclete nuns that they are the choir of women led by Miriam, the maiden companions of the bride of the Song of Songs, and the women of the Gospel who with Mary Magdalene witnessed to and proclaimed the resurrection of the Lord.

The Bride's *Epithalamicum*

Despite this, various expressions in stanzas 3-6 are reminiscent of Abelard's other Paraclete songs. The very first words of the bride's song (stanza 3 of the sequence):

> *In montibus hic ecce saliens*
> *Ecce venit, colles transiliens*

unquestionably correspond to Song of Songs 2:8:

> . . . *ecce iste venit,*
> *saliens in montibus, transiliens colles.*

But stanza one of Abelard's Ascension hymn was inspired by the same text from the Song:

In montibus hic saliens[131]	*Epithalamica*
In montibus hic	*In montibus his* ecce
saliens	*saliens*
venit, colles	ecce *venit, colles*
transiliens,	*transiliens;*
Sponsam vocat	*per fenestras ad me*
de montis vertice:	*respiciens*
Surge, Soror,	*per cancellos dicit,*
et me iam sequere.	*prospiciens:*
He comes leaping	Behold! he comes leaping
upon the mountains,	upon the mountains.
He comes, springing over the	Behold! he comes
hills,	skipping over the hills
He calls his bride	Gazing upon me through the
	windows,
Arise, sister, and follow	looking through the lattices,
me now.	he says:

Remove the two-fold *ecce* from the sequence, and the first two lines are identical to those of the hymn.

As Waddell has recognized, we probably have to concede this identity to coincidence; they are just minor modifications of the Song.[132] Anyone reordering Vulgate words for the sake of rhyme and meter very likely would come up with these same lines. Abelard does, however, rearrange the Song of Songs passages in *chreia*-like form for purposes of persuasion. This reshaping serves Abelard's goal of 'sequencing' the nuns through the Old and New Testament stories and cultivating and nurturing a

131. Hymn 46; CLS 9:67; PL 178:1795; AH 48:181; HP 2:133; translation adapted from Freeland, *Hymns,* 77–78 (Hymn 62).

132. Waddell, '*Epithalamica*', 261.

specific symbolic world. *Epithalamica*, like *Virgines castae*, was fashioned to lead Heloise and her nuns through Scripture and patristic texts to their own vocation at the Paraclete.

In the light of Abelard's sermons telling of Magdalene's experience of Christ's empty tomb, the connection of stanzas 7-8 with Pope Gregory's Homily on Mary Magdalene at the empty tomb[133] makes perfect sense. Both the pope and *le Mestre* point to Mary's distress at finding the tomb empty. Likewise, the bride of the sequence seeks, but does not find her bridegroom. He, 'passing through, had already gone away' (*at ille transiens iam declinaverat*, stanza 5). Anxious and burning with zeal, the bride— like Gregory's and Abelard's Mary Magdalene—looks hither and thither for her beloved. Finally she passes—just as the bridegroom had—beyond the walls of the city and the watchmen and finds her beloved.

Transiens, 'passing over', is a key concept for Abelard. In Waddell's words:, 'it encapsulates the entire paschal mystery of the Lord who makes us pass with himself through and beyond death and mortality into life and immortality'.[134] In his Easter sermon Abelard makes much of Christ passing from this world to his Father:

> In the Pascha of old, the Lord passed through Egypt and slayed the first born, liberating his people through crossing the Red Sea; this solemn celebration is called the Passover (*transitus*). Immediately it is declared also that the day of the Lord's Resurrection corresponds with the Pascha. Having died and passed over in Christ, human nature is changed from mortality to immortality, from corruption to incorruption. The Lord passed over at a certain time and events were set in motion that immediately changed what was before; for instance, when he made what was mortal immortal and changed what was corruptible and passable or mutable to its contrary. This "Passover", so to speak, the Evangelist considers saying, 'Jesus knowing that his hour had come

133. See the scribal analysis above, Chapter Two, 62–65.
134. Waddell, 'Epithalamica', 262.

and that he would cross from this world to his Father, and
so on.' (Jn 13:1)[135]

In this sermon Abelard also juxtaposes, much as he does in stanzas 7-8 of *Epithalamica*, the woe of separation from, and the joy
of (re)union with, Christ. Abelard rings the changes on the topic
of delay and fulfillment:

> What wonder, therefore, if we pass those two days of the
> Lord's suffering and burial chiefly in the grieving of com-
> passion, so that after the weeping, laughter may be all the
> more dear.[136]

Epithalamica's couplets of weeping and laughter bear the
stamp of Abelard's preaching. In his pre-lenten sermon for Septuagesima Sunday[137] he makes much of Ecclesiastes 3:4, *Tempus
flendi / tempus ridendi*, 'A time for weeping / a time for laughing'.
As in his Easter sermon, he interprets the biblical verse eschato-
logically, leading his audience to the end-time consummation of
the present and the arrival of the heavenly Jerusalem. Until that
day, the Paraclete nuns can only weep. Sin and, even more, delay
bring tears. One day there will be joy and laughter.[138]

---

135. PL 178:485D-486A: *In veteri quippe Pascha, Dominus per Egpytum transiens, primogenitis interfectis, et per transitum maris Rubris populum suum liberans,
de nomine transitus hanc solemnitatem insignivit. Praesens quoque Dominicae resurrectionis dies non incongrue Pascha dicitur. Ipsa quippe immutatio humanae naturae
de mortalitate ad immortalitatem, de corruptione ad incorruptionem, quidam in Christo
transitus et motus fuit. Transit quippe in aliam statim, et quodammodo movetur, quia
in aliud quam prius fuerat, commutatur; veluti cum quod mortale erat fit immortale, et
quod corruptibile et passibile sive mutabile in contrarium vertitur. Hunc quidem transitum et evangelista considerans: sciens, inquit, Jesus, quia venit hora ejus, ut transeat
ex hor mundo ad Patrem, etc.* (Jn. 13:1).

136. PL 178:485D-486A: *Quid igitur mirum, si et biduum illud Dominicae pas-
sionis ac sepulturae in luctu compassionis praecipue ducimus, ut post fletum gratior
habeatur risus, nec jam Dominicae pressurae recordemur, resurrectionis gloria super-
veniente?*

137. Sermon 6; PL 178:425B-430C.

138. PL 178:430B.

The delay/fulfillment and tears/laughter couplets that feature so prominently in these sermons and in the sequence, Abelard also made central in the first of his hymns for the Sacred Triduum (Maundy Thursday, Good Friday, Holy Saturday).[139] He begins the opening stanza of his hymn for the first nocturn with a reference to this night for weeping: *Haec nox, carissimi, nox illa flebilis . . .* (This is the night, most beloved, the woeful night.)[140] This lamentation continues throughout his Triduum hymns with hymn 44 for Nocturn 3, declaring:

> *Nox ista flebilis prasensque triduum,*
> *quo demorabitur fletus ad vesperum*
> *donec laetitiae mane gratissimum,*
> *surgente Domino, sit moestis redditum.*

> For woeful is this night and the present triduum,
> wherein weeping tarries at evening until,
> at the Lord's rising, the most dear morningtide of gladness
> be restored to those who mourn.[141]

Even for the Lauds hymn for an ordinary Sunday, Abelard uses the same language for the same ideas. In *Advenit veritas* he speaks of death having turned to life and tears to joy; and, as in *Epithalamica*, this transformation results from Christ's resurrection:

> *Transacto Flebili de morte Vespere*
> *cum vita redditur Mane Laetitae*
> *resurgit dominus, apparent aneli,*
> *custodes fugiunt splendore territi.*

> Evening has meaning, as death in its dolefulness;
> life is resurgent with dawn in its joyfulness.
> God has arisen, the angels are witnesses.
> Guards are in fear, for the splendor is luminous.[142]

---

139. CLS 9:144-159; HP 2:105-126.

140. Hymn 106: CLS 9:145-146; AH 48:107-109; HP 2:105, 107, 108; Freeland, *Hymns* 41, 67.

141. CLS 145; HP 2:109.

142. Hymn 10: CLS 9:21; PL 178:1779; AH 48:150; HP 2:36; Freeland, 42.

Abelard concludes all fifteen of his hymns for Good Friday and Holy Saturday with a doxological reference to the 'laughter of paschal grace'.

> *Tu tibi compati sic nos fac, domine,*
> *tue participes ut simus glorie,*
> *Sic praesens triddum in luctuc ducere*
> *ut risum tribuas paschalis gratiae.*

> Lord, make us worthy to share in your pain,
> thus have a part in the joy of your reign.
> Present in grief while the long hours wane,
> so may we laugh with the joy we regain.[143]

From our cultural analysis, we see that Abelard was especially sensitive to the rhetorical power of the Song of Songs in forming identity. As the great drama of heavenly love, the Song requires enactment on the part of every soul; specifically, it calls for the Paraclete audience—as a collective choir and as individual members within their choral body—to appropriate the bride's words by responding to the bridegroom's utterance as to the very words of Christ. The Song provides a narrative by which the Paraclete Abbey and each of its members can discover and define their bridal self by seeking marriage with Christ and assuming their role in God's heavenly nuptial celebration. In *Virgines castae* and *Epithalamica* Abelard articulates Christ's tropological utterance. The Paraclete singer/auditor could never be a mere listener, objectifying the discourse of the *Sponsa et Sponsus*; Abelard insisted that she make the bride's song her own subjective song and lift her own virginal voice in longing praise of her Beloved.

The nun's emotional response to Christ allowed her, in Astell's words, 'to have a "sexual" experience of God—this, a surpassing sense of personal completion by him in body and soul—without the mediation of a man arousing those feelings first on a lower, directly physical level'.[144] Hence, as Abelard

143. Hymn 107: CL 9:147; AH 48:172; HP 2: 220, 110; Freeland, *Hymn*, 68 (Hymn 42).

144. Astell, *Song*, 63.

perceives it, the Paraclete nun's virginity is wrapped up in 'both her renunciation of sexual complementarity at the human level and her entering into a marriage with God that fulfills her personally (and therefore also sexually) at a higher level'.[145] The emotions she experiences in union with God, Astell observes, 'are similar and dissimilar to those of a woman coupled with a man—similar in kind, dissimilar in their unmixed purity and intensity. Each soul is called to marriage with God--a union realized imperfectly on earth, perfectly only in heaven.'[146]

Spiritual marriage with Christ runs like a thread of gold through all of Abelard's Paraclete works. His sermons, hymns, and letters fit together with *Virgines castae* and *Epithalamica* like the warp and woof of a fine tapestry. The evidence that Abelard composed all the elements of this great bridal fabric is simply overwhelming. Our detailed analysis of the sequences' oral-scribal intertexture, their poetry and music, and now their cultural texture reveals a web of connections between Abelard's Paraclete *liturgica* that is meticulous. Taken together, Abelard's sermons, hymns, letters and sequences reveal a master liturgist, a persuasive preacher, and insightful exegete—in short, a person with a breadth of skill and depth of understanding that fully accords with the brilliance long associated with Abelard.

145. Astell, *Song*, 63.
146. Astell, *Song*, 63.

6

THE BRIDE OF CHRIST

Nulla uiris doctis sentencia cercior ista est:
non nos commendant exteriora deo.
Ex habitu non sanctus eris, potes esse superbus . . . .

There is no idea that learned men accept as more certain
truth than this: external things do not commend us to God.
Your habit may make you proud, but not saintly . . . .

—*Peter Abelard*[1]

Nihil enim minus in nostra est potestate quam animus, eique
magis obedire cogimur quam imperare possimus.

Nothing is less within our power than the heart; we are
compelled to obey it much more than we are able to command it.

—*Heloise*[2]

THROUGH A CULTURAL ANALYSIS of *Virgines castae* and
Epithalamica we have seen Abelard hard at work shaping
and reinforcing the identity of the Paraclete community. At the core of the nuns' *sensus communis* stands Christ, the

1. *Carmen ad Astralabium: A Critical Edition*, ed. José M. A. Rubingh-Boscher
(Groningen: J.M.A. Rubingh-Boscher, 1987) 123, lines 301–303. This poem of
moral advice in elegiac distichs was written by Abelard for his son Astralabe.
2. Muckle, 'Letters', 241.

heavenly bridegroom. At his side stands his queen with her virginal attendants. *Virgines castae* makes quite clear that this queen
is the Virgin Mary and that her retinue includes every chaste soul
who embraces Christ as the beloved. Through his two sequences
and other Paraclete works, Abelard teaches that the supreme
Virgin radiates her presence on all virgins who follow her, transforming them through imitation into her own likeness. She is the
guide by whom every virginal soul finds its bridal self and enters
into the chamber of the heavenly bridegroom.

Abelard strongly suggests that at the Paraclete the embodiment of the Virgin Mary, Miriam of the Old Testament, Mary
Magdalene, Thecla, Agnes, Agatha, Lucy, Paula, Eustochium, and
every virginal bride of Christ is the abbess, Heloise. Heloise is a
moral catalyst within her community, called to inspire her nuns
with profound love for God.[3] When her nuns look at her, they
should see far more than a single holy woman. She is a foil, a kind
of transparency, through which past lives are 'sequenced' into the
present and present lives make past experience their own.

Abbess Heloise was expected to embody the nature and purpose of the christian life before her nuns. She was a living book,
the epitome of all the texts—the Paraclete Rule, the Bible, the
writings of the Church Fathers, breviaries, ordinals, Abelard's *liturgica*—that scripted the performance of the Divine Office at the
Paraclete. Led by Heloise, the nuns day after day celebrated a
liturgy—much of which had been composed by Abelard. The
nuns sang, read, heard, and memorized sacred texts for the sake
of learning to exercise and to develop the christian virtues of
willing obedience, proper desire, deep contrition, and loving humility. Abbess Heloise was called to display these virtues; she was
to be a scrupulous teacher, a firm director, and an earnest conduc-
tor, as well as an exemplary model. Her model was the Supreme
Virgin, the Virgin Mary, who summed up for Abelard all that

---

3. On christian exemplars, see Peter Brown, 'The Saint as Exemplar in Late
Antiquity', *Saints and Virtues*, ed. J. S. Hawley (Berkeley: University of California Press, 1987) 9.

Heloise should be.[4] Such a role placed a high calling upon Heloise; it was a vocation that many leaders in her day believed she accepted, but that Abelard believed she had not fully embraced.[5]

In this final chapter we shall consider how *Virgines castae* and *Epithalamica* figure into the historical intertexture of Abelard and Heloise. Historical intertexture, as defined by Vernon Robbins, refers to the 'textualization' of specific events that have occurred at specific times.[6] *Virgines castae* and *Epithalamica* give insight into Abelard's interpretation of two historical events in Heloise's life. When she took the vows of a nun, she became the bride of Christ. When she became an abbess, she became mother to a particular group of virginal brides and was responsible for guiding them into the embrace of Christ. Abelard's Paraclete writings reveal that he sought to persuade Heloise that these two events called her to a self-understanding that she could not deny without putting her very soul in jeopardy.

Heloise's marriages to Abelard and to Christ figure deeply in the letters exchanged between Heloise and Abelard. We learn from Abelard's *Historia calamitatum* that marriage and identity were both subjects they hotly debated in the early days of their relationship. In this letter of consolation, Abelard relates how he sought to right the horrendous wrong he had committed in seducing Heloise by promising her uncle Fulbert that he would marry her. Heloise resisted Abelard's proposal of marriage because, she argued, the married state would simply be at odds with the proper *ethos* of a philosopher. Abelard was a philosopher;

4. My thought in this paragraph has been deeply shaped by Asad, *Genealogies*, 125–167.

5. On the on-going debate over whether Heloise ever whole-heartedly committed herself to being a nun, see Linda Georgianna, 'Any Corner of Heaven: Heloise's Critique of Monasticism', *Mediæval Studies* 49 (1987) 221–53; Linda S. Kauffman, *Discourses of Desire: Gender, Genre, and Epistolary Fictions* (Ithaca: Cornell University Press, 1986); and Barbara Newman, 'Authority, Authenticity, and the Repression of Heloise', *Journal of Medieval and Renaissance Studies* 22 (1992) 121–157.

6. Vernon K. Robbins, *The Tapestry of Early Christian Discourse: Rhetoric, Society, and Ideology* (New York: Routledge, 1996) 119–120.

philosophers do not marry; therefore, Abelard must abstain from marrying her. Abelard's true identity rested in being a philosopher and teacher, not in being a husband and father.

Many years later the roles of the couple were reversed. Then Abelard resisted what he perceived as Heloise's stubborn refusal to accept the inner motives of the monastic life while externally carrying out her duties as abbess. He sought to persuade her to see the tragedies of their lives and their affair as God chastening and drawing them both to himself. Abelard's argument did not end with his letters. He used his hymns, sermons, *planctus*, and sequences to persuade the abbess to see herself, not as his former wife or mistress, suffering for wrecking a great man's life, but as Christ's bride. As such, she had honors and joys that far exceeded any that Abelard could have offered her or himself achieved in this life. Heloise should set her affections upon Christ, her true lover. Illustrating this debate over marriage and identity as well as determining the place of *Virgines castae* and *Epithalamica* in Abelard's rhetorical strategy requires us to revisit the famous story of Abelard and Heloise.

Abelard's seduction of Heloise, as he himself relates years later, was a sufficiently vile affair that he quite likely would have included his premonastic self among the *incestus* of *Virgines castae*, those 'incestuous' men who prey upon virgins. When he discovered Heloise and set about having his way with her, he had not the least trace of Christ's love for virgins. Nothing but lust and arrogance guided his action. In his *Historia calamitatum*, he tells of coldly calculating the seduction of the young woman who was known throughout France for her great learning: 'I considered all the usual attractions for a lover and decided she was the one to bring to my bed, confident that I should have an easy success'.[7]

A thirty-seven year old parisian Master, Abelard was now celebrated by his admirers as the most learned philosopher since Aristotle; he was 'at last at the top of the greasy pole' of the pa-

---

7. Muckle, 'Consolation', 182–183. Radice, 66.

risian intellectual world.[8] 'Knowing the girl's knowledge and love of letters', he wrote, 'I thought she would be all the more ready to consent . . .'[9] With his piercing exactitude of mind, Abelard had triumphed over some of the greatest intellects of his day—some of them his own teachers. Now he wished to have 'jocund intercourse' with Heloise and add the seduction of the most praised woman of France to his accomplishments.[10]

As Christ appoints angels to stand guard around his virgins (*Virgines castae*, stanza 8), so Heloise's guardian, her uncle Fulbert, like Abelard a canon of Notre-Dame, kept watch over her. Fulbert believed he had taken every precaution to protect her against predatory men. Whereas medieval male honor had a certain flexibility and could sometimes be regained, female honor was absolute; once lost it was gone forever. Any sexual offense, however slight, on a woman's part would destroy not only her own honor, but that of the male head of her paternal kin group as well. Fulbert and Heloise lived in a world in which the sexual purity of females was embedded in the honor of some male. Men were responsible for keeping watch over their females, lest they both be publicly shamed. Should a wife, a mother, or a daughter be violated, the deceived husband, father, or son became the object of public ridicule and dishonor, and took it upon himself to avenge the outrage committed against his household. Fulbert clearly had deep personal and social reasons for protecting Heloise. His honor, social recognition, and standing rested in part upon his protecting the virginity of Heloise.[11]

---

8. Clanchy, *Abelard*, 74.

9. Muckle, 'Consolation', 183; Radice, 66.

10. Muckle, 'Consolation', 183: . . . *et sic semper iocundis interesse colloquiis.* See Clanchy, *Abelard*, 134.

11. See Georges Duby, ed. *A History of Private Life*, 2: *Revelations of the Medieval World* (Cambridge, Massachusetts: Harvard University Press, 1988); and Marc Bloch, *Feudal Society*, trans. L. A. Manyon (Chicago: University of Chicago Press, 1961). Biblical scholars have begun to recognize the profound importance of honor in ancient and modern non-westernized Mediterranean society. For an excellent introduction to honor and other dimensions of pre-industrial social

Abelard informs us that Fulbert had done more than protect Heloise within the walls of his home; he had done 'everything in his power to advance her education in letters'.[12] Abelard knew that Fulbert took great pride in his niece's learning and guessed that he would not hesitate to have one of Paris's greatest minds further her education. Abelard wrote: 'he gave me complete charge over the girl, so that I could devote all the leisure time left me by my school to teaching her by day and night, and if I found her idle I was to punish her severely'.[13] Their studies not only permitted Abelard entrance into Fulbert's house; they also allowed teacher and student to withdraw in private. Abelard's previous reputation for chastity made him appear a trustworthy shepherd. But Fulbert 'had entrusted a tender lamb to a ravening wolf.'[14] Soon, their books open before them, they were exchanging words of love rather than of scholarship, and kissing more than teaching. 'In short,' writes Abelard, 'our desires left no stage of love-making untried'.[15]

After having seduced Heloise, Abelard was no longer the cold, calculating person he had been. He not only mastered her heart, she captured his. The two became passionate lovers. The wild unicorn came to rest in Heloise's lap—and soon his vulnerable flesh would feel the awful blow of his enemies. Once Fulbert learned of what was taking place under his own roof, he separated the two lovers. Surely the well-educated Heloise was familiar with the Song of Songs and perhaps, as she longed for the return of her beloved, she reflected on the pain and grief the bride experienced.[16] Abelard tells us that they were filled with lament and

---

life, see Jerome H. Neyrey, ed., *The Social World of Luke-Acts: Models for Interpretation* (Peabody: Hendrickson Publishers, 1991).

12. Muckle, 'Consolation', 183; Radice, 66.

13. Muckle, 'Consolation', 183; Radice, 67.

14. Muckle, 'Consolation', 183; Radice, 67.

15. Muckle, 'Consolation', 184–185; Radice, 67–68.

16. On Heloise' early knowledge of the Song of Songs, see Constance J. Mews, *The Lost Love Letters of Abelard and Heloise: Perceptions of Dialogue in Twelfth-Century France* (New York: Plagrace, 2001).

distress over one another's troubles. They both knew the pain of separation. Yet, writes Abelard, 'separation drew our hearts still closer while frustration inflamed our passion even more'.[17]

Together they had experienced a burning love for one another. Apart, the flames only increased. A thousand times in her heart and mind—like the bride of the Song of Songs and *Epithalamica*—Heloise zealously sought her beloved by night. What joy must have been theirs when they found a way to reunite! Heloise knew by experience the desolation and the joy that Abelard would later attribute to the bride in Stanzas 7 and 8 of the *Epithalamica*.

Iam video quod optaveram,	Now I see what I had hoped for,
iam tenco quod amaveram	now I cling to what I had loved;
iam redo quae sic fleveram	now I laugh at what I had wept for:
plus gaudeo quam dolueram	I rejoice more than I had grieved.
Risi mane, flevi nocte	I laughed at morn, I wept at night;
mane risi, nocte flevi	At morn I laughed, at night I wept.
Noctem insomnem dolor duxerat	Grief had caused a sleepless night,
quem vehemetem amor fecerat;	which love had made passionate;
dilatione votum creverat,	desire intensified through delay until
donec amantem amans vistat.	the Lover visited lover.
Plausus die, planctus nocte.	Joy comes by day, lamentation by night;
die plausus, nocte planctus.	By day rejoicing, by night lamentation.

Surely Heloise knew the bride's story of sorrow and joy long before becoming a nun. Embedded in her memory, the words of the bride in the Canticle may well have helped her come to terms with her experience with Abelard.

17. Muckle, 'Consolation', 184; Radice, 69.

In suggesting these links between Heloise's story and the bride's story of the Song of Songs, I am drawing on the valuable insights of Mary Carruthers into the medieval way of reading and experiencing life, especially life's tragedies. We know that Heloise identified with Pompey's wife Cornelia, who wished to sacrifice herself to take away her husband's shame before the gods and his people[18] Heloise desired to sacrifice herself to remove Abelard's shame. If indeed Heloise knew the bride's story in the Song of Songs, she may well have identified with the bride's experiences of lost love, separation, shame, and grief—feelings common among medieval women (and men). Eventually Heloise found herself pregnant.[19] She wrote Abelard, who wasted no time. One night when her uncle was away, he removed her secretly from Fulbert's house and sent her straightaway to his own family. When Fulbert returned and found no Heloise, he was overwrought with grief and mortification. Eventually, Abelard went to the miserable man and begged Fulbert's forgiveness, and 'offered him satisfaction in a form he could never have hoped for: I would marry the girl I had wronged.'[20] All Abelard asked was that the marriage should be kept secret so that his reputation as a philosopher would not be damaged. Fulbert agreed. But Heloise resisted the marriage with all the erudition she could muster.

Here we detect another interesting echo between the story of Abelard and Heloise and the sequence *Virgines castae*. Both reflect the same disparaging attitude towards marriage found in the chief of western monastic teachers, Saint Jerome. The Heloise of the *Historia calamitatum* presents christian and pagan anti-marriage arguments taken from Jerome's works. Her arguments are directed to Abelard, and she is precise as to what marriage will cost him: the *ethos* of a philosopher.

18.Muckle, 'Consolation', 190–191; Radice 76–77. See also, Carruthers, *Memory*, 178–180.

19. Heloise gave birth to a son in 1118 and called him Astrolabe. The boy was raised by Abelard's sister at le Pallet, where Abelard had been reared. Heloise asked Peter the Venerable *c*. 1144 to find Astrolabe a prebend.

20. Muckle, 'Consolation', 185; Radice, 69–70.

The anti-marriage rhetoric of *Virgines castae* is directed to women. Abelard borrows Jerome's advice to the young virgin Eustochium to list particular marital woes that every virgin avoids by choosing Christ as her husband. As we shall see, in their arguments against marriage both Abelard and Heloise were ultimately concerned about proper self-understanding.

Either Abelard had taught Heloise well about the philosophical life, or perhaps she had long known of it through her wide classical reading. Invoking the Apostle Paul, Saint Jerome, and the philosopher Theophrastus,[21] she exhorted Abelard not to betray the philosophic ideal by marrying.[22] Philosophers are born to serve humankind and clerics the Church. Being both, Abelard had no business marrying. Paul and Jerome had counseled their followers against wedlock. The greatest of pagan philosophers, Seneca, had advised Lucilius that philosophy is not a subject for idle moments. Only by rejecting worldly distractions—not least cradles, spindles, and nursemaids—can the philosopher find lady wisdom. 'What Heloise desired from the man she loved was, therefore, a state of life worthy of his stature as a philosopher', Gilson wrote.[23] 'He must choose between being master of himself or living in servitude, between practicing continence in order to have the right to attend to philosophy as a free man or of renouncing it and no longer teaching an ideal which he must admit being incapable of practicing'.[24] He had to stand before his students as the embodiment of what he taught.

By seeking marriage Abelard was making a temporary aberration a permanent path. In the *Historia calamitatum* Abelard himself redacted Heloise's beautifully crafted speech against their marriage. Yet, as Peter Dronke has shown, Heloise is known

21. A long fragment of his treatise *De nuptiis* appears in Jerome, *Adversus Jovinianus* 1.47; PL 23:288-291.

22. Muckle, 'Consolation', 186–187; Radice, 70–72.

23. Gilson, *Heloise and Abelard*, 26.

24. Gilson, *Heloise and Abelard*, 31.

to have had great oratorical skills.[25] She was a student of the rhetorical tradition as it had been mediated through Abelard and her argument reflects her (and his) commitment to the classic understanding of an orator, as described by Saint Augustine in his *De doctrina christiana*. The teacher cannot be all technique and style, the bishop of Hippo had written. He, or she, must be a person of moral content and embody his, or her, own teaching: 'But whatever may be the majesty of the style, the life of the speaker will count for more in securing the hearer's compliance'.[26] Heloise knew that Abelard could not play the philosopher before his students, who would see right through his act. Marriage was simply out of the question.

Perhaps lust and love blinded Abelard. Or perhaps his offer 'was his means of making reparation for his grievous transgression of the moral law. Thus the price of his morality demanded the sacrifice of his reputation as a cleric and philosopher.'[27] Heloise knew that Abelard would soon grow weary of playing the husband-philosopher; his greatness, like that of every philosopher before him, rested upon his practicing what he preached.

If we judge from his remarks in his *Historia calamitatum*, Abelard was less concerned with doing penance before God than with his social standing before Heloise's uncle Fulbert and others in authority. He is quite explicit that he resisted Heloise's arguments against marriage because he wished to make amends, conciliate, and render satisfaction before her uncle.[28] He knew that he had horribly wronged Fulbert's personal honor through

25. See Peter Dronke, *Women Writers of the Middle Ages: A Critical Study of Texts from Perpetua (+203) to Marguerite Porete (+1310)* (Cambridge: Cambridge University Press, 1984) 107–143; and *idem.*, 'Heloise's Problemata and Letters: Some Questions of form and Content,' in *Petrus Abaelardus (1079–1142) Person, Werk und Wirkung, ed. Rudolf Thomas* (Trier: Paulinus-Verlag, 1980), 53–73; and Linda S. Kauffman, *Discourses of Desire: Gender, Genre, and Epistolary Fictions* (Ithaca: Cornell University Press, 1986) 62–89.

26. *De doctina christiana* 4.27.57; PL 34:120-121.

27. Paul L. Williams, *The Moral Philosophy of Peter Abailard* (Lanham: University Press of America) 31.

28. Muckle, 'Consolation', 185–186; Radice, 70.

his seduction. He had betrayed Fulbert's trust in his own house; and he had violated a virgin, an irreversible crime.

He and Fulbert lived in a world in which a man's honor rested on both his self-valuation *and* the approbation of his social group. The identity of Heloise, as of every respectable woman in the medieval world, was embedded in her male guardian's honor. Her intellectual attainments gained her a certain personal honor but when she was under Fulbert's roof, her accomplishments brought *him* great respect and honor.

Abelard knew exactly what his affair with Heloise and betrayal of Fulbert had cost the uncle. Abelard's father was a knight, and knighthood was fundamentally about the gaining and maintaining of honor. Indeed, Abelard tells his readers at the opening of the *Historia calamitatum*: 'I was so carried away by my love of learning that I renounced the glory of a soldier's life, made over my inheritance and rights of the eldest son to my brothers, and withdrew from the court of Mars in order to kneel at the feet of Minerva.'[29]

Even so, the spirit of Mars remained with him. The young Abelard had seen himself as a knight armed with the piercing lance of dialectic. Having challenged and defeated some of the greatest minds of his day, he had swelled with pride at his great honor. But his betrayal had brought Heloise's uncle Fulbert great personal dishonor. In his own humiliating defeat Abelard recognized that he must right the *social* wrong he had perpetrated upon Fulbert. The knight Abelard knew that he must at least render some satisfaction to Fulbert. That is at least a significant part of why he resisted Heloise protestations against marriage.

Heloise worshipped Abelard too much to do anything other than what he wished. They were married secretly in the presence of Fulbert and some of their friends and then went their separate ways, meeting only occasionally and clandestinely. The clandestine marriage did not remove Fulbert's dishonor. He soon—dishonorably—reneged on his promise of secrecy and began spreading

29. Muckle, 'Consolation', 175–76; Radice, 58.

news of the marriage. Out of deference to Abelard, Heloise denied her uncle's word and, once again, Abelard whisked his beloved damsel away—this time 'to a convent of nuns in the town near Paris called Argenteuil, where she had been brought up and educated as a small girl.'[30] To squelch mounting rumors, he had her clothed in the habit of a novice.

Fulbert concluded that Abelard had betrayed him and was ridding himself of Heloise by forcing her to become a nun. Fulbert got his revenge, setting his servants upon Abelard by night; 'they cut off the parts of my body whereby I had committed the wrong of which they complained'.[31] As the unicorn's weakness for virgins led to his capture and de-horning, so Abelard fell for Heloise and lost his manhood to her uncle's revenge. Castrated and humiliated, Abelard sought shelter in the enclosed world of the monastic life.[32] Heloise, his obedient wife, had already agreed to become a nun.

Abelard would probably never have become a monk but for his 'misfortune'. He felt no interior call from God to 'religion'; as M. T. Clanchy has summed up his situation:

> No lay person could be described as *religiosus*, however devout he or she might be, and within the clergy a distinction was made between seculars and monks. The secular (literally the 'world') clergy were the Church's ministers, ranging from the minor orders of porters and acolytes through the major orders of deacons and priests up to the bishops and archbishops. The monks, who aimed to be other-worldly and dedicated to pure prayer, were reputed to be the only truly 'religious' people among either clergy or laity.[33]

Abelard fled to the cloister to escape his shame before the world; Heloise took the veil out of deference to Abelard and in grief over

30. Muckle, 'Consolation', 189; Radice, 74.

31. Muckle, 'Consolation', 189–190; Radice, 75.

32. Two of the men who perpetrated the crime were punished with blinding and castration. It also appears that his cathedral chapter punished Fulbert with at least a temporary exile. See Mews, *Lost Love*, 148.

33. Clanchy, *Abelard*, 211.

causing Abelard's downfall. Both entered monastic life without any sense of vocation. Once again, Abelard and Heloise were confronted with the question of *ethos*.

Once a monk, Abelard eventually gave himself completely to God. Having been willing to live a double life, embracing philosophy by day and wife by night, he now wished only to be embraced by God. Later, he would confess his adoration of Christ to Heloise:

> I do not wish to be a philosopher if it means conflicting with Paul, nor to be an Aristotle if it cuts me off from Christ. For there is no other name under heaven whereby I must be saved. I adore Christ who sits on the right hand of the Father.[34]

Heloise, by contrast, even after some fifteen years as a nun and abbess, declared that she regarded her monastic vows as an expiation offered to the great philosopher whom she had brought down into disgrace through marriage: 'Not devotion to religion but your command alone drew me, young as I was, to embrace the severities of monastic life'.[35] God owes her no reward for taking the veil, she unequivocally declares, for from her entrance into religion she has done nothing for him. 'I can expect no reward from God, for I am sure that up to now I have done nothing out of love for Him'.[36]

For all the years of their separation, the abbess of the Paraclete had been laboring not for God but for Abelard. Only for him did she suffer the austerities of monastic rigor; only memory of his embrace and her continual love for him brought happiness

---

34. Letter XVII; PL 178:375C: *Nolo sic esse philosophus, ut recalcitrem Paulo. Non sic esse aristoteles, ut secludat a Christo.* This confession is preserved only in an open letter by one of Abelard's pupils, Berengar of Poitiers (Radice, 271, n. 2).

35. Muckle, 'Letters', 72: *Quam quidem iuvenculam ad monasticae conversationis asperitatem, non religionis devotio sed tua tantum pertraxit iussio.*

36. Muckle, 'Letters', 72: *Nulla mihi super hoc merces exspectanda est a Deo cuius adhuc amore nihil me constat egisse.*

and consolation.[37] As Gilson observed: 'what others call giving themselves to God was for her but another way of giving herself to him [Abelard] . . .'.[38]

> God knows, I would not have hesitated to follow you or to precede you into hell itself (*ad Vulcania loca*) if you had given the order. My heart was not my own, but yours. Even now, more than ever before, if it is not with you it is nowhere, for you are its very existence. So, I pray you, let my poor heart be happy with you. And it will be happy with you if it finds you gentle, if you render it grace for grace, little things for great, words for things. Remember, I beg you, everything I have done; and weigh out all that you owe me. When I delighted with you in carnal pleasures (*libido*), many wondered why I did it, whether it was for concupiscence or for love. But now my last state shows my true beginning, and I now forgo all pleasures only to obey your will. Truly, I reserved nothing for myself but to be yours before everything, and such I am to this very moment.[39]

Heloise's heart still belonged to Abelard and only Abelard. In a great flood of confession she declares to Abelard her continued longing for their old mode of existence, 'lest he come to think that Heloise had found in the cloister the calm, the peace, and the consolations of divine love.'[40] Heloise's anguish was nothing

37. PL 178:184C.

38. Gilson, *Heloise and Abelard*, 93.

39. Muckle, 'Letters', 173: *Aeque autem Deus scit ad Vulcania loca te properantem praecedere vel sequi pro iussu to minime dubitarem. Non enim mecum animus sed tecum erat. Sed et nunc maxime si tecum non est, nusquam est. Esse vero sine te nequaquam potest. Sed ut tecum bene sit age, obsecro. Bene autem tecum fuerit, si te propitium invenerit, si gratiam referas pro gratia, modica pro magnis, verba pro rebus. Utinam, delects, tua de me dilectio minus confideret ut sollicitior esset. Sed quo to amplius nunc securum reddidi, negligentiorem sustineo. Memento, obsecro, quae fecerim et quanta debeas attende. Dum tecum carnali fruerer voluptate, utrum id amore vel libidine agerem incertum pluribus habebatur. Nunc autem finis indicat quo id inchoaverim principio. Omnes denique mihi voluptates interdixi ut tuae parerem voluntati. Nihil mihi reservavi nisi sic tuam nunc praecipue fieri.*

40. Gilson, *Heloise and Abelard*, 93.

short of 'the distress of a worshiper forsaken by her god. The comparison is not too strong, for although Heloise never dared write it, she never ceases to suggest it.'[41] She thought first of, lived first for, and hoped first in Abelard:

> At every stage of my life up to now, as God knows, I have feared to offend you rather than God, and tried to please you more than him. It was your command, not love of God which made me take the religious habit.[42]

Abbess Heloise, in her devotion to Abelard, must have been surprised to encounter the devoted monk Abelard. 'Totally bent on loving God, he had bowed before the transforming *conversio* of religious profession,' writes Gilson.[43] Time, grace, and the habits of the monastic life had changed Abelard after marriage into a lover of God. Heloise by contrast had changed little. Abelard realized to his terror that the abbess of the Paraclete was not only the same Heloise he had known in the world but also a Heloise full of reproach for God.

She had never accepted their separation as God's judgment on their actions. For years she had churned in her mind the question,

> Why had God spared us in fornication only to punish us in marriage? . . . But when we amended our unlawful conduct by what was lawful, and atoned for the shame of fornication by an honourable marriage, then the Lord in his anger laid his hand heavily upon us, and would not permit a chaste union though he had long tolerated one which was unchaste.[44]

41. Gilson, *Heloise and Abelard*, 93.

42. Letter 3; Muckle, 'Letters', 81: *In omni autem (Deus scit) vitae meae statu, te magis adhunc offendere quam Deum vereror; tibi placere amplius quam ipsi appeto. Tua me ad religionis habitum iussio, non divina traxit dilectio.* Radice, 134.

43. Gilson, *Heloise and Abelard*, 70.

44. Muckle, 'Letters', 79: *Ut autem illicita licitis correximus, et honore coniugii turpitudinem fornicationis operuimes, ira Domini manum suam super nos vehementer aggravavit, et immacultum non pertulit torum qui diu ante sustinuerat pollutum.* Radice, 130.

After their marriage the two had not shared the joys of matrimony, but had 'parted and were leading chaste lives. . . .'[45] In recompense for a just marriage they had unjustly suffered severe grief: having expiated his sin through marriage Abelard had been stricken with a punishment worthy only of someone caught in adultery. Unforgiveness grew large in Heloise's heart. Her unhappy soul admitted to Abelard, 'I can find no penitence whereby to appease God, whom I always accuse of the greatest cruelty in regard to this outrage'.[46]

Moreover, Heloise found it impossible to do penance for past pleasures while her heart continued to long for them in the present. To Abelard she wrote: 'people say I am chaste, because they have not discovered that I am a hypocrite. They consider purity of the flesh a virtue, though it belongs not to the body but to the soul. I can win praise in the eyes of men but deserve none before God.'[47] Outward confession and mortification of the body were easy; uprooting from her heart the desire for supreme carnal pleasures was beyond her strength, or her wishes.[48] To Abelard she cried, 'Nothing is less within our power than the heart; we are compelled to obey it much more than we are able to command it'.[49]

In insisting that external appearance is no guarantor of inner virtue, Heloise was rejecting one of the core ethical beliefs of the cathedral schools and monastic institutions of the tenth through the twelfth centuries, and revealing how deeply her education in the classics had shaped her moral thinking.[50] Heloise had

45. Muckle, 'Letters', 79.

46. Muckle, 'Letters', 80; Radice, 132.

47. Muckle, 'Letters', 81: *Castam me praedicnt qui non deprehendunt hypocritam. Munditiam carnis conferunt in virtutem, cum non sit corporis, sed animi virtus. Aliquid laudis apud homines habens, nihil apud Deum mereor, qui cordis et renum probator est, et in abscondito videt.* Cf. Jerome, *De perpetua virginitate beatae Mariae* [=*contra Helvidium*]; PL 23:214A.

48. Muckle, 'Letters', 80.

49. *Nihil enim minus in nostra est potestate quam animus, eique magis obedire cogimur quam imperare possimus.* Muckle, 'Letters', 241.

50. See Stephen Jaeger, *The Envy of Angels: Cathedral Schools and Social Ideals in Medieval Europe, 950–1200* (Philadelphia: University of Pennsylvania Press,

learned many years before from Abelard that intentions, not external deeds, damn or grace the soul. God judges the intentions; humans judge only deeds. Her knowledge of this truth led her to admit:

> At every stage of my life up to now, as God knows, I have feared to offend you rather than God, and tried to please you more than him. It was your command, not love of God, which made me take the veil. Look at the unhappy life I lead, pitiable beyond any other, if in this world I must endure so much in vain, with no hope of future reward. For a long time my pretense deceived you, as it did many, so that you mistook hypocrisy for piety.[51]

Abelard, now a monk inwardly as well as outwardly and regarding himself as a brother to Heloise, determined to rid the Paraclete abbess of these misguided sentiments. To her he declared his acceptance of emasculation as just punishment:

1994) 118. Cathedral school masters attended to their students' posture, gait, gestures, speech, table manners, clothing, in an effort to form their inner dispositions, from outside to inside the human body and soul. Though monastic institutions to some degree cultivated a different set of external virtues among their members, they, too, looked on outward appearances as evidence of inner grace. For both traditions 'the motion of the body is perhaps the most visible means of registering the inner state: the way of gesturing and walking (external *motus*) indicates the way of feeling or the inner state.'

51. Muckle, 'Letters', 81: *Et hoc fortassis aliquo modo laudibile, et Deo acceptabile quoquo modo videtur, si quis videlicet exterioris operis exemplo quacumque intentione non sit ecclesiae scandalo, nec iam per ipsum apud infideles nomen Domini blasphemetur, nec apud carnales professionis suae ordo infametur. Atque hoc quoque nonnullum est divinae gratiae donum, ex cuius videlicet munere venit non solum bona facere, sed etiam a malis abstinere. Sed frustra istud praecedit, ubi illud non succedit, sicut scriptum est: Declina a malo, et fac bonum. Et frustra utrumque geritur quod amore Dei non agitur. In omni autem (Deus scit) vitae meae statu, te magis adhuc offendere quam Deum vereor; tibi placere amplius quam ipsi appeto. Tua me ad religionis habitum iussio, non divina traxit dilectio. Vide quam infelicem, et omnibus miserabiliorem ducam vitam, si tanta hic frustra sustineo, nihil habitura remunerationis in futuro. Diu te, sicut et multos, simulatio mea fefellit ut religioni deputares hypocrisim.* Translation Radice, 134.

How just was God's justice that punished me in the part
of my body by which I had sinned! How just was the betrayal chosen by the one whom I had betrayed, to repay
treachery with treachery![52]

But Abelard's castration had deeply wounded Heloise's faith in
the goodness of God. Abelard was determined to convince her
that it had instead revealed God's ineffable love.

See then, my beloved, see how with the dragnets of his mercy
the Lord has fished us up from the depth of this dangerous
sea, and from the abyss of what a Charybdis he has saved our
shipwrecked selves, although we were unwilling, so that each
of us may justly break out in that cry: 'The Lord takes thought
for me'. Think and think again of the great perils in which we
were and from which the Lord rescued us; tell always with
the deepest gratitude how much the Lord has done for our
souls. Comfort by our example any unrighteous who despair
of God's goodness, so that all may know what may be done
for those who ask with prayer, when such benefits are granted
sinners even against their will. Consider the magnanimous
design of God's mercy for us, the compassion with which the
Lord directed his judgement towards our chastisement, the
wisdom whereby he mead use of evil itself and mercifully set
aside our impiety, so that by a wholly justified wound in a
single part of my body might heal two souls.[53]

---

52. Muckle, 'Consolation', 190: *Quam justo Dei judicio in illa corporis mei
portione plecterer, in qua deliqueram. Quam justa proditione is quem antea prodideram,
vicem mihi retulisset.*

53. Muckle, 'Letters', 88-89: *Attende, itaque, attende, charissima, quibus mi-
sericordiae suae retibus a profundo hius tam periculosi maris now Dominus piscaverit,
et a quantae Charibdis voragine naufragos licet invitos extraxerit, ut merito uterque
nostrum in perrumpere posse videatur vocem: 'Dominus sollicitus est mei.' Cogita et
recogita, in quantis ipsi nos periculis constituti eramus, et a quantis now eruerit Dominus: et narra semper cum summa gratiarum actione quanta fecit Dominus animae
nostrae; et quoslibet iniquos de bonitate Domini desperantes nostro consolare exemplo,
ut advertant omnes quid supplicantibus atque petentibus fiat, cum tam peccatoribus et
invitis tanta praestentur beneficia. Perpende altissimum in nobis divinae consilium pietatis, et quam misericorditer judicium suum Dominus in correptionem verterit, et quam*

Heloise, however, remained tormented by her past relationship with Abelard and her inability to banish pleasurable memories of their love.

> In truth, the pleasures of love, which you and I shared, were so sweet to me that they can never displease me, so that I cannot discipline my mind by erasing them from my memory. Which ever way I turn, they are forever pressing themselves before my eyes with their wanton desires. They do not spare me from these longings even when I sleep. Even during the solemnities of the mass, when one's prayers should be purer, the obscene visions of these desires so captivate my tawdry soul that I am more preoccupied with their lewdness than my prayers. I ought to groan over the sins I have committed, but I rather sigh for what I have lost. Everything we did and also the times and places are stamped on my heart along with your image, so that I live through it all again with you. Even in sleep I know no respite.[54]

Awake or asleep Heloise longed for Abelard to come leaping over mountains to her, to hear his voice utter the words, 'Arise my friend, make haste'. For the years of their separation she had been trapped in a long tearful search for her beloved. Heloise knew in the deepest way the pathos of the literal level of the Song of Songs and Abelard's sequences.

---

prudenter malis quoque ipsis usus sit, et impietatem pie deposuerit, ut unius parits corporis mei justissima plage duabus mederetur animabus. Radice, 146–147.

54. Muckle, 'Letters', 80–81: *In tantum vero illae, quas pariter exercuimus, amantium voluptates dulces mihi fuerunt ut nec displicere mihi, nec vix a memoria labi possint. Quocumque loco me vertam, semper se oculis meis cum suis ingerunt desideriis. Nec etiam dormienti suis illusionibus parcunt. Inter ipsa missarum solemnia, ubi purior esse debet oratio, obscena earum voluptatum phantasmata ita sibi penitus miserrimam captivant animam ut turpitudinibus illis magis quam orationi vacem. Quae cum ingemiscere debeam de commissis, suspiro potius de amissis. Nec solum quae egimus, sed loca pariter et tempora in quibus haec egimus, ita tecum nostro infixa sunt animo, ut in pisis omnia tecum agam, nec dormiens etiam ab his quiesam.* Radice, 133.

This study has focused on Abelard's thought, voice, and vision for Heloise and her nuns. Only in the last several pages have we heard Heloise. Until Constant J. Mews[55] connected with Abelard and Heloise a collection of anonymous love letters between a male teacher of no small fame and influence and a female student of notable learning, our Heloise sources were limited to her few letters to Abelard.

The collection edited by Mews consists of one hundred thirteen prose and poetic letters that were probably copied at Clairvaux around 1471 from an older manuscript (perhaps in Heloise hand) now lost.[56] The copyist was a certain Johannes de Vepria (*c.* 1445–*c.* 1518), a monk and cataloger of books and papers in the library of the community. Just as the profound links between Abelard and Heloise's monastic correspondence and the sequences *Virgines castae* and *Epithalamica* have led Waddell and now me to suggest abelardian authorship, so Mews' comparison of these anonymous letters with the couple's monastic letters has led him to conclude that 'Their language is so close to that of other writings of Abelard and Heloise that there seems no reason to doubt their authorship. These letters help confirm the authenticity of the famous correspondence of Abelard and Heloise.'[57] Much as I have argued for Abelard's authorship of the sequences *Virgines castae* and *Epithalamica*, Mews has written regarding the de Vepria manuscript:

> To argue that the love letters constitute a literary fiction demands that we postulate the existence of an author with an astonishingly intimate knowledge of their attitudes, vocabulary, and prose style. . . . These letters must have been written by Abelard and Heloise. When we compare the exchange copied by Johannes de Vepria to poems written about Abelard and Heloise from the twelfth century, or other love letters from the period, we simply do not find

55. Mews, *Lost Love*, 143. In Mews' judgment the letter writers' attitudes, vocabulary, prose and poetic styles point to Abelard as the teacher and Heloise as his student.

56. Mews, *Lost Love*, 8–11, and 181ff.

57. Mews, *Lost Love*, 176.

anything approaching the depth and sophistication of this exchange. The contrasting perceptions of love in these love letters are so similar to those evident in the Abelard-Heloise letters, that it seems most unlikely that they could have been written by a male disciple of Abelard intimately familiar with his master's philosophical vocabulary. The only student of Abelard in a position to record this exchange was Heloise.[58]

These early love letters help us escape the profound rhetorical force of Abelard's *Historica calamitatum*. In his powerful autobiography Abelard sought publicly to reveal his break from his infamous past. Purged of all sexual impurity, he had learned the hard way how to set his affections on God alone. He had recognized that his own lustful arrogance had led to his humiliation. In the earlier de Vepria correspondence the male lover and teacher writes of his 'love' for his female student in terms of passion and seduction; he sees love for the woman as wonderfully intoxicating. But, as Mew writes, in the last of these love letters the man (Abelard) has already begun to move towards a more conventional male mind-set, suggesting 'that he has been seduced by the charms of her beauty, noble birth, and behavior, as if these are all external qualities. The conventional stereotype of women as the source of seduction, encountered so often in ecclesiastical documents from the twelfth century, surfaces both in this final poem and in the *Historica calamitatum*.'[59] By the time he wrote the *Historica calamitatum* Abelard had fully adopted the ecclesiastical male attitude toward women:

> He was anxious to maintain a public image of respectability in a monastic environment which considered any intimate association with a woman dangerous. By identifying himself as an ascetic teacher like Origen, famous for having castrated himself, he sought to re-assert himself as a teacher, unmoved by feminine distraction. Just as he saw the spirit

58. Mews, *Lost Love*, 143.
59. Mews, *Lost Love*, 83.

triumphing over the flesh, so he saw reason as triumphing over the senses.[60]

Heloise—as we heard earlier—had her own voice, a voice with rhetorical force. In the letters she sent in response to Abelard's *Historica calamitatum*, Heloise is far more than a forgotten and broken lover. Her frustration with Abelard's distancing himself from her caused her great pain. Her love for him had not died; it had remained strong and she continued to long for intimacy. There is evidence that after their marriage and entrance into the monastic life,[61] Abelard did keep in contact with Heloise, but he no longer had intimate conversation with her. In neither set of letters does the woman (Heloise) understand the affair as the debauchery that Abelard declared it to be in his *Historica calamitatum*.

Heloise was deeply wounded that Abelard had reduced their relationship to lust, pollution, and carnal seduction. They had known true love; at least, Heloise had loved Abelard with the friendship that Cicero had long ago described as true, deep, and complete.[62] *Amicitia*, the friendship that binds intimates in the common pursuit of understanding and goodness, had characterized the true depths of their relationship. Although Abelard denied it in his *Historica calamitatum*, Heloise was sure that he had shared this mutuality. But now, well after marriage and entrance into monastic life, Abelard considered mutual love inordinate, unthinkable, something impossible between a man and a woman. Cicero had never conceived of such friendship between the sexes. It was Heloise who had experienced such a possibility. In her letters that follow Abelard's *Historica calamitatum*, Heloise pushed

60. Mews, *Lost Love*, 149.

61. See Clanchy, *Abelard*, 249–253.

62. Cicero, *De amicita*; translated as *On Friendship* by Michael Grant, in *On the Good Life* (Harmondsworth: Penguin, 1971) 172–227. The latin text and translation are in *On Old Age. On Friendship. On Divination.*, W. A. Falconer, The Loeb Classical Library 20 (Cambridge: Harvard University Press, 1923). For discussion of Heloise's use of Cicero's *De amicitis*, see Mew, *Lost Love*, 124–138.

Abelard to remember and rekindle that friendship of mind and soul that they had once shared. She saw no contradiction between a mutual love between herself and Abelard and her monastic state and leadership. She appealed to Abelard as Paula and Eustochium had questioned their mentor and spiritual friend Jerome, reasoning that, if Paul and Thecla had known spiritual friendship, Abelard and Heloise could do the same—even after all *they*—not just Abelard—had suffered.

Abelard, however, yielded nothing to the past; his address to her is all forward looking. In her first letter response to Abelard's *Historica calamitatum*, Heloise uses many expressions of *amicitia* to signal 'her desire to return to the intimate dialogue that Abelard had once lavished on her in the past'.[63] She expressly reminds Abelard of the many letters they had once exchanged, and she addresses Abelard as 'dearly beloved' (*dilectissime*) and as her 'only one' (*unice*)—language, as Mews shows, that Abelard had used in his earlier love letters to Heloise.

Abelard will not look back; he replies by 'correcting' her greeting. Mews has masterfully summed up this volley of exchange between the two as follows:

> . . . he emphasizes that he now relates to her in Christ, rather than as an individual: 'To Heloise, his beloved sister in Christ, Abelard, her brother in the same' (*Heloise, dilectissime sorori sue in Christo, Abaelardus, frater ejus in ipso*). She responds in her next letter by cleverly combining the notions of singularity conveyed by *unicus* with his emphasis that they are greeting each other in Christ: 'To her only one after Christ, she who is his alone in Christ' (*Unico suo post Christum, unica sua in Christo*). She accepts that her relationship with him is in Christ, but she wants to communicate with him as an individual, the way he used to speak to her. As if to drive home her frustration, she then chides Abelard for putting the name of Heloise before his own, contrary to the convention of how a superior should address an inferior. If

63. Mews, *Lost Love*, 123.

he does not want to engage with her at a personal level, he should begin 'Abelard to Heloise'. She points out that he is employing an epistolary convention normally used by friends in correspondence, but is not actually addressing her as an individual. Abelard counters in his second reply by re-emphasizing the general terms in which he wishes to address her. 'To the Bride of Christ, the servant of the same' (*Sponse Christ, servus ejusdem*). There is an ambiguity here, as he could be defining himself as the servant of Christ or as the servant of the bride of Christ. He repeats this theme in the farewell to his letter. As if in direct rejoinder to such a general greeting, she replaces *unicus/unica* in her earlier greeting by invoking the two different ways they used as lovers to address each other: 'To him who is hers specially, she who is his singularly' (*suo specialiter, sua singulariter*).[64]

In the end, Heloise's efforts to convince Abelard to meet her on old terms seem to have failed. She finally gave up and accepted that Abelard would relate to her only as a spiritual daughter, the mother of nuns, and the bride of Christ. She began to try to persuade him to write her spiritual letters and songs. She asks him for work related to her direction of the Paraclete nuns: hymns, sermons, a rule for nuns, a history of the origin of nuns.

And now we find ourselves back where we began. Yet now we can see that Heloise saw no real contradiction between her deep affection for Abelard and her monastic commitments. But Abelard did. He was willing to relate to Heloise after their marriage and monastic consecration only on the spiritual level of the Song of Songs, and other texts that scripted Heloise as Christ's bride.

Through *Virgines castae* Abelard sought to open up an alternative mode of being to Heloise. She was, in his opinion, stuck on the dangerous literal level of the language of love. The life to which Abelard, the monk-spiritual guide, pointed Heloise by his sequences existed beyond sensual and carnal love to love's fulfil-

---

64. Mews, *Lost Love*, 123–124.

ment in union with God. This marriage would be similar in kind to her love for Abelard, but dissimilar in its unmixed purity and intensity.

Heloise, surely he thought, was cutting herself off from the very reality to which her monastic vows had initiated her. As a nun and abbess, she was Christ's bride. And, as Abelard's sequence (stanzas 9-11) reveals, Christ embraces his beloved virgin upon their nuptial bed.

Dormit in istis	In these [beds]
Christus cum illis	Christ sleeps with them [the virgins]
felix hic somnus	happy the slumber [and]
requires dulcis	sweet the repose
quo cum fovetur	in which the faithful virgin
virgo fidelis	is caressed
inter amplexus	in the embraces
sponsi caelestis	of the heavenly bridegroom
Dextera sponsi	The right hand of the bridegroom
sponsa complexa	clasps his bride
capiti laeva	His left hand cradles her head
dormit submissa	While wakeful in heart
pervigil corde	she sleeps in body
corpore dormit	and she quietly slumbers
et sponsi grato	on the loving breast
sinu quiescit	of her bridegroom
Approbans somnum	Favoring her
Sponsus beatam	sleep the Sponsus
inquietari	Does not let
prohibet illam	the blessed one
ne suscitetis	be disquieted
inquit dilectam	Do not awaken my beloved,
dum ipsa volet	thus quiet
ita quietam	till she wishes.

The heavenly Bridegroom watches over the peaceful sleep of his beloved. Abelard wants Heloise to see that, once she releases her grip on their past love, she will find Christ himself holding her in his loving arms. Only by giving herself wholly, both body and soul, to her bridegroom will she find rest from her torments.

Once upon a time Abelard had written Heloise passionate letters and love-lyrics calculated to win her complete affection and commitment. Now, long after marriage, separation, and entrance into religious life, his letters and sacred songs were designed to direct her heart away from himself toward Christ, her true lover and bridegroom. In Heloise's torments Abelard found God's work of love. He sought to persuade her that her temptations did not mock her role as abbess; rather they were God's means of purifying and strengthening her character. His struggle with the flesh ended with his castration and no reward awaits him. To her, however—if she struggles for both of them—God promises a martyr's crown. Marriage made them one flesh; her merits will also be his. Her glory will become his glory.

> We are, in fact, one in Christ, one in body by the law of matrimony. Whatever is yours, I think, cannot fail to be mine also. Christ is yours, because you have been made his spouse . . . from this I have increasing confidence in your defense of our case in His court of law, so that I might obtain from your prayers what I am unable to secure through my own.[65]

In Letter Four Abelard does not mince words about who Heloise now is. Previously the wife of a poor lowly mortal, Heloise now enjoys the bed of the King of Kings. It was fitting, writes Abelard, that he address Heloise, now the bride of 'my Lord', as 'my Lady', just as Jerome had addressed Eustochium:[66] The Lady Heloise is now at Christ's side as his bride; and the lady abbess has in her train a throng of virgin followers.

65. Muckle, 'Letters', 93: *Unum quippe sumus in Christo, una per legem matrimonii caro. Quidquid est tuum, mihi non atbitror alienum. Tuus autem est Christus, quia facta es sponsa eius. . . . Unde et de tuo nobis quod ipsum patrocinio amplius confidimus, ut id obtineam ex tua quod possum ex oratione propria.*

66. Epistle 22.2; PL 22:395. Muckle, 'Letters', 83; Radice, 137.

Abelard turns next to Psalm 44 further to describe Heloise's relationship to Christ. As the queen and bride in heaven, she is exalted to the right hand of the king. Because 'wives are better able than their households to intercede with their husbands, being ladies rather than servants,' Abelard would have Heloise to remember him before her heavenly husband. He reminds her that her privileged relationship to Christ is illustrated when

> the Psalmist says of the queen and bride of the King of kings: 'On your right stands the queen,' as if it were clearly stated that she is nearest to her husband and close to his side, and moves forward with him, while all the rest stand apart or follow behind.[67]

Here Abelard has cast Heloise in the same bridal role as is portrayed in both *Epithalamica* and *Virgines castae*. As a nun, she is the bride of Christ. She is like the ethiopian bride of the Canticles: black but lovely.[68] Her outer garb is coarse and black, like the mourning dress worn by widows who weep for their dead husbands. Outwardly she weeps like Mary Magdalene at the Lord's tomb. As *Epithalamica* reveals, separation from her beloved seems too much to bear. Her afflictions of body and soul are but the chastening of her gentle bridegroom, who strikes only to correct, wounds only to heal, humbles only to lift up. Abelard insists that Heloise interpret the sufferings of her life as God's mercy.

> God himself has thought fit to raise us up from the contamination of this filth and the pleasures of this mire and draw us to him by force—the same force whereby he chose to strike and convert Paul—and by our example perhaps to

67. Muckle, 'Letters', 83: *In quarum quidem typo regina illa et summi regis sponsa diligenter describitur, cum in psalmo dicitur: Astitit regina a dextris tuis, etc. Ac si aperte dicatur, ista iuncto latere, sponso familiarissime adhaeret et pariter incedit, ceteris omnibus quasi a longe absistentibus vel subsequentibus.* Radice, 138.

68. Letter 4; Muckle, 'Letters', 83: *De huius excellentia praerogativae sponsa in Canticis exsultans illa, ut ita dicam, quam Moyses duxit, Aethiopissa dicit: Nigra sum, sed formosa filiae Heirusalem. Ideo dilexit me rex et introduxit me in cubiculum suum.* Radice, 138.

deter from our audacity others who are also trained in letters.[69]

Her outward blackness cannot compare to her white and lovely interior, Abelard continues. Her inner self, her true self, thirsts for Christ her bridegroom, not for earthly things. Her humility is not false like that of the foolish virgins. Her self-denial is not only outward; it penetrates into the very whiteness of her bones and teeth. That is why she can and should lead her virginal chorus in singing psalms, hymns, and canticles. Because of her purity she is raised to Christ's bed, 'to that secret place of peace and contemplation, and into the bed, of which she [the bride of the Canticles] says elsewhere, "Night after night on my bed I have sought my true love.'"[70] This is the same bed of contemplation so cherished by the bride of *Virgines castae*.

Upon this bed Heloise has conceived and borne many spiritual daughters to her Lord. Like the bride of *Virgines castae*, she has not abandoned herself 'to the defilement of carnal pleasures only to bear in suffering a few children for the world.'[71] Rather, as abbess of the Paraclete, Heloise has 'delivered in exultation numerous progeny for heaven!'[72] As abbess she has and does turn 'the curse of Eve into the blessing of Mary'.[73]

The Supreme Virgin—is indeed the Mother of God—, who has led in her train an innumerable host of virgins—every one of whom she has led to Christ's bed chamber. As abbess Heloise follows Mary's procession; she leads her own daughters forward

69. Muckle, 'Letters', 91: *Ipse now a sontagiis huiuis caeni, a voluptabris hius luti dignatus est erigere, et ad seipsum vi quadam attrahere, qua percussum voluit paulum vonvertere, et hoc ipso fortassis exemlo nostro alios quoque litterarum peritos ab hac deterrere praesumptione.* Radice, 150.

70. Muckle, 'Letters', 84–85: *Bene etiam, quia nigra est, ut diximus,et formosa, dilectam et introductam se dicit in cubiculum regis, id est, in secretum vel quietem contemplationis, et lectulum illum de quo eadem alibi dicit: In lectulo meo per noctes quaesivi quem diligit anima mea.* Radice, 140.

71. Muckle, 'Letters', 90; Radice, 150.

72. Muckle, 'Letters', 90; Radice, 150.

73. Muckle, 'Letters', 90; Radice, 150.

as she walks at the side of her bridegroom. Heloise's heart and deeds are not hers alone, Abelard exhorted; she must give both to Christ and be a model for her nuns.

In fact, Abelard would have Heloise imitate all of the Marys of Scripture. Our study of *Epithalamica* revealed that Abelard's tropological interpretation of Miriam and Mary Magdalene casts them both in the role of a song leader directing a troupe of singers. Abelard is explicit that Mary Magdalene, like Miriam of old, was the first to sing of what she had been the first to see. Like the two Marys, Heloise, as abbess of the Paraclete, is graced with the duty and the honor of leading her virginal band in singing a heavenly canticle. She is the bride of Abelard's sequences, teaching her bridal song to her young virgins.

By his sequences and other Paraclete *liturgica*, as well as by his letters and hymns, I contend, Abelard is trying to convince Heloise that it is not enough outwardly to appear as abbess while remaining in love with him. She cannot play abbess by day and be his lover by night, even if it is only in the deepest chambers of her heart. Abelard insists that the *ethos* of an abbess requires her full commitment. Indeed, in the Rule for Nuns he had sent to Heloise, he wrote,

> What damage to souls will there be if she who is the authority over religion is lacking in religion herself? For it is sufficient for her subordinates if each of them displays a single virtue, but in her examples of all the virtues should shine out, so that she can be a living example of all she enjoins on the others, and not contradict her precepts by her morals, nor destroy by her own deeds what she builds in words; in order that the word of correction may not fall away from her lips when she is ashamed to correct in others the errors she is known to commit herself.[74]

---

74. McLaughlin, 'Rule', 254: *Quantum vero est animarum damnum si minor in religione fuerit quae religionis praeest magisterio? Singulis quippe subjectis singulas virtutes exhibere sufficit. In hac autem omnia exempla debent eminere virtutum ut omnia quae aliis praeceperit propriis praeveniat exemplis ne ipsa quae praecipit moribus oppug-*

As he puts it, 'anyone whose life is despised must see his preaching and teaching condemned as well'.[75] She must abandon her obsession with him and experience Christ as her husband and beloved. If she seeks true love, then she should turn to Christ. 'It is he,' argues Abelard, 'who truly loved you, not I.'[76]

> My love, which brought us both to sin, should be called lust, not love. I took my fill of my wretched pleasures in you, and this was the sum total of my love. You say I suffered for you, and perhaps that is true, but it was really through you, and even this, unwillingly; nor for love of you but under compulsion, and to bring you not salvation but sorrow. But he suffered truly for your salvation, on your behalf of his own free will, and by his suffering he cures all sickness and removes all suffering. To him, I beseech you, not to me, should be directed all your devotion, all your compassion, all your remorse. Weep for the injustice of the great cruelty inflicted on him, not for the just and righteous payment demanded of me, or rather, as I said, the supreme grace granted us both. For you are unrighteous if you do not love righteousness, and most unrighteous if you consciously oppose the will, or more truly, the boundless grace of God. Mourn for your Saviour and Redeemer, not for the seducer who defiled you, for the Master who died for you, not for the servant who lives and, indeed, for the first time is truly freed from death.[77]

---

net et quod verbis aedificat factis ipsa destruat et de ore suo verbum correctionis auferatur cum ipsa in aliis erubescat corrigere quae constat eam committere. Radice, 202.

75. McLaughlin, 'Rule,' 254; Radice, 203.

76. *Amabat te ille veraciter, non ego*; Muckle, 'Letters', 92; Radice, 153.

77. Muckle, 'Letters', 92: *Amor meus, qui utrumque nostrum peccatis involvebat, concupiscentia, non amor dicendus est. Miseras in te meas voluptates implebam, et hoc erat totum quod amabam. Pro te, inquis, passus sum et fortassis verum est, sed magis per te, et hoc ipsum invitus, non amore tui, sed coactione mei, nec ad tuam salutem, sed ad dolorem. Ille vero salubriter, ille pro te sponte passus est qui passione sua omnem curat languorem, omnem removet passionem. In hoc, obsecro, non in me tua tota sit devotio, tota compassio, tota compunctio. Dole in tam innocentem tatae crudelitatis perpetratam iniquitatem, non iustam in me aequitatis vindictam, immo gratiam,*

Indeed, it was through the incarnation that God sought to draw all the affections of carnal humans toward his saving love, helpless as they were to love him in any other way, and then to raise them gradually to a true spiritual love.[78]

With these words Abelard brought his argument to its climax: Heloise puts her soul in jeopardy by setting her affections on him and lamenting his sufferings. It is idolatry and Abelard will have none of it. He has accepted God's judgment upon his flesh as grace and embraced the monastic life as his calling. He now implores Heloise to do likewise, lest in the end she be found unrighteous. Her habit of heart must match her habit of dress. It is not enough that she outwardly goes about her duties as abbess. She must embrace the monastic life as her vocation. She cannot be mother to the Paraclete nuns and continue to brood over her past with Abelard. She must live *after* marriage; she must see herself as Christ's bride. By day and by night she must follow the steps of the bride of *Epithalamica*. Her weeping should be for her beloved Saviour and her joy should be at his presence. In his narrow bed of contemplation she should strive to dwell. As the bride of *Virgines castae*, she shall find true love and rest only in Christ's embrace.

In his effort to persuade Heloise to embrace Christ, Abelard did not hesitate to use the dangerous literal level of such texts as the Song of Songs or to evoke memories of human love. Like Bernard of Clairvaux, the spiritual director of the Paraclete knew that memories of sensual pleasure and desire for human love

---

ut dictum est, in utrosque non iustam in me aequitatis vindictam, immo gratiam, ut dictum est, in utrosque summam. Iniqua enim es, si aequitatem non amas, et iniquissima, si voluntati, immo tantae gratiae Dei scienter es abversa. Plange tuum reparatorem, non corruptorem, redemptorem, non scortatorem, pro te mortuum Dominum, non viventem servum, immo nunc primum de morte vere liberatum. Radice, 153.

78. My language here is derived from Saint Bernard's explanation of the incarnation in his sermons on the Song of Songs [especially Sermon 20; see *Bernard of Clairvaux: On the Song of Songs*, Cistercian Fathers series 4 (Spencer-Kalamazoo: Cistercian Publications, 1971) 147–155], but it no less captures Abelard's very sentiments.

cannot be dealt with by simple rejection. As Talal Asad has written, 'an authoritative redescription of pleasurable memory was necessary'.[79] Abelard offered this authoritative redescription through his sequences and other Paraclete *liturgica*. As he well knew, the liturgy is an indispensable means of forming the nuns to love God above all else and to persuade Heloise to embrace Christ as her true bridegroom. Union with him is not wholly unlike human love, yet of a different quality. The goal of the monastic life was to transform (not suppress) sensual desire into desire for God. This task required the skillful deployment of biblical and patristic language that we have seen in Abelard's *liturgica* and closely examined in his sequences *Virgines castae* and *Epithalamica*.

By a study of these two sequences we have been able to probe the texture of Abelard and Heloise's relationship. Because of their deep love for one another, they used all their rhetorical skill to teach and to move the other to a more faithful living of their lives. The young Heloise could not bear to see Abelard throw away his life as a philosopher by marriage, even to her. And the aged Abelard could not allow Heloise to throw away her eternal life by idolizing him. She had to see herself rightly as Christ's bride. To achieve this end, he marshaled his every rhetorical skill, seeking through sermons, hymns, *planctus*, and sequences to persuade her to embrace her role as abbess of the Paraclete with all her heart, soul, and mind.

79. Asad, *Genealogies*, 145.

EPILOGUE

Cum bene quis moritus persolvit debita cuncta

A good death pays all debits.

—*Peter Abelard*[1]

In his sacrorum operum exercitiis, eum adventus illius aeuangelici uisiutatoris reperit, . . . uigilantem inuenit. Inuenit eum uere uigilantem, et ad aeternitatis muptias, non ut fatuam sed ut sapientem uirginem euocauit.

. . . when the Visitor of the Gospels came to find him [Abelard], . . . he found him truly awake, and summoned him to the wedding of eternal life as a wise, not a foolish virgin.

—*Peter the Venerable*[2]

Virgines castae and *Epithalamica* have carried us deeply into the symbolic world of Abelard, the founder and then spiritual director of the Abbey of the Paraclete. Abelard the academic has aged into the monk; in his hymns and sequences he reveals himself less a dialectician and more a rhetorician. Nothing observed here

---

1. *Carmen ad Astralabium: A Critical Edition*, ed. José M. A. Rubingh-Boscher (Groningen: J.M.A. Rubingh-Boscher, 1987) p. 141, line 615.
2. Letter 115, to Heloise, *The Letters of Peter the Venerable*, ed. Giles Constable, 2 vols. (Cambridge: Harvard University Press, 1967) 1:307.

suggests that Abelard's academic prowess and dialectical skill had faded; he was and remained an exceptional master of both dialectic and rhetoric. This study has given us, however, a glimpse of an Abelard who emerged in the years following castration and conversion to the monastic life. Once in that world, Abelard embraced its core symbols of humble chastity, love of God, and marriage to Christ; its reality for him became deeply ordered by texts such as the Song of Songs and Psalm 44.

Virgines castae and *Epithalamica*, along with the many Paraclete works tied to them reveal the depth to which the symbolic world of the monastic tradition had penetrated Abelard's soul. He had drunk deeply from a great ocean of christian ascetics: Ambrose, Cyprian of Carthage, Gregory the Great, and especially Jerome. He had so consumed and assimilated the symbols, metaphors, and arguments of his sources that their meanings became an expression of his own thought. In both sequences we have seen his masterful skill at arranging, elaborating, ornamenting, and setting to music his invented material. Poetry and music combine with technical wonder for affective appeal; united word and melody produce an artfulness and beauty that Abelard used to reach deep within and to move the souls of Heloise and her nuns. Through his rhetorical skills he wove song and words together to make a bridal tapestry for the brides of Christ, his Paraclete nuns.

Abelard focused on the tropological significance of virginity and the love of God, directing his sequences to the concrete life situation of the Paraclete nuns and their abbess. He used the affective force of *Virgines castae* and *Epithalamica* and the biblical and nonbiblical sources in them to move the Paraclete nuns to love Christ as their bridegroom. In these songs we see, not the cantankerous philosopher of abelardian lore, but the poet, composer, rhetorician and monk. Among his Paraclete nuns, Abelard was not the rampaging unicorn, but the unicorn at rest among maidens.

By emphasizing the tropological significance of the Song of Songs and Psalm 44, this Abelard placed himself in the company

of such twelfth-century preachers and theologians as Anselm of
Laon, Bruno of Segni, Rupert of Deutz, Honorius of Autun, Philip
of Harveng, Gilbert of Poitiers, William of Saint Thierry, Gilbert
of Hoyland, John of Ford, Thomas the Cistercian, Alan of Lille,
and Bernard of Clairvaux. Abelard died as a monk and was celebrated by the abbot of Cluny as a model for others. Upon Abelard's death on 21 Apri 1142, at the age of roughly sixty-three,
Peter the Venerable (*c.* 1092–1156; abbot from 1122–1156), perhaps
the greatest prelate in Europe at his time apart from the pope,
wrote Heloise, paying tribute to the simplicity, piety, and devotion of the aged Abelard:

> The nature and extent of the saintliness, humility and devo-
> tion of his life among us, to which Cluny can bear witness,
> cannot briefly be told. I do not remember seeing anyone, I
> think, who was his equal in conduct and manner I
> often marveled, and when he walked in front of me with
> the others in the usual processional order, I almost stood
> still in astonishment that a man who bore so great and dis-
> tinguished a name could thus humble and abase himself.
> And because some who profess the religious life want un-
> necessary extravagance even in the habits they wear, he was
> completely frugal in such matters, content with a simple
> garment of each sort, seeking nothing more. He was the
> same as regards food and drink and anything for his bodily
> needs, and condemned by word and by his living example,
> for himself as well as for others, not merely what was su-
> perfluous, but everything except the barest necessities. His
> reading was continuous, his prayer assiduous, his silence
> perpetual, except when informal conference amongst the
> brothers or a public sermon addressed to them in assembly
> on sacred subjects compelled him to speak. He was present
> at the holy Sacraments, offering the sacrifice of the immortal
> Lamb to God whenever he could, and indeed, almost with-
> out interruption. . . . In such a way this simple, upright
> man lived among us, fearing God and shunning evil; and
> in this way, I repeat, he stayed for some time, dedicating
> the last days of this life to God. . . . He was engaged on

such holy occupations when the Visitor of the Gospels came
to find him, and found him awake, not asleep like so many;
found him truly awake, and summoned him to the wedding
of eternal life as a wise, not a foolish virgin.[3]

The Abbot of Cluny—surely no mean judge of inward conversion—assures Heloise that Abelard had truly taken to heart the
habits that marked him as a monk, and had died a good death.
His physical bearing revealed the state of his inner life. His
humble monk's habit bore witness to an internal disposition to
the good. His silence and speech were but outward expressions
of his inner well-being. All of this epideictic language could be
read as little more than the typical conceits spoken over the passing of a comrade. But our study suggests otherwise. *Virgines
castae* and *Epithalamica* as well as Abelard's other Paraclete *liturgica* attest to a truly converted Abelard—however present his
fateful penchant for making enemies had remained throughout
his life—, an Abelard engaged in furthering the spiritual life of

3. Letter 115; Constable, *The Letters of Peter the Venerable*, 1:306-307; trans.
Radice, 282–283: *Cuius sanctae, humili ac deuotae inter nos conuersationi, quod quan-
tumue Cluniacus testimonium ferat, breuis sermo non explicat. Nisi enim fallor, non re-
colo uidisse me illi in humilitatis habitu et gestu simillem. . . . Cumque in magno illo
fratrum nostrorum grege, me compellente gradum superiorem teneret, ultimus omnium
uestitu incultissimo uidebatur. Mirabar sepe, et in processionibus eo me cum reliquis
pro more praecaedente, pene stupebam, tanti tamque famosi nominis hominem, sic se
ipsum contempnere, sic se abiicere posse. Et quia sunt quidam religionis professores
qui ipsum quem gerunt habitum religiosum nimis esse cupiunt sumptuosum, erat ille
prorsus parcus in istis et cuiusque generis simplici ueste contentus, nil ultra quaerebat.
Hoc et in cibo, hoc et in potu, hoc et in omni cura corporis sui seruabat, et non dico
superflua, sed et cuncta nisi ualde necessaria, tam in se quam in omnibus, uerbo pariter
et uita dampnabat. Lectio erat ei continua, oratio frequens, silentium iuge, nisi cum
aut fratrum familiaris collatio, aut ad ipsos in conuentu de diuinis publicus sermo eum
loqui urgebant. Sacramenta caelestia, immortalis agni sacfificium deo offerendo prout
proterat frequentabat, immo postquam litteris et labore meo, apostolicae gratiae reddi-
tus est, pene continuabat. . . . In his sacrorum operum exercitiis, eum aduentus illius
aeuangelici uisitatoris reperit, nec eum ut multos dormientem sed uigilantem inuenit.
Inuenit eum uere uigilantem, et ad aeternitatis nuptias, non ut fatuam, sed ut sapientem uirginem euocauit. . . .*

those in his charge. Peter the Venerable assured Heloise that years of monastic training had resulted in harmony between Abelard's outer behavior and inner motives. Abelard could hope for nothing greater for Heloise than that she, too, die a good death.

The picture of the Father Founder drawn here remains incomplete. Until the sort of study attempted here is extended to include *all* of Abelard's contributions to the liturgical life of the Paraclete, an understanding of the mature and aged Abelard will continue to elude us. Secondary literature will continue to describe him largely in terms of his early life, his academic accomplishments, and the enmities he created. He will remain the champion of reason over faith, dialectics over authority, and scholastic over monastic theology.

Those who are fascinated by Peter Abelard's *entire* life and thought must follow his work up to the very point of his good death. Our work has been greatly assisted by Chrysogonus Waddell's study of the Paraclete liturgical books; he has discovered and preserved the tattered and faded pieces of the Paraclete liturgical life. This study has sorted some of those pieces of Abelard's liturgical contributions to the Paraclete, and has confirmed and buttressed Waddell's argument for abelardian authorship of the two sequence hymns, *Virgines castae* and *Epithalamica*.

By taking his sequences as a center point, we have shown that Abelard wove them together with his hymns and sermons from a range of shared topics linked to virginity and marriage to Christ. Active words that express movement of soul and body, like singing, offering, loving, embracing, rejoicing, lamenting, and marrying, portray the themes that form this tapestry. This language created and nurtured a culture of belief and practice at the Paraclete. Abelard's sequences displayed before the Paraclete nuns the ideas and actions Abelard thought central to their identity as virgin brides of Christ. Abelard gave Heloise and her nuns more than the physical space of the Paraclete Abbey; he created through the tapestry of his Paraclete *liturgica* a symbolic world in which the nuns could live and move and have their being.

MUSIC GLOSSARY

Commas and colons   subphrases which result from the combining of *syllabae*.

Distinctions   complete musical phrases formed from the joining of sub-phrases

Flex   a term used by some medieval theories for a particular pitch in a mode that functions as a light pause or cadential point.

Measured Singing   the lengthening of pitches used in reading a text aloud. As most medieval texts did not include punctuation, readers and singers supplied both the textual and musical punctuation.

Mixed modes   combining authentic and plagal forms of a mode and thereby extending the chant's tonal range.

Mode, modal forms   in medieval music there are two modes: 'authentic' and 'plagal'. Authentic modes begin with the final note and proceed from the final up to its octave. The plagal form begins with the fourth note below the final and proceeds up to the fifth note above the final. A chant might be in the D form of the plagal mode, which means that its range is roughly from the fourth note below the final to the fifth note above the final.

Musical syntax	arises from musical *syllabae*, commas, colons, *distinctiones*, and *periodi*.
Neume	notational signs used in medieval chant. Neumatic notation includes signs for single tones as well as groups of two, three, or more tones. The square-shaped character of the neume dates from the thirteenth century.
Periodus	musical phrases joined together to form a complete melody.
Reciting tone	see Structural tones
Structural tones	those tones that give a mode its particular form. A 'd' mode is built around the note d and has at least one other structural tone, 'a'. This 'a' is the mode's reciting tone, the pitch upon which psalms in the d mode were sung.
Syllabae	the joining of *voces* to form melodic gestures.
Voces	individual pitches; a single pitch is a *vox*.

SELECTED BIBLIOGRAPHY

Manuscript Sources

Bruxelles, Bibliothèque royale, MS 10147–58.

Chaumont, Bibliothèque municipale, MS 31.

Paris, Bibliothèque Nationale, MS nouv. acq. Lat. 3126.

Paris, Bibliothèque Nationale, MS français 14410.

Primary Sources

Abelard, Peter. 'Abelard's Letter of Consolation to a Friend'. Ed. J. T. Muckle. *Mediæval Studies* 12 (1950) 163–213.

———. 'Abelard's Rule of Religious Women'. Ed. T. P. McLaughlin. *Mediçæval Studies* 18 (1956) 241–292.

———. *Carmen ad Astralabium: A Critical Edition*. José M. A. Rubingh-Boscher, ed. Groningen: J. M. A. Rubingh-Boscher, 1987.

———. *Hymn Collections from the Paraclete. Edition*. Chrysogonus Waddell, ed. Cistercian Liturgy Series 9. Trappist, Kentucky: Gethsemani Abbey—Kalamazoo, Cistercian Publications, 1987.

———. *The Hymns of Abelard in English Verse*. Translated and introduced by Sister Jane Patricia [Freeland]. New York: University Press of America, 1986.

———. *Petri Abaelardi Paeripatetici Palatini Hymnarius Paraclitensis sive hymnorum libelli tres ad fidem codicum Bruxellensis et Calmontani*. Commentary and annotations by G. M. Dreves. Paris, 1891. Reprinted in *Medium Aevium—Collana di Studi e Testi B*. Scriptores V/2. Bologna: Giuseppe Vecchi, 1970. Also reprinted without commentary and annotations in *Analecta Hymnica*, Volume 48:141-223. Leipzig, 1905.

———. *Peter Abelard's Hymnarius Paraclitensis. II. The Hymnarius Paraclitensis. Text and Notes*. Intro. and annotated by Joseph Szövérffy. Albany, New York: Classical Folia Editions, 1975.

———. *Sermones*. Patrologia cursus completus series latina. Volume 178, columns 379–610. Paris, 1844–.

Abelard, Peter and Heloise. *The Letters of Abelard and Heloise*. Translated and introduced by Betty Radice. New York: Penguin Books, 1974.

———. *The Letters of Abelard and Heloise*. Translated and edited by C. K. Scott Moncrieff. New York: Knopf, 1942.

———. 'The Letters of Heloise on Religious Life and Abelard's First Reply'. Ed. J. T. Muckle. *Mediæval Studies* 17 (1955) 240–281.

———. 'The Personal Letters between Abelard and Heloise: Introduction, Authenticity, and Text'. Ed. J. T. Muckle. *Mediçval Studies* 15 (1953) 47–94.

Analecta hymnica medii aevi. G. M. Dreves and C. Blume, edd. 55 volumes. Leipzig: 1886–1922. Volumes 8 and 48.

Bernard of Clairvaux. *On the Song of Songs*. 4 volumes. Translated Kilian Walsh and Irene Edmonds. Kalamazoo: Cistercian Publications, 1971–1980.

———. *Sermones super Cantica Canticorum*. 2 volumes. Edd. J. Leclercq, C. H. Talbot, H.M. Rochais. *Sancti Bernardi Opera,* 1–2. Rome: Editiones Cistercienses, 1957–1958.

Cicero, *On Old Age. On Friendship. On Divination*. Text and translation W. A. Falconer, The Loeb Classical Library 20. Cambridge: Harvard University Press, 1923.

———. *On Friendship*. In *On the God Life*. Translated Michael Grant. Harmondsworth: Penguin, 1971. Pp. 172–227

Cyprian of Carthage. *De habitu virginum*. English translation, *The Dress of Virgins*, by R. E. Wallis. Ante-Nicene Fathers series, volume 8:430-436. Rpt Grand Rapids: Eerdmans, 1983.

Hock, Ronald, and Edward N. O'Neil, introduction, translation, and edition. *The* Chreia *in Ancient Rhetoric. Volume I. The Progymnasmata, Texts and Translations 27*. Graeco-Roman Religion Series 9. Atlanta: Scholars Press, 1986.

Hurst, Dom David, translator. *Gregory the Great: Forty Gospel Homilies*. Cistercian Studies Series, 123. Kalamazoo: Cistercian Publications, 1990.

Jerome. *Against Jovinian*. Library of Nicene and Post-Nicene Fathers series 2. Volume 4:346-416. Rpt Grand Rapids: Eerdmans, 1983.

Jacobus de Voragine. *The Golden Legend: Readings on the Saints*. Translated William Granger Ryan. 2 volumes. Princeton: Princeton University Press, 1993.

John of Salisbury. *The Metalogicon of John of Salisbury: A Twelfth-Century Defense of the Verbal and Logical Arts of the Trivium*. Translation, introduction and notes by Daviel D. McGarry. Westport: Greenwood Press, 1982.

Menander. *Menander Rhetor*. Edited with translation and commentary by D. A. Russell and N. G. Wilson. Oxford: Clarendon Press, 1981.

Origen. *Origen. The Song of Songs Commentary and Homilies*. Ancient Christian Writers series, 26. New York: Newman Press, 1957.

Ovid. *Ovid. Metamorphoses*. 2 Volumes. Loeb Classical Library, 3–4. Cambridge: Harvard University Press, 1916.

Paraclete Breviary: IIIA Edition. Kalendar and Temporal Cycle. Ed. Chrysogonus Waddell. Cistercian Liturgy Series 5. Trappist, Kentucky: Gethsemani Abbey—Kalamazoo: Cistercian Publications, 1985.

The Paraclete Breviary: IIIB Edition. The Sanctoral Cycle. Ed. Chrysogonus Waddell. Cistercian Liturgy Series 6. Trappist, Kentucky: Gethesemani Abbey—Kalamazoo: Cistercian Publications, 1985.

The Paraclete Breviary: IIIC Edition. Common of Saints, Varia, Indices. Ed. Chrysogonus Waddell. Cistercian Liturgy Series 7. Trappist, Kentucky: Gethsemani Abbey—Kalamazoo: Cistercian Publications, 1985.

Patrologiae cursus completes: Series Latina, ed. Jacques P. Migne, 222 volumes. Paris, 1844–1902.

Pelagius. *Viginitatis laus*. In Patrologiae cursus completus, series latina. Volume 30, columns 163–175. Paris, 1844–. English translation in B. R. Rees, *The Letters of Pelagius and His Followers*. Woodbridge: Boydell Press, 1991. Pp. 71–87.

Peter the Venerable. *The Letters of Peter the Venerable*. 2 volumes. Edited Giles Constable. Cambridge: Harvard University Press, 1967.

Pseudo-Cicero. *Rhetorica ad Herennium*. Translated Harry Caplan. Loeb Classical Library. Cambridge: Harvard University Press, 1954.

Walpole, A. S., ed. *Early Latin Hymns: With Introduction and Notes*. Hildesheim: Georg Olms Verlagsbuchhandlung, 1966.

SECONDARY SOURCES

Abelson, Paul. *The Seven Liberal Arts: A Study in Medieval Culture*. Columbia University Teachers College Contributions to Education, no. 11. New York: Teachers College Columbia University, 1906.

Apel, Willi. *Gregorian Chant*. Bloomington, Indiana: Indiana University Press, 1958.

Asad, Talad. *Genealogies of Religion: Discipline and Reasons of Power in Christianity and Islam*. Baltimore: The Johns Hopkins University Press, 1993.

Astell, Ann W. *The Song of Songs in the Middle Ages*. Ithaca: Cornell University Press, 1990.

Barré, H. *Prières anciennes de l'Occident à la Mère du Sauveur*. Paris: P. Letheilleux, 1963.

Baldwin, C. S. *Medieval Rhetoric and Poetic (to 1400), Interpreted from Representative Works*. New York, 1928; rpt. Gloucester, Massachusetts, 1959.

Baltzell, Jane. 'Rhetorical "Amplification" and "Abbreviation" and the Structure of Medieval Narrative'. *Pacific Coast Philology* 2 (1967) 32–39.

Baumstark, Anton. *Comparative Liturgiology*. London: A. R. Mowbray, 1958.

Benton, John F. 'Fraud, Fiction and Borrowing in the Correspondence of Abelard and Heloise'. *Pierre Abélard—Pierre le Vénérable. Les courants philosophiques, littéraires et artistiques en occident au milieu du XIIe siècle. Abbaye de Cluny 2 au 9 juillet 1972*, 469–511. Paris: Editions du CNRS, 1975.

———. 'Nicholas of Clairvaux and the Twelfth-Century Sequence, with Special Reference to Adam of St. Victor'. *Traditio* 18 (1962) 149–180.

———. 'A Reconsideration of the Authenticity of the Correspondence of Abelard and Heloise'. In Rudolf Thomas, ed., *Petrus Abaelardus (1079–1142) Person, Werk und Wirkung*. Trier: Paulinus-Verlag, 1980. Pages 41–52.

———. 'The Style of the *Historia Calamitatum*: A Preliminary Test of Authenticity'. *Viator* 6 (1975) 1–8.

Beer, Rüdiger Robert. *Unicorn: Myth and Reality*. New York: Van Nostrand Reinhold Company, 1977.

Bliese, John. 'The Study of Rhetoric in the Twelfth Century'. *Quarterly Journal of Speech* 63 (1977) 364–383.

Blume, Friedrich, ed. *Die Musik in Geschichte und Gegenwart*. Kassel: Bärenreiter, 1949–79. *S.v.* 'Prosa,' 'Sequenze (Gesang),' and 'Tropus,' by Bruno Stäblein.

Bloch, Marc. *Feudal Society*. 2 volumes. Chicago: University of Chicago Press, 1961.

Bolgar, R. P. *The Classical Heritage and Its Beneficiaries*. Cambridge: Cambridge University Press, 1954.

Bonner, Stanley F. *Education in Ancient Rome*. Berkeley: University of California Press, 1977.

Bower, Calvin M. 'The Grammatical Model of Musical Understanding in the Middle Ages'. *Hermeneutics and Medieval Culture*. Edd. Patrick J. Gallacher and Helen Damico. Albany: State University of New York Press, 1989. Pp. 133–145.

Brooke, Christopher. *The Medieval Idea of Marriage*. Oxford: Clarendon Press, 1989.

Brown, Peter. *The Body and Society: Men, Women and Sexual Renunciation in Early Christianity*. Lectures on the History of Religion 13. New York: Columbia University Press, 1988.

———. 'The Notion of Virginity in the Early Church'. *Christian Spirituality: Origins to the Twelfth Century*. Edd. Bernard McGinn and John Meyendorff. World Spirituality: An Encyclopedic History of the Religious Quest. Volume 16. New York: Crossroad, 1985. Pages 427–443.

———. 'The Saint as Exemplar in Late Antiquity'. J. S. Hawley, ed. *Saints and Virtues*. Berkeley: University of California Press, 1987. Pages 3–14.

Brundage, James A. *Law, Sex, and Christian Society in Medieval Europe*. Chicago: University of Chicago Press, 1987.

Bugge, John. *'Virginitas': An Essay in the History of a Medieval Ideal*. Archives internationales d'histoire des idées, series minor, 17. The Hague: Martinus Nijhoff, 1975.

Bynum, Carolyn Walker. *Docere Verbo et Exemplo: An Aspect of Twelfth-Century Spirituality*. Harvard Theological Studies, 31. Missoula, Montana: Scholars Press, 1979.

———. *Jesus as Mother: Studies in the Spirituality of the High Middle Ages*. Berkeley and Los Angeles: University of California Press, 1982.

———. *The Resurrection of the Body in Western Christianity, 200–1336*. New York: Columbia University Press, 1995.

Carruthers, Mary. *The Book of Memory: A Study of Memory in Medieval Culture*. Cambridge Studies in Medieval Literature 10. Cambridge: Cambridge University Press, 1990.

Chavasse, Claude. *The Bride of Christ: An Enquiry into the Nuptial Element in Early Christianity*. London: The Religious Book Club, 1939.

Chenu, Marie-Dominique. *Nature, Man, and Society in the Twelfth Century*. Edited and translated Jerome Taylor and Lester Little. Chicago: University of Chicago, 1968. Rpt. Toronto: University of Toronto Press, 1997.

Clanchy, M. T. *Abelard: A Medieval Life*. Oxford: Blackwell, 1997.

Connelly, Joseph. *Hymns of the Roman Liturgy*. Westminster: Newman Press, 1957.

Copeland, Rita. *Rhetoric, Hermeneutics, and Translation in the Middle Ages: Academic Traditions and Vernacular Texts*. Cambridge Studies in Medieval Literature. Cambridge: Cambridge University Press, 1991.

Crocker, Richard. L. *The Early Medieval Sequence*. Berkeley and Los Angeles: University of California Press, 1977.

———. 'Medieval Chant'. *The New Oxford History of Music: The Early Middles Ages to 1300*. Edd. Richard Crocker and David Hiley. Volume 2:225-307. Second edition. Oxford: Oxford Press, 1990.

———. 'The Sequence'. Wulf Arlt *et al.*, edd. *Gattungen der Musik in Einzeldarstellung: Gedankschrift Leo Schrade*, 269-322. Bern: Francke, 1973.

———. 'The Troping Hypothesis'. *Musical Quarterly* 52 (1969) 183-203.

Crocker L., Richard and David Hiley, edd. *New Oxford History of Music*. Volume 2: *The Early Middle Ages to 1300*. Oxford: Oxford University Press, 1989, 2nd. edition.

Crocker L., Richard and John Caldwell. 'Sequence'. *The New Grove Encyclopedia of Music and Musicians*. Volume 17:141-153. London-Washington, 1990.

Culpepper, Robert H. *Interpreting the Atonement*. Grand Rapids, Michigan: Eerdmans, 1966.

Cunningham. David S. *Faithful Persuasion; In Aid of a Rhetoric of Christian Theology*. Notre Dame: University of Notre Dame Press, 1990.

Delahaye, P. 'Le dossier anti-matrimonia de l'*Adversus Jovianum* et son influence sur quelques écrits latins du XIIe siècle'. *Mediæval Studies* 13 (1951) 70–75.

Diehl, Patrick S. *The Medieval European Religious Lyric: An Ars Poetica*. Berkeley: University of California Press, 1985.

Douglas, Mary. *Natural Symbols: Explorations in Cosmology*. New York: Routledge, 1970.

Dronke, Peter. *Abelard and Heloise in Medieval Testimonies*. Glasgow: University of Glasgow Press, 1976.

———. 'The Beginnings of the Sequence'. *Beiträge Zur Geschichte der Deutschen Sprache und Literatur* 29 (1965) 278–95. Reprinted in Dronke, Peter, *The Medieval Poet and His World*. Storia e Letteratura, Raccolta di Studi e Testi, 164. Rome, 1984. Pages 115–144.

———. 'Heloise and Marianne: Some Reconsiderations'. *Romanische Forschungen* 72 (1960) 236–240.

————. 'Heloise's *Problemata* and *Letters*: Some Questions of Form and Content'. Rudolf Thomas, ed. *Petrus Abaelardus (1079–1142) Person, Werk und Wirkung*. Trier: Paulinus-Verlag, 1980. Pages 53–73.

————. ed. *A History of Twelfth-Century Western Philosophy*. Cambridge: Cambridge University Press, 1988.

————. *Latin and Vernacular Poets of the Middle Ages*. Vermont: Gower Publishing Company, 1991.

————. *Medieval Latin and the Rise of European Love-Lyric*. Oxford: Oxford University Press, 1957. 2 vols.

————. *The Medieval Poet and His World*. Storia e Letteratura, Raccolta di Studi e Testi, 164. Rome, 1984.

————. 'Mediaeval Rhetoric'. *The Medieval World*, Literature and Western Civilization, volume 11. London, 1973. Pages 315–345.

————. *Poetic Individuality in the Middle Ages: New Departures in Poetry, 1000–1150*. Oxford: Clarendon Press, 1970.

————. 'Types of Poetic Art in Tropes', in Gabriel Silagi, ed., *Liturgische Trope: Referate zweier Colloquien des Corpus Troporum in München (1983) und Canterbury (1983)*. Münchener Beiträge zur Mediävistik und Renaissance-Forschung, 26. Munich: Arbeo-Gesellschaft, 1985. Pages 1–23.

————. '*Virgines caste*'. *Lateinische Dichtungen des X. und XI. Jahrhunderts: Festgabe für Walther Bulst zum 80. Geburtstag, 93–117*. Heidelberg: Lambert Schneider, 1981; rpt Peter Dronke. *Latin and Vernacular Poets of the Middle Ages*. Chapter Six. Brookfield, Vermont: Gower Publishing Company, 1991.

————. *Women Writers of the Middle Ages. A Critical Study of Texts from Perpetua († 203) to Marguerite Porete († 1310)*. Cambridge: Cambridge University Press, 1984.

Duby, Georges. *The Chivalrous Society*. Translated Cynthia Postan. Berkeley: University of California Press, 1977.

————. *Dames du XIIe siècle: Héloïse, Aliénor, Iseut, et quelques autres*. Paris: Gallimard, 1993.

————. ed. *A History of Private Life II: Revelations of the Medieval World*. Cambridge, Massachusetts: Belknap Press of Harvard University Press, 1988.

————. *Love and Marriage in the Middle Ages*. Translated Jane Dunnett. Chicago: University of Chicago Press, 1994.

Elliott, Dyan. *Spiritual Marriage: Sexual Abstinence in Medieval Wedlock*. Princeton: Princeton University Press, 1993.

Evans, Robert F. *Pelagius: Inquiries and Reappraisals*. London: Adam & Charles Black, 1968.

Eynde, Davien Van den Eynde, 'Le receuil des sermons de Pierre Abelard'. *Antonianum* 37 (1962) 17–54.

Falk, Marcia. *Love Lyrics from the Bible: A Translation and Literary Study of the Song of Songs*. Sheffield, UK: Almond Press, 1982.

Fassler, Margot E. 'Accent, Meter, and Rhythm in Medieval Treatises '*De Rithmis*''. *Journal of Musicology* 5 (1987) 164–190.

———. 'The Disappearance of the Proper Tropes and the Rise of the Late Sequence: New Evidence from Chartres', in László Dobszay, Péter Halász, János Mezei, and Gábor Prószéky, edd. *Cantus Planus: The Conference Report of the Chant Study Group of the International Musicological Society, Held in Pécs, Hungary, Sept., 1990*. Budapest, 1992. Pages 319–335.

———. *The Gothic Song: Victorine Sequences and Augustinian Reform in Twelfth-Century Paris*. Cambridge Studies in Medieval and Renaissance Music. Cambridge: Cambridge University Press, 1993.

———. 'Musical Exegesis in the Sequences of Adam and the Canons of St. Victor'. Ph.D. Dissertation, Cornell University. 1983.

———. 'The Office of the Cantor in Early Western Monastic Rules and Customaries: A Preliminary Investigation'. *Early Music History* 5 (1985) 29–51.

———. 'Who Was Adam of St. Victor? The Evidence of the Sequence Manuscripts'. *Journal of the American Musicological Society* 37 (1984) 233–269.

Ferrante, Joan M. 'The Education of Women in the Middle Ages in Theory, Fact, and Fantasy'. Patricia H Labalme, ed., *Beyond their Sex: Learned Women of the European Past, 9–42*. New York: New York University Press, 1980.

Flynn, William T. 'Paris, Bibliothèque de l'Arsenal, MS 1169: The Hermeneutics of Eleventh-Century Burgundian Tropes, and Their Implications'. Ph.D. Dissertation, Duke University, 1992.

Foley, Edward B. 'The "Libri Ordinarii": An Introduction'. *Ephemerides Liturgicae* 102 (1988) 129–139.

Gallacher, Parick J. and Helen Damico, eds. *Hermeneutics and Medieval Culture*. Albany, New York: State University of New York Press, 1989.

Gauss, Julia. 'Das Religionsgespräch von Abaelard'. *Theologische Zeitschrift* 27 (1971) 30–36.

Georgianna, Linda. 'Any Corner of Heaven: Heloise's Critique of Monasticism'. *Mediæval Studies* 49 (1987) 221–53.

Gillingham, Bryan. *Medieval Polyphonic Sequences: An Anthology*. Musicological Studies volume 45. Ottawa: Institute of Medieval Music, 1985.

Gilson, Etienne. *Heloise and Abelard*. University of Michigan Press, 1960; rpt 1968.

Giusberti, Franco. *Materials for a Study on Twelfth-Century Scholasticism*. Naples, 1982.

Gold, Penny Schine. *The Lady and the Virgin: Image, Attitude, and Experience in Twelfth-Century France*. Chicago, 1985.

Handschin, J. 'Trope, Sequence, and Conductus'. *New Oxford History of Music II: Early Music up to 1300*. Ed. A. Hughes. Oxford: Oxford Press, 1954. Pages 128–174.

Harper, John. *The Forms and Orders of Western Liturgy from the Tenth to the Eighteenth Century: A Historical Introduction and Guide for Students and Musicians*. Oxford: Clarendon Press, 1991.

Haskins, Charles Homer. *The Renaissance of the Twelfth Century*. Cambridge, Massachusetts: Harvard University Press, 1927. Cleveland: World Publishing, Meridian, 1957.

Hiley, David. 'Cluny, Sequences, and Tropes', in Claudio Leonardi and Enrico Menesto, edd. *La Tradizione dei Tropi Liturgici: Atti Dei Convegni Sui Tropi Liturgici Parigi-Perugia Organizzati Dal Corpus Troporum*, 125-138. Spoleto, 1990.

———. 'The Rhymed Sequence in England: A Preliminary Survey'. *Musicologie Médiévale: Notations et Séquences*, 227–246. Paris, 1987.

———. 'Rouen, Bibliothèque Municipale, MS 249 (A. 280) and the Early Paris Repertory of Ordinary Mass Chants and Sequences'. *Music and Letters* 70 (1989) 467–482.

———. *Western Plainchant: A Handbook*. Oxford: Oxford University Press, 1995. Huglo, Michel. 'Abélard, poète et musicien'. *Cahiers de civilisation médiévale* 22 (1979) 349–361.

———. 'Un Nouveau Prosaire Nivernais'. *Ephemerides Liturgicae* 71 (1957) 3–30.

———. 'Origine et Diffusion de la Séquence Parisienne (ou Séquence de Second Époque)'. *Musicologie Médiévale: Notations et Séquences*, 209–212. Paris, 1987.

———. 'On the Origins of the Troper-Proser'. *Journal of the Plainsong and Medieval Music Society* 2 (1979) 11–19.

Husmann, H. 'Sequenz und Prosa'. *Annales musicologiques* 2 (1954) 61–91.

Jaeger, C. Stephen. *The Envy of Angels: Cathedral Schools and Social Ideals in Medieval Europe, 950–1200*. Philadelphia: University of Pennsylvania Press, 1994.

Johnson, Elizabeth A. 'Marian Devotion in the Western Church'. *Christian Spirituality: High Middle Ages and Reformation*. Ed. Jill Raitt. World Spirituality series. New York: Crossroad, 1988.

Johnson, L. T. *The Writings of the New Testament: An Interpretation*. Philadelphia: Fortress Press, 1986.

Johnson, Mark. *Moral Implications of Cognitive Science for Ethics*. Chicago: University of Chicago Press, 1993.

Jolivet, Jean. *Arts du language et théologie chez Abélard*. Paris, 1969.

Jonsson, Ritva, and Leo Treitler. 'Medieval Music and Language: A Reconsideration of the Relationship'. *Music and Language*. Studies in the History of Music, 1. New York: Broude Brothers, 1983. Pages 1–23.

Kamuf, Peggy. *Fictions of Feminine Desire: Disclosures of Heloise*. Lincoln: University of Nebraska Press, 1982.

Kaske, R. E., in collaboration with Arthur Groos and Michael W. Twomey. *Medieval Christian Literary Imagery: A Guide to Interpretation*. Toronto Medieval Bibliographies, 11. Toronto: University of Toronto Press, 1988.

Kauffman, Linda S. *Discourses of Desire: Gender, Genre, and Epistolary Fictions*. Ithaca: Cornell University Press, 1986.

Kearney, Eileen. 'Master Peter Abelard, Expositor of Sacred Scripture: An Analysis of Abelard's Approach to Biblical Exposition in Selected Writings on Scripture'. Ph.D. diss. Marquette University, 1980.

———. 'Peter Abelard as Biblical Commentator: A Study of the Expositio in Hexaemeron'. Rudolf Thomas, ed. *Petrus Abaelardus (1079–1142): Person, Werk und Wirkung*, 199–210. Trier: Paulinus-Verlag, 1980.

Kelly, Douglas. *The Arts of Poetry and Prose*. Typologie des sources du moyen age Occidental. Brepols, 1991.

———. 'Rhetoric in French Literature: Topical Invention in Medieval French Literature'. J. J. Murphy, ed. *Medieval Eloquence: Studies in the Theory and Practice of Medieval Rhetoric*, pp. 231–251. Berkeley: University of California Press, 1978.

———. 'The Scope of the Treatment of Composition in the Twelfth- and Thirteenth-Century Arts of Poetry'. *Speculum* 41 (1966) 271–276.

————. 'Theory of Composition in Medieval Narrative Poetry and Geoffrey of Vinsauf's *Poetria Nova*'. *Mediæval Studies* 31 (1969) 117–148.

Kelly, J. N. D. *Jerome: His Life, Writings, and Controversies*. New York: Harper and Row, 1975.

Kennedy, George A. *Classical Rhetoric and Its Christian and Secular Tradition from Ancient to Modern Times*. Chapel Hill: University of North Carolina Press, 1980.

————. *New Testament Interpretation as Rhetorical Criticism*. Chapel Hill: University of North Carolina Press, 1984.

Lakoff, George and Mark Johnson. *Metaphors We Live By*. Chicago: University of Chicago Press, 1980.

Leclercq, Jean. '*Ad ipsam sophiam Christum*. Le témoinage monastique d'Abélard'. Fritz Hoffman, Leo Scheffczyk, Konrad Feiereis, edd. *Sapienter ordinare*. Festgabe für Erich Kleineidam, 179–198. Leipzig, 1969; and in *Revue d'ascétique et de mystique* 46 (1970) 161–182.

————. 'Écrits Monastiques sur la Bible Aux IX–XII Siècle'. *Monastic Studies* 15 (1953) 95–106.

————, '*Lectulus*. Variazioni sul un tema biblico nella tradizione monastica'. In C. Vagagini and G. Penco, edd. *Bibbia e Spiritualita*, 417–436. Rome, 1967.

————. *The Love of Learning and the Desire for God: A Study of Monastic Culture*. Translated Catharine Misrahi. New York: Fordam University Press, 1961.

————. *Monks on Marriage: A Twelfth-Century View*. New York: Seabury Press, 1982.

————. *Monks and Love in Twelfth Century France*. Oxford: Clarendon Press, 1979.

Lewis, C. S. *The Allegory of Love: A Study in Medieval Tradition*. Oxford: Oxford University Press, 1936.

————. *The Discarded Image: An Introduction to Medieval and Renaissance Literature*. Cambridge: Cambridge University Press, 1964.

de Lubac, Henri. *L'exégèse médiévale: Les quatre sens de l'écriture*. 4 volumes. Paris: Aubier, 1959–1961.

————. *Medieval Exegesis, Volume I: The Four Senses of Scripture*. Translated Mark Sebanc. Grand Rapids: Eerdmans, 1998.

Luscombe, David E. 'The *Letters* of Heloise and Abelard since "Cluny 1972"'. *Petrus Abaelardus (1079–1142). Person, Werk und Wirkung*. Ed. Rudolf Thomas. Trierer Theologische Studien. Trier: Paulinus-Verlag, 1980.

————. *The School of Peter Abelard: The Influence of Abelard's Thought in the Early Scholastic Period*. Cambridge: Cambridge University Press, 1969.

MacIntryre, Alasdair. *After Virtue*. Notre Dame: Notre Dame Univesity Press, 1984.

Mack, Burton L. *Anecdotes and Arguments: The* Chreia *in Antiquity and Early Christianity*. Occasional Papers 10. Claremont, California: Institute for Antiquity and Christianity, 1987.

————. *Rhetoric and the New Testament*. Guides to Biblical Scholarship series. Minneapolis: Fortress Press, 1990.

Mack, Burton L., and Vernon K. Robbins. *Patterns of Persuasion in the Gospels*. Sonoma, California: Polebridge Press, 1989.

Malina, Bruce J. and Jerome H. Neyrey. *Portraits of Paul: An Archaeology of Ancient Personality*. Louisville: Westminster John Knox Press, 1996.

Matter, E. Ann. *The Voice of My Beloved: The Song of Songs in Western Medieval Christianity*. Philadelphia: University of Pensylvania Press, 1990.

McKeon, R. 'Rhetoric in the Middle Ages'. *Speculum* 17 (1942) 1–32.

McKinnon, James, ed. *Antiquity and the Middle Ages: From Ancient Greece to the 15th Century*. Music and Society. New Jersey: Prentice Hall, 1990.

McLaughlin, Mary Martin. 'Abelard as Autobiographer: The Motives and Meaning of His "Story of Calamities"', *Speculum* 42 (1967) 463–488.

————. 'Peter Abelard and the Dignity of Women: Twelfth Century "Feminism" in Theory and Practice'. In *Pierre Abélard Pierre Le Vénérable: Les Courants Philosophiques, Littéraires et Artistiques en Occident au Milieu du XII Siècle*. Paris, 1975. Pages 287–333.

Murphy, James J., ed. *Medieval Eloquence: Studies in the Theory and Practice of Medieval Rhetoric*. Berkeley: University of California Press, 1978.

————. *Rhetoric in the Middle Ages: A History of Rhetorical Theory from St. Augustine to the Renaissance*. Berkeley: University of California Press, 1974.

Meerseman, G. G. *Der Hymnos Akathistos im Abendland*. Freiburg, Schweiz: Universitätsverlag, 1960.

Mews, Constant J. 'La bibliothèque du Paraclet du XIIIe siècle à la Révolution'. *Studia monastica* 27 (1985) 31–60.

————. 'On Dating the Writings of Peter Abelard'. *Archives d'histoire doctrinale et littéraire du Moyen Age* 52 (1985) 73–134.

————. *The Lost Love Letters of Heloise and Abelard: Perceptions of Dialogue in Twelfth-Century France*. New York: Pralgrave, 2001.

Morrison, Karl F. *Tradition and Authority in the Western Church, 300–1140*. Princeton: Princeton University Press, 1969.

Newman, Barbara. 'Authority, Authenticity, and the Repression of Heloise. *Journal of Medieval and Renaissance Studies* 22 (1992) 121–157.

————. 'Introduction'. *Saint Hildegard of Bingen: Symphonia, A Critical Edition of the* Symphonia armonie celestium revelationum *[Symphony of the Harmony of Celestial Revelations]*. Ithaca: Cornell University Press, 1988. Pages 1–63.

Neyrey, Jerome H., ed. *The Social World of Luke-Acts: Models for Interpretation*. Peabody, Massachusetts: Hendrickson Publishers, 1991.

O'Banion, John D. *Reorienting Rhetoric: The Dialectic of List and Story*. University Park: Pennsylvania State University Press, 1992.

Odelman, Eva. 'Comment a-t-on Appelé les Tropes? Observations sur les Rubrics Des Tropes Des Xe et XIe Siècles'. *Cahiers de Civilization Médiéval* 18 (1975) 15–36.

Perelmann, Ch. and L. Olbrechts-Tyteca. *The New Rhetoric: A Treatise on Argumentation*. Notre Dame: University of Notre Dame, 1969.

Pernoud, Régine. *Heloise and Abelard*. New York: Stein and Day, 1973.

Raby, F. J. E. *A History of Christian-Latin Poetry from the Beginnings to the Close of the Middle Ages*. Oxford: Oxford University Press, 1953.

Rees, B. R., ed. *The Letters of Pelagius and His Followers*. Woodbridge: Boydell Press, 1991.

————. *Pelagius: A Reluctant Heretic*. Woodbridge: Boydell Press, 1988.

Reichel, Georgius. *Quaestiones Progymnasmaticae*. Ph.D. Dissertation. Leipzig, 1909.

Reynolds, Philip Lyndon. *Marriage in the Western Church: The Christianization of Marriage During the Patristic & Early Medieval Periods*. Leiden: E. J. Brill, 1994.

Robbins, Vernon K. *Jesus the Teacher: A Socio-Rhetorical Interpretation of Mark*. Minneapolis: Fortress Press, 1992.

————. *Exploring the Texture of Texts: A Guide to Socio-Rhetorical Interpretation*. Valley Forge, Pennsylvania: Trinity International Press, 1996.

————. *The Tapestry of Early Christian Discourse: Rhetoric, Society, and Ideology*. New York: Routledge, 1996.

Ryle, Stephen. 'The Sequence: Reflections on Literature and Liturgy'. In Francis Cairns, ed., *Papers of the Liverpool Latin Seminar 1976: Classical Latin Poetry/Medieval Latin Poetry/Greek Poetry.* Liverpool, 1977. Pages 171–182.

Sedgwick, W. B. 'The Style and Vocabulary of the Latin Arts of Poetry of the Twelfth and Thirteenth Century'. *Speculum* 3 (1928) 349–381.

Silvestre, Hubert. 'Le Ms Bruxellensis 10147-58 (s. XII-XIII) et son "compendium artis picturae"'. *Bulletin de la Commission royale d'histoire* 119 (1954) 95–140.

———. 'A propos d'une édition récente de l'*Hymnarius Paraclitensis* d' Abélard'. *Scriptorium* 32 (1978) 91–100.

Smalley, Beryl. *The Study of the Bible in the Middle Ages.* Oxford: Basil Blackwell, 1952; 3rd edition, 1983.

Smith, Susan L. *The Power of Women: A Topos in Medieval Art and Literature.* Philadelphia: University of Pennsylvania Press, 1995.

Spanke, Hans. 'Aus der Vorgeschichte und Frühgeschichte der Sequenz'. *Zeitschrift für deutsches Altertum und deutsche Literatur* 71 (1934) 1–39.

———. 'Die Kompositionskunst der Sequenzen Adams von St. Viktor'. *Studi Medievali* 14 (1941) 1–29.

———. 'Fortschritte in der Geschicte mittelalterlicher Musik. Zur Geschichte der Sequenz und ihrer Nebenformen'. *Historisches Vierteljahrschrift* 27 (1932) 374–389.

———. 'St. Martial-Studien,' in *Zeitschrift für französische Sprache und Literatur*, 54 (1931) 282–422; 56 (1932) 450–478.

Stäblein, Bruno. *Monumenta Monodica Medii Aevi.* Band I: *Hymnen* (1): 342 (melody 590). Kassel and Basel: Bärenreiter-Verlag, 1956.

———. 'Sequenz'. *Die Musik in Geschichte und Gegenwart,* 12 (1965) 522–549.

———. 'Zur Frühgeschichte der Sequenz'. *Archiv für Musikwissenschaft,* 18 (1961) 1–33.

Steiner, Ruth. 'The Prosulae of the Ms Paris BN F. Lat. 1118'. *Journal of the American Musicological Society* 22 (1969) 367–393.

Stevens, John. *Words and Music in the Middle Ages: Song, Narrative, Dance and Drama, 1050–1350.* Cambridge: Cambridge University Press, 1986.

Sticca, Sandro. *The 'Planctus Mariae' in the Dramatic Tradition of the Middle Ages.* Translated Joseph R. Berrigan. Athens: University of Georgia Press, 1988.

Szövérffy, Joseph. *A Concise History of Medieval Latin Hymnody: Religious Lyrics Between Antiquity and Humanism.* Leiden, 1985.

————. 'False Use of Unfitting Hymns: Some Ideas Shared by Peter the Venerable, Peter Abelard, and Heloise'. *Revue Bénédictine* 89 (1979) 187–199.

————. 'A Mirror of Medieval Culture: St. Peter Hymns of the Middle Ages'. *Transactions of the Connecticut Academy of Arts and Sciences* 42 (1965) 97–403.

————. *Peter Abelard's Hymnarius Paraclitensis*. Wetteren, Belgium: Cultura Press, 1975.

Treitler, Leo. 'Reading and Singing: On the Genesis of Occidental Music-writing'. In Iain Fenlon, ed. *Early Music History*, no. 4. Cambridge: Cambridge University Press, 1984. Pages 135–208.

Turner, Denys. *Eros and Allegory: Medieval Exegesis of the Song of Songs*. Cistercian Studies Series 156. Kalamazoo: Cistercian Publications, 1995.

Van Deusen, Nancy. *Music at Nevers Cathedral: Principal Sources of Medieval Chant*. Institute of Medieval Studies: Musicological Studies, 30. Henryville, Pennsylvania: Institute of Mediaeval Music, 1980.

————. 'Origins of a Significant Medieval Genre: The musical "Trope" up to the Twelfth Century'. *Rhetorica* 3 (1985) 245–267.

————. 'The Sequence Repertory of Nevers Cathedral'. *Basler Studien zur Interpretation der Alten Musik*, 44–59. Forum musicologicum, volume 2. Winterthur, 1982.

————. 'The Use and Significance of the Sequence'. *Musica Disciplina* 40 (1986) 5–47.

Van den Eynde, Damien. 'Le recueil des sermons de Pierre Abelard'. *Antonianum* 37 (1962) 17–54.

de Vogüé, Adalbert. 'Marie chez les Vièrges du sixième siècle; Césaire d' Arles et Grégoire le Grand'. *Benedictina*, 33 (1986) 79–91.

Waddell, Chrysogonus. 'Abelard and the Chaste Virgins'. Unpublished Essay.

————. 'Epithalamica: An Easter Sequence by Peter Abelard'. *Musical Quarterly* 72 (1986) 239–271.

————. *Hymn Collections from the Paraclete I. Introduction and Commentary*. Cistercian Liturgical Series 8. Trappist, Kentucky: Gethsemani Abbey—Kalamazoo: Cistercian Publications, 1989.

————. *The Old French Paraclete Ordinary and the Paraclete Breviary I. Introduction and Commentary*. Cistercian Liturgical Series 3. Trappist, Kentucky: Gethsemani Abbey—Kalamazoo: Cistercian Publications, 1985.

————. 'Peter Abelard as Creator of Liturgical Texts'. Rudolf Thomas, ed. *Petrus Abaelardus (1079–1142). Person, Werk und Wirkung,* 267–286. Trierer Theologische Studien. Trier: Paulinus-Verlag, 1980.

————. 'Peter Abelard's *Letter 10* and Cistercian Liturgical Reform'. John R. Sommerfeldt, ed. *Studies in Medieval Cistercian History,* 2. Cistercian Studies Series 24. Pp. 75–86. Kalamazoo: Cistercian Publications, 1976.

————. 'St. Bernard and the Cistercian Office at the Abbey of the Paraclete'. E. Rozanne Elder and John R. Sommerfeldt, edd. *The Chimaera of His Age: Studies on Bernard of Clairvaux.* Cistercian Studies Series, 63. Kalamazoo: Cistercian Publications, 1980. Pages 76–121.

Walters, Anne Elizabeth. 'Music and Liturgy at the Abbey of Saint-Denis, 567–1567: A Survey of Primary Sources'. Ph.D. dissertation, Yale University. 1985.

Weingart, Richard E. *The Logic of Divine Love: A Critical Analysis of the Soteriology of Abailard.* Oxford: Clarendon Press, 1970.

Weinrich, Lorenz. 'Peter Abaelard as Musician'. *The Musical Quarterly* 55 (1969) 295–312, 464–486.

Williams, Paul L. *The Moral Philosophy of Peter Abelard.* Lanham, Maryland: University Press of America, 1980.

Wright, Craig. *Music and Ceremony at Notre Dame of Paris, 500–1550.* Cambridge Studies in Music. Cambridge: Cambridge University Press, 1989.

Yearley, Janthia. 'A Bibliography of Planctus in Latin, Provencal, French, German, English, Italian, Catalan, and Gallician-Portuguese from the Time of Bede to the Early Fifteenth Century'. *Journal of the Plainsong and Medieval Music Society* 4 (1981) 12–52.

INDEX OF BIBLICAL TEXTS

GENERAL INDEX

Abelard, *see* Peter Abelard

Abbreviation, 60

Accentuation, 163–166, 171–175, 195–198

Adam of Saint-Victor, 167, 196–197

affectus, 94, 112, 114, 218, 246

Agnes, Saint, Office of, 65

Alan of Lille, 246, 309

Alcuin, 48

Alleluia (chant), xxi, 34, 150, 153

All Saints Day, 89

Ambrose, Saint, 33, 38, 76, 169, 308; *De virginibus*, 55–56, 255; *Iesu corona virginum*, 87–88

amica (friend), 213

amicitia (friendship), 296–298

amplificatio, 136

anaphora 145, 215

analogy, 116–119, 132

anima (soul), 245–246

Anselm of Laon, 246, 309

antithesis, 145

Aphthonius of Antioch, 129 (n. 40)

apostrophe, 145

Aquinas, Saint Thomas, 46

Argenteuil, convent of 1 (n. 2); refectory at, 223

Aristotle, 148, 278

Asad, Talad, xxix (n. 22); 4 (n. 15), 277 (n. 4), 306; concerning monastic life, 51

Asella, 11

Astell, Ann W., xxx (n. 24), 49–50, 94 (n. 92), 95, 246 (n. 74), 247, 273–274

Augustine of Hippo, definition of "hymn", xxiv, 169; *De doctrina christiana*, 284

Augustinian Order, and adult recruits, 48–49

Babb, Warren, 178 (n. 38)

Baltzell, Jane, 98 (n. 3)

Barré, H., 223 (n. 8)

Baumstark, Anton, 261 (n. 117)

Bede, The Venerable, 48

Beer, Rüdiger Robert, 91–93

Benton, John F., 11–12

Berengar of Poitiers, letter preserving Abelard's preference for Christ over Aristotle, 287 (n. 34)

Bernard of Chartres, 130–132, 144

Bernard of Clairvaux, 48, 50, 246, 305 (n. 78), 305, 309; and Song of Songs, 51, 247; hymnal of, 11, 47, 25; critical of liturgical practices at Paraclete, 169–170

Betrothal, 57

Bloch, Marc, 279 (n. 11)

Blume, Friedrich, 177 (n. 37)

Bower, Calvin, 175, 176 (n. 35), 177 (n. 36), 182 (n. 42, n. 43), 184 (n. 45)